Dog Days at the White House

Dog Days at the White House

The Outrageous Memoirs of the Presidential Kennel Keeper

Traphes Bryant

with **Frances Spatz Leighton**

Macmillan Publishing Co., Inc.
New York
Collier Macmillan Publishers
London

*This book is dedicated to
man's best friend—women.*

Copyright © 1975 by Traphes Bryant and Frances Spatz Leighton

Macmillan Publishing Co., Inc.
866 Third Avenue, New York, N.Y. 10022
Collier Macmillan Canada, Ltd.

Library of Congress Cataloging in Publication Data

Bryant, Traphes.
Dog days at the White House.

1. Presidents—United States—Biography.   2.   Presidents—United States—Wives.
3.   Washington, D.C. White House.   4.   Bryant, Traphes.   5.   Dogs—Anecdotes,
facetiae, satire, etc.   I.   Leighton, Frances Spatz.   II.   Title.
E840.6.B79   973'.00992   75-6504
ISBN 0-02-517990-X

Third Printing 1975

Printed in the United States of America

Contents

Acknowledgments
vii

Prologue
ix

Introduction
3

I

Of Jack and Ike and Harry
and Dick and Dogs and Dames and Ducks
7

II

Lyndon Baines Johnson
83

III

Richard M. Nixon
235

Epilogue
332

Index
333

v

Acknowledgments

First and foremost I wish to thank my wife, Doris, whom I tease a lot but who has helped me tremendously on this book in spite of it.

Special credit should also be given to the talented White House photographers, whose photographs add luster to every President's public image—and luster to this book: Chief Robert Knudsen, Cecil W. Stoughton, Abbe Rowe, Frank Wolfe, Mike Geisinger, Yoichi ("Okie") Okamoto, Ollie Atkins, Jack Kightlinger, Ricardo Thomas, and David Kennerly. Kennerly deserves special mention for keeping American tradition intact by getting dogless President Ford a dog.

Prologue

The story goes that God spoke to the new President. And God said, "I have good news and bad. The good news is that you *will* be permitted to bring your dog, your cat, or whatever to the White House—there is no lease restriction."

"Oh, thank you, Sir," said the new President, "and what is the bad news?"

"The bad news is that the dog will be happier there than you."
It's true. It's true.

How do I know? Because I was the invisible man, the dogkeeper who was always around the inner sanctums of the White House—in the living rooms, the bedrooms, the kitchens, and even the fabled Oval Office. Usually the dogs were with me. Sometimes they weren't, because I was there in my other capacity, electrician.

I have seen Presidents as few others have seen them, some literally with their pants off. I saw them in moments of tension and relaxation, exuberance and sorrow, and in their angry cussing moments just before they put their public masks back on.

And I've kept a diary!

Introduction

I don't have a dog of my own.

I'm still in the recovery room after years of taking care of presidential dogs. I've had them all—jumpers and bumpers and biters and kissers. I've been wetted and shedded and sat on by the pampered pets of the White House since the Kennedy administration. I've been torn, shorn, and worn. I've had Presidents scream at me and pat me and shake my hand gratefully, all because of dogs.

And wouldn't you know it, after I had retired as far away from Washington as I could get, fate put me next to a neighbor with seven dogs, all of whom have adopted me and one of whom has taken up night residence on my doorstep.

One President almost took a poke at me because he thought I was getting too chummy with his wife. I was only getting chummy with his dog. I've shed real tears comforting and being comforted by a presidential daughter after her dog met an untimely death at the White House.

And yet when the reigning dogs were about to disappear from my life at the end of each administration, on the day known around the White House as "the changing of the guard," it hasn't been easy to toss them a last steak bone saved by my wife, Doris, and start getting chummy with a new set of dogs. You can't change loyalties that fast between high noon and 1:00 P.M. on a January 20th.

It dawned on me, somewhere along the line after Kennedy turned over his dogs to me, that I was getting the damned doggiest view of Presidents a human could get. So I started keeping a diary. Dog lovers weren't the only people I had in mind. Sure, they'd like to compare their dog adventures with those of the Presidents. But White House watchers, too, would want to hear what I'd found out on the inside—all those people who wonder if everything actually is as glossy-perfect as it seems.

And historians, who know what to make of little things, may like to put these together with what they already know and come up

3

with new meanings and new conclusions about the lives of the Presidents.

I mean such things as their love lives, and how they treat their wives, their secretaries, their families, their dogs, their help. And the backstairs things that go on that never get into the papers or books —those were the things I wanted to record for posterity. At least it was different.

I could score high in an oddball kind of quiz:

Which presidential daughter liked to shock the staff with how well she could cuss?

Which President liked to skinny-dip in the pool—with doggie and/or female companions?

Which President said he'd rather sleep with his dog than with anybody?

Which President was pathetically afraid of his dog's opinion of him?

If you don't know the answers, if you're curious about the unbelievable occupants of the White House—and they're all slightly unbelievable—read on. My White House diary may shatter your view of recent history.

As I mentioned, I first started taking notes when I landed in the doghouse during the Kennedy administration. It just seemed the thing to do because such a fuss was being made about White House staffers writing their memoirs after they quit. The furor began with the publication of the book *My Thirty Years Backstairs at the White House,* an instant best-seller. The tell-all girl was Lillian Rogers Parks, the maid-seamstress I used to talk with when I would see her leaving the White House on crutches—the result of childhood polio.

Hell, I thought, where there's smoke there's fire. I kept my ears and eyes open and my mouth shut and almost every day while the stuff was fresh in my mind I'd make a few notes. Nothing fancy. Just plain talk.

When Jacqueline Kennedy read Lillian's book, she added to the uproar and probably the book's sales as well by making everybody on the household staff sign an agreement that they wouldn't write about the White House after they got out. Nobody thought of me. I didn't sign any agreement. And even if I had, lawyers now say you can't make it stick. History will out.

4

History did out, in a flood of books, including one by Jackie's own secretary, Mary Barelli Gallagher. Mary had gotten help in pulling her book together from the same writer who had helped Lillian—Fran Leighton, a news gal who'd already done an article or two on me for Sunday supplements.

So one night on impulse, during the Nixon administration, I caught Fran in the Blue Room where the President and First Lady were chatting with guests. My job was to hold a quartz light on the First Family for the cameraman. I put the light down and left my post for a few minutes—a high crime, but I was desperate. We walked quickly to the Red Room and I asked her if she would like to help me with my book, since I would soon be leaving the White House. She asked me to drop by for coffee at her office at the National Press Building—"and bring the diary!"

I've always been lucky. It was sheer luck that brought me to the White House in the first place.

I grew up in the West Virginia coal-mining area, and after high school I got my first job as an electrician's helper, climbing poles to string high-tension wires outside the mines. On weekends, when the mines were closed, I went down about a mile underground to work on the substations that bring power to the mines. Then one day I decided it would be nice to have a safer, steadier job, so I went to work at the Norfolk Naval Shipyard. The Navy sent me to Hawaii, where as a civilian I helped repair the ships damaged in the 1941 Japanese attack on our naval base at Pearl Harbor.

That lucky star certainly hung over me at Pearl Harbor. A torpedo plane narrowly missed killing me. It was all in the matter of a moment's decision. I had been walking across the base when a friend drove by in a jeep and yelled. "Hey, Traphes, come on, I'll take you where you're going." I waved him on. For some strange reason I felt compelled to keep walking. Had I gone with him, I would be dead.

The same lucky star had led me to volunteer for the White House assignment. After World War II, I had gone to work for the General Services Administration as a maintenance man at the Navy Building in Washington, D.C. One day someone called out, "Hey, they need an electrician at the White House. Any volunteers?" Several men volunteered, but I got the job.

If I hadn't volunteered, I never would have had a chance to

5

work in the White House, starting in 1951, first as a day-shift, then a night-shift electrician, and eventually as an electrician *plus* keeper of the White House dogs.

I

Of Jack and Ike
and Harry and Dick
and Dogs and Dames
and Ducks

1

Those early days at the White House were mighty rough, and I never knew when I would be fired. The Usher's Office was very rigid about how all maintenance people were to conduct themselves and keep in the good graces of the First Ladies.

I'd hardly started working in the White House when I got into trouble in the First Lady's bathroom. The Trumans had just moved back from Blair House. As I replaced a burned-out fluorescent tube, I noticed that the frosted glass that diffused the light had some dirt inside, and I figured I would help the housekeepers out. So I reached over and took the washcloth from the ledge of the bathtub and cleaned the glass. This dirtied the washcloth a bit, so I rinsed it out as best I could.

In about an hour I had been summoned to the Usher's Office where Head Usher Howell G. Crim chewed me out a good ten minutes for having touched Mrs. Truman's personal washcloth, and for a few of those minutes my job was in jeopardy. He said that Mrs. Truman was very much distressed that anyone would handle her personal washcloth.

When I had sweated enough, he patted me on the shoulder and sent me on my way with the observation that the lesson I'd had would probably save me from getting into worse trouble later. "And from now on, Bryant," he admonished, "carry your own damn rags."

By the time the Trumans moved out and the Eisenhowers moved in, I thought I'd learned exactly what to do with every light. The White House, for example, has a Grand Staircase, down which the President and his official guests descend for the formal picture-taking ceremonies before a formal dinner begins. So-called landing lights run down each side of the stairway. My first day on the job during the new Eisenhower administration, I turned out those lights as usual for the night.

Again the Usher's Office summoned me. "Why did you turn off the Grand Staircase lights?" Crim wanted to know. "Didn't you get the new instructions on how we handle lights?"

"I don't need new instructions," I said. "I already know about the Grand Staircase lights. Mrs. Truman said those lights are to be turned off at night."

Mr. Crim turned crimson. "Mr. Bryant," he said, "as of January twentieth, Mrs. Truman no longer resides in the Mansion." As he talked, it looked once again as if *my job* no longer resided in the Mansion either. I'm happy to say that eventually I became older and wiser and Crim's good friend.

But just as that happened, he retired and I had a new man to contend with, James B. West—called JB. Then JB retired, and for the rest of my days at the White House, Chief Usher Rex Scouten had the job of laying down the law to me—or trying to.

When President Kennedy made me official dogkeeper, I thought the assignment would last a few weeks. But it lasted ten years, until I retired from the White House during the Nixon administration. Each succeeding President wanted the old system continued—first President Johnson, then President Nixon. I think what they liked best was the way I trained the dogs to meet the presidential helicopter, no matter what time of the day or night it arrived.

I had done it once or twice as a gag for Kennedy, standing there with a row of dogs when he got off the helicopter. He had smiled broadly and greeted the dogs as if they were his distinguished hosts. Then I had quit doing it because I didn't want to overdo a good thing. But President Kennedy, getting off the copter, missed the canine greeting and actually ordered me to have the dogs there to greet him from then on.

Before the Kennedys catapulted into the White House, I had survived the Truman and the Eisenhower administrations—not, however, as a dogkeeper. Ike had a dog, Heidi, whom he couldn't control worth beans, and Truman did not care for pets. I have a hazy recollection of seeing a mopey-looking mixed-breed dog around for a short time before Truman palmed him off on someone. The Trumans were such a close family that they treated each other as pets.

Even President Truman, though, felt the need to be friendly with a little animal; he tried to make a pet of a certain squirrel, slipping it bits of food under the table when the family ate outside.

Then came Eisenhower, who couldn't stand squirrels because they had the gall to dig into the velvety grass of his golf green to hide nuts. Sometimes he would be putting and the ball looked like it was going into the hole, but it would roll right on past. After a few repetitions, he would rush over and look into the hole, only to find the squirrels had filled it solidly with nuts. His face would turn red and he'd shake his club and yell, "Get those goddamn squirrels out of here."

And many's the bagful we did. Capital Parks Service's maintenance crew, which oversees the grounds, set cages that did not harm the squirrels. Captives were escorted to other parks in the city, which caused great merriment among the White House help. Once an angry citizen brought back a bagful, claiming they had set up housekeeping in his front yard.

Much has been written about Truman's salty language and his no-nonsense personality. All that is true, and I can also add that he was a very impatient man around the house. If you didn't do something instantly, he would grab it and do it himself.

Once I got a call that a light bulb was out in his bedroom. I took a three-way bulb—50/100/150—to his room, but he was all tensed up. Before I could insert it, he snatched it out of my hand, saying, "Give me the damn thing. I'll do it. I'll do it."

His valet, Mr. Prettyman, looked at me and shrugged as if to say, "What can we do with him?" Truman thrust the old bulb at me, and Prettyman and I stood watching as the President did his own handiwork.

But Truman was an angel compared with Eisenhower. Ike would not have a moment's patience with me or anyone. When Give 'Em Hell Harry cussed it sounded kind of humorous, but when Ike's temper flared we all cringed. Even when he was leaving the White House, Ike was still very abrupt. Moaney had promised me that when the President left the White House he would give me one of his hats. So when the President was packing things up in his room I went upstairs and reminded Moaney. Moaney told me to go right into the President's bedroom and ask him.

I said, "No, I can't do that. I'm a White House employee. I can't just go in uninvited."

So Moaney went in and I heard him say, "Mr. Bryant wants one of your hats as a souvenir." I heard the President sputter and curse a while and then say with great annoyance, "Go ahead and give him the goddamn hat."

I was standing near the elevator door, just across the hall from the presidential bedroom, and I felt like calling out, "If it's that much trouble, just skip it." But I didn't, and in a minute Moaney had picked one out for me and was handing it to me with a little smile of understanding. Since it was so grudgingly given I couldn't stand to have the hat around, so I gave it to my brother-in-law.

Truman had a way of cussing that made his words into some kind of a joke so that you half forgave him. For example, I recall Truman's White House gang snickering because after Truman fired General Douglas MacArthur—or maybe just before—he called him "that dumb son of a bitch."

But the cuss words weren't what made the statement funny. What made everyone laugh was what he added: "I didn't fire him because he was a dumb son of a bitch, because that's not against the law for generals. If it was, half of them would be in jail."

LBJ could also be pretty humorous in the ornery way he could chew someone out, telling him, "You've got the stubborness of a water buffalo and the brains of an ass." That still meant he was being good-natured. But if he said, "Well, goddamn it, *now hear this!* You get your ass over here!" then you were really in trouble. The phrase "now hear this" meant you'd better be listening.

The man who really surprised me in the field of expletives was Nixon, because he had always acted holier than thou and had said right out, during the campaign of 1968, that he certainly didn't want to be another cussing President like Truman.

One of the first things I learned after Nixon moved into the White House was that he could cuss as well as the next President, and some of his language was pretty raunchy. "That guy has brass balls" was his angry way of saying someone had a lot of nerve, and he also favored "bastard," as in "those damn liberal bastards."

In LBJ's day the White House staff had a standard comment about his cussing. "The President doesn't use four-letter words," we'd say, "he makes do with three." "Ass" was clearly his pet term. "You're dumber than a mule's ass," he'd say. "Get your ass moving." "I'll have your ass if you don't do such and such." "You goof this up one more time and I'll have your ass." The President's all-time favorite punch line, "Aw, you don't know your ass from your elbow," came into play any time he wanted to tell a man how dumb he was.

President Kennedy cussed like a little boy caught with a stolen apple. He thought saying "Damn it to hell" or "Let the damn thing alone" was pretty risqué. When he mentioned someone he and his friends didn't like, he might refer to him as "that prick." To tell a friend off, he'd say, "Oh, go screw yourself," just as he probably did back in "Hahvaad."

As if the Presidents hadn't enough trouble with friends and associates, all the Presidents I have known have had some variety of in-law or family problem.

When Harry Truman was in office, it seemed to me that Mrs. Wallace, Bess Truman's mother, felt she came first. President Truman and his wife seemed to be constantly straining to see to her comfort.

This wouldn't have been so important if she had been only an occasional guest, but Mrs. Wallace lived with the Trumans until she died and her attitude always conveyed the message that she was not President Truman's Number One fan. Still, he continually tried to win her over.

She was hard to please. I remember when the White House was being repaired and the Trumans lived in Blair House, Mrs. Wallace was always complaining that it wasn't warm enough and I was frequently called on to heat up a room for her. Finally I installed an electric heater for her. Then she was dissatisfied with the lighting and I put in a special reading lamp.

JFK's problem was that he was caught in the middle of competition between Jacqueline and her sisters- and mother-in-law. It seemed to me that Kennedy was doing his best to keep his sisters and mother from feeling they were taking a back seat to the glamorous Jackie. Meanwhile Jackie also felt the pressure of trying to live up to such an energetic family and once told me she felt tired even trying to keep up.

She felt tired and she looked tired and she said, "Bryant, if you think keeping up with dogs is 'triffic' pressure, you should try having my job of keeping up with my in-laws."

With the Johnson family, the in-law problem was the President's brother, Sam Houston Johnson. LBJ loved and feared him. With a few drinks in him, there was no telling what Sam Houston might say that was embarrassing or painful to the Prez, even if it was the truth.

Brother Sam was frequently "between jobs" and would stay at the

13

White House for weeks on end, during which time LBJ felt he had to give him some sort of job.

Presidents Eisenhower and Nixon also faced problems involving brothers—mostly making sure their brothers had jobs that did not embarrass the White House or didn't seem to be based on their White House connection. President Nixon was so worried about one of his brothers that, it was later revealed, he ordered a tap on his phone to be sure he wasn't getting into any trouble.

2

Everything changes around the White House—the people on the scene, the cast of dogs, and even the character of the White House rooms. Margaret's bedroom used to be where the second-floor kitchen is now. The present family dining room was her sitting room.

Some Presidents liked cooking with electricity. In Kennedy's time the kitchen was converted to gas. The Nixons used gas for cooking, electricity for baking. President Ford makes his breakfast with a toaster.

Kennedy loved to swim. Every President I knew had used the pool or thrown it open to his friends. Even Truman. But Nixon slapped a floor over it and made it into a press room. As part of the conversion he had to cover over the seascape mural that Kennedy was so fond of and that Ambassador Kennedy had paid an artist a pretty penny to paint on the walls enclosing the pool.

I can see that mural of the New England shore now. And I can see the pool full of balls and things to throw to Charlie and the children. During the day Charlie, Caroline's dog, would be the President's usual swimming companion—Charlie and the President's trusted aide, Dave Powers.

Various Presidents searched out different rooms for working. LBJ liked his noisy West Wing office, with everyone staying late to keep him company. Nixon first preferred to go alone with his dog, Timahoe, to the Executive Office Building—probably because his own office was bugged. Then he took a fancy to the second-floor Lincoln Room study, using it for his night office.

Each President had a different idea of where his pets should be housed. Eisenhower had a standard-type doghouse near his office. The Kennedys kept their pets in the Bouquet Room, which was on the ground floor between the President's office suite and the Mansion.

When Lyndon Johnson saw the pitiful accommodations available for dogs, he ordered a fancy doghouse built that grew more extravagant every time he brought a friend out to look at it. The story has been told of how Lyndon Johnson could never be satisfied with the way his shower worked and spent thousands of taxpayers' dollars installing new and stronger shower systems. But that was nothing compared with how particular he was about his personal doghouse, as you will see later from my diary.

Then came Nixon, who was perfectly satisfied with the living quarters for the dogs King Timahoe, Pasha, and Vicky, except for one important detail. The kennels were too close to the house and he couldn't stand noise. He was almost pathological about it. I spent many nights following his orders concerning methods of trying to keep the dogs quiet.

Then came Ford, with a cat. He looked the dog runs over and, friends tell me, said, "Who needs kennels? Wouldn't a swimming pool be much nicer there?"

While he was still pondering the question, the President's seventeen-year-old daughter, Susan, and his official White House photographer, David Kennerly, took matters in hand and gave the President an eight-month-old golden retriever with the gutsy name of Liberty. I sighed with relief. I knew the American way of governing hadn't changed. The country was still safe for dogs and dog lovers.

Electricity was another theme that was treated differently by each President. LBJ, as everyone knew, was a fanatic about light bulbs. Now and then I would note something down in this regard in my diary:

6/9/64   As I was bringing the dogs out for the 10 P.M. walk, the President turned out the light in the Bouquet Room. He was coming to the Mansion from his office. Luckily I had a flashlight.

It was important to have a flashlight around during the Johnson administration. The President was forever turning the lights out on me. He never looked around to see who needed light.

But then came the Nixons, and one of the first things Mrs. Nixon did as her contribution to White House tradition and the happiness of tourists was to have giant floodlights trained on the White House all night long. I hardly needed a flashlight any more. I used to smile as I'd wonder what LBJ must be muttering to himself as he read about those floodlights.

Lyndon Johnson once reported that he was saving $2,000 a month on the electric bill at the White House, and some reporter said, "Yes, and adding it to his telephone bill."

So you see how things changed from administration to administration. Take television as the perfect illustration. Sets came and went. The Kennedys hated TV. When they came in, we electricians had to take out about a dozen sets. The Eisenhowers before them had planted TV sets all around the living quarters. I remember that we, the White House employees, would watch television on a set in the West Hall so that we could hear Eisenhower coming up on the elevator. When we heard the elevator, we would turn it off and run into the pantry.

The Eisenhowers could hardly eat a meal by themselves without watching television. They ate on trays, like a couple of kids, glued to the set. You could almost bet they were watching a Western, and sure enough, soon would come the bang of guns and the sound of hoofbeats.

For the record, the Eisenhowers were the first presidential family to have color TV. I remember I got a call once that the color set was out of order. It was a Sunday and I was the electrician on duty. When I got to the West Hall, Ike was fuming. The President said, "Let the goddamn thing go." But since the First Lady wanted her mother, Mrs. Doud, who was visiting, to have color TV, I went ahead and switched a couple of tubes. I wasn't used to color and I didn't know much about color sets. The picture came out looking very dark. I remember how Mrs. Doud's prejudice showed when she commented on the picture I was getting. "It looks like a bunch of niggers," she whispered to us. The President heard but didn't comment.

For history's sake I should tell exactly what happened when color TV came to the White House. The RCA people sent a top man all the way from New York to adjust the set. He showed me how the controls worked and clued me in on how to take care of it. Under instructions from his company, he was waiting to show the President and Mamie how to operate it, and I was not supposed to leave him there alone. We both waited all afternoon, but Ike and Mamie didn't show. The RCA man was nervous as a kitten. He was supposed to take a full report back to his office in New York as to how the President had reacted. I told him he could wait in a reception room, but he didn't want to budge. He told me he couldn't go back without his report. Finally he agreed after I promised to call him when the President arrived.

I did not get to show it to the President until ten that night, and I was too bushed to bother reporting to the RCA man. I went to the Usher's Office and said, "I'm shipping out." The next day I learned that at eleven-thirty that night they had found the RCA man still waiting for his report.

Ike had no patience when it came to movies or watching television. He would not watch something just because someone else liked it. If he didn't like it he would jump up and stalk out. Eisenhower wanted action. He ordered all the Westerns, and we would show them in the White House before they were released in the local theaters.

Paul Fischer, who used to operate the movie projector at the White House theater, would call me up and say, "We've got a good one tonight," and I would be part of the audience watching it. But if there were too many women in the picture or if there was too much love-making the President would get up and leave.

He would tell Paul, "Let the Secret Service and the rest of the fellows watch it. It's not for me," and he'd go. For some reason he had taken a dislike to Robert Mitchum. If by chance a movie slipped in with Robert Mitchum in it he would curse and jump up, saying, "I can't stand that S.O.B. Let the other fellows watch." And off he'd go.

For just these emergencies he'd have stacks of Western paperbacks in his room and he'd read himself to sleep. Zane Grey was his favorite. I saw a Zane Grey book in Peoples Drug Store not long ago, and for a brief moment I felt that I was back working at the White House and I was on lunch hour.

Nixon would never watch himself on television if he could help it; it made him nervous. But Lyndon Johnson would sit like a king with four sets on in a row, watching himself. He loved it. There he'd be, throwing out comments and switching the sound from one to another, or keeping several sets on together, with the sound turned up loud.

The very day Johnson left, while the parade was still going on, the order was already being carried out to remove a bunch of TV sets. It was very funny when some of the White House staff watching the Inaugural parade suddenly found themselves looking at a blank wall as TV sets were yanked out.

Kennedy and Nixon had at least one thing in common. Both loved a fire in the fireplace. When I was at Hyannis Port and the President was expected to fly up on a Friday, Jacqueline asked me, "Can you have a nice, cozy fire in the living room? I want things to be particularly nice."

I racked up the logs and went to the basement and found some small pieces of wood to help start the fire. Then I got a can of charcoal lighter fluid from the cook and sprayed the logs. The President arrived sooner than expected, but I used a newspaper to warm the chimney draft and had the fire roaring before he got into the room.

With all his money, it was the little things he liked—a fire to watch, the feeling of ocean spray on his face. And he liked to stand around with his hands in his pockets.

It amused President Kennedy that I shared this bad habit, and he would call out, "Hey, what have you got in your pockets?" Once he commented, "During the campaign everybody kept telling me to get my hands out of my pockets, but I said, 'What the hell am I supposed to do with them?' "

Kennedy was a mystery man to me. I never could quite figure him out—was he fun-loving or ultraserious? Just as you thought he was one, he was the other. He could change like mercury.

But one thing is sure, he was more earthy than people realized. I'll never forget the day he stepped out of the pool and put his foot right square in some of Charlie's dog dung. I held my breath for the explosion. But not a curse word left his lips. He looked down, just sort of smiled, and kept on going. It didn't bother him a bit.

There was a lot of tenderness in him. When Pushinka had her pups, Jacqueline cut up newspapers and lined a box for them so it would be soft for the puppies. The President would always stop to inspect them and ask me questions like, "Will their eyes change color when they get older?"

When he had his feud with the New York *Herald-Tribune* and banned it from the White House, I got a copy of the *Trib* one day and cut it up and lined the box with it, leaving the name of the paper hanging over the top so the President would be sure to see it. Sure enough, he grinned from ear to ear and nodded approval.

He said not a word until he was walking away, and then he called back, "It's finally found its proper use."

One thing all the Presidents I knew had in common—none was completely happy or satisfied, despite their exalted position as President. A couple even told me that they envied me.

I used to feel sorry for Eisenhower, alone on his putting green or with only his valet for company. He seemed a very lonely man. He was happiest when his grandson, David, came to visit him.

Truman I felt sorry for because he had so many enemies. He tried to act thick-skinned, but backstairs and on the White House lawns we White House workers sometimes commented that it was a shame he could only count on two sure fans—Bess and Margaret. When he was reelected it was the greatest ego boost he could have had. It's a pity he didn't live quite long enough to see himself become an idol.

Harry Truman often consoled himself with a bottle of bourbon—I. W. Harper, undiluted and no chaser. On one poker-playing cruise with his cronies on the presidential yacht he hit the bottle so heavily that Bess had to be phoned and consulted about what to do. She was in Missouri, but when she heard he was on a bender, she came right back and straightened him out.

I also think Harry Truman had one of the most unusual idiosyncrasies of any President—he kept a private liquor supply in his personal bathroom. I'm not sure Bess knew it was there. In fact, I seriously doubt it.

LBJ was always telling me he'd like to change places with me and "get a vacation." He'd say, "Mr. Bryant, where can I apply for a job like yours? I want to take off like you do and go on a hunting trip."

Once even John F. Kennedy, with all he had going for him, said, "Bryant, I envy you your life. How would you like to change places? I'll take care of the dogs if you'll take care of the country."

I said, "I don't know, Mr. President. Looks to me like you've got a pretty good job."

He sighed and said, "Well, it's got some advantages. At least I can walk home to lunch."

In Ike's day, the staff would see him on the putting green and call the White House "the White House Country Club." But his administration also had the hardest-working man I ever saw at the White House. That was Sherman Adams, a man who later came under a cloud because he accepted what seems like a trivial gift by today's standards—a vicuña coat.

In those days I was the early-shift electrician, and the first thing I would do was check Sherman Adams' office, hoping to get there ahead of him and turn on the lights. Though I wasn't supposed to be there until seven-thirty, I'd try to get there by seven to turn on lights and equipment for him, which was my job. Usually I'd be embarrassed to find him there ahead of me, hard at work before 7:00 A.M.

3

President Kennedy certainly seemed to enjoy his women. I don't know for sure about Marilyn Monroe, but I did hear backstairs talk, after he was dead, that during his visits to California he had enjoyed a few discreet meetings with her at a private home.

I never saw her around the White House and I never heard talk of her being either an official or "O.R."—off the record—guest there in his administration, even though she once sang "Happy birthday, Mr. President, happy birthday to you" to him in New York's Madison Square Garden.

But this much I can tell you: he did enjoy having beautiful women around him at the White House and he did entertain them when Jackie was away. There was a conspiracy of silence to protect his secrets from Jacqueline and to keep her from finding out. The newspapers would tell how First Lady Jacqueline was off on another trip, but what they didn't report was how anxious the President sometimes was to see her go. And what consternation there sometimes was when she returned unexpectedly.

I remember one time it was a beautiful tall blond girl skinny-dipping in the pool with him. JFK liked to swim nude and so did some of the girls who popped in to visit him. But this particular girl must have been just waiting for the First Lady to be on her way. She came in the South West Gate and straight to the South Portico, and a trusted aide met her there. He walked her through the Diplomatic Room and along the Colonnade, as if he were taking her to the President's office, but instead he took her to the gymnasium, where she shed her clothes and went to the pool.

Jack Kennedy was already there, lounging naked beside the pool and sipping a daiquiri. Sometimes one or two from a group of trusted staff aides and friends would join Kennedy in the pool, and often there would be just one other male and female to make up a foursome. This time there were several girls and several male friends.

I was there that night because the tall girl had taken a notion she wanted to pet the famous space dog, Pushinka. So I brought the little Russian mongrel to the aide who had escorted her in. The aide kept hurrying the girl along, saying, "The President is waiting for you. He's getting impatient. You can't keep a President waiting, you know." But she insisted on playing with the dog, saying, "Jack won't mind waiting."

While all this was going on, Mrs. Kennedy was supposed to have gone to Atoka, Virginia. But the First Lady circled back because she had forgotten something—or maybe she just had a hunch. Bobby Kennedy was also there. Well, suddenly the ushers were sounding the alarm, and first thing I knew naked bodies were scurrying every which way.

It was easy to get rid of bodies, but gathering up the drinks was another matter and the help had a time clearing away the evidence —like highball glasses. Only the President remained in the pool.

As I remember it, Jacqueline seemed not to notice anything amiss. Soon word came that she was getting back into her car, and then that it had driven off. But just in case, the President swam alone in the pool for a while.

Thinking of this incident reminds me that Jackie wasn't the only one who influenced the décor of the White House—I helped bring about one small alteration myself. When the President noticed that some of us male workers were standing outside the glass door watching him swimming nude with mixed company, he ordered the door to the pool changed to frosted glass. The President always did try to be discreet. He tried to have as few household people as possible know whom he was entertaining. The way he would work it was this. After Jacqueline would leave on one of her numerous outings, he would tell the kitchen help to prepare some food and drinks and just leave them. Then he would tell the waiters they could go home. "I can take care of it," he'd say. What he liked on these occasions was little wiener sausages with bacon wrapped around them. They were kept in a portable warmer. And a pitcher of daiquiris was kept in the refrigerator. JFK liked them.

And usually when he wanted to be alone with his female company, JFK passed the word that the private family quarters on the second floor were off-limits. One night I got word not to go upstairs after the First Lady left. But somehow, thinking of an electrical

23

appliance I had to fix, it slipped my mind and I accidentally went up. I was headed for the third floor anyway, the floor above the living quarters, but the elevator stopped by itself at 2. I could hear lovey-dovey talk. Another man went to the second floor to see if the gas was off in the kitchen—it had been a problem and a bit of a danger. When he stepped out of the back elevator he saw a naked woman walking from the kitchen.

When Jackie was away, riding the elevator was hazardous duty, as this diary entry shows:

Just as the elevator door opened, a naked blond office girl ran through the hall between the second-floor kitchen and the door leading to the West Hall. Her breasts were swinging as she ran by. There was nothing to do but to get out fast and push the basement buttons.

It was natural for us to exchange information backstairs so that we would know how to handle ourselves. But while the Kennedys were in the White House I told no one outside the White House—not even my wife.

The way I heard it, the shots in the arm or hip that the President took every day for his health had the side effect of making him feel very sexy. I don't know how *he* felt, but I do know how the women of the White House reacted to him—half the secretaries and other women around him would gladly have stood in line outside his bedroom door. Some would kiddingly tell me what they would give "for only one night with that man."

They may not have gotten anywhere near his bedroom but they were delighted to help him relax as best they could in the office. Kennedy had an unusual way of relaxing at the end of the day. I found out because my hours officially were three-thirty to eleven-thirty at night, and frequently ended up at midnight or later. Here's the way I described it in my diary, when I was writing down some of my memories after Kennedy had been assassinated.

I'd be out at the C-9 Post* with the dogs and I'd tell the policeman, "Well, I see the President is getting his brush job." The policeman would laugh and say, "I wish she'd come out and fix my hair that way." The girl, a pretty office girl, would take her time, brush Jack Kennedy's hair very

*Every station at which a White House policeman stands guard is designated by a letter-number combination. Policemen are rotated so that the same policeman may stand guard at several posts or stations on the same day.

slow, back and forth, back and forth, brush the sides, brush the back. He'd be sitting at his desk in the office. Maybe working. It relaxed him to have his hair brushed.

I liked Kennedy. I didn't set myself up as his judge. I figured he had his reasons for whatever he did. Also, I liked Jacqueline Kennedy. I liked her a lot. I don't want to give the impression she was some kind of angel. I remember one particular White House party. Mrs. K. was loaded on champagne and flung her shoes off. I looked through the ushers' window, which guests don't know is a one-way mirror, and saw her kick her shoes off while dancing under the chandelier in the main lobby, officially called the Grand Entrance Hall. That's where the good dance floor is, and the Marine Band plays out there. The Usher's Office adjoins the main lobby, just inside the North Portico—what you would call a front porch.

Getting back to that party, Jacqueline seemed to flirt with every guy she danced with—making eyes, throwing her head back lovey-dovey. All the men danced with her. I could see that some of the female guests were plenty jealous. I'll bet their husbands had some explaining to do that night.

She didn't flirt with me, but she did make me feel like a man and someone especially important to her.

For some reason she chose me to help her with various chores, maybe because I understood her—or tried to—and sympathized with her need to feel that she was doing things for herself. I remember Mrs. K. had me help her move a gigantic dollhouse from one side of Caroline's room to the other. I wanted to do it alone but the First Lady pushed right along with me, tugging and huffing and puffing and enjoying the effort.

Once she had the dogs out in the station wagon. She liked to take her big German shepherd to one of the parks and run and hike with him. This time she was waiting for a Secret Service man who would accompany her. She asked me for a cigarette and I didn't have one. I was smoking cigars. I jokingly held one out to her and she giggled. Then I said I'd go get her a cigarette. She said, "No, please, let me." She jumped out and went to the Usher's Office and got her own cigarettes.

I think as marriages go, her marriage to the President wasn't too bad. They had a lot going for them. They both loved their kids and, I think, each other, very much. They were always looking out for each other, sometimes protectively, sometimes trying to think up little surprises. And they did not air their problems in front of the household staff.

When they had anything to say to each other they took walks together inside and outside the White House grounds, no matter what the weather. Sometimes I brought them a dog or two to walk with them. I could tell when they were squabbling with each other, or were just sullen.

Even in the rain or snow I'd find them making their late-night rounds. No umbrella. She with a scarf over her head. He bare-headed. No tourist would take a second look and the Secret Service men kept a discreet distance, usually in a car. It would be dark and rainy. Either Clipper or Charlie would be on a leash. Or both.

What tourist would dream that a President and First Lady were walking a dog? When the Kennedys were happy and playful they didn't want to use a leash, but I would insist, sometimes not so gently, saying I was sure the dog would run into traffic and be run over. Jacqueline would be slightly annoyed with me. She prided herself on her control over dogs. She personally had taken her dogs to the U.S. Park Service's Dog Obedience School, watching the trainers and participating, and now she felt she could make any dog heel and obey. But when I acted tough, she would look resignedly at the President and say, "Oh, all right, Bryant"—pronouncing my name in her appealing little-girl voice—"give it here."

The President never interfered. I felt he enjoyed the little byplay.

I was sure that the Kennedys' dogs were somehow helpful in their marriage, a means they had of communicating with each other in a close and affectionate way.

The White House can be such a lonely place that some presidential couples have given most of their affection to their pets. At times President Warren Harding showed much more affection toward his dog than he did toward his wife, with whom he was frequently feuding. That overindulged dog was Laddie Boy, an arrogant aire-dale who had his own social calendar and his own chair to sit on at cabinet meetings.

Once Laddie Boy presided at a birthday party for himself to which neighborhood dogs had been invited. The birthday cake was made of layers of dog biscuits topped with icing.

According to Lillian Rogers Parks, whose mother, Maggie, worked for the Hardings as a maid, Laddie Boy helped the Hardings over the rough spots. When they were not speaking to each other, the President and First Lady would communicate to each other by addressing to Laddie Boy the remarks they meant for each other.

When the Kennedys came to the White House, they owned just one dog, Charlie, a Welsh terrier. But gifts of dogs descended on them. The one that caused the greatest commotion was Pushinka, a present from Premier Khrushchev. Before the offspring of the Russian space dog, Strelka, could be given the run of the place, she had to be checked through security as a possible dog spy. After all, she might have been wired for sound or have an electronic "bug" implanted in her. But she didn't. She passed inspection A-OK.

I remember I took the furry little mutt to the second floor and sat on the floor in Caroline's room as Caroline and John-John shyly reached out. I was worried because the newcomer was a little temperamental. I'm glad I was careful. Later, little Anthony Radziwill, the children's cousin, son of Prince and Princess Radziwill, almost got his nose bitten by Pushinka while visiting the White House.

I told Rex Scouten, the usher, that I didn't want to be responsible if the dog bit the children. He said it wasn't my responsibility, as they had a nurse, Maud Shaw, and a Secret Service man. But that didn't impress me. I was always alert and would put my finger under Pushinka's collar when she snapped.

At this first meeting between the children and Pushinka, toddler John-John said, "Take me Daddy." He wanted me to take him and his new dog to his daddy's private bedroom. I told him he could go if he wanted to, but that "I can't go unless your daddy calls." He thought that over, then ran to his father's room, and I could hear them hollering and laughing inside.

But getting back to White House pets, the Kennedys had every kind of pet and the papers were always writing that the White House harbored a menagerie. They were right. It was like a way station for the zoo, which is where many gift animals to the Kennedys—like deer and snakes and bears—went. Most of these potentially dangerous gifts Caroline never saw because her father had a hard time denying her anything, once she had her heart set on it.

Even so, the Kennedys really had a houseful and a yardful: ponies and parakeets and cats and ducks and rabbits and guinea pigs. And

27

of course the dogs. First on the list was feisty litle Charlie. Born in 1958, he was a Welsh terrier who rode herd on the much bigger Clipper, snatching things right out of his mouth. He thought he had a right. He'd gone through the election with the President, and had moved into the White House with the Kennedys straight from their Georgetown home.

Pushinka came next, born in 1960 to the Russian space dog, Strelka. As I mentioned before, she was the gift of Premier Nikita Khrushchev. When her own puppies were born, JFK called them "pupniks."

Then the President's father, Ambassador Joseph Kennedy, gave Jacqueline a German shepherd, Clipper, born June 9, 1962.

The Prime Minister of Ireland, Eamon de Valera, gave the President Shannon, an Irish cocker spaniel, born June 15, 1963.

Another citizen of Ireland, this one a Dublin priest with the same family name, Kennedy, sent the President a tremendous wolfhound named Wolf, born May 19, 1963. Wolf liked people, but hated dogs. The place was getting crowded.

The President favored Charlie, and Charlie was Number One dog, and the other dogs better believe it. He knew all about presidential precedence and gave a growl any time a dog preceded him through a doorway, which naturally amused the President.

From the beginning, everything about the glamorous Kennedy family and menagerie fascinated the public.

People stopped to watch through the fence as Caroline's pony, Macaroni, and John-John's pony, Leprechaun, ambled around the yard munching grass. Then Vice President Johnson gave the children what they needed like a third thumb—a third pony, Tex. Tex was a wild one. He thought he was still in Texas, on the ranch near Johnson City. The White House grounds were certainly not big enough for him.

Once Tex almost ran over me. I was helping Mr. Adams, the engineer, round up the ponies, and Tex was about to trample me under. I ducked behind a tree just in time. We had a devil of a time getting the little demon in his stall. Adams was in charge of the horses just as I was in charge of smaller pets.

One horsey incident that tickled me a lot involved Macaroni and JFK. This day, for some reason, Macaroni wandered over to the presidential office window and stood staring at the President. And the President, just as solemnly, stared back. Or, as LBJ would say, "They eyeballed each other."

All of a sudden the President got up, opened his door, and motioned for the pony to come in. Macaroni stood considering the invitation, turned snooty, and walked away. I'm kind of sorry she did. It would have been the first time a horse entered the White House since the Teddy Roosevelt kids sneaked a pony named Algonquin to the second-floor bedroom of their brother Archie, who was sick in bed with measles. As it was, Macaroni made history in a more cultural way by having a symphony named for her. Looking back, I think it was fortunate that Caroline had so many pets because the animals gradually acclimated little Caroline to accept the shock of death in her little world.

I remember when Caroline's canary, Robin, died and was buried in the Rose Garden. This was Caroline's first funeral and she thought it was fun. She always took friends to see the marker.

Then there was a family of hamsters, like something out of a Greek tragedy. First one hamster drowned itself in the President's tub. Then others were eaten by their father. But the final act beat all—the mother hamster killed the father and then died herself, probably of indigestion. What an atmosphere for a child! I think Caroline learned a lot about tragedy from this—the hard way.

Caroline also felt a loss when her mother gave her pet cat, Tom Kitten, to Mary Gallagher, her personal secretary. The cat hair was bothering the President's allergy. He was allergic to dog hair as well, but the difference was that the dogs stayed out of the way and slept in the Bouquet Room, and Tom Kitten was always underfoot. When Tom Kitten died, Caroline went to Mary's house to see the little grave with its marker.

There almost was another funeral when Charlie caught a duck and nearly killed it. He wouldn't let go. Officer Peters managed to get it away before its last gasp and Caroline was much relieved. Charlie jumped in the fountain to cool off, feeling no guilt at all, but the poor duck stuck to dry land. Charlie was too good a swimmer.

I was a little upset, after the President died, that Shannon was the only dog kept. That may have been diplomatically proper, but Charlie was like one of the family and Pushinka was his lady love. Charlie had been with Caroline since she was a baby. It was terrible to separate them. After all, how much dog food could Charlie eat?

I think all the dogs should have stayed as one happy family, for the children's sake. Not only did Caroline and little John lose their father and all the staff they were used to, but they lost all their pets except one.

It had been strictly Jacqueline's decision.

When it came time to leave the White House, Jacqueline Kennedy made it clear she didn't want the trouble or the expense of taking care of all the dogs.

I hate to say it but I have found that some First Families can be rather heartless when it is a question of their convenience or when they have to dip into their own pockets.

But that doesn't mean I don't like First Families. It just means they have warts like the rest of us—some that don't show.

Getting back to happier times, it was the love life of the Kennedy dogs that resulted in my getting to visit Hyannis Port and see the clan together.

What happened was that Charlie had fallen in love with Pushinka, with predictable results. Jacqueline and the children—Caroline and John-John—had gone to Hyannis Port for the summer, and Pushinka had had puppies. Jackie helped Caroline name them Blackie and White Tip and Butterfly and Streaker. As usual she was ahead of the fashions, since being a "streaker" didn't become the rage till 1974.

The President wanted to stage a big surprise for the children, so he asked me whether I would mind taking Pushinka and her pups to Hyannis Port.

I hardly bothered to pack a bag, thinking I would be right back. I remember I flew up on a military plane with the Filipino cooks.

My dramatic entrance with the dogs was carefully staged by the President himself. I had to stay hidden with them at the Secret Service trailer until the President called for me. The joy of the children was something to behold. And they were soon all romping at oceanside.

The Secret Service got me a room at the Anchor Inn, a rooming house for tourists with a view of the village post office. I would have my meals at the Kennedy home in the kitchen. Every day I would look after the dogs and be company for the children, and eventually, like top dog Charlie, I truly felt a part of the family, making myself very much at home.

I used to arrive from my motel between six and six-thirty in the morning to feed the dogs so they wouldn't awaken Mrs. Kennedy and the children. Then I would put the coffeepot on and make coffee, as the cooks made it too weak.

We certainly kept the vets at Hyannis busy. Mrs. Kennedy's sister, Princess Radziwill, was there and told me one of the dogs, Shannon, had a warm nose. So I took Shannon to the vet, who kept the dog overnight. No chances are taken with presidential dogs.

One of my jobs on arrival at the Kennedy compound was to find quarters for all the dogs—quarters that were to the dogs' liking. I gave Shannon a comfy corner in a hall. I made a place for Pushinka and her pups in the basement, and during the day they played in a section fenced in with a brick wall. Charlie slept wherever he liked in the house. He knew he was people—or better.

Just when I had all the dogs squared away, word came that another Kennedy dog was arriving. I rushed to the Barnstable airport to pick up Wolf, the Irish wolfhound. Two men and a young boy had flown the dog from New York in a small plane. I gave each of them one of President Kennedy's tie clasps with the PT boat on it. JFK often saw me giving away his tie pins and approved this act of generosity.

I finally found the temperamental Wolf a place to sleep in the garage.

One time I was driving Pushinka and the pups to the vet when I glanced in the back seat and saw only three pups. I stopped the car and searched all over. Only three pups. I thought I'd have a heart attack. I was sure the fourth had climbed out the window. What would I tell Caroline? Then I heard a little snort and found the prize crawler down under the front seat. What a relief!

Whenever I took a dog to the vet in Hyannis Port, we would wait our turn, as we didn't want to pull rank over the other dogs. I knew that was the way Jackie would want it. Washington was a different matter—there I pulled rank—but in Massachusetts the Kennedys played it very humble. Arthur M. Bernstein, the presidential vet, was at the Yarmouth Animal Hospital in West Yarmouth, Massachusetts. A very good man. He performed an operation on Clipper's hip and showed me the x-rays.

With no one to play with, John-John would turn to me. I used to let him ride on my back and play horse. As we played around on the beach he was happy and without a care, but I felt uneasy—in fact, mighty uncomfortable—because I could see the Russian fishing boats off Squaw Island. Luckily, I had brought along my telescope for a pastime and I ended up loaning it to the Secret Service to use at their guard post.

Some of the Kennedy dogs were really wild. For example, Jackie's German shepherd, Clipper, was afraid of helicopters. When he heard one, one day, he tore the screen door, bolting right through it.

The Kennedys were in a rented house—Brambletide. A thousand dollars a month, a maid told me. I didn't think it was worth it.

I became friendly with the owner of the Anchor Inn—I still get a Christmas card from her each year. It was a happy month. I remember how, all day, life at the rented house centered around the puppies. The children would romp and tumble about with the dogs. The First Lady was anxious for them to learn to handle dogs with kindness. I was more concerned about how the dogs handled the children.

I stayed in Hyannis Port for a month at the request of President Kennedy. The Usher's Office was most annoyed. They had wanted to send someone else but had to send the keeper of the dogs instead, since no one bucks the President. The Usher's Office is the nerve center of the White House, greeting guests and running the kitchens, handling the housekeeping and the maintenance of the President's house; only the President or First Lady can tell the ushers what to do.

I have only one sad memory of those days. It concerns Jacqueline, who was very pregnant. I was horrified to see her swimming in high waves at Squaw Island in her condition a few days before having her last baby—Patrick, the baby who did not survive the first days of his life.

I'll take that back, there was one other sad sight—the President's father in a wheelchair.

I was especially touched by the way the President tried to communicate with his father, Ambassador Joseph Kennedy. Every day the President would show his father the dogs, but one day I got all choked up when he put a puppy in his father's lap and his father seemed to respond. This was in June 1963. In November not the father but the son was dead.

The night they brought Kennedy's body to the White House, I was on duty. I did not see him. It was a sealed casket. Somehow, all

I could think of was the way the President had kidded about my being called a presidential aide by a Boston newspaper. Over and over again the scene went through my mind. He was heading for a helicopter at Hyannis Port with his press secretary, Pierre Salinger, walking beside him puffing a big cigar. "I hear you are now my presidential aide for taking care of the dogs," the President said to me a bit sternly; then both men laughed. Somehow that kept going through my mind—the laugh, the grin, the crinkled eyes.

And now looking back I remember so many other things. The President scolding me for letting Clipper chase balls and sticks. I'd thought he'd be pleased at the new trick. I was training the dog outside and tossed a ball a few times for him to catch. The President had glasses on, reading a letter, when he looked out the window and saw us. He came to the window, then sent Mrs. Kennedy out to get me. She said, "Bryant, the President wants to talk to you," and I thought, How young she sounds.

When I got up to the house, the President said sternly, "I don't want you to throw sticks and teach him to run after balls."

I assured the President it wouldn't happen again. I went straight to the Secret Service and they notified all the men not to throw sticks and not to play with this particular dog here at Hyannis Port or at the White House. Later I found out why the President had gotten so excited. The President had been practicing his golf swing and Clipper had leaped for the club when he had it over his shoulder. Clipper had almost succeeded in dislocating the presidential arm. The President ended up swinging club *and* dog.

I had to smile. It reminded me of Eisenhower and his golfing problems. Instead of having a dog retrieve the balls, Ike gave the job to his valet, Sergeant Moaney. Many times while walking through the White House grounds I saw Ike hitting golf balls while Moaney chased them.

Sometimes President Eisenhower hit the ball so hard that he would shatter a street light across the street from the South Grounds. You could hear the glass protector tinkle. Instead of being conscience-stricken about it, Ike would chortle, "I got that one." When he got through, we would go out and I would replace the bulb. Eventually the city got tired of replacing glass protectors and put in plastic ones.

I have a souvenir ball—one that scored a bull's eye on the street

33

light. The lawnmower chewed up many others. Speaking of things being chewed up, I remember how Ike's golf shoes would chew up the cork tile border around his office rug. The housekeeping staff would tear their hair but they couldn't say anything. Nobody tells a President he can't wear spikes in the house. So now and then they would just quietly replace a few tiles.

4

Did Kennedy play around much at the White House? Yes, he did. Every time one of his feminine guests left, the help would scour the rooms for hairpins and bobby pins. Kennedy was following a tradition established by a lot of earlier Presidents.

More than once I heard talk in the White House of how Woodrow Wilson had played around after his first wife died. According to the story, the President's doctor, Cary Grayson, was so worried that rumors would sweep the country about a "playboy in the White House" that he introduced him to a widow he considered suitable for marriage, Edith Bolling Galt. Luckily the meeting "took."

President Wilson proposed. Nevertheless, he had such a wild reputation that a joke went the rounds of Washington, and even today people occasionally resurrect it at the White House while reviewing the love lives of the Presidents.

Question: What did Mrs. Galt say when President Wilson proposed to her?

Answer: Nothing. She was so surprised she fell out of bed.

There's still talk about a packet of love letters that Wilson is supposed to have exchanged with some other woman before Edith Galt entered his life. At the time people thought the letters had damaging material that might keep him from being reelected. But the best letters weren't revealed and never have been. The lady in question clammed up. She was rumored to have received a gift of money from a close friend of the President. One of the President's daughters sought to counteract the bad publicity by gathering and publishing his love letters to her mother, his first wife.

And what about the shocking White House romance of another very sexy President in the 1880's, Grover Cleveland? That story has it that President Cleveland was romancing his ward, Frances Folsom, daughter of his old law partner and his responsibility since she was eleven.

The President tried hard to keep his feelings about the pretty girl

35

a secret, but as every President learns, no secrets survive for long in the White House. On the night of June 2, 1886, President Cleveland, who was pushing fifty, filled the Blue Room with flowers and made Frances, who was twenty-one or twenty-two years old—versions differ—his bride, with only a few close friends and his Cabinet present.

When Eisenhower moved into the White House, backstairs talk began immediately about his wartime relations with his W.A.A.F driver and how he gifted her with pretty gowns from Paris. The story told was that five-star General Ike really cared deeply about his chauffeur, Kay Summersby, and that he wanted to divorce Mamie to marry her. At Mamie's request, people said, General Marshall, the Chief of Staff, sent Ike's son John to be his father's aide, in order to help save the marriage. The strategy worked.

Scratch almost any President and you will find a bit of a lady's man. Even McKinley, with his reputation as a stiffneck, had a fine eye for the ladies. When he was President, he supposedly taught a parrot to tell the difference between men and women. Every time a female approached the parrot would shriek, "Look at the pretty girl!" But McKinley didn't need a parrot to tell him.

LBJ loved women, too. Within my sight he confined himself to grabbing an occasional kiss, but the talk backstairs and among his aides was that he didn't stop just there a few times when he'd gone driving off into the night with some charmer—usually on his way to the presidential yacht. He was even said to have "inherited" two very pretty girl reporters from Kennedy. At least, they were LBJ's favorites and he would mention one or the other to me as "all woman" or "a lot of woman" and even accord them the ultimate compliment he ordinarily reserved for his favorite dog, Yuki, telling me they were "pretty as a polecat."

At a party LBJ would back a pretty girl off in a corner and sweep her off her feet by telling her, "You're the prettiest thing I've ever seen." What he didn't add was "since yesterday." Sometimes he'd tell the gal who caught his eye to step into the next room away from the noise, where they could hold a "serious discussion."

She may have been serious. He wasn't. If ever there was a kissing President, it was he. When he got into the party spirit at a White House dance, someone had to get the lipstick off him. Lady Bird would be on the alert to break it up. She'd say kind of plaintively,

"You're wanted over there, Lyndon. You're neglecting some of your friends." She found safety in numbers. As long as the President was kidding all the girls, she was safe.

Once Lyndon Johnson actually got jealous of *me*! I'll tell you about it later. The point I want to make now is that LBJ was a sexy man. He told me so and I'm willing to take his word for it. Lady Bird frequently slept in LBJ's bed. I would go up to deliver the dogs and she would be tucked under the covers.

After Johnson died, I read somewhere that Lady Bird was interviewed about her husband's playful way with the girls and you could tell that she had understood him all the time. Asked about her husband's flirtations, Lady Bird said, "He got a lot of solace and happiness and inspiration from women," and admitted Lyndon was "a flirt and a ladies' man."

Then she said something that showed her true humility. "I hope that I was reasonable. And if all those ladies had some good points that I didn't have, I hope that I had the good sense to try to learn by it."

When it comes to the Nixons, what can I say? Pat Nixon herself admitted she could not sleep in the same bed with the President because he was too fretful—kept waking up, dictating into a Dictaphone, turning lights off and on. But more on that later.

There was nothing fretful about Kennedy and his sleep habits. He enjoyed his bed—day or night.

And he certainly enjoyed women, as I can attest by my own eyes. He would often kid with his male staff about women. An item from my diary shows his style of banter:

Dave Powers once asked the President what he would like to have for his birthday. He named a TV actress from California. His wish was granted.

Even President Ford commented on Jack Kennedy's obsession with girls. They used to have offices across the hall from each other when Kennedy was a congressman. After Ford became President and was still in his "honeymoon stage" with the press, I read that he had reminisced with a newspaperman about those days. Congressman Kennedy would come in, he said, prop his feet up on Ford's desk, and sit around talking about his favorite theme. As Ford put it, "He always talked about one subject—girls."

One of Kennedy's girlfriends commented that he was the only man she knew who could make love with one eye on his watch.

Even so, there were sudden exits and Jackie once found a woman's undergarment tucked in a pillowcase. She delicately held it out to her husband between thumb and forefinger—about the way you hold a worm—saying, "Would you please shop around and see who these belong to? They're not my size."

Some newspaper and magazine articles say Marilyn Monroe was smuggled into the White House. If so, I'm sorry I missed her. But the gals I did see were not bad. Not bad at all. Even though his wife was brunette, his girls all seemed to be blonde—and one was a near redhead. The backstairs help used to mutter, "Why can't he make it easier for us? Why do we always have to be searching for blonde hairs and blond bobby pins? Why can't he get himself a steady brunette?"

With Kennedy, the story was that in spite of his marriage to Jacqueline, he had never given up his bachelorhood. Many people have heard the rumor that Joseph Kennedy, the President's father, gave Jackie one million dollars in return for her promise not to divorce his son while he was running for the Presidency, or if he made it, as long as he was in the White House.

Less widely known was the theory of just what the straw might have been that broke the camel's back and prompted the gift in the first place. After all, Jack had been the playboy of the Western world for some time before the campaign began, and Jackie hadn't made waves.

The story around the White House was that the blow she finally could not forgive had come when a fifteen-year-old babysitter accused the senator of making her pregnant. That, Jackie was quoted to have said, was the limit beyond the limit. It was also, supposedly, what the ambassador was trying to soothe her for.

Despite all the stories I've heard about other past Presidents, I doubt we will ever have another one like Kennedy. I even heard him say to one of his buddies, "I'm not through with a girl till I've had her three ways."

There was something else interesting about Kennedy's pre-White House escapades. When he and a congressional buddy used to get a hotel room in another city, they would get two girls and trade

38

around. Nowadays he would be called a "swinger." Then he was called just plain wild.

Even Jackie realized that her husband wouldn't be satisfied with just one woman. I used to think how amazed the country would be to find out that Jacqueline Kennedy, supposedly the most desirable and exciting woman in the whole world, couldn't keep her husband content. It really wasn't her fault. Another man would have desired nothing more than the opportunity to stay close to her in the White House or wherever she was. But Kennedy's way, or his previous training, simply made him different. As every dogkeeper says, "You can't teach an old dog new tricks."

Jackie sought a little solace herself—a close friend she could talk to and let her hair down with. One such comforter was the famous economist and ambassador to India, John Kenneth Galbraith.

Once when Jackie was traveling with Galbraith on an official visit, the word was Jack became afraid he would lose ground with her himself, and she would get too much sympathy, so he called her to come back to the White House.

And he did that again, insiders knew, when she was on the luxury yacht of Aristotle Onassis, with her sister, Princess Lee Radziwill.

Some people may have mentioned it, but I never saw anybody point out the full significance of the fact that when President Kennedy died, one of the men at the White House comforting Jacqueline was Aristotle Onassis, whose yacht she had been on not too long before.

So when she later married him, she was marrying an old, old friend, not someone who had just entered her life. Backstairs at the White House, though we were amazed she had married a foreigner, once we got used to that thought we were not surprised that it was Onassis.

And I'll tell you another thing that seemed without significance at the time, but important looking back. My wife, Doris, reminded me after the news of the Onassis marriage exploded in the headlines that we had seen Onassis at the commissioning of the aircraft carrier *John F. Kennedy* when Robert McNamara had been the speaker. "Don't you remember," Doris said, "when Jackie Kennedy came up and talked to you, she suddenly swung around and said rather excitedly to a strange-looking, rather short, gray-haired man, 'Oh, Ari, I didn't know *you* were here!'" So evidently the friendship had been going on for quite some time before anyone paid any attention.

One might ask, "How come Kennedy got away with his romantic escapades, and few stories ever came out?" The answer is simple. Politics on a high level is a club. You protect the club member. Henry Cabot Lodge, for example, who was a close friend of LBJ, once ran against Kennedy. That was when Kennedy was a congressman, running for senator. During the campaign, so the story goes, Lodge's people came across a picture showing Jack Kennedy and a blonde, both naked, lying on a beach. Lodge could have worked the picture for a lot of mileage, but when it was shown to Congressman Kennedy, he just laughed and said, "Oh, yes, I remember her. Naw, Henry won't use that." And he didn't. As I said, politics is a club.

For some reason Kennedy liked soft romantic music coming from under him when he was in bed. The Army Signal Corps installed stereo speakers under his bed and the President also had a stereo speaker mounted on the second-floor balcony. One day someone switched the balcony speaker on loud and German martial music suddenly blared out over the South Lawn. I'm not sure what the tourists thought, but Pushinka, Clipper, and Charlie figured it was a carnival and started barking loudly. I called the usher and someone quickly cut the speakers off.

After Kennedy died, LBJ ordered the stereo ripped out. He liked the sound of telephones and his own voice better. I'd come into his bedroom at any hour, bringing or picking up a dog, and he'd be talking and laughing on the phone or cussing someone out. I'd wonder how the guy on the other end could take so much abuse.

5

They ought to have little plaques on the White House lawn—
HERE IS WHERE PRESIDENT KENNEDY AND JOHN-JOHN ROLLED ON THE
GRASS or HERE IS WHERE FIRST LADY PAT NIXON WAS KNOCKED TO THE
GROUND BY KING TIMAHOE—and I hope future generations wouldn't
assume that King Tim was a foreign monarch.

Actually Kennedy was the only President I knew who loved to
get down on the ground. Three First Ladies did—Jackie and Pat
and Lady Bird—but JFK was the only President I ever saw do it.
He would sit on the golf green and play with the pups and he would
tumble John-John there.

One day John-John was crying because Charlie, the Welsh terrier,
was missing. The President asked me where Charlie was, and I told
him he had been chasing squirrels and had one treed. Little John's
lip quivered. The President didn't say anything, but later I was
summoned to his office, where quite severely he ordered me to keep
the dogs more available to the children. Incidentally, Jacqueline
hated to hear people call her son John-John, but everyone did, even
the press. And she told me she detested the nickname "Jackie"; she
wanted to be "Jacqueline" at all times.

Late-summer afternoons I sometimes get a lump in my throat as
I watch the sun setting and think back to those Kennedy days—so
happy in retrospect. I especially remember the President's dog-and-
kid ritual because I was there and saw the tumble of animals and
little people that resulted. At dusk if he was still working in his
office, the President would come out and clap his hands. All activity
stopped—playing, running, jumping—and then dogs and children
would rush for him with barks and shrieks of joy. As they milled
about, he'd give the dogs dog candy, and Evelyn Lincoln, his secretary, would hand out authorized goodies to the children—JFK's own
two children and their little friends and cousins present at the time.

JFK would tease Caroline, looking all around at the dogs—
Charlie, Pushinka, the puppies, and Clipper—and saying, "But,
Caroline, where's the blue whale?" The blue whale was imaginary

but Caroline would say, "He's got a cold today," or, "Oh, Daddy, you're hiding him behind you."

Once a story made the rounds that JFK had taken the children out on the presidential yacht—the *Honey Fitz*—and brought along his good friend Franklin D. Roosevelt, Jr., who liked to relax on the boat in his socks. The President was telling his blue-whale story and FDR, Jr., was just as fascinated as the children were. Suddenly the President deviated from the story line, saying, "And the thing the blue whale likes to eat most is a dirty sock." With that he reached over and pulled Franklin's sock off and threw it in the water.

Roosevelt just slouched there, not knowing what to say, but Caroline peered over the rail and exclaimed, "The whale got it." Kennedy nodded and said, "But the only thing the blue whale likes better than one sock is two socks," and he reached over and grabbed the other one off Roosevelt's foot, tossing it overboard, too. That finally stirred Franklin up enough to say, "Hey, I hope the blue whale isn't waiting for pants for dessert."

Kennedy would do anything for his children. Anything but lift them. It hurt his manly pride that doctors didn't let him do much lifting because of his bad back. About the only time he ever looked a little jealous was when someone else would lift his kids and toss them in the air. Or let them play horsey on his back, as I sometimes did.

The only way JFK could roughhouse with them at all was to lie with his back flat on the ground or floor and pretend to fight them off. Caroline and John-John would crawl over him or climb up and stand on his knees. Lying this way, if he felt especially good, he would lift John-John high above him. But this was rare.

The White House has a terrible effect on children. I can't think of any kids it hasn't spoiled, with the possible exception of Julie Eisenhower. And the reason I think she wasn't spoiled by it was that she was already married when the Nixons moved in.

Even Margaret Truman threw her weight around and was more or less feared by the staff. If she wanted a piano moved to another room you had better move it that instant. She played hard to get and made photographers really work to get her picture. Their discomfort amused her.

I was very fond of Luci Johnson, probably my favorite White

House brat, but I must admit she was publicity-mad. I think it's like opium—the need for publicity after kids get a taste of it. Once Luci had her picture taken with a huge snake around her neck. She was visiting a reptile farm and was probably making sure the event would be recorded for history. It was. The next day that picture made all the papers.

Luci also liked to cuss like a trooper to see if she could shock anyone. Anyone backstairs at the White House, that is.

The Nixon girls thought nothing of keeping the White House kitchen staff on duty extra hours in case they wanted something. Kids tend to get a little helpless with all that service around.

Even little John-John got the idea of how important he was. He could demand, even order. I noted in my diary how one time Mr. West, the chauffeur of the Secretary of Defense, Robert McNamara, was sitting in the limousine waiting for his boss.

Little John Kennedy came up and poked his knee and asked him what he was doing. Mr. West said, "Reading a fishing book."

John-John ordered Mr. West to drive him around the South Grounds Circle. West told him he couldn't do it because he had to wait for Mr. McNamara.

John-John drew himself up and warned Mr. West, "You'd better do it, or my daddy will make you."

And he might have!

Caroline, too, had only to ask and her daddy attempted to grant her slightest wish. As I've mentioned before, when they moved into the White House, the Kennedys ordered all the TV sets taken out. But they hadn't reckoned on Caroline, who set up a wail because she wanted to see Lassie. So the President ordered me to rush a portable TV set into the West Hall for Caroline. It had rabbit ears and did not connect with the roof antenna. It could be moved out of sight when company came.

The President was putty in Caroline's hands. Caroline wasn't supposed to eat candy without authorization. One day the President saw her munching away, and he asked her sternly if she was eating candy. She wouldn't answer. He asked her again and she just looked a little guilty but still didn't answer.

"Come on, Caroline," her daddy said, his face breaking into a little grin, "you can answer yes, no, or maybe."

One thing that perturbed Caroline about her father was that she couldn't get money out of him. Once on an outing Caroline talked her daddy into letting her and all her friends have candy, with a limit of five cents apiece. As frequently happened, JFK didn't have a cent in his pocket. He looked kind of sheepish and borrowed a dollar from the Secret Service man. Caroline scolded him, saying, "Daddy, you shouldn't go into a store without money." To which he said, "It's all right if you go with rich friends," and he grinned at the agent.

I liked seeing all the Kennedys, great and small, congregating at the White House, looking so healthy and slim and athletic—it seemed like a coeducational locker room. Especially when all the little nieces and nephews were there—Jean's and Eunice's and Bobby's and Ted's. The President was as friendly with them as with his own two kids, and often mentioned them in his humorous comments on events. When he was criticized for making his own brother, Robert, Attorney General, for example, he told a group, "Talking about jobs for relatives, Master Robert Kennedy, who is four years old, came to see me today, but I told him we already had an Attorney General."

I dearly loved Caroline Kennedy—she was a little doll. But she could also be a little pain in the neck. She fancied herself the social arbiter of me and the dogs and was forever telling me that something I was doing wasn't polite. "You gave Clipper a dog biscuit and you didn't give one to Charlie. That's not polite." Or, "You only petted three puppies. That's not fair."

I could pet two dogs at a time, but it was difficult to pet four at once. With up to nine dogs in the Kennedy household, anyone would have had trouble. Especially since White House dogs get so spoiled they start competing for attention like children. Caroline's dog, Charlie, was jealous of Wolf, the President's dog. Clipper was jealous of Shannon. Pushinka was jealous of everybody, including her four puppies—Blackie, Butterfly, White Tip, and Streaker.

I remember the Eisenhowers had similar problems.

Ike's weimaraner, Heidi, detested Spunky, a little Scottie that Ike's grandson, David, brought with him on visits. Heidi would jump all over Spunky and would have to be put out of sight when David was coming. David—now married to Julie Nixon—was the apple of everyone's eye and ran the roost when he was at the White House: his grandfather, his grandmother, his little sisters, the kitchen help. No one ever thought of telling David not to bring his dog.

44

Leaving Spunky home probably wouldn't have helped anyway because Heidi was so jealous of her position with the President that she resented the First Lady. Whenever Mamie approached the President, Heidi would jump all over her to keep them apart.

Poor Heidi kept being shuffled back and forth to Gettysburg, but the President would get lonely for his dog and order her brought back, dispatching a chauffeur-driven limousine.

But getting back to Caroline Kennedy, of all my failings and errors she ever sought to correct, the worst, in her five-year-old opinion, was the trick I used to teach Pushinka to climb the ladder to Caroline's tree house.

What happened is that one day President Kennedy spotted Pushinka hurrying up the ladder to the tree house, walking across the platform, and then sliding down a chute on the other side. He laughed heartily and asked, "How in the world did you ever get a dog to do that?"

I showed him a peanut in my hand. "No problem, Mr. President. I just moved a peanut up the ladder one step at a time and Pushinka followed the peanut. She'll do anything for a peanut. The same goes for the trip down. She knows there is always a peanut at the bottom of the slide."

As he watched Pushinka slide down and collect her payment several times, the President shook his head, amazed, and asked me to have some pictures made of it. He said, "That's worth six million votes right there."

Apparently he made a big thing of it with Jackie and Caroline because the very next day Caroline started scolding me about feeding peanuts to Pushinka and told me her mommy said it was very bad for a dog to eat peanuts. And yes, daddy, too, said it was very bad for a dog to eat peanuts. She wouldn't let up until I promised I would be very careful about how *many* peanuts I gave Pushinka. And she kept checking up on me until one time I told her, "Caroline, you better watch out. You're getting to sound like a common scold."

I read somewhere that Caroline, now a teenager, was considering becoming a nun. I have to smile because at age five she showed little sign of any such inclination. I remember one day her father shaking his head as he told me that Caroline had spent the whole time in church making faces and mouthing words at the parishioners over his shoulder. "I didn't think it was a funny sermon," the President said, "but everyone else was finding it uproarious." When he

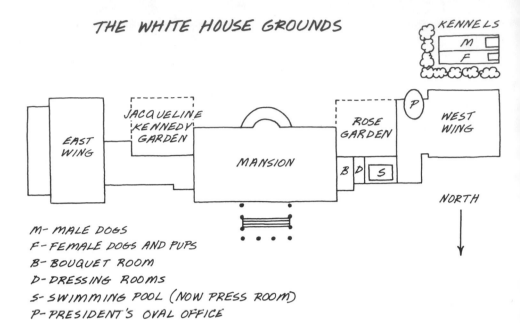

THE WHITE HOUSE GROUNDS

M— MALE DOGS
F— FEMALE DOGS AND PUPS
B— BOUQUET ROOM
D— DRESSING ROOMS
S— SWIMMING POOL (NOW PRESS ROOM)
P— PRESIDENT'S OVAL OFFICE

turned around, he saw that Caroline was holding her own service in a lighter vein, energetically moving her lips and making faces as the priest spoke.

Not only that, but she was a bit of an exhibitionist. One day at Hyannis Port I heard excited squealing and looked up at the upstairs bedroom windows. The little boys spending the night were all in one bedroom, and the little girls were in another bedroom facing theirs. I think the children of the President's sister, Patricia, who was then married to movie star Peter Lawford, were there, and so was the young son of Provi, Jackie's maid. The cause of the squealing was that Caroline was doing a little striptease and streaking back and forth in front of her window to the delight of the boys.

I told a Secret Service man to check into what was going on. I felt my duty went no further than that; if Jacqueline's special Secret Service man, Clint Hill, thought the First Lady should know what was going on upstairs, he should be the one to tell her.

Few people have the courage to tattle on a White House kid— not to a President or First Lady.

White House children may be the stars of their own little show, but deep down most of those I have known have suffered loneliness.

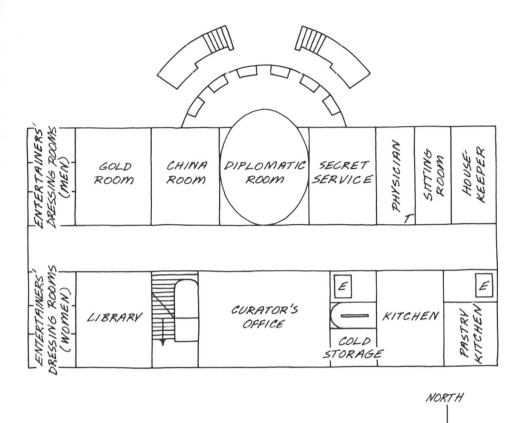

T—TRAPHES BRYANT'S ELECTRIC
SHOP IS DIRECTLY UNDER
PHYSICIAN'S OFFICE
(BASEMENT MEZZANINE)

NORTH

GROUND FLOOR PLAN
WHITE HOUSE

There's never a boy or girl next door who can just wander over to the White House and get acquainted. As Luci Johnson once told me, "You have to be pushy to have any friends at the White House. No one will call you any more. *You* have to call *them*." That was her problem, and she solved it by doing the calling. Lynda Bird was shyer, so she suffered more loneliness than Luci.

Jackie Kennedy tried to lick the problem of finding playmates for Caroline by running a nursery school at the White House. Presidential parents tend to feel guilty and try to make it up to their children by pampering and indulging them.

47

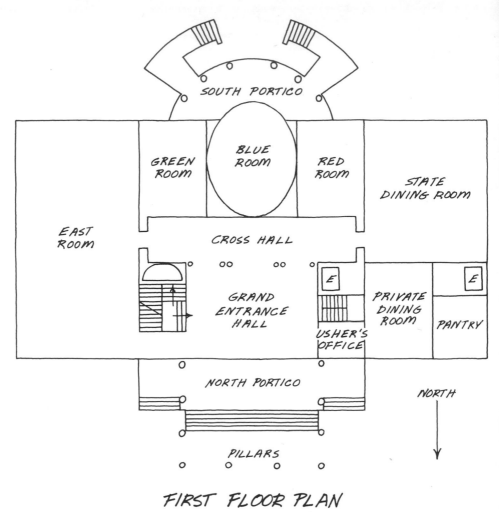

FIRST FLOOR PLAN
WHITE HOUSE

Even as far back as Lincoln, Presidents realized there was a barrier between their own children and other children and tried to solve it with pets. Pets and children come first, and Presidents haven't cared how it looks to the rest of the world.

Lincoln, when he took his family to Soldier's Home—used temporarily for a summer White House—some miles from the Capitol, piled his son Tad's two goats in the carriage along with everyone else. A shocked aide haughtily suggested that perhaps goats

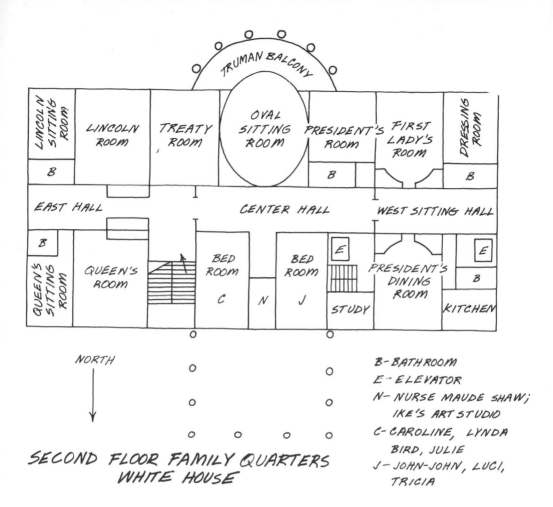

SECOND FLOOR FAMILY QUARTERS
WHITE HOUSE

B – BATHROOM
E – ELEVATOR
N – NURSE MAUDE SHAW; IKE'S ART STUDIO
C – CAROLINE, LYNDA BIRD, JULIE
J – JOHN-JOHN, LUCI, TRICIA

should not be allowed in a presidential carriage, but Lincoln said innocently, "Why not? There's plenty of room in here." The goats went. The aide stayed behind.

LBJ was in the tradition of Lincoln when it came to pets. His dogs rode in the limousine and LBJ didn't care which famous people or aides or chauffeurs or family members frowned their disapproval. Anyone who didn't like it—and some didn't, when they were on their way to a trip on the yacht—moved over to another car, if more than one limo was going, and joined the President at dockside.

I've seen a lot of children come and go at the White House and I've noticed that all presidential parents try to keep them from being

49

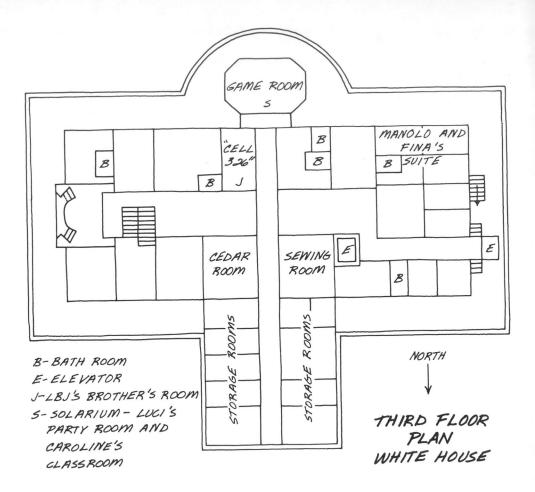

GAME ROOM
S

"CELL 3-26"

B J

B

B

MANOLO AND FINA'S SUITE

B

B

CEDAR ROOM

SEWING ROOM

E

E

B

STORAGE ROOMS

STORAGE ROOMS

B - BATH ROOM
E - ELEVATOR
J - LBJ's BROTHER's ROOM
S - SOLARIUM - LUCI's
    PARTY ROOM AND
    CAROLINE'S
    CLASSROOM

NORTH

THIRD FLOOR
PLAN
WHITE HOUSE

spoiled. Facts are facts, however, and the White House is not the place to raise an unspoiled child. The prize may go to Luci Johnson, who once kept a Secret Service man, a chauffeur, and a limousine waiting eight hours.

Naturally the White House staff tires of catering to the whims of the presidential offspring, especially if they don't seem grateful for the endless help and pampering they get. But after a few tangles with the brats, every employee learns that it's easier just to go along and do what they want than it is to try to change them.

Once Tricia felt like eating a hot dog. Poor Chef Haller searched the second-floor kitchens, refrigerators and deep freeze, the first-floor pantry, and the ground floor vault of freezers but could not find one. Plenty of roasts, steaks, legs of lamb, hamburgers, you name it, but zero on hot dogs. Stores were closed. Finally Haller went to a vending machine in the West Wing used by the office help and put money in it. Out came the hot dog. He rushed it to the kitchen, reheated it, served it to her. She said it was the best hot dog she'd ever had. Haller left the room muttering under his breath. Adding injury to insult, he had paid for the hot dog out of his own pocket.

Julie was my favorite Nixon because she was most friendly and thoughtful of others. She would always thank me when I had taken care of something for her dog, Vicky. But I never got as personally involved with any of the Nixons as with the Johnsons. The Nixons were just trained never to let their guard down with the employees.

The three Presidents I knew who had marriageable daughters seemed always to be worried about them. The word backstairs was that Margaret Truman was forever being humiliated by her father sending Secret Service men after her when she stayed out late, busting up any chance for romance.

Lyndon Johnson, who confided in me now and then on the subject of Lynda Bird, didn't rest easy until she had given up her Hollywood "part-time" boyfriend, George Hamilton, and found "a nice feller who's around full time and who she can count on." But until that day Lynda had to put up with a lot of paternal flak—in the form of LBJ's humor—about her Hollywood jet-setting style.

Then came Nixon, and the word backstairs at the White House was that "King Richard" would like nothing better than a royal British princeling for a son-in-law. As you will see, when Prince Charles arrived for a visit, even King Timahoe lost his crown— worse, was thrown into the White House equivalent of the Tower of London. But Tricia crossed up her father's plans by holding out for the man she loved, Ed Cox.

6

Each First Lady had her specialty—something she cared about in a very particular way. Something the staff would be very aware of because of its importance to her.

With Lady Bird Johnson, it was sunshine and her ceramic Doughty birds. She wanted things in the family quarters of the White House painted yellow, the color of sunshine, and into that sunshine she brought her collection of Doughty birds, giving her, she said, "that happy feeling of sunshine and birds everywhere."

When she moved to the White House, Lady Bird hand-carried her two most precious possessions: a portrait of Sam Rayburn, who had helped her husband in his early political days, and her Doughty birds—each one worth $1,100 or more.

With Jackie Kennedy, it was flowers, flowers, everywhere flowers. She wanted them to look as if they had just been picked in some field, and these bouquets meant so much to her that they were photographed, each and every day, as a guide for the White House florists of future First Ladies.

When I'd walk through Jackie's White House, gone were the formal pink roses and carnations set off by fern that Mamie had ordered. Instead, flowers and grasses I'd never seen in the White House before made it look like a pretty meadow.

With Mamie Eisenhower, the special emphasis was on rugs. All the carpeting had to be perfect, as if no foot had ever trod there, and the staff learned to walk around a rug before a party.

So you can imagine how she felt when Heidi, for reasons known best to herself, and maybe the President whose dog she was, chose to decorate the $20,000 rug in the Diplomatic Reception Room. When Mamie saw what had happened, she stayed up nearly all night working with housekeeping staff trying to get the stain out. No luck. Then she had the rug dyed but the acid still showed through, so the rug and Heidi were banished—the rug permanently, the dog until she could be forgiven.

Mamie endeared herself to me because, when she gave a little gift, she actually wrapped the gift and wrote the card herself. And she really knew how to pick a present that you could cherish and use. Practical things. Various Christmases I received from her linen handkerchiefs, a silver bottle opener, crystal coasters, a leather telephone book cover, and *wearable* neckties.

And it was she who insisted that all the White House crew come visit the First Family at their summer home—Gettysburg—something I can't imagine any other First Lady doing. I'll never forget that day—Ike and Mamie being just plain folks and having their pictures snapped standing with various employees while a friend would handle the Brownie camera. All went well till the wife of an engineer got carried away. It happened while Ike was showing some of us the garden. Spotting a row of onions, the engineer's wife literally ordered the President to dig some for her so she could take them home. He pretended he didn't hear. She repeated it.

I fought back my laughter as I saw the President get ready to explode. Then suddenly he gulped and damned if he didn't kneel down and pull her an armful of nice green onions.

Getting back to Christmas presents, Jacqueline Kennedy was another First Lady whose gifts reflected her individual personality. Several years she gave me and others on her staff lovely photographs of the interiors of rooms that she had redecorated, such as the Green Room. And another Christmas present from her that I particularly cherish is an exterior shot of ducks on the White House lawn. I'm not sure we will ever have ducks on the White House lawn again, but on the wall in my house, there they always are.

Pat Nixon had the good idea of sharing some of the White House treasures with us by giving us beautifully reproduced copies of the portraits of Presidents that hang there, such as the standing figure of Teddy Roosevelt and the seated, brooding figure of Abraham Lincoln.

A few years earlier, Lady Bird Johnson had given us a print of a watercolor painting showing a White House tree. Mrs. Johnson had written an eloquent legend that goes with it:

Tall and graceful, with fan-shaped crowns of finely subdividing branches, the American elm has long been favored as an ornamental stately shade tree. A few days before Christmas 1913, President Woodrow Wilson took a moment from the affairs of state to plant this symbol of peace and serenity which today shades the North Portico of the White House.

I look at that tree and read her words often and feel a surge of nostalgia as I see her signature under it as well as that of Lyndon B. Johnson, and the cheerful comment, "Our warmest best wishes for a joyous holiday season and a bright and prosperous New Year, 1966."

It was a joyous holiday, and my wife and I took great pride in knowing the Johnsons, especially when a chauffeur drove up and surprised us with a package of the famous Lyndon Johnson deer-meat sausage and some homemade bread baked from Lady Bird's own recipe.

Lyndon Johnson and his family were the only presidential family to send gifts not just while they were at the White House but after they left it. The Christmas before he died, for example, LBJ sent me a copy of his book *The Vantage Point*. And Luci has sent me quaint gifts like a painting on wood of herself and the dogs running on the lawn.

Hearing Lyndon Johnson talk about his ranch and seeing Dwight Eisenhower's farm with its pond and its mallards made me decide that when I retired from the White House I, too, wanted a country place of my own. I was born under a lucky star. The first farm Doris and I looked at had a duck pond even larger than Ike's, plenty of land, and all the rest—it was even near another historic landmark, the Appomattox Court House. I said, "I'll take it."

That's where I am today, paddling around my acre pond in a boat and feeding the mallards lettuce from the barrel of my shotgun. They have nothing to fear from the gun—it's for killing snakes. To them it's just a thing that you stuff lettuce into.

As the time grew close for me to leave the White House, after twenty years, I started to get nostalgic. I didn't know how I was going to adjust to a life that didn't include Presidents, First Ladies, Secret Service men, chauffeurs, dogs, high-powered presidential assistants and aides, kings and queens dropping in by helicopter, prime ministers and ambassadors milling about on the lawn and pausing to shake hands with an overindulged dog at the invitation of a beaming Chief Executive.

Who can say how much White House dogs have influenced American history? How many Presidents have they helped keep a balanced perspective on life, and thus make better decisions? How often have they made it easier for a President to win friends for the country, influence royalty, or win an election? I'd say a lot.

Dogs have also been important in helping Presidents ease the tremendous pressure of the job. The clearest example I can think of is the Cuban missile crisis. I was there in Jack Kennedy's office that day. Everything was in an uproar. I was ten feet from Kennedy's desk as Pierre Salinger ran around the office taking messages and issuing orders while the President sat looking awfully worried. There was talk about the Russian fleet coming in and our fleet blocking them off. It looked like war.

Out of the blue, Kennedy suddenly called for Charlie to be brought to his office. He petted the dog, and it seemed to relieve his tension. Then he signaled me to take Charlie out.

Dogs even have helped many a presidential candidate past a tight situation. George McGovern had a dog named Atticus, and it was some help for him to be able to hold up one of the comic ATTICUS FOR VICE PRESIDENT signs when he suffered the embarrassment of having to ask his running mate, Tom Eagleton, to withdraw from the ticket.

McGovern's opponent in that race, Richard Nixon, had gotten where he was partly because of his effective use twenty years earlier of his dog Checkers in a speech defending himself against attacks on his financial backing. At the time it seemed iffy whether he would be permitted to remain on Eisenhower's ticket as the vice presidential candidate, but the "Checkers speech" saved him.

After Nixon had been elected a second time and things started to turn sour, a joke circulated in the White House to the effect that Checkers did the country a bad turn and should have let Nixon sink or swim on his own qualifications.

Dogs have had a big impact on the moods and actions of our Presidents, and I'm proud of the years I spent trying to make things go smoother for them. My brothers Bill and Doug are still surprised when they think how I went in one door of the White House an electrician and came out another a dogkeeper, but they've gotten many a kick out of my career. Doug, for example, was startled one time as he was watching the movie *The President's Analyst* and I suddenly appeared in it, walking the Johnson dogs on the South

Lawn, with the White House in the background. And Bill, until recently mayor of Summersville, West Virginia, was pleased to be able to welcome Lyndon Johnson to the dedication of a flood-control dam with a speech that included a wry reference, much appreciated by the crowd, to the President's high-priced dogkeeper. Incidents like these were probably what decided them that maybe I hadn't done so badly after all.

Sometimes as I row around on my pond, I get a little misty-eyed as I remember all the adventures I had at the White House, all the laughs, all the teasing I had to endure at the hands of LBJ, all the emotional moments I shared with the White House children—Caroline, John-John, Luci, Lynda Bird, Tricia. And I remember the First Ladies: Mamie, with her heart of gold; Bess, with her shy smile, trying to find a place to hide to stay out of the limelight; Lady Bird, with her Southern drawl and her preoccupation with looking after her husband; Pat Nixon, with her delicate thinness that made you think a breeze could blow her over. And then I remember Jacqueline. Yes, I'm afraid that of all the First Ladies, Jacqueline was my favorite.

Why wouldn't she be? In spite of her great beauty, wealth and position, she always treated me more as a friend than an employee, and thanked me as if I were doing her a great favor by helping her. Another thing, she always introduced me to anyone who happened to be around, no matter how important they were—kings and queens, it made no difference.

Lady Bird Johnson followed Jackie's lead in introducing me to her guests, but when Pat Nixon became First Lady, she seemed to feel this kind of familiarity was no longer appropriate.

Somehow I always felt like a conspirator with Jacqueline, if only in confounding the press and the rest of the White House staff. Instead of walking ahead, she would insist on walking with me and talking with me as if we were old friends. Once, seeing the dark looks on the ushers' faces as we walked this way to her waiting helicopter, I said, "Are you sure you want me to do this?" She laughed and said, "Come on, you'll be all right." So I walked close beside her as White House employees glowered and reporters made notes.

When the snow is on the ground in winter, I can almost see Jacqueline Kennedy with a horse and sleigh, driving the children around the South Lawn of the White House. I wonder if the White House will ever see such scenes of youth and beauty again.

Jackie with the dogs was a sight to see. She liked them, I think, because they gave her an excuse to run and exercise. But her first love was horses, and with them she really came alive. When President Ayub Khan of Pakistan gave her the beautiful mount named Sardar that she had ridden on a visit to his country, she was almost as finicky about its care as George Washington had been about his favorite horse. The Father of Our Country cared so much about his white horse, the story goes, that he would have the grooms apply a coat of whitening paint to its body the night before an important occasion, so that, dried and brushed, his horse would startle people with its gleaming beauty. And he would have its hooves manicured and touched up with black paint to intensify the effect.

Jacqueline was also very tender with all the ponies around the White House. She was always afraid someone would hurt them. I told her she was lucky there was a fence around the White House so tourists couldn't pull hairs from their tails for good luck. That's what happened to the horse President Zachary Taylor used to have grazing on the White House lawn. Strangers would come up behind and pull out a hair from "Old Whitey's" tail.

Jackie wasn't perfect. She had her pet hates, too. She particularly hated "those damn nosy reporters" and would get her feathers ruffled when they printed inside information about anything pertaining to her private life. Several times she called me over and warned me to keep things secret. For example, one day she told me heatedly, "Bryant, don't give Helen Thomas any information about the dogs. Not a damn thing!" She went on: "I am sick of her stories and I don't want you to give Helen Thomas a damn thing."

Mrs. Kennedy feared Helen Thomas of the UPI more than any other reporter because she was forever scooping her colleagues about Mrs. Kennedy's clothes. That was the thing Jackie was probably the most sensitive about. So when Helen started bothering the Press Information Office to find out if one of the Kennedy dogs was pregnant, that was the last thing Jacqueline was going to let her find out. "Remember, I don't want you to give Helen Thomas a damn thing," she repeated. I was torn between the two of them. I wanted to help the First Lady, but Helen kept cornering me on the White House grounds and I had been friendly with her for a long time. I wanted to hint to her that Pushinka was pregnant, but I didn't dare. Instead I kidded her, saying, "How would you feel if everybody asked you about your sex life?"

Helen got her story all right, but not from me.

It was amusing to watch the First Lady fuss and fume and knock herself out with her restoration projects and her search for perfection. She was always trying to improve on the beauty of the White House, and sometimes stubbed her toe. One disaster that stands out in my mind above the others occurred when Jacqueline had a set of historic and precious old chairs carefully restored for the family dining room.

And the first time her husband and his legislative leaders sat down on them to hold a breakfast meeting, two of the chairs collapsed—one being the President's. The men on either side of the President grabbed him just before he hit the floor, but poor Larry O'Brien—the same poor Larry O'Brien who years later would be chief target of the Watergate bugging at Democratic headquarters—wasn't that lucky. He crashed through the chair and was sprawled on the floor, to the embarrassment of everybody. Especially JFK. Luckily he wasn't hurt.

Then Jackie wanted a tighter fence put all around the South Lawn so that the dogs couldn't get out. The outdoor men got some ratty-looking chicken wire, dipped it in black paint, and wired it to the iron picket fence. It looked terrible from the beginning and even worse after the tourists started standing on it and breaking it down while they were trying to get better pictures of the White House and Caroline playing around the yard with her dog Charlie.

The Kennedys had a special feeling about dogs—a dog could do no wrong. As my diary tells it:

A White House policeman asked me if my foot was wet. I said, "No, it's not raining." He grinned and I looked down and Charlie was just putting his hind leg down. Then Charlie did the same thing on Mrs. Kennedy. She was wearing long trousers.

JFK actually loved dogs much more than Jacqueline did, and even though he was allergic to animal fur—though much more to cats' than dogs'—he insisted that the children have all the dogs they wanted.

I refuse to believe it was a publicity stunt that inspired him to start the tradition of having a dog on hand to greet him when his helicopter landed. True, it was good for photographers to have that human-interest picture, but I think JFK really got a kick out of being welcomed back to the White House by a dog. Others were thrilled to be greeted by the President; the President in turn wanted to be greeted by a dog. He was never too tired to pet the dog I would have there as he came off the ramp, and he would always say something to me, such as, "Are they giving you a hard time, Bryant? Are they eating well?" He'd be satisfied with a "Yes, sir, Mr. President."

I think one reason Jackie liked me was that I didn't take her and her projects too seriously. Everybody was always being terribly serious around her and acting as if getting a certain antique for the White House was the most important event in the world. But I would just kid around about it and warn her not to sit on that chair if she didn't want a pile of sawdust.

Or I'd say, "I see a trickle of sawdust down the corner of that chest." And she'd laugh and pretend disgust, saying, "Oh, Bryant."

I have never seen an exercise bug like First Lady Jacqueline. Outsiders didn't realize how hard Jackie Kennedy worked to keep in shape. Exercise, exercise. I uncovered the trampoline for her after she returned from Hyannis Port in the fateful summer of '63. It was one of her first orders. This was right after her baby died.

She was always exercising; she loved tennis, horseback riding, and just running with the dogs. But she wanted it kept secret. She once told me, "Don't ever tell Helen Thomas or the rest of those witches anything about how I keep fit—not even that I walk the dogs."

But I remember once when Jackie wanted publicity, even if it meant being nice to Helen Thomas, and that was when she had a "triffic" idea of how to find homes for two of Pushinka's puppies. She talked it over with me.

The idea was that she would sponsor an essay contest for children all over the country. The winner would get a dog. Did I think a child would be good to the dog? she wanted to know. I assured her that most children are very good to their dogs—"treat them better than they do their parents." She smiled at that. Also, I pointed out, since everyone in the community would know about the dog and how it had come from the White House, everyone would have an eye on it. Of course they'd treat the dog well—they wouldn't dare do otherwise.

That seemed to reassure the First Lady. And then she had

another idea to make sure the dog would be well cared for. She would make it the whole point of the contest—the child would tell how the dog would be treated.

Jackie got the idea because kids were already writing letters about dogs to the President. One letter in particular, from a little boy somewhere out West, had tickled his funny bone—both for spelling and content. So when his staff showed it to me in his office, I made this copy.

Dear Mr. President,

Please don't throw this leter away until you read it. When you were runing for President my sister and I held banners that said "VOTE FOR KENNEDY" and we sang a song, "Kennedy in the White House, Nixon in the garbage can"

You are dong a good job and we love you.

I read in the newspaper that Carylon's dog had puppys. My sister has been dying for a puppie. Do you think Carylon will mind very much if she gave us a puppie? It will have a good home. Do you know what it means to get a puppie from the President of the United States?

All the best,
Tom

Jacqueline's contest produced an avalanche of replies. After thousands of letters were sifted through, two kids were given puppies, and a third Pushinka pup went to the children of the President's sister Patricia Lawford. I don't recall who got the fourth.

I didn't save the winning letters, but a damn funny one that unfortunately didn't win was unsigned and promised the kid would "raise the dog to be a Democrat and bite Republicans." I always figured that one was a ringer, probably sent by someone working at the White House, someone like Pierre Salinger.

After the assassination of her husband, while Mrs. Kennedy was still at the White House, Pushinka came in heat again. I had to know whether she wanted her bred. I saw Mrs. Kennedy getting off the helicopter one day and thought that would be a good time to ask her. When the ramp opened, she fairly flew down the steps and to the White House. I never saw her do that before. She ran so fast, she had to hold out her hands to keep from crashing into the wall at the Diplomatic Entrance on the south side of the White House.

I was standing at the South Portico. Jacqueline seemed anxious to see the dogs. I asked her then about whether to breed Pushinka.

She said, "Oh, let Charlie have some fun." Charlie had been the father of the first litter.

For some reason I double-checked with Mr. Hill, her Secret Service man. He went over and talked with her for a moment; then he came back and said, "No, don't start anything. We have enough trouble."

It was all over. Her mood had changed.

Even before the tragedy—in June 1963, in fact—Jacqueline Kennedy said that she wanted me to have Pushinka as my own dog. She said, "Pushinka loves you. You should have her." I thanked her for the offer and said I would have to think about it because my wife and I were moving to a new apartment.

When the President was assassinated, everybody wanted Pushinka. She was world-famous. Again Jacqueline said I should have her and again I asked for time to think about it.

Then Irvin Williams, the Head Gardener, told me that Mrs. Kennedy had asked him to check with me and find out whether I had made up my mind yet. She had told him that if I still didn't want Pushinka, he could have her.

There is a tragic footnote to the story. I am looking at the entry now in my diary:

10/6/66   Mr. Williams told me Pushinka had a pup from being bred with a poodle. His eight-year-old daughter dropped the pup as she was opening a refrigerator door. It cracked its skull when she dropped it. I feel badly for Pushinka.

I remember also that I was gripped with the eerie feeling that the Kennedy bad luck was still continuing.

If you worked at the Kennedys' White House you learned that one command contradicted another. One day the White House police and Secret Service men were telling me Mrs. Kennedy's orders: "This area is off-limits to the dogs." The next day the President was countermanding it. He motioned me into his office and asked me what the schedule was for letting the dogs exercise. I told him I took them out four times a day. And that I tried to keep them out of areas that were off-limits to them.

He said, "Forget that. Let the dogs run free." After that they had the run of his office and of the house, especially Caroline's room.

Her room was one of the prettiest a little girl could have, painted the color of sunshine, with the great dollhouse she could crawl into and a tremendous collection of stuffed animals all around.

Caroline wasn't the only White House child to collect stuffed creatures, of course. Margaret Truman did, too, even as an adult. Margaret's bed was a sea of stuffed animals, and they were all around the room as if Margaret, in the loneliness of an only child, needed them for company.

But the Kennedy children spent more time thinking about live animals than stuffed ones. New animals kept appearing and disappearing. When Jackie got the idea it would be nice for the children to have ducks in the South Fountain, ducks were brought in, and the children were fascinated as they paddled about. Unfortunately, nobody had reckoned on Charlie, who'd plunge right in and swim after them, and gave them no peace, as I mentioned earlier. The last act for the ducks came when they started gobbling the tulip sprouts at the South Fountain as if they were grass. Mrs. Kennedy gave up and out they went.

Charlie had another trick that did not endear him to the laborers at the White House. I don't know where he learned it. He would slip up behind a worker digging a ditch or spading the ground and bite him in the seat of the pants or grab his leg. Then he would run like hell, leaving the man cursing in pain and rubbing his wound. Sometimes Charlie drew blood.

But nobody wanted to take it to the President. I guess they figured if they couldn't get along with Charlie and it was a choice of who would go, Charlie would stay. The President laughed like crazy at everything Charlie did. Like taking a running jump into the President's convertible. Or catching a ball while swimming with the President in the pool.

When the children were there, incidentally, the President did not swim in the buff.

For a man who liked to swim naked, the President was a very formal man. I never saw him kiss his wife when in public. Only in their private moments did he act affectionate with her. But he did treat her with a lot of courtesy and attention in public, and the public loved it. Women would tell me, "Boy, I wish I had a man who paid attention to me like that." I didn't disillusion them by saying that sometimes the only time they had together for long stretches was in public places.

There was always something funny happening around the White House in the Kennedy days—even cases of mistaken identity seemed hilarious. One day President Kennedy walked through the Bouquet Room on his way to the pool. He said, "Hi, Charlie, how are you?" Charles Pecora, Mrs. Paul Mellon's head gardener who was helping Jacqueline, was in the Bouquet Room. He said, "Fine, Mr. President." I could see he was amazed at the President's friendliness and at the fact that the President knew his name. The President was a little startled too. He was speaking to Charlie the dog, who was lying down in his path. He had never set eyes on the visiting gardener before.

I think this incident gave Jacqueline Kennedy one of the best laughs she ever had at the White House, and looking back, I must say she deserved a few.

7

I'll tell you why I'd rather be a dog at the White House than a President. Presidents, after their short honeymoon is over—and Gerald Ford made some kind of a record with a honeymoon that lasted only a couple of weeks—have to take a lot of abuse from everyone. Dogs, on the other hand, take no abuse from anyone, including the President.

If I had to make one generalization about Presidents on the basis of what I observed at the White House, it would be that no President ever thinks anyone but himself has the right qualifications for the Presidency. In fact, most of the ones I knew acted as if they didn't think their successors—or predecessors—were playing with a full deck.

You could compose a round robin about it. Truman hates Nixon. Ike hates Truman. LBJ hates Ford. Kennedy hates LBJ. Nixon hates Truman. LBJ hates Kennedy, and on and on and on.

You heard it all if you worked at the White House and kept your ears open—how the Presidents couldn't stand one another. And how they hurt one another under the guise of humor.

I was there, for example, when President Johnson was hurt—simply crushed—at the way former President Eisenhower was making fun of him in the newspapers. "He was my guest and he ate my food, and I invited him here to ask his advice," said Johnson sadly. "That's the highest compliment you can pay a man, to ask his advice, and now he says this."

What Ike had said to reporters after their meeting was that much of Johnson's domestic program was "just plain nuts."

The press thought that was mighty humorous. LBJ thought the statement was "mighty irresponsible," in fact, "a stupid comment, just plain stupid, and mighty irresponsible in these troubled times." Then he added, "Well, considering the man, I might have known it."

Truman probably turned over in his grave all through the Watergate disclosures about President Nixon. I vividly remember Truman saying to some colleagues during the latter part of his administration, when Nixon was running on the Republican ticket with Ike, "That son of a bitch Dickie Nixon is incapable of an honest act. If they ever let him be President, he'll have the country in ruins in six months."

The aides laughed. And though I wasn't supposed to overhear, since in those days I was only "sticking in light bulbs" and laying cables, I almost laughed out loud, too. I thought, There he goes again, trying to be funny.

Nixon hadn't sounded so funny in 1954, however, when he called Truman a "traitor to the high principles in which many of the nation's Democrats believe." President Truman heard only the first part of that sentence, or at least had only paid attention to the label of "traitor," and was in turn quoted as saying he'd punch Nixon in the nose on sight. At the White House we laughed and said, "Oh-oh, they're still at it."

Truman later made a very funny comment about Nixon to Merle Miller during an interview that was being taped for a TV series. The series didn't come off, but Miller turned the material into a splendid book. "I never would call Nixon a son of a bitch," Truman declared, "because he claims to be a self-made man."

LBJ didn't know that Ford would become President when he said of him, "The only trouble with Jerry Ford is he played too many football games with his helmet off. That guy can't walk and chew gum at the same time." When Ford became President through a flock of circumstances, I could just imagine LBJ turning over in his grave, too. The nerve of his old adversary from Capitol Hill, becoming the thirty-eighth President of the United States!

Yet when Lady Bird broke ground in September, 1974 for a park near Washington that would feature a stone with some other immortal words by LBJ carved on it, President Ford was there to speak in highest praise of the dead President. He might well have skipped the ceremony, since he knew his wife was going into the hospital the next day for cancer tests, but he played the game. Now that's "club loyalty," as it's called in Washington.

As for Jack Kennedy's feelings about LBJ, I can only report what I heard around his office in 1963, when people were starting to talk about 1964 and speculating about whether LBJ would again be his running mate.

I heard his brain trusters tell each other, "We've got to get that Texas corn pone out of here before he uses the Vice Presidency as a springboard into the White House in '68," or words to that effect. And I specifically heard one Kennedy aide ask another, "How would you like to work for *him*?" as if that would be the worst thing that could happen to a man. And then they laughed and laughed as they recalled how during a visit to Pakistan the then Vice President had gotten so chummy with a camel driver that he'd invited him to the United States on the spot and had entertained him royally in Washington and at the LBJ ranch. They seemed to think LBJ would make a laughingstock of the White House and maybe bring over the camel driver from Pakistan to run the country.

Someone said, "Ho-ho, that Texas corn pone would probably make him his top foreign advisor." And someone else said, "No, LBJ'd make him Secretary of State."

At least one senator has stepped forward in recent years to say Kennedy told him he had someone else in mind for the Vice Presidency for his second term. I believe it. I remember his aides saying one time that even First Lady Jacqueline didn't want LBJ again—adding that "Jack won't pay any attention to her, of course, but for once she's right."

The Kennedy "brains" cited FDR as their precedent for dumping LBJ. Roosevelt had changed Vice Presidents in midstream, they said, so the country wouldn't hold it against Kennedy if he followed that example and turned from LBJ to someone else. I believe it was a senator, not a governor, that they mentioned as a good possibility to be picked as the new Vice President. I didn't write the name down, and have cussed myself out for it since. At that time my diary notes weren't a daily thing. After the Kennedy assassination shook me up in 1963, I started writing things down on a regular basis. Every night, in fact, I'd go through my midnight ritual—which sometimes became my 2:00 A.M. ritual—sitting down in my apartment after I got home from work at the White House, with my milk and crackers and my notebook, and recording the highlights of my day before going to bed.

I can remember that in this conversation of JFK's staff and cronies, someone also said that if FDR hadn't had the good sense to switch to Senator Harry Truman, "That left-winger Henry Wallace would have been President." Another man responded that

"Jack" wasn't so sure whether a "left-winger was any worse than a Pendergast machine man."

I had been in the White House in 1960 when Eisenhower's aides were stewing over the fact that Ike had stalled so long about endorsing Richard Nixon as the man to succeed him that it was almost too late to do any good. For that matter, at no time during his Vice President's first run for the Presidency was Ike's endorsement of him really *hearty*.

And the same thing happened with LBJ and his Vice President, Hubert Humphrey, in 1968. Lyndon just dragged his feet and never did come out and say that the world and the country needed HHH.

I can also remember when President Truman didn't think John F. Kennedy had the qualifications for the Presidency either. Truman was *not* a great admirer of Jack Kennedy, any way you looked at it. He bluntly said he wasn't the man for the job, and the person he was talking to had passed the comment along to some aides of Eisenhower. The aides laughed like hell because Truman was really up against it—he couldn't stand Kennedy *or* Nixon. Sometime later I read that Truman had been asked if he were worried about Kennedy being a Catholic and taking orders from the Pope, and he grumpily retorted, "It's not the Pope I'm worried about, it's the pop."

As for Eisenhower's feelings about Truman, and vice versa, everyone knows they couldn't stand each other. Many of us on the household staff heaved a genuine sigh of relief when Ike finally came to the White House and picked up the outgoing President on Inauguration Day, 1953. It had looked as if Ike might not even consent to ride in the same car with Truman to the Capitol, as was traditional.

LBJ figured you were on duty around the clock, and he didn't care how many hours it took a man to get a job done. He even seemed to think you were always present in the White House, and in my case, I sometimes thought the same thing. But while he expected you to work long hours, that was no sign he wanted anyone to work slow.

On the contrary. LBJ wanted everyone on the public payroll to jump when he gave an order. He was like a tornado himself and he tried to speed everyone else up to the same fever pitch. "Move it, damn it, move your ass," he'd exclaim, or he'd ask, "When are you going to get the lead out of your ass?" He didn't often have to remind me to speed up because I learned to be there with his dogs almost as fast as he could even *think* he wanted to see them.

Usually the President didn't have time for dogs until noon, after I had arrived on the job. But one day while I was off duty the President sent for the dogs. It took a long, long time for the ushers to locate someone to get the dogs and for the dogs to be taken over to the Mansion.

Unfortunately, the man they had hit upon was the fattest of the engineers, who tipped the scales at 250 lb. LBJ had a thing about fat and assumed that anyone with an ounce of overweight moved like "molasses in January." When he arrived a half-hour later with the dogs the President was fuming at the delay, cursing under his breath about having Traphes' ass. But as soon as he saw the heavy-set engineer with the dogs, he said disgustedly, "Oh, it's *you*. No wonder!" as if that explained everything.

For a while, "Oh, it's *you*, no wonder" became a popular expression backstairs at the White House for anyone who was goofing up. Or keeping someone waiting.

Of all the Presidents I observed, LBJ was by far the hardest-working, and he expected the same of his aides. In fact, even when he slipped away to take an early evening nap and then went back to the office to work until ten o'clock supper, he'd expect a few of his aides to be still there and "hustling," as he called it.

Joe Laitin, a press aide, was one of those unlucky fellows the Prez was always keeping his eye on. It really was a compliment and meant the Prez liked Laitin around and liked to hear his thinking. But sometimes LBJ's friendship could be pretty exhausting for the recipient, as Laitin was finding out.

Poor Joe Laitin was always getting it in the neck. One time the President was looking for him. It was fairly late in the evening and Joe had gone out for a sandwich to hold him up. When he got back to the White House, the police told him the Prez was very angry and had said he'd have his ass if he came back again and couldn't find him at his desk. Joe, exhausted, said, "Yes, and you haven't found me yet. I've gone home." And he turned and kept walking, right out of the gate.

That time Joe Laitin reached his limit, but usually he did whatever he was asked, and more.

I was the same way. One tries to please a President. One tries to please his family. I have strung Christmas lights, inside the White House and out. I've passed out the presidential gifts at Christmas gatherings and even opened up the presidential packages.

I have fixed the President's elevator when it got balky, and have helped set up lighting for White House weddings and parties and historic ceremonies.

I have strung miles of wiring in various parts of the White House, and raised and lowered floodlights to suit the whim of various Presidents at press conferences and picture sessions. For Johnson the lights had to be high. For other Presidents, they had to be low, medium, or well-done.

It was in my role as electrician since Truman's time, helping photographers take their pictures of the President during relaxed at-home occasions and during important State visits, that I learned how concerned every President has been with his image. Truman worked like a son of a gun at the White House and never wore those wild sport shirts everyone talked about. But as soon as he got away from the White House, he wanted very much to maintain the image of a relaxed President and always put on the gaudiest shirts he could find so the photographers could catch "the man of leisure."

After Truman, who didn't have much vanity about his looks, every President seemed to get more finicky about how he appeared and about having the White House photographer record his every movement.

LBJ had a great personal photographer named Yoichi Okamoto, whom everyone called "Okie." He also had a few other photographers and he kept them all busy. He wanted his dogs recorded as well as himself.

The funny thing was that LBJ didn't care how ugly some pictures were and he even exposed his belly and invited photographers to take a picture of his gall-bladder-operation scar. But when it came to photographing his face, he always maneuvered to be photographed from the left side. Okie and the regulars around the White House knew this and wouldn't dream of approaching the President with a camera from anywhere but the left side.

Richard Nixon had Ollie Atkins, formerly with the *Saturday Evening Post*, as his main photographer. Chief Knudson was another. President Nixon didn't care what side he was photographed from and he didn't even mind if a picture emphasized the unusual shape of his nose. In fact, he liked to mention it, saying, "The ski nose never hurt Bob Hope." Bob Hope, incidentally, was one of the President's favorite guests.

The picture session I remember best from the Nixon years happened when the President ordered us to get pictures of King Timahoe swimming in the South Fountain. How beautifully he swam! If only President Nixon had liked to swim as well as his pet, instead of flooring over the White House pool and using the space for more and more intricate press announcements that were delivered for him by his press secretary, Ron Ziegler.

Both as kennel keeper and electrician moving around the White House and grounds, I had a really excellent opportunity to tune into the world of the Presidents, and see how they work and play.

Every President, I recall, had a special friend he trusted completely. A friend he could let his hair down and kid around with, and not worry about how it would sound. Dave Powers was such a friend to Kennedy. I remember Kennedy and Powers sitting nude at poolside, and Powers telling the President one wild Irish joke after another. Strangely enough, most of his favorite jokes seemed to be about death and funerals and drunken Irish wakes.

I remember one of them—at least I remember approximately how it went. Powers was the master, and I wouldn't try to compete with him in telling an Irish story. This one he'd tell over and over.

It had something to do with an Irishman in Dublin named Mike, who drunkenly shows up at the wake of a man he had never met. Mike could practically smell liquor from a block away and always managed to be at the right place at the right time.

The widow was greatly impressed with this man she'd never seen before but who spoke so eloquently in praise of her husband and so tearfully about his demise.

"Oh, now, and I can see it's that you were Paddy's best friend," said the widow. "And so I must ask you now, for I have no one else to lean on, what shall we do? Shall we go now to bury him?"

"Bury him? Hell, no!" roared the stranger. "Let's stuff the bum and keep the party rolling."

Knowing how JFK loved stories that laughed at death, I really think he must have looked down and shaken his head over all the tears that fell when he died, and all the mourning and show of sorrow.

Next to Dave Powers, Kennedy was most amused by Pierre Salinger, his press secretary, and by John Kenneth Galbraith, who used to send him memos from India, when he was ambassador there, that got widely quoted around the White House. One Galbraith witticism that tickled JFK especially concerned some matter that was supposed to remain secret.

In his memo, marked "For the President's Eyes Only," Galbraith said the matter "was about as confidential as mass sodomy in the New York subway during rush hour."

Lyndon Johnson had more friends than any President I have known. I don't know who ranked highest with him, but surely his top aide, Joseph Califano—who later became legal counsel of the Democratic party—was one of them. And so was Willard Deason, a Texas friend whom he named to the Interstate Commerce Commission. LBJ loved to regale both of them with political stories, especially about vote stealing and illegal elections. That was his specialty.

I think his favorite tale, though I can't recall it word for word, was about a little Texas-Mexican boy, Manuel, who is crying as if his heart would break when a friend comes along and asks him why.

"I'm crying because my father was in town last week and didn't even come to see me," Manuel manages to stammer out.

His friend is amazed to hear this, and starts to scold the boy, telling him, "Don't be silly, Manuel, you know your father is dead. We went to his funeral together. How could he have been in town last week?"

"I know about the funeral," says Manuel, still sobbing. "But my father *was* here. I *know* he was here because he voted three times. But he didn't come to see me."

Johnson loved the folksy expressions of the Southwest and lost no chance to use them around me. I think it made him feel he was back at the ranch. He would say, "Well, I'd better get in and eat now, my coffee's been saucered and blown."

When his popularity had fallen and he had to go face people he knew hated his guts, he'd mutter, "Nobody wants to be a skunk at a garden party." He always fought pain with humor.

Lady Bird had her own expressions and Lyndon enjoyed hearing

71

her use them. I remember when he was furious about everyone trying to help him get rid of some of his dogs—at times he had as many as eleven at the White House—she soothed him, saying, "Now, Lyndon, you'll still have more dogs than you can say grace over." It was her favorite expression—and his!

Nixon's humor had to do with the situation right at hand. He thought it was very funny when he would introduce himself as "President Eisenhower's grandson's father-in-law, Dick Nixon."

He and Bebe Rebozo had a big joke going about an "in and out" martini which Rebozo would make for his famous friend. It was sort of a ritual. First Bebe would put the ice cubes in the cocktail shaker. Then he would pour vermouth into the shaker and swing it once around and ceremoniously pour all the vermouth out, to the amusement of the President. Then he would add the gin. The President would laugh heartily as he took his first sip of his "in and out!"

Bebe Rebozo was, of course, Nixon's long-time friend, and Nixon turned to him for quiet understanding and humor. Often I would see them getting in the car together to go for a ride in the yacht, which was Nixon's way of relaxing.

Sometimes they would simply jump in the car and take a ride together in the evening, not to go to the boat, but just to drive for the pleasure of it. Or to talk.

Of the First Ladies I knew, Jackie Kennedy had the best sense of humor. Her staff would dare anything to amuse Jackie, even after the death of her premature baby, Patrick Bouvier.

In fact, the way I knew Jackie had recovered from the death of her baby was that one day she planned a birthday party for her social secretary, Nancy Tuckerman, and arranged an elaborate gag. She had the Chief Usher, James West, put on one of her wigs and a dress and pose as the housemother that the First Lady and Nancy had had back at Miss Porter's School. A lot of Jackie's friends and staff also took the time to learn the old school song. To round out the festivities, Nancy Hough, a girl from the Curator's office, dressed up like Jackie and imitated her voice to a T. This Nancy was famous around the White House for her Jackie imitation and her ability to trick people on the phone into thinking Jackie was giving them some kind of crazy instructions.

The party was a great success. When Nancy Tuckerman came in, she was led to the front of the room by "housemother" West, the group sang the old school song, and Nancy Hough, decked out in another Jackie wig, greeted her in a whispery Jackie voice.

Miss Tuckerman was stunned and everybody exploded in laughter.

I doubt that any other First Lady was ever as playful or put on a better show at the White House than Jacqueline—whether it was coming up with a live monkey for Caroline's birthday party, or getting humans to make monkeys of themselves for her own party.

I really have Lyndon Johnson to thank for getting me interested in the history of the White House pet population.

In fact, one day he said to me, "With all the pictures you are getting of me and my dogs, you could write something up and have yourself a book." I didn't tell him that I already had notebooks full of "write something up" or that he was a major star in my cast of characters. But my efforts to document contemporary history are not the way I got started on the history of pets past.

What happened is that on another occasion LBJ came up with a strange assignment for me. "Listen, Mr. Bryant," he said, "I want you to do something for me, but I don't want any talk of it around here. Especially don't talk about it to Liz Carpenter or I'll have your ass."

We were outside on the White House lawn. LBJ looked around to be sure no one was listening; then he said, "There's a strange rumor around here that General Lafayette brought an alligator with him as a pet when he came to the White House. Now I'd say that's like bringing a skunk to a garden party. So would you just have your wife look that up for me at a library somewhere and just say she needs the information for you. Leave me out of it."

LBJ thought my wife was thrown into the bargain of having me around and he never hesitated to give her an assignment—such as the strange sewing assignment I'll mention later in Part Two. The fact that she was a brainy woman, and had a responsible job as a data systems analyst for the Defense Department, never stopped him. She was a *married* woman, wasn't she? A wife did these little services.

Doris was a little too busy to delve deeply into history, so I passed the research assignment along to a reporter who thought the material was for the book I was planning to write—which of course it now becomes. Eventually she came up with the information about

73

the alligator and I forwarded it to LBJ, who very typically didn't say thank you, but did say to tell my wife he found it mighty interesting.

The story we uncovered is that when Lafayette paid his triumphal visit to the United States in the 1820s, once he'd toured around a bit, he stayed as a guest of President John Quincy Adams at the White House. People everywhere had given him gifts to take back to France, and one of the gifts was an alligator, which was kept at the White House in the same drafty room that Abigail Adams used to hang her washing in, the East Room.

That's how I started studying the history of the White House animal world. I kept at it, and made good use of many things I learned. When Lyndon Johnson's dog Yuki began accompanying the President in song, I was able to tell him that Jefferson had done duets with his pet, too. He would play the violin and his mockingbird would whistle an accompaniment. Jefferson had a lot of fun with his mockingbird and even taught it to imitate a dog and a cat.

Since Doris was so interested in birds, I leaned a little heavy on bird stories and found out that President McKinley had a bird who could whistle the line "Yankee Doodle came to town." It probably was the same parrot who had such an eye for the girls.

When the Teddy Roosevelt family moved into the White House, the lawns turned into a jungle of pets and wildlife. The old Rough Rider used to keep a record in his diary of the birds he'd see around the White House grounds. It was a red-letter day for him when he saw a pair of cuckoos. His daughter Alice, however, went him one better as an animal fancier. She kept a snake, named "Emily Spinach" after an aunt, and took the damned thing with her visiting, just to shock people.

When I saw Alice Roosevelt Longworth at the White House, in her late eighties but still spry and still trying to shock people with her spicy comments about famous people, I almost asked her, in the interest of history, what ever became of Miss Spinach. I didn't have the nerve, but I figure there's probably an unmarked grave somewhere on the White House grounds, along with Caroline Kennedy's marker for her bird, Robin.

President Lincoln was both a dog and cat man. He let son Tad have a dog and son Willie have a cat. Lincoln got a big kick out of the fact that both critters gave birth to offspring the same day.

Knowing that Jerry Ford was moving into the White House with no backup but a single, solitary Siamese cat named Shan, I wanted to write him a letter assuring him that he was not unique in history and that other Presidents had dared to like cats. Calvin Coolidge was one. He had two canaries—Nip and Tuck—and two dogs—Rob Roy and Prudence Prim—but going against tradition, his favorite pet was an alley cat named Tiger.

The cat had come strolling in from Pennsylvania Avenue one day and adopted "Silent Cal" as his master. On many a summer day thereafter the President would sit silently on a bench outside the White House, petting his cat and thinking about the state of the country, no doubt.

Tiger occupies a special niche in pet history because he strayed away and President Coolidge became the first President to use that new-fangled contraption, the radio, to send out a plea for help in finding a lost animal.

The new invention proved its worth when someone heard his message and did find old Tiger not too far away, trying to make friends at the building which was then the Navy Department.

8

The President of the United States is surrounded by danger. The real threats to his life are bad enough, and tight security is maintained at the White House to protect him. But the very need for vigilance around the clock leads everyone to imagine dangers that don't exist, at least not yet. Presidents usually tolerate the situation pretty well but sometimes they get impatient.

From time to time an airplane buzzes the White House and the country gets concerned. During every administration I served in at the White House, we always had a fear that some foreign object would come hurtling down.

It was something we would not talk about to reporters but we were always on the lookout. The Truman administration actually installed proper bomb shelters. If a plane or other object made the White House catch on fire, the President could be whisked underground in seconds.

I was not at Nixon's White House when the helicopter flown by a twenty-year-old Fort Meade helicopter mechanic landed on the South Grounds in a hail of shotgun pellets. Or when the would-be hijacker at the Baltimore-Washington International Airport killed himself because his plan to nose-dive into the White House backfired. But reading about those incidents while safe at my retirement hideaway, I thought, "Oh-oh, it's finally happening."

I can remember any number of tense moments when planes ventured too close, even though all pilots know that the air space over the White House and the grounds near it is out of bounds and violating this rule can get them into severe trouble.

I am happy to learn that the White House guards are now armed with Redeye antiaircraft missiles. Each missile has an infrared heat-seeking warhead which will guide it straight to the engine exhaust of any plane that tries a trick in the future.

When I was at the White House, the police would grab field glasses and take down the numbers on any planes that came too close. Every object appearing on the horizon had to be identified and reports on violations went to the proper Federal aviation authority.

I remember once we were all alerted to danger from above. A plane was somewhere overhead and White House policeman Hanson was trying to spot it through field glasses. He was under the South Portico awning training his glasses upwards and he finally spotted it—a plane with something trailing behind. It was a tense moment and then came the relief of laughter. The plane belonged to an awning company and it was dragging an ad.

Hanson quickly phoned in his report and I'm sure the pilot learned about air regulations in a hurry.

I remember another time President Kennedy almost lost his life on the White House lawn in his own helicopter. A rush of wind almost dashed his helicopter into a tree. The incident was hushed up and did not get into the papers.

And once there was a fire on Nixon's helicopter. Fortunately it was on the ground. He simply took another.

Lots of times I ponder President Kennedy's assassination. It's ironic that at the time it happened, all kinds of evidence existed that Lee Harvey Oswald was a dangerous nut. He had sent threatening letters to the governor of Texas, John Connally, and to a Texas senator, John Tower. Yet nobody bothered to check up on his whereabouts when Kennedy went to Texas. Because he had never threatened the President.

In my mind there is some question about whether he was after Governor Connally, who happened to be riding with the President, or Kennedy himself. Far from being the crack shot the papers made him out to be, Oswald may have been a lousy shot, aiming at one man and killing another.

It's hard to know anything with certainty when you deal with madmen. That's why we were trained to report instantly any strange behavior on the part of someone entering the White House grounds. Now and then I reported odd behavior that I noticed, but I seldom knew the end of the story.

The healthy mind sometimes fails to see the danger in mental disease. Sick people can seem completely harmless and sort of funny when they come up to the White House grounds and try to get in by pretending they belong there or have some message for the President or First Lady. One man came as Jesus Christ bearing an important message for President Eisenhower about the Secret of Fatima.

At other times men came up to the gate with the illusion they were Jackie Kennedy's husband, without even being concerned that that meant they were also President of the United States. And one woman was sure she was "the real Jacqueline Kennedy"; she wanted the White House police to go in and drag out the imposter in there trying to take her place.

In the Johnson administration a man arrived at the gate insisting he was there to pick up a package containing a million dollars left for him by LBJ. He reminded me of a man in President Kennedy's time who said a bank had sent him to get the President's co-signature so he could withdraw his own million dollars from his account.

The trait the would-be White House gate-crashers all seem to have in common is that they talk a blue streak and don't listen. The Secret Service once told me that it really doesn't matter which President is in office, they all get the same number of dingbats and deranged visitors—about fifty a year.

But threats through the mail and over the phone are a different matter, and once, toward the end of his term, LBJ said he was averaging three thousand threats on his life per month.

After Arthur Bremer shot Governor George Wallace, he said he had planned to shoot President Nixon instead and he had intended to yell, "A penny for your thoughts!" as he pulled the trigger. That was weird, but typical.

It's hard to spot a real nut among the harmless ones, which may be part of the reason Presidents get to feeling they are immune to danger and lead a charmed life. I wasn't at all surprised to read that Nixon was unperturbed when a plot to assassinate him was uncovered in New Orleans while he was visiting that city. He just went on about his business.

Lyndon Johnson was the worst President I ever knew about flaunting danger and charging into crowds to shake hands. Once when the papers were taking him to task for it, he said to me, "I'm not a hermit and I'm not going to live like one." Lyndon didn't even like the Secret Service men to follow his car too closely, and in Texas when they did he yelled back at them, "If you don't get away from me, I'm gonna shoot out your tires."

The one time I risked trying to warn John F. Kennedy to be a little careful about shaking hands in crowds, I said, "It could be dangerous out there, Mr. President. There are all kinds of nuts out there." He just smiled and answered, "Naw, Bryant, you've got more danger right here when you get between a couple of those dogs."

At the time it seemed pretty funny because the President's dog, Wolf, and Jacqueline's dog, Clipper, were growling at each other and I had them both on leash.

All the people around Kennedy knew he was relaxed about security, and sometimes the security men got a little relaxed themselves. One fall afternoon during the Kennedy administration, an agent and a policeman on duty at one of the gates were trying to enjoy the finer things of life. The agent was reading a book and the policeman was listening to a Redskin game on a transistor radio, which naturally was against regulations.

A voice called out, "What's the score?" The policeman thought it was the agent asking and was in the middle of answering when he realized he was talking to the President. The book was snapped shut and the transistor radio was cut off immediately as both men jumped up. But President Kennedy grinned and motioned the policeman to turn the radio back on. "As you were, men," he said.

Truman's walks made the men around him a nervous wreck. His famous last words before some Puerto Rican nationalists tried to assassinate him at Blair House were being quoted by one and all when I went to work for the White House—"Who'd want to shoot me?"

We've had so many tragedies and attempted murders in recent years, it's easier now to tighten security if it seems to be relaxing. Strangers at the gate and airplanes drifting overhead aren't the only targets for scrutiny—every parcel delivered gets a rigorous going-over.

Take the matter of food. I think it's time the public finally knew they can't send gifts of food to the White House—it's destroyed.

Though the White House pretends gift food gets sent to the needy, it can't be because no one has the time to test it all. There's too much danger of producing the headline WHITE HOUSE GIFT FOOD POISONS THREE AT OLD FOLKS HOME.

The only way anyone can get a gift of food to a President or First Lady is to hand-carry it or send it to them by way of a trusted aide.

That reminds me of the time LBJ blew his top over some blintzes that Mrs. Robert McNamara had made for him. LBJ loved them, and now and then she would send them along when the Secretary of Defense was coming to the White House to see the President. He would give them to someone like Liz Carpenter, Lady Bird's aide, who would know how to handle them.

But one time, being in a hurry, Secretary McNamara simply gave the blintzes to a policeman, saying they were for the President. The policeman in turn gave them to the Secret Service, who quickly destroyed the food, as usual.

When McNamara asked the President how he'd liked the blintzes, there was the devil to pay. "What in the hell happened to my cheese blintzes?" LBJ demanded, and after a full report proceeded to cuss out the Secret Service man for not letting him lead any kind of normal life. "You leave my food alone," he said. "Use that thing on top of your head that's supposed to have a brain. Did you think the Secretary of Defense is going to kill me?"

While the staff is busy checking out sacks of blintzes, the Secret Service is checking the staff. Check and recheck. Once the Secret Service found that a workman at the White House had been involved in a little moonshine operation, a fact he had somehow neglected to mention on his application for government employment. So suddenly out he went, and started working elsewhere.

Liquor and the other good things of life sometimes caused as much difficulty at the White House as unsolicited food. A household helper of Jackie Kennedy's got so plastered on her day off that when she returned to the White House at day's end, she came stumbling up the steps of the North Portico in her stocking feet and carrying her shoes, happy as a lark. Leaving the cabdriver waiting.

This flaunted an absolute rule that nobody but presidential family and guests and White House security people used the pillared North Portico, the White House's front entrance on the Pennsylvania Avenue side—with the occasional exception of me, if accompanied by a presidential dog, the President, or both.

The ushers were immensely relieved that no one from the presidential family had seen the tipsy helper and led her to the servant's elevator as she warbled happily to herself. The ushers even had to pay her cab fare.

She was lucky that didn't get her fired on the spot. But her days were numbered anyway because she had another little bad habit—

that of inviting the White House maintenance men up to her third-floor live-in room. Once she even invited an usher, who tried to tell her his wife would not appreciate it. She didn't care, she said, because he was "adorable." Thereafter, every time I wanted to get a rise out of that usher, I'd phone him, and when I was sure I had the right man, I'd say, "Is this Adorable? I want to speak to Adorable in the Usher's Office." And he'd howl with laughter.

All the social activities going on at the White House turned the head of a pretty secretary during the Johnson years. First she invited herself to a State Dinner. Then she attended a movie which Lynda had ordered for herself and friends. My diary shows that the secretary "left the White House very suddenly and for good."

Most White House employees manage to keep on a steady keel and efficiently help the President meet the needs of the country as they arise. Presidents usually appreciate their dedication, and know what they are up against. I remember being in President Johnson's office when war dissenters staged a sit-down strike in the White House theater. They came through as tourists and just sat down. There was a big debate going on in the President's office on whether to lift them out.

I can see it now, the President standing there listening to various aides say what they thought was "correct procedure." "Hell, how are you going to do it without getting into trouble?" he kept asking. The President had his four TV sets on with news, waiting to see whether the newscasters had pictures of the sit-down. They didn't.

The staff eventually found a way to end the impasse.

Then there was a different kind of gate-crashing that never made the papers. An army of rats who weren't satisfied with their food rations lived across the street in Lafayette Park. Their persistent attempts to join the party were carefully kept from First Ladies who might have been squeamish.

Unfortunately, Mrs. Truman once encountered a little crasher and the exterminators were called. A lot of good it did. When I was leaving the White House grounds for the last time in the Nixon administration, I met the good old exterminator on his way in, come to do his duty.

Knowing the vast network of tunnels and cableways under the White House, I can only say it's a losing game. The rats never had it better.

81

II
Lyndon Baines Johnson

9

I well remember the last time I saw President Kennedy. Just before he went on that fateful Dallas trip in November 1963, he called to me as he was coming out of the White House gym, wearing a bathrobe. I was walking with Wolf, the Irish wolfhound. JFK told me that Charlie had snapped at Caroline in his office. He looked worried. That was the last time I heard his voice. Two days later he was dead.

I thought I could never feel emotion about a President again, never laugh with one, never feel close to one. Surely never feel any particular friendship. How wrong I was.

The days of transition from Kennedy to Johnson were as hard on me as they were on anyone else—harder. I was losing a dog and gaining a President I didn't know. Not only didn't I know him, I didn't think I wanted to know him.

He wasn't boyish or good-natured or quick-witted like Kennedy and I heard him cussing out the help when things weren't done fast enough. He was a perfectionist, and from the beginning lights were on at all hours in the presidential office.

At first everything reminded me of Kennedy. A month after the President's assassination, Frank Sinatra's son, Frank, Jr., was kidnapped from a gambling resort at Lake Tahoe, Nevada. The singer paid almost a quarter of a million dollars for his boy's release. Frank at one time had been a good friend of the Kennedys.

But as the weeks rolled by I began to realize that everything that had been associated with the Kennedys was now out. Sinatra and his "Rat Pack" clique of friends were out.

The New Frontier was out, the Great Society was in.

Terriers were out and beagles were in.

Jackie pink was out, Lady Bird yellow was in.

Chowder was out and chili was in.

The Georgetown crowd was out; Perle Mesta and Scooter Miller, an old friend of Lady Bird's, were in.

Toddlers were out and teenagers were in. Not only that, but collecting ordinary dolls, as Caroline had done, was out. Now you had to collect historic dolls; Lynda Bird had several that were a couple of hundred years old.

French was out and the Spanish language was in. So were all the Spanish-speaking embassies, especially Mexico's.

Johnson had a different set of showbiz buddies—Carol Channing and Hugh O'Brian were his favorites. Eventually, in about a year, we had a Hollywood character in on-and-off residence—the teenagers' idol, George Hamilton.

I was aware LBJ was less than thrilled about "Georgie boy," as he called him, and I liked the Prez for that. Hamilton was so slicked down and shiny he looked unreal. LBJ said it first, muttering to me one time as he saw George coming through the gates, "Christ, he looks like he was put together by a ladies' club committee."

It had taken me a while to discover that the President did have a sense of humor—a bit rough, but all his own. As he got used to me, more and more he seemed to relax by ribbing me. Here's a typical diary entry:

3/10/65 I washed Blanco and Him. Him chewed a six-inch length of rug in President's office. The Prez returned by helicopter at 9:15 P.M. The Prez said he would send me a bill for damage. I think he was kidding. The Prez took Him to the second floor for few minutes to keep him company on an errand. The Prez sure loves Him.

The President loved all dogs that wore his brand, even Blanco, that beautiful but dumb rare white collie who was so inbred, he hardly knew his paw from his tail.

A few days later I added another note in my diary:

3/14/65 Him chewed the same strip of President's rug. Now two feet.

The rug was getting ratty-looking. This time the President said, "Mr. Bryant, I'm starting to keep books on all this destruction. At the end of the year we're going to have to settle up." And again he took Him along with him to the second-floor family quarters just as if Him had been an angel and not a devil.

He said over his shoulder, "I'm getting you a set of weaving instructions."

It went on for days. I tried to avoid trouble by keeping the dogs away from their master, but according to my diary:

3/23/65   The President saw me in the West Lobby with the dogs. In a hurt voice, he wanted to know why I didn't bring them to his office. The dogs and I trailed along with the President. We went to Marvin Watson's office, then to the Press Information Office, then the President's Oval Office. He told me to bring a leash for Blanco and to get two bones from the White House kitchen. He gave the bones to the dogs. The dogs stayed in his office for two hours. I was called back to get them and the President told me to look at Him. He was almost asleep on the divan. The President started ribbing me and asked me about the rug that looked all chewed up. A TV reporter was with the President. I said it was probably done by the TV people during his telephone call to the two-man space ship. The President told me that I knew better than that. He obviously wanted the reporter to hear it from me. So I told the President Him had chewed on the rug—as if he didn't know.

I guess that's what started our friendship. Any man who felt about dogs the way he did would have won me over. And he didn't limit his enthusiasm just to dogs. When he drove around his ranch, an old buck deer he called George would sidle up to the car and he would feed him through the window. He'd carry goodies in his pockets for everyone—candy for kids, lapel pins for men, Unipets (flavored vitamin treats) for dogs, sugar cubes for horses, deer, and mules.

President Johnson was the greatest pet lover I have ever known— and possibly the greatest pet lover of all our Presidents. True, George Washington pampered his horses, President Jefferson trained a mockingbird to sit on his shoulder while he worked, and also to meow like a cat, and President Harding taught his dog to sit on a chair and attend Cabinet meetings.

But they were pikers compared with President Johnson. Animals for LBJ were a way of life, sometimes an exotic one. While he was Vice President, Lyndon had a dog named Old Beagle. When Old Beagle died, LBJ had him cremated and kept the ashes in a box over the refrigerator.

He felt so strongly about Old Beagle's passing, he couldn't bring himself just to throw the ashes out. Emotions were a familiar staple at the White House during his administration—everyone around him was entitled to express them, even the cook.

And so when Zephyr Wright, the family cook, found out what was in that small box on the shelf above the refrigerator, she blew a fuse. "Get that damn dog out of here," she said, and Old Beagle was laid to rest in a corner of the family burial plot at the ranch.

I don't think the President ever got over the death of any of his dogs. When Her died from eating a stone, I made a notation in my records:

Her died after surgery—November 27, 1964.

As soon as the story hit the newspapers, more than three hundred offers of beagle dogs and puppies came rolling in. All were turned down with thanks. But one lonely beagle arrived anyway at National Airport, a cute brown and white female whose owner in Rushville, Nebraska, hadn't gotten his rejection in time. Liz Carpenter thought the man was just making an offer, like everyone else, until she heard the dog was about to arrive at the airport and would be awaiting instructions.

So the pup got royal treatment, a ride in a White House chauffeur-driven limousine. But instead of bringing it to the White House where LBJ might have become emotionally involved, the chauffeur whisked it to Fort Myer where it was fed and pampered, then sent back from whence it came.

LBJ was touched and sent the man—E. D. Hollstein—a picture of himself holding Him and Her with the inscription "From one dog lover to another."

Some dog lovers will want to know exactly how a dog came to be eating stones at the White House.

What happened was that while I was away on vacation, usher Rex Scouten had the Capital Parks people put a small fenced runway area for dogs below the tennis courts on the South Lawn. They dumped some rocks and trash in there to keep the dogs' feet from getting muddy. If they had used fine gravel, a dog could have swallowed it, but these bigger stones were trouble for Her, who must have started playing with one out of curiosity or boredom.

Her was rushed to Fort Myer, which had good veterinary facilities. Dr. Ralph Chadwick operated and told me all about it. He said Her had survived the operation. After resting a bit, she had gotten up, walked a few steps, and fallen down. She died a short time later.

The news was almost more than LBJ could stand to hear. I felt miserable about it. Luci did too, and took to her bed with a cold, which I was sure was partially emotional—because Luci loved Her very much.

The President and I took Him, the surviving beagle, and Blanco to visit Luci. Him jumped on the bed and whimpered a little. LBJ, never one to keep things bottled up, came right out and asked Luci if she thought the dogs were suffering because they missed Her.

"Yes," Luci answered sadly, the tears starting to fill her eyes.

As the President and I walked back down the hall, trying to ease the pain, trying to lay the blame somewhere, anywhere, he burst out at me, "Damn it, why didn't *you* take better care of Her? Why did you let it happen?"

I was stunned. "Mr. President," I said, "I was on vacation when the dog died."

He went on as if he hadn't heard me. "You should have taken better care of Her!" I had to get away. I said, "Come on, Blanco! Come here, Him." I got into the elevator with the dogs, went down to the ground floor, and walked to the White House kennel, where I could control my emotions.

After that, I campaigned to have the dog facilities at the White House improved. I wanted the runway put elsewhere, near the President's office, and favored moving the dogs from the Bouquet Room to their own quarters. Eventually a proper doghouse was built with a Dutch door so the President could bring dignitaries around for a look, open the top gate, and reach in to pet the dogs without their getting loose.

Not everyone at the White House was as enthusiastic as the President and I were to see the dogs romping about. John Pustka, the man who took care of the dogs on the morning shift until I arrived after lunch, hated to chase dogs. He had diabetes and I think it made him a little bit cranky. Once the President asked John to let the dogs out, and then a few minutes later told him, "Go round them up and bring them back."

John glared at the President and snapped, "You turned them loose, *you* go get them yourself!" The President was so shocked he said nothing. Not at the time, nor later, or Pustka would have been transferred away from the White House immediately. The only way I found out myself was that Pustka told me.

As soon as I could, I casually mentioned to the President that John had diabetes. The President looked at me and just nodded.

President Johnson generously understood Mr. Pustka, but it is true that he could be vindictive over little things. Once without much notice he visited an air base at Harlingen, Texas. When his plane landed, he was met by a hearse instead of a limousine. Everything had happened so fast that the townspeople had not come up with a limousine in time. I can't myself believe they did it as a joke, but LBJ was so furious, according to the story that made the rounds, that he closed the air base, using a more acceptable reason for publication, of course—economy. Years later I visited Harlingen and it was still the talk of the town.

That was one of the other sides of the dog lover.

The Johnsons arrived at the White House with just two dogs, the beagles Him and Her. Luci drove them over herself from The Elms, the vice presidential home that had once belonged to LBJ's friend Perle Mesta, the "hostess with the mostess."

The collie Blanco was soon added—a gift from a little girl in Illinois, as I recall. LBJ loved gifts, especially unusual gifts, as much as the next man. But he could see a problem coming up, because the sight of a President with two beagles gave everyone the idea of offering him still another pet.

So LBJ announced that his white collie would be symbolic of all the wonderful dogs he had been offered by Americans everywhere. All other dogs would be returned to their senders.

This was a statesmanlike decision, but the White House was always awash with dogs, anyway. The beagles had litters of puppies, for one thing, and even the ones that were given away tended to keep returning until they made the White House into a dog motel.

Lyndon made angry sounds about it but the truth was he loved them all. Even Blanco, the overbred collie who turned out to be practically a eunuch. But he didn't really love another dog as much as he'd loved Old Beagle until one afternoon toward the end of his days in the White House Luci brought a little mutt named Yuki into his life. Touchingly it was Yuki, not a human being, who was with him when he died.

I know Yuki, who is still in retirement at the ranch, commuting between there and Luci's home in Austin, must still be grieving for the President. They were inseparable at the White House, and afterward.

I remember President Johnson one time personally opening the door to the main ground-floor kitchen because Yuki wanted to go in. Frankie Blair, a clean-up man, didn't realize what was going on and chased Yuki out. President Johnson then went into the kitchen and asked Frankie, "Has Yuki eaten his dinner?"

Frankie said, "Yes, Mr. President."

President Johnson said, "Well, Yuki says he hasn't eaten. Are you trying to call my dog a liar?"

During the Johnson administration I continued to record the birth dates of the White House dogs, their trips to and from the vet's, and their medical problems, just as I'd done for President Kennedy's pack.

How far away it all seems now, looking at some of those Kennedy records.

BORN:		
Charlie		1958
Pushinka	(Russia)	1960
Clipper	June 9,	1962
Wolf	May 19,	1963
Shannon	June 15,	1963
Pups	June 15,	1963

Other charts bear witness that at the time of the Kennedy assassination, dog life was going on as usual—Pushinka in heat again; Wolf and Shannon having rabies shots; Charlie acting snappish.

And then the LBJ dog records begin:

BORN:
Him and Her   June 27, 1963
Blanco   September, 1963
Him's pups: 1 male and 5 females, born in Austin, Texas, 10/21/65
Him and Her sired from Jackson 11th ("Little Beagle"), and Fsurdies
      Clementine (mother).

Few people, including President Johnson, knew Blanco's real name:

Blanco—Registered as Leader Blair Jamie of Edlin.

In spite of his fancy moniker, and maybe because of his fancy breeding, Blanco kept the vets hopping.

Rabies vaccination: 11-29-63
Tag number: 5840
Named: Blanco

12-13-63	Distemper, hepatitis, and leptospirosis vaccine.
12-13-63	Stool sample to vet.
	Diagnosis: Worms.
12-16-63	Blanco has round- and hookworms.
12-17-63	Blanco sent to Friendship Hospital and treated for round- and hookworms and bathed.
	Blanco due for Booster shot on the first week in 1964.
12-17-63	President autographed picture of Blanco and myself.
12-18-63	Blanco had loose tooth pulled, returned to the White House.
1-3-64	Blanco treated for worms. Vet says was caught in time.
1-3-64	Distemper and hepatitis and leptospirosis.
1-7-64	Bathed.
1-8-64	Stool sample taken.
1-9-64	Sample okay—no worms. Dogs moved to same room.
1-15-64	Stool sample for worms check sent to vet.
1-18-64	No worms.
2-4-64	Sample stool.
2-5-64	No worms.
2-7-64	Sent to vets for bath.
2-12-64	Bought a collar and traffic leader.
2-12-64	Rabies certificate tag: #153.
	Vet checkup and shots.
	City dog tag: #20.
3-4-64	Stool sample.
3-9-64	Blanco has coccidiosis.
3-10-64	Colonel Chadwick, Fort Myer, in charge of White House dogs.
3-18-64	Blanco to Fort Myer for checkup. Stool to be checked.
3-18-64	Colonel Chadwick sent a letter with instructions and medicine for Blanco. Copy given to President Johnson for night reading.
3-23-64	Stool sent to vet.
3-24-64	Colonel Chadwick and three lieutenants visited and checked Blanco. They looked at Him and Her. Wanted all dogs brought in for further tests.
3-25-64	All dogs to vets.

Similar records were kept for Him and Her.

How Luci and the President loved those dogs! The Johnsons were evenly divided into two groups: those who loved dogs, and those who merely liked dogs—and sometimes barely that. Lady Bird and Lynda Bird viewed the President's and Luci's doggie ways with amused tolerance. Or disgust, depending on their mood.

Now and then Lady Bird threw up her hands in horror and said, "What can I do with Lyndon?" The answer, of course, was nothing.

To be around Lyndon Johnson you had to take a lot of abuse. That is, if he liked you. If he didn't, you were simply ignored. Or worse, if he got really angry, his tongue was like a whiplash.

One Sunday morning Lyndon Johnson told his valet, who told the doorman, Harrison, that he might decide to go to church. The doorman, thinking that he was doing the President a favor, told a Secret Service man that the President was going to church. The Secret Service got busy and had a limousine and a squad of Secret Service men on stand-by for the President. They didn't know it, but that particular Sunday the President had planned to walk to a church near the White House, St. John's Episcopal.

When he saw the Secret Service and the limousine outside he asked the Secret Service man how come. The Secret Service man said that the doorman had informed him. The President approached the doorman and said, "When I want you to be my mouthpiece, I will push your button. So you mind your business and operate the elevator."

Nothing infuriated Lyndon Johnson more, I noticed, than someone trying to do his thinking for him.

The same principle applied if anyone speculated that a certain man was to be appointed to a position by the President. He would then become the last man he'd appoint. Once the President grumbled, "I see the opposition is planting stories of who I'm going to appoint. Yep, I see his enemies are trying to make sure he doesn't get the job. I ought to fool them, damn it. I hate to be maneuvered that way."

Frankly I don't remember who the appointee in question was or whether he got the job. But the odds are strong he didn't.

On another occasion a Secret Service man rested something for a minute on a corner of the President's desk. LBJ, who liked to see the top of his desk looking neat and who couldn't stand packages that were the slightest bit messy, bellowed, "What son of a bitch put that package on my desk?" The Secret Service man reached over and took the package and meekly apologized.

Johnson was bigger and louder than life, and from the beginning I knew that everybody around the White House was going to have trouble with him. He had a short fuse and a quick temper. You

93

knew he was angry when he kicked the elevator door. He and Ike both came up with this trick, and they didn't learn it from each other.

One day LBJ sat down on his commode and broke the seat. All hell broke lose. As fast as possible a larger commode was installed with an extra-large-size wooden seat. After that, he'd often brag to his male friends about his special toilet, tailored to fit presidential specifications. And he would add, "Now don't anyone dare say it's to fit the Number One ass of the nation."

LBJ liked bathroom humor, and he knew how to wring a story dry. As the weeks went by, he became the world's greatest expert on toilet seats. He knew the good points and the bad points of all the kinds he could have had—plastic, nonplastic, bamboo, flowered, Grecian, or Early American. His listeners would begin by chuckling at this display of expertise, and end up roaring with laughter.

I recall another bit of horseplay in which LBJ would accuse a friend—a famous Texas architect who designed the American embassy in Mexico, and whose firm renovated the Johnson ranch house—of permanently damaging the presidential spine. The cause of said damage was the position of the toilet-paper holder in the President's bathroom at the ranch.

Even though his friend had not *personally* supervised the placement of the toilet-paper dispenser, every time he came to the White House for a visit, he would be treated to a replay—in front of an eager audience—of how LBJ had to twist himself out of shape to reach the most out-of-the-way toilet-paper holder ever conceived by the mind of man. Still, the President couldn't have been all that displeased because he chose the same architect, R. Max Brooks, as half of the team that designed the LBJ Library, the other half being Gordon Bunshaft of New York.

Another of President Johnson's favorite themes was his shower. I don't know how many people he complained to, or how many friends were marched into his bathroom to see the most obstinate shower in the Western world, but it must have run to dozens.

Lyndon, who had a rubdown nearly every day and loved it almost as much as he loved his dogs, liked to take a shower that amounted to a second treatment. When he was Vice President and living in The Elms, he had enjoyed a super-powerful multi-nozzle shower that drove needlelike jets of water over every part of his body.

He just wanted the same thing at the White House, that's all. But it wasn't so simple. Several times the White House shower was changed; special pumps were installed and experts examined The Elms' shower to learn its secret. No good—the President went on griping and no one could ever get the shower jets strong enough to suit him.

As far as I could see, the White House shower had been made strong enough to throw a lesser man down, but to the very end of his term in office, LBJ grumbled about that "damned weak White House shower." Complaining was his fun and games, and he loved every minute of it.

Lyndon Johnson could be very generous. But at all times he fully expected his generosity to produce the intended result. One time he gave a press secretary, Joe Laitin, a radio. A few days later he called Laitin at 7:30 A.M. to ask if he'd caught the 7:00 A.M. radio news.

Joe said no, he hadn't had the radio on.

Lyndon sounded very annoyed and asked, "Well, didn't I give you a radio so you could hear the morning news?"

Joe patiently answered yes, he was most grateful for it.

The President wasn't satisfied. "Damn it, I can't understand you," he exploded. "If you aren't going to use it, just give it back."

Laitin started to apologize but bang, the President hung up.

It was hard to know what gift LBJ would like to receive himself. A wastebasket, hand-decorated by a friend of Lady Bird's, rated so high that he said to me, "It's too good for the White House. I'm keeping it home on the ranch for my boat."

Another gift that really hit home was one he received from W. Marvin Watson after he made him Postmaster General. Watson was an old friend of Johnson's from Texas and he decided to give LBJ a copy of every stamp that had come out since LBJ came to Washington in 1935 with his first government job—in the NYA.

Watson thought it would be easy, but it turned out the Post Office no longer had many of the stamps and he had to buy them at inflated prices from stamp dealers. The most he paid for any one stamp was $10 for a $5 Hamilton stamp, but before he was finished he was about $120 out of pocket.

That was the kind of gift Johnson liked, however. A gift that required thinking.

Sometimes LBJ was fantastically generous with the people he liked. But he was not above dickering for a real bargain. On his last trip to Rome before leaving the Presidency, this trait suddenly surfaced, much to the embarrassment of an agent in his party.

"That bum," the Secret Service man told me, "went to an art display and tried to get the price down. He wanted the stuff for the LBJ Library. And by God, he did get the price down. And then he was so anxious to get his bargains home he bypassed the crowds waiting for him by using a viaduct that took him right to the airport. I tell you he was a demon that day."

About the time LBJ announced he wasn't going to run again he really got testy. Once I came into the room just as he exploded: "They shot me down. The only difference between the Kennedy assassination and mine is that I am still alive and feeling it." He was talking about Vietnam and how nobody was rallying round him to support his position.

I remember when the papers were giving Johnson unmitigated hell every time he turned around. George Christian, his top PR man, said to the press, "Okay, you guys, you just go ahead and pour it on. But one of these days you're going to miss him."

And I'll bet they do.

I hated to see LBJ lose his popularity, going from cock of the walk to bottom of the barnyard well. Strangely enough, the decline had begun with his beagles, Him and Her, in an incident that ended the new President's honeymoon with the press and with a lot of the dog-loving public. He'd been hailed for his tax cuts, great new civil rights legislation, and countless other achievements. He'd even settled a railroad strike and gotten the Chamber of Commerce on his side.

And then in a flash everything changed. Or as one reporter—Mary McGrory—put it, "A yelp ended a winning streak."

The incident I'm talking about was the ear-pulling, and many people asked me about it. "You're the dogkeeper, why didn't you stop him?" they'd wonder. As long as I was at the White House, I kept still. I figured LBJ had $30,000-a-year advisors to tell him what he should or shouldn't do if he cared about his image.

But that's all over now—LBJ is gone, I'm retired, and I can finally say what I had the bad luck to see. Yes, I was there the day the

President picked up his little beagle Him by the ears. I cringed to hear the dog yelping. It all happened April 27, 1964, at C-9 Post, right outside the President's office. He had been meeting there with some balance of payments experts, and as a relief from financial talk, he took them for a walk around the yard. A swarm of reporters and photographers followed, as usual.

What the President was trying to do was please the photographers by getting the dogs to do a trick. Lyndon Johnson was such a tall man he had to bend way over even to get near a beagle. So he was bending over and just took hold of Him by the most convenient handle, his ears, probably thinking of some Texas story about a farmer lifting his dog that way. Even when he heard the yelps, the President didn't seem to realize that anything was wrong. He just matter-of-factly explained that pulling their ears was good for the dogs, and that everyone who knew dogs liked to hear them yelp.

What the President didn't remember, or know, is that you can only try this lift-'em-by-the-ears trick with a puppy. Old-time farmers and hunters start to pick up a pup by the ears and if it yelps, they stop and pick up one that doesn't. Puppies are light, but grown dogs have more weight than their ears can comfortably support.

Even as the episode unfolded—with the dog yelping and the flash bulbs popping—I knew the fat was in the fire. Or to quote a favorite expression of Lyndon's, "the ox was in the ditch," and it was going to make news. I had just gotten some good stories in the papers about the presidential dogs, and now this! I felt sorry for both the President and the dog.

Johnson probably never knew that Nixon, as soon as he entered office, used the ear-pulling incident for a gag to amuse his Republican friends. You will read about it later in my diary.

After LBJ's goof, the White House was flooded with mail. Some defended the President; most condemned him. Reporters around the world were going to dog experts to poll their opinion on beagle ear-pulling. Veterinarians were anti-President on the matter. So were the National Beagle Club, the American Kennel Club, and the American Society for the Prevention of Cruelty to Animals.

But Bernard Workman, the chairman of the Canine Defense League in London, defended him. A clipping quoted him as saying, "I don't believe that a beagle comes to any harm by picking it up by the ears. Their ears are particularly strong."

When I showed it to the President he still didn't ask me, his dog-keeper, whether I thought he'd done right, which was a tipoff to me he really knew it had been a mistake. And since he didn't ask, I didn't volunteer. I just listened as he defended himself some more. "You know, Bryant, it's good for these dogs to bark. They have things too soft around here; they've got to exercise those lungs in case I take them hunting. Where else does a dog get such treatment as I give them? They lead a better life than I do. Hell, they even have their teeth cleaned for them."

I said, "Why don't you call a press conference and tell the reporters?"

"Oh, hell," he said, "I can't teach those guys anything. Half of them don't know their ass from their elbow. They're too ignorant. You can't teach anything to a shut mind. But I never thought a dog would do me in."

Then he got his second wind and decided to use the incident to his own advantage. "The only thing that saves my sanity is humor," he had told me. So I wasn't surprised that when he spoke to a group of Jewish clothing workers in New York City, he said, "I've been warned that you are mad at me because I pulled the ears of a *bagel.*" He came back beaming and said, "They loved it. I went from *beagle* to *bagel* and let the bagel share the blame."

Now it can be told that the much-publicized April 27 ear-pulling wasn't the only time he pulled the dogs' ears. A few days later he went to the trouble of showing some tourists how he had lifted his dog by the ears, and again Him yelped. A tourist laughed and called out, "That was off the record."

My diary shows another item about a year later:

3/15/65 The President called for the dogs in front of his office. He twisted Him's ear and Him yelped. President petted Him before going to the Capitol to make a civil rights speech. I took Blanco to the second floor. Linda took Him. The President told me to bring them both out in fifteen minutes.

To the end of his term he still persisted in pulling the dogs' ears just to prove they really "liked it." The Prez hated to be wrong.

LBJ wove a lot of fun and games into his days as President but life wasn't all beer and skittles or dogs and shower nozzles, even in his early years in the White House. Some terrible moments passed in

98

the President's official life. One of the worst involved Walter Jenkins, an aide I had often seen around. He was a hard worker and LBJ's closest friend and assistant, and his daughter, Beth, was sixteen-year-old Luci's best friend. Sometimes the two families ate together on the Truman Balcony.

But on October 7, 1964, everything changed within a short half-hour. Jenkins was attending an opening of *Newsweek*'s new Washington office. Suddenly, about seven o'clock, according to the story that circulated the White House, he ducked out. Half an hour later he was arrested at the YMCA men's room for disorderly conduct of the type associated with homosexuals. It turned out the police had peepholes at the Y John and picked up a lot of homosexuals that way.

Lyndon Johnson and the whole White House staff were in shock. Jenkins was out, and LBJ explained to a startled public that he was sorely grieved and that all he could say was that Jenkins had lately been under great stress.

A different scandal, this one involving Bobby Baker, the Senate Majority Secretary and LBJ's old protégé from his days on the Hill, threatened the President much more seriously. Baker was charged with using LBJ connections to get kickbacks on contracts and otherwise feather his own nest, and the President was so distraught he rushed to the office of his old mentor, House Speaker John W. McCormack, for advice. He was sure he'd be blamed for Bobby's sins, according to the inside story, and blurted out that he would be the first President to go to jail.

LBJ was so agonized he didn't even notice that others were listening in. Anyway, nothing stays secret very long in Washington. Whatever advice Speaker McCormack gave him must have been right. LBJ came through unscathed. Only Baker went to jail.

10

It's hard to know how much credit LBJ's dogs deserve for his landslide victory in the November 1964 presidential election. I'd say they deserve a lot, and I was their advance man and PR representative. I soldered LBJ tieclasps with the motto LBJ FOR THE USA on the collar of every dog I could get my hands on, and I mean every dog that passed through the White House gate, not just our permanent residents. I also plastered large LBJ FOR THE USA signs on the dogs, draped them with blankets carrying the same message, and took them to the White House gates to meet the voters.

Somebody on the President's staff complained that I was spending too much time campaigning. The Secret Service didn't like my activities, either, so one of them raised a new objection. "I don't want Him and Bryant over there at the South West Gate where the President goes out on his way to church," he said. "Bryant's attracting too many tourists."

The President called me in that night. "Have you been showing my dogs to the tourists?" he asked me.

I was cagey. For all I knew I was in deep trouble, so I just answered "Yes, Mr. President," and volunteered nothing further. He kept probing and I kept being noncommittal until he asked me how the dogs were behaving themselves. "Fine," I said, "but when I took them to the South West Gate the officer told me I can't show the dogs down there."

I'd seen that the President was losing his temper, and this did it. "Goddamn it, now hear this," he bellowed. "You tell that captain that you can take the dogs anywhere you damn well want on these White House grounds. And tell him the President said you can go *anywhere, anytime,* you want to and to keep his damn nose out of it."

So I went over, picked up the phone, called the captain, and told him approximately what the President had said. "All right," he replied. "There will be no more problem." But his voice was coated with ice.

It was full steam ahead on the campaign:

Oct./64   Made footprints of Blanco, Him, and Her from an ink pad.
I photographed the footprints with a picture of President and his dogs,
to be sent to children who request one. Every child has voting-age
parents.

Dressed Him and Her up with huge eight-inch LBJ FOR THE USA campaign badges under their chins and babies' bibs saying, "We'd vote for
LBJ," in crazy kiddish print. Chief Knudsen made pictures and released
to newspapers.

Nov./64   Now in final days before the election, Him and Her wore their
big LBJ FOR THE USA signs, campaign posters and everything "LBJ" that
I could tie on them, including balloons. A young couple pushing a baby
in a carriage on the street south of the fountains saw me near the fence
walking the dogs. The young man said, "We are for Goldwater." About
this time the dogs spotted another dog across the park. They started
barking loudly. The young man said that he must have said the wrong
thing. So the young couple left in a hurry. The crowd laughed when he
said he was for Goldwater, so I'd say LBJ is safe.

Though I wasn't a Goldwater man, I did like the senator's dry
sense of humor. He said he was grateful for the job offers Lyndon
had given him during the campaign—librarian in Sitka, Alaska, or
file clerk in the town of his choice in Indonesia. That's one joke
cracked by somebody besides himself that made LBJ laugh.

Of course the President helped a little himself in getting reelected.
He sure knew how to give a campaign speech and he started early,
slipping in a political pitch as far back as February 1964 while in
Florida to open the construction of a barge canal. Then on St. Patrick's Day the next month he said in a speech, "I woke up this morning and suddenly realized that the Irish have taken over the government—and I like it." The line was immediately on everyone's lips
around the White House, except that we left off the last part. I
thought about this—LBJ and his Irishmen—years later when Nixon
came into office and it seemed as if the Germans had replaced them.

I also recall LBJ observing that the Democratic party was so
peaceful, the fighting Irish might move to the Republican party
"where the feuding is really going on."

The thing I noticed about President Johnson's speeches was that
they gave people a vision of a forever greater America. LBJ was
always talking about the American dream and how a man could still

rise to the top from the humblest beginnings. Kennedy had built dreams, too. One time when JFK was walking the White House grounds, thinking aloud, he blurted out, "A politician is a dream merchant." Then he thought a moment and added, "But he must back up the dream." It's my theory that Nixon's speeches failed to kindle warmth in a lot of people because they didn't hold out a dream.

The really touching moment of the 1964 election involved Robert Kennedy. The story around the White House was that Bobby wanted to be Vice President so bad he could taste it, and LBJ wanted him to know that he didn't have a chance so he would stop counting on it. LBJ just didn't want any more competition from the Kennedy family—he felt it was time to be the star of the show himself. They had a talk one day at the White House and Johnson told Bobby straight out that he was *not* his choice.

Bobby just looked at him and didn't say a word. LBJ then tried to soften the blow and offered him any job he wanted, like ambassador, and it was Bobby's turn to say, no, thanks. He said he liked his job as Attorney General.

Hubert Humphrey knew right along that he was going to be the one chosen as LBJ's running mate, so he could afford to be relaxed and make jokes about it. When LBJ and Hubert were together, if Pierre Salinger or anybody else appeared at the door, Hubert would say, "Oh, here's so-and-so—he looks just like a vice presidential candidate to me." And everyone would laugh.

I wonder what would have happened if Bobby had been Vice President. Maybe he'd be alive today. Maybe he'd even have made President.

I know the papers tried to describe LBJ as an uncouth tough guy with the hide of a rhinoceros. Uncouth now and then, maybe. But thick-skinned, no. In fact, I used to feel sorry for him because he was so thin-skinned. Men seem to let down their reserve when they are around their dogs, and as the President's dogkeeper, I sometimes had a better chance than anyone else to see what was bothering him.

A lot of things hurt Lyndon Johnson's feelings. He was stung, for example, when the press poked fun at a speech by his special assistant, Jack Valenti. Valenti, now head of the Motion Picture Association, had praised LBJ to the heavens and said in effect that he slept better knowing Johnson was in the White House.

Some columnists hinted darkly that the President must have forced Valenti to say those things and the Washington *Post* cartoonist, Herblock, really got under LBJ's skin with a sketch showing the White House in the background, the President with a bullwhip, and his poor aides with welts on their backs.

"They are trying to make me out a fool," he burst out to everyone and no one in particular. "But just remember this. A fool is nothing more than human being acting like a human being and letting the world see he is acting like a human being."

Humor was LBJ's comfort, and pretty soon I heard him kidding pretty Mary Margaret, Jack Valenti's wife, saying, "Jack is going to make another speech and get me into some more cartoons." And for a while he went around asking his political friends if they didn't want him to lend them Valenti to make a speech for them.

Then there was the matter of the ADA. LBJ was hurt when the Americans for Democratic Action blasted him in February 1965, despite what he felt were his great plans and achievements. Lyndon was particularly proud of his battle against want and inequity, yet the ADA said he'd declared only "a verbal war on poverty" with his Great Society and planned to back it up with "a budget of timid numbers."

"In politics," he commented as he patted his dogs, "it's just a matter of who you'd rather antagonize, this group or that. If the ADA grades you A, the John Birch Society grades you F."

Everyone around the White House went under the President's grading system. A bill before Congress was only a grade C. If he liked a dress, he'd give it a grade A or B+. His daughters caught on and were using the grading system. Lynda Bird, whom he flattered by consulting about his drafts for speeches, would tell him the speech was a grade C or grade B, but that a few changes could help it. Once his speech was given, however, his family would always grade it an A or A+. They were very loyal.

Friends had to bear up under the grading system as well. He gave architect Max Brooks' toilet-paper dispenser a D, his White House shower a flat F.

Lyndon used humor time and again in coping with the women in his life. For example, when he wanted his wife to buy more expensive dresses to be an even greater asset to him, he tricked her into it by offering to buy her two very expensive dresses if she bought herself one more at the same price. She couldn't resist a bargain like that.

103

Humor helped him, too, when "Lucy" Johnson made history in February 1965 by changing one letter of her name. The President was baffled by it; he was also slightly annoyed that she didn't tell him first and that she didn't think the name he and her mother had given her was good enough. But he hid his emotion in humor, saying, "Lucy thinks 'Luci' is a proper old spelling of the word. I'd hate to let her loose on the English language." She was a freshman at the National Cathedral School at the time and had been made honorary student chairman of the National Symphony Orchestra. The announcement called her "Luci" and a footnote explained, "Miss Johnson prefers this spelling of her name." LBJ learned of it when the newspapers pounced on the story.

I asked Luci about it and she said, "I've been spelling it that way for years but nobody paid attention. That's the world for you. They have to see everything in print. Even my father." The funny thing was that though she wanted a modern spelling of her name, she still was curtsying to her elders like an old-fashioned girl. When her father teased her about her curtsy she said, "I can't stop. But I'm trying to. My knee gets a reflex action when I meet the older generation, Daddy."

Luci would do anything to get her father's approval. The little punkin even took credit for teaching Blanco to shake hands after I'd trained him in two sessions. After asking me how I had done it, she proudly told LBJ she did it that way herself. Maybe to please and compliment Luci for what she felt was her accomplishment, LBJ never failed to shake hands with Blanco when he arrived at or was leaving the White House, by car or helicopter. It was a kind of solemn ceremony, Blanco looking very dignified about it and LBJ not cracking a smile.

LBJ often expressed his feelings in a roundabout way. When you'd done something he liked, he'd "brag on you" to a third person or find some other indirect way to let you know that he was pleased. When Luci brought home Yuki, the stray dog he loved more than any other and would have suffered the most to lose, LBJ never came right out and asked Luci for him. He just kept putting off letting Luci take him home with her.

And when I complimented him on his landslide victory in 1964, he didn't brag about it but told a story as if to pooh-pooh his popularity and make fun of himself and politics. The story concerned a

Texas state senator who telephoned his friend, a local judge, to tell him that the Senate had just voted to abolish his court as part of an economy drive.

The judge was completely dumfounded and sputtered and asked if there had at least been a hearing about it.

"Oh yes," said the senator. "We held a hearing, all right."

"But who in the world could you find to testify against me?" demanded the judge.

"Well," said the senator, "the head of the Bar Association testified."

"Just wait a minute," said the judge, "let me tell you about that joker. He's nothing but a shyster lawyer, and his daddy was too."

"Well," said the senator, "the mayor of your town also testified."

"Hold on," said the judge. "You can't count on anything he says. He stole his way into office. He padded the ballot boxes and counted most votes three times, the rest of the votes twice."

"But your banker testified as well," said the senator.

"Are you going to trust that banker?" wailed the judge. "He's the worst one of all—he's been charging usury rates just like his daddy and granddaddy before him."

Finally the senator laughed and admitted he'd made the whole thing up. The court wasn't abolished and there'd been no hearing.

The judge broke into sobs. "Now why," he asked, "did you go and make me say those things about the three dearest friends I have?"

Lyndon loved to tell stories and he had a sense of humor, but his fanaticism about saving electricity was no prank. He kept making news with his damn bulbs, and my diary records other incidents that never got noticed—how he'd go from one end of the White House to the other and plunge us all in sudden darkness, even in the carpenter's shop and my electrical shop. It became fashionable across the country and also a laughing matter to turn off the lights, and LBJ earned the richly deserved nickname "Light Bulb Lyndon."

When his brother, Sam Houston, was staying on the third floor, LBJ would burst into his room to see if he'd fallen asleep with the light on. Then he would wake him up and demand to know if Sam Houston was working for him or for the light company.

His mania just increased when a February 1964 report showed a one-month drop in the White House electricity bill to $3,100 from the previous month's $4,900. He could have saved a lot more if he'd switched off the three or four TV sets he had on most of the time, but he never tired of listening to himself talk.

What a change it was when Nixon came in and hated to see himself on television. Maybe he had a point.

While Lyndon tracked down electricity wasters, Lady Bird was making news herself with her beautification projects, traveling to every nook and outpost in the country and giving awards to cities and towns for their beautification achievements. The story around the White House was that Liz Carpenter, her smart and sassy press secretary, and Bess Abell, her beautiful and able social secretary, had helped her come up with the beautification scheme. A problem Lady Bird faced when she came to the White House was that Jackie Kennedy had made such a spectacular success of fixing up the interior of the place that anything Lady Bird tried would be interpreted as me-tooism. So when the new First Lady happened to voice despair at the plague of billboards ruining the landscape everywhere she went, the three of them came up with the ambitious project of beautifying not just the White House but, as LBJ put it, "the whole outdoors—of the whole damn country."

And to a great extent, she succeeded.

What the world didn't know is that Lyndon was often glad Lady Bird was busy with her beautification programs because that was the only way he could have some privacy. "When you work and live in the same house, that's a hell of a lot of being together," he said. "You almost have to get away now and again to see what's on the other side of the bars."

Lady Bird knew his need to feel free and never let herself interfere in his plans. She was happy—actually grateful, it seemed to me —just to be included.

LBJ, of course, was the real star in my life—Lady Bird, Lynda Bird, and Luci were only supporting characters that periodically crossed the White House stage. But sometimes I would pay Lady Bird the same tribute I paid the President and have the dogs out to welcome her when she came home by helicopter and the President was busy elsewhere. At first she couldn't believe this ceremony was for her and would ask me whether the President was getting ready to take off. She had been in her husband's shadow so long, it took some time for her to get used to being a star in her own right.

Lady Bird didn't want people to think she was too perfect. She admitted that she had a temper and that after she had blown her stack she felt sick inside. "I just hate myself then," she said once.

She needn't have worried about the staff thinking she was perfect. They didn't. But they did feel she was long-suffering, having to put up with the quirks of LBJ, and they gave her high marks for it.

Interpretations vary. Expert Lady Bird watchers at the White House figured the First Lady understood Lyndon better than anyone else did, and painted just the picture of herself she wanted. She'd tell everyone that her husband and daughters came first and not to worry one little bit about her. This somehow made Lyndon feel strong and free—free to work and play as he chose. But behind the picture she was actually a very clever woman. And a strong First Lady, feared and catered to just as much as any of her predecessors.

Lady Bird never seemed to object no matter how many pretty secretaries and friends and wives of aides her husband surrounded himself with. But I soon learned and the White House was soon abuzz with the word that nobody better come between her and Lyndon.

When it came down to it, she was fiercely proud of her position as First Lady and the untarnished picture in history of herself and Lyndon as a happily married couple. Which they were. They really were warm and loving together. But the only trouble was, Lyndon was warm and loving with a lot of other pretty women—usually blondes.

You wouldn't believe the sort of stories that made the rounds of some of the White House intimates pretending to describe LBJ's wild life on Capitol Hill and as Vice President. That LBJ had gotten one girl pregnant. That LBJ had sired one child out of wedlock. That LBJ couldn't let any pretty girl alone.

I remember someone told how a very highly qualified girl had applied for a particular job in his office but that LBJ had turned her down for only one reason—she wasn't a bit pretty.

I know he had an absolute obsession about every woman making herself look as beautiful as possible, and he sent his own wife and daughters and some of his secretaries to the New York make-up man Eddie Senz to learn how to apply their make-up and to choose the particular hair style that was best for each of them.

After seeing a pretty White House secretary go tripping by, LBJ once startled me by commenting, "I can't help it. I put a high mark on beauty. I can't stand an ugly woman around or a fat one who looks like a cow that's gonna step on her own udder."

As for the nasty rumors, they were no surprise—I'd heard the same things about John F. Kennedy. I remember when a researcher browsing through a genealogy book came across a shocking reference to JFK's earlier days. You can't find the book in the Library of Congress any more. All copies have disappeared. But I managed to get a copy of the book's key page, and here's the reference that caused the talk:

Durie (Kerr) Malcolm . . . born Kerr but took the name of her step-father. She first married Firmin Desloge, IV. They were divorced. Durie then married F. John Bersbach. They were divorced, and she married, third, John F. Kennedy, son of Joseph P. Kennedy, one-time Ambassador to England. (There were no children of the second and third marriage. One child, Durie, by the first.)*

The way I heard it, JFK never denied that he had known the gal or dated her. He just said he hadn't married her. Or at least a White House spokesman said it for him, quoting President Kennedy as saying, "There's nothing to it, of course." Some insiders said that if he had married her and later had the marriage quietly annulled, it would have been the same in the eyes of the Church as never having been married at all.

I don't know. I'm just saying what stories went around the White House.

Some of the stories that made the rounds of the White House about LBJ weren't just concerned with the good old days on the Hill. One was that he not only preached civil rights and equal opportunity when he got to the White House, he also practiced it. He was said to be fond of his black secretary, whom he had found working at the White House in the office of his assistant, Ted Reardon, and had promoted to his own office.

Gerry Whittington was her name—short for Geraldine—and she was one of the most beautiful girls I had ever seen. LBJ made her one of his private secretaries and took her with him sometimes, as when he was making a speech at Howard University.

*The Blauvelt Family Genealogy, by Louis Blauvelt, privately published in 1957.

108

I don't know what happened, but eventually Gerry was switched over to the State Department, where she had a good job in the Office of Protocol.

Lady Bird kept an eagle eye on what was going on and always seemed to know when to step in and move. Quick and neat and polite. For example, one gal who got cut off so fast it made her head swim was Barbara Howar, a damned good-looking blonde. Her trouble was that she had bragged too much about her closeness to the President and she had tried to move in as best friend of the family. She was advising the girls on what to wear. She was helping run the wedding plans for Luci. She was talking to the press. And the worst mistake of all, she was flashing around a picture of herself dancing with Lyndon.

Suddenly she was out. Lady Bird canceled a big, glamorous party Barbara Howar was giving for the bride-to-be, a party on the rooftop of the Washington Hotel, near the White House. Barbara wasn't helping the girls buy clothes any more, either. One story was that Barbara Howar was caught sitting on the presidential lap. She insisted she had fallen over the rug when she was approaching the desk. But that left a question about what she was doing on the wrong side of the desk.

Lady Bird could be tough when she had to be. The iron hand in the silken glove. So could the two women who were the First Lady's protectors and eyes and ears—social secretary Bess Abell and press secretary Liz Carpenter. Both had known her for many years before the White House.

An entry in my diary reminds me of a typical episode. It features Bess Abell, but if I hunted awhile I'm sure I could find something similar for Liz. The Johnsons were going to have a small dinner in the private dining room on the second floor. The butler, Robert Few, had been told to prepare for sixteen people, and he did. Later he got word to change the table to seventeen guests, and he did that, too.

Then just a little before the guests were to arrive, Bess Abell came to the dining room and smilingly told him to quick, change the table, there would be eighteen guests, but to stand ready in case the President brought along even more people.

Robert Few exploded. "Fix the damn table yourself," he snapped.

Bess got angry and called the Usher's Office. Robert was soon thereafter transferred to the Treasury Department.

But getting back to Lady B, as some called her backstairs at the White House, someone said Lady B ought to hang a sign in all the pretty White House secretaries' offices saying YOU CAN PLAY WITH LYNDON BUT YOU CANNOT TAKE HIM HOME WITH YOU.

The trouble was, nobody had to take Lyndon home. He took them with *him*. He entertained, sometimes nightly, on the presidential yacht, the *Sequoia,* and made up his own guest list.

The stories coming off his boat showed he liked to cozy up with at least one and preferably two pretty girls clinging to his arms and listening to him as he spun his yarns or teased them about their "ugly husbands" or "ugly boyfriends," with whom, LBJ lamented, he could not compete. Liquor on the boat was the best—scotch for the Prez, anything else anyone wanted—and so was the service. And the rule of the boat was that everything was off the record.

The presidential yacht was a real burden for the First Lady. She tried to go with her husband every time she could, but sometimes he went off without her, willy-nilly. I can remember seeing Lady Bird return exhausted from some beautification trip only to find Lyndon was not there to welcome her as she stepped off the helicopter—as she always tried to be there for him—but was on the yacht, and a little hurt look would cross her face. She knew that old boat was her competition.

Once I said to one of the staff how sorry I was that Lyndon had gotten away when he knew she would be coming in by helicopter, and the aide said, "Don't worry about it. This is the way they play, Texas style. Lady Bird can take care of herself."

Lady Bird was the businesswoman of the family, and Lyndon never forgot it. She would shut herself up in her room to work on her ledgers and letters and nobody better intrude. If they did, they were given a very cool reception. She liked to take care of her own accounts, and she was quoted as saying, "I wouldn't have a joint checking account with the Angel Gabriel."

Another cool character was Lynda, who had the brains of her father and the personality of her mother. I once said to someone who worked upstairs in the family quarters that I felt sorry for Lynda because she never got excited about anything.

"Are you kidding?" came the reply. "Lynda is a volcano belching ice." I realized this was right later when Lynda had a fight with her mother and came haughtily out and walked angrily around the White House grounds in icy silence. She could spit ice at a moment's notice, and she often spit ice at photographers. Her pet hate at the White House was the same as Margaret Truman's had been—photographers.

Once during a political convention Luci tried to imitate her sister by being difficult with photographers, and ran out into the surf to evade them. But she was such fun and so cute about it that the photographers got into the spirit of it and waded out after her in their trousers.

Luci loved to cuss like her father, damning this and damning that and using a few choice four-letter words, but it was a kid show-off thing. Luci was so full of love for the world you never had to worry about her. It was Lynda who could say the things that hurt.

When the Johnson women first came to the White House it looked to me as if all of them were trying to be carbon copies of Jacqueline Kennedy. When dressed up they wore their hair the way she did and the same kind of sleeveless dresses. Luci even put on a little whispery voice that she must have known was pure Jackie. But gradually the memory of Jackie faded and each woman in the LBJ family began developing as a distinct personality. Luci was emerging as a complete flirt. She even flirted with me if she wanted me to run an errand. She could get anyone to do anything for her just by tilting her head and giving them a slow smile and an innocent gaze. But when she was angry she could stamp her foot and say, "Damn it, when I want something done, I want something done." She liked to cuss to shock the White House staff, but with LBJ she was flirtatious and all little girl. He couldn't say no to her. But he could be tough with Lynda Bird.

He wanted Lynda Bird to lose weight, dress more appealingly, and learn to make up to fellows. "Why do the boys always prefer Luci?" he asked me once. I said, "Well, Mr. President, Lynda wears her brains outside. Maybe she'd better wear them only in her head." He nodded yes. Then he muttered, "I can't reason with her."

Luci and Lynda were on-again, off-again friends. They were more competitive than people realized. I think one reason Lynda latched onto Hollywood star George Hamilton and hung on even when their romance looked like an endless dead-end road was that she wanted to be one up on Luci. A backstairs story held that Lynda had never

111

forgiven Luci for something she once said about her hope chest. "You don't need a hope chest," taunted Luci, who always had boyfriends galore. "You'll never get to use it." Lynda was furious. Sisters have disputes and then forget it, but I always did think Lynda danced attendance on Hamilton and let him make her over just to show Luci what she could do. If Luci was jealous, she was good at hiding it.

It was obvious to a lot of people at the White House that Lynda envied Luci her ability to make up to people or to let herself go and do a wild dance if she felt like it. When Lynda would say, "Here comes Watusi Luci," it wasn't a compliment or a joke. She was trying to put her sister down.

The way the White House crowd figured it, Lynda hated to have her picture taken because she didn't want to be compared with Luci. After moving to the White House, Lynda went out of her way for a while to look like a schlump when she didn't have to dress up to attend something. She herself told the story of how she'd gone to a fancy Washington store to buy a lamp for her new room in the White House. The clerk didn't realize who she was, judged her by her appearance, and suggested she could find a less expensive lamp at another store. Speechless for once, Lynda simply left the store and the haughty clerk.

Luci, on the other hand, could always look bandbox right, cute, and cuddly, even barefoot. Looking at her and at the other LBJ women, I used to think how well the Secret Service had labeled them in giving them code names so no one would know what they were talking about:

Lady Bird was Victoria. The perfectly proper woman.

Luci was Venus.

Lynda was Velvet—I would always mentally add "in an iron glove."

Lynda Bird, unlike Luci, never seemed to be able to yield, and handled herself a bit stiffly. Her father once wondered aloud what to do about her, how to make her more agreeable to the kind of strong man he wanted her to find. This was before Lynda's Hollywood phase. LBJ put it bluntly—"Lynda always wants to be in charge," he said. She always picked someone she could handle—her alliances didn't stick. The story was that if a fellow had one fight with Lynda Bird, he was out in the cold, she wanted nothing more to do with him. Whereas Luci would squabble around with her boy-friends and just act natural.

Both girls ran through quite a few boyfriends in those early months at the White House. Luci had a boyfriend named Jack Olsen who invited her to be his guest at the University of Wisconsin. The visit killed the romance. As the White House staff got the story, coping with mobs when he was with Luci and being spied on by re-porters, friends, strangers, and Secret Service men gave Olsen ulcers. He gave her up for his health.

Then there was Paul Betz, a medical student, who also dropped out early in the game. He was Luci's boyfriend just before Pat Nugent.

Luci was always flying into tears. She would shed tears when a boyfriend left the White House to go back to college, till his next visit. She would shed tears when Daddy Lyndon said she couldn't have her way. Which wasn't often. She'd start sobbing and fling her-self into his lap and nine times out of ten he'd say, "All right, you can go do it this time, but don't ask again."

Lynda didn't use tears. She was all dignity, which some called haughtiness. When she came to the White House she was engaged to Bernard Rosenbach. Rosenbach, a Catholic, was assumed by some people to be Jewish, because of his name, and this was said to bother Lynda, who was Episcopalian like her mother. The engagement broke off about five months later. What Lynda couldn't cope with, Luci could—a change of religion. In fact, when Luci was becoming a Catholic, she told me, "I can't explain the peace I feel. I am hap-piest when I am in a Catholic church."

I never did find out what George Hamilton's religion was, but when Lynda was eventually married, it was to an Episcopalian.

Luci really did take religion seriously. She not only embraced the Catholic Church but she used her father's trick of making the church a part of the White House. For a while I almost stumbled over all the priests walking around the White House with Luci. They ate with her, they walked with her, they talked with her. And they even attended a beer party she gave in her own fun room, the Solarium, to celebrate after she officially became Catholic.

Everyone pressed food and drink on me at that party of Luci's, but though I ate more than my share, I can truly say I never drank a drop while on duty. On this occasion, as a Baptist, I was surprised to see the priests take off their jackets and dig into the beer. Before the party Luci asked if her daddy would be there or was going to Texas. I don't recall whether she wanted to see him or was afraid he would disapprove of her beer-drinking.

But being religious didn't cramp Luci's style or her love for loud music and wild dancing. My diary shows:

Luci has two radio antennas on her limousine. There is one radio for the driver and one FM radio for Luci mounted on top shelf behind the rear seat. Her driver says she turns it on full blast and listens to teenage-style music. He says it almost drives him nuts.

Lynda was much more secretive than Luci and seldom had me around during her parties. And she didn't seem to go in for the amount of entertaining Luci did. Some said when Lynda entertained, she liked it to be for princesses of foreign lands.

Lynda certainly was delighted when her father sent her as his envoy to Greece to attend the royal wedding of Princess Anne Marie. However, word around the White House was that the Greek royal family was a little miffed that the American President had sent only a slip of a girl to cope with their royal guests—about a dozen reigning monarchs—as well as other heads of state.

So the situation was already sensitive when Drew Pearson published a column poking fun at Lynda Bird's costume. I saved the clipping, dated September 23, 1964, and here's the key passage:

And the chief topic of conversation at the royal wedding reception was why Lynda didn't take off the silk coverall that looked like an old-fashioned dust protector. Bejeweled royalty watched as Lynda caromed over the dance floor and wondered what Lynda was trying to hide under that silk raincoat.

"Christ," LBJ exploded to a trusted friend after reading him the article, "is he trying to say my daughter is pregnant? Why doesn't the bastard attack me? Why my daughter? He's lower than a lizard's belly, and I'd like to nail his hide to the barn door."

No matter how the President criticized his daughter, he didn't want outsiders doing it, and we almost had another Harry Truman —daughter Margaret—Paul Hume case. But unlike Truman, who reacted to music critic Hume's unflattering notice about his daughter's singing by writing him in straight man-talk to the effect that he'd cut his balls off if he ever got near him, LBJ did nothing so

114

obvious, and I even saw Pearson invited to various functions and chatting amiably with the President.

When Lynda Bird finally emerged as the White House beauty-in-residence, thanks to the make-up tricks she learned from George Hamilton's friend George Masters, a make-up expert, she played it to the hilt. She was regal and stunning. And soon thereafter she took a glamorous job as a writer for *McCall's* magazine.

It's one of the small ironies of history that though Walter Jenkins had brought troubled times to the Johnsons when he was picked up as a deviate in the YMCA, a member of his family helped Luci to find real happiness. Walter's daughter Beth introduced Luci to two great boyfriends in a row—Paul Betz, who got Luci interested in becoming a Catholic, and Patrick J. Nugent, Beth's fellow student at Marquette University in Milwaukee, the man Luci was to marry.

Beth had a feeling about Luci and Pat being right for each other, and when they met, seventeen-year-old Luci was so struck that she broke off with Paul, the twenty-year-old pre-med student whose pin she had been wearing for about a year.

Luci's greatest triumph, and one she loved to talk about, happened early in June 1965, when she went to Marquette University, danced at the senior prom, even went picknicking, and nobody recognized her. As she told me long afterwards, "You should have seen me in my disguise. Nobody knew it was me and people were running around asking if anyone had seen Luci Johnson—there was a rumor Luci Johnson was around."

The way Luci did it was to wear a blonde wig and different make-up and get down on the floor of automobiles to avoid being noticed when they passed reporters. Three Secret Service men were with her, but they just helped her with her hide-and-seek.

The name Luci used during her big disguise was Amy Nunn. Nunn was easy for her to remember, feeling as she did about Catholicism. It was also the name of one of her favorite Secret Service men.

Only one person ever recognized her, she said, and that was a member of the faculty, on the morning of the prom. She was sure he would give the whole thing away, and she called Nugent to say she was canceling. Luci said Pat sounded just like her father when he told her, "No, honey, you can't give up now. You *are* going!"

So Luci went to the prom in her blonde wig, and told me later she "had the most wonderful time of my life. For once I knew what it was like to be just like anyone else and nobody staring at me because of my daddy."

In tribute to the Johnson family, I want to say they never turned their backs on the Jenkins family, and every once in a while there would still be an off-the-record dinner for them at the White House. Sometimes it would be just a luncheon on the balcony and sometimes a dinner inside. And Luci continued to invite Beth to the White House as if nothing had happened.

11

You are now stepping through the time machine of my diary to the year 1965. LBJ has been safely elected to office with the greatest landslide ever and seems to be surviving the greatest Inaugural ball —as a matter of fact, five of them. Luci Johnson is much amused at one ball that a look-alike named Robin Murphy is being pursued by photographers even more than she.

LBJ is amused at a security flap. Two teenagers who didn't even know an inauguration was going on were arrested openly carrying shotguns down the street. They were on their way to hunt squirrels in Virginia, and fortunately had their hunting licenses along.

Lady Bird is not amused that Lyndon has danced about a half-hour with Barbara Howar, crushed in a tight embrace by the crowd on the dance floor and not wanting to be rescued. He is supposedly rewarding Barbara for having helped Lady Bird on the Lady Bird Special campaign train by playing hairdresser and waving prettily at crowds.

Now the time machine skips forward to March and the staff is grumbling because for the sake of economy they must continue to use LBJ's old vice presidential stationery for scratch paper and notes until it is all gone.

And I am grumbling to my diary about the way the White House staff is treating me concerning one of my coats.

3/24/65 I had the dogs out for a walk at 5:00 P.M. President called for the dogs. He fed them one Unipet apiece. Blanco got excited, wanted more, and bit three holes in my thirty-five-dollar jacket and scraped the skin on my left arm. I went to the doctor's office. I reported the coat damage to Usher Carter.

3/25/65 Rex Scouten of the Usher's Office says the White House cannot pay for coat damage—there is nothing in the budget to cover it.

Every day someone else got into the act:

Presidential aide Marvin Watson wants a full report, including estimate of cost to repair the coat.

Usher Carter sent word he wants to discuss the coat matter further. So does the Housekeeper's Office.

I couldn't be bothered and wore the coat the way it was, to the delight of the President. "Mr. Bryant," he'd holler, "why is your sleeve torn? Why are you keeping my dogs fat? Why are buttons missing from your coat?"

He knew the answers. It just gave him a chance to let off a little steam. I finally gave the coat to the janitor in my apartment building rather than hear it razzed so much. When he saw the coat missing, LBJ was very generous and wanted me to buy a new coat and let him pay for it.

I said no, thanks. I wasn't about to put a price tag on my feeling for the President.

4/4/65 Helicopter from Camp David, 10:10 P.M. The President walked Blanco and Him off chopper and returned the dogs to me before going into the Mansion. He said the dogs ran in the woods, chased chipmunks, and barked at the Camp David sentries. "The dogs had a nice trip," he said. "I did all the work. Where do I go to get a job as dog?"

4/6/65 Mr. Scouten called me at home and said the President wanted Blanco to put on some weight. He is too slender. Colonel Ralph Chadwick, the vet, called me and said he would give Blanco a tranquilizer and put him on hamburger. 7:30 P.M., the President called for the dogs on the second floor. He took the guests on a tour of the West Hall, Mrs. Johnson's bedroom, his bedroom, and the Oval Room. Him jumped on Mrs. Johnson's bed, pulled some threads on a satin comforter. The President put the blame on me. I told the President I just got through feeding the dogs ice cream and hamburger. He said it was no wonder his grocery bill was so high. He said if this keeps up, the President will be on dog food and the presidential dogs will be on steak.

4/12/74 Senator Robert Kennedy saw me with the dogs on the South Grounds. He waved a greeting to me.

Every time I saw Bobby Kennedy I thought about how LBJ owed his Presidency to Bobby's brother, Jack. The inside story around the White House was that when someone at the 1960 Democratic Convention told the then Senate Majority Leader Johnson that nominee JFK was going to ask him to be his running mate, Lyndon had just two words to say: "Oh, shit." It just shows how human nature is and how quickly a "blushing bride" politician can say yes once someone really pops the question.

4/14/65 The President flew over flood and tornado areas of the midwest (Indiana, Ohio, and Minnesota). He returned by helicopter. As he got off he took Him to the second floor for a meeting with Willy Brandt of Germany. The Prez went to the office about 8:20 P.M. to work. He asked me if the dogs had been good. I told the President that Him wanted to get aboard the chopper when he landed, as Him missed him while he was on his trip. The President is the busiest man I know.

4/15/65 I almost got a trip. The President told me he wanted to take both dogs to Texas. It was raining. I had the dogs under the South Portico canopy. The President took Him. I told the President I would get Blanco aboard. Both dogs jumped up immediately on the padded seats across from the President's chair. I made them get down and put them in the rear of the chopper. Someone had pulled up the ladder and closed the door. I was trapped. Nobody seemed to care. Finally Marvin Watson took pity on me and told the pilot to let me off.

4/19/65 I'm worried about Blanco. He came back from Texas a bundle of nerves. The President walked dogs off the helicopter at 7:45 P.M. I met Blanco at the foot of the ladder. The President walked Him into the Diplomatic Room. Blanco acted jumpy.

The President told me he wanted me to put some weight on Blanco. He said Blanco is too scared. He wants someone with Blanco during the day to quiet his nervousness. I told the ushers and Colonel Chadwick after the helicopters left. The ushers do not like idea of being baby-sitters to a dog. Plenty of cussing. I took the dogs for some exercise on the grass.

Blanco took a leak on one of the round pads the helicopter lands on. An angry air control man hollered at Blanco. I told the control man, "That's what Blanco thinks of your helicopters." He started cussing us out. To calm the control man I turned off the helicopter landing lights on the South Grounds, which saved him a walk.

4/20/65 Blanco and Him went to Fort Myer and had their teeth cleaned. Lynda played with the dogs on the presidential golf green. I had Blanco and Him on the North Portico for the arrival of Prime Minister Aldo Moro of Italy. Gave Blanco a tranquilizer.

4/21/65 1:45 P.M.—I went in early to help at a picture-taking session. The President took reporters and photographers three trips around the South Grounds. I sat Him at the wheel of a tractor. UPI took a picture.

4/22/65 Had the dogs across the roadway while Lady B dedicated the Jacqueline Kennedy Garden. The Prez came and stayed a few minutes, then took Him to visit his secretary's office. Usher Scouten said someone

119

informed him that the dogs and I had tramped on the tulip beds. I said I'd heard no complaint from the gardeners. The dogs drank from the South Fountain while walking with the Prez and reporters. Later Blanco watered the tulips in the Jacqueline Kennedy Garden. He was rededicating it.

4/23/65 Juanita Roberts, the President's secretary, told me to pawprint Blanco and Him to add to the [new] picture of the Prez.

4/24/65 President took Him to Camp David.

4/25/65 Him returned at 5:15 to the White House with LBJ and Lady Bird. I had Blanco at the South Portico. The Prez came off the chopper with Him. Him growled at Blanco. The President asked me why. I told the Prez Him was jealous of Blanco coming toward President. Lynda said Him had a big time at Camp David. Later the President sent word he wants Him's toenails clipped. Luci returned from Norfolk where she was crowned Azalea Queen. She petted both dogs and said they were nice and clean. The President is proud of her. He says he always knew she was a queen. Blanco bit engineer Simmons. Blanco exhibiting a dangerous temperament.

4/26/65 Him went to the vet's at Fort Myer and got his toenails clipped. *Life* photographer Miller took a shot of Him sitting on a big new hassock in the West Lobby. I soldered LBJ tags to the dog collars.

4/27/65 The President told me Him slept with him in Texas. He asked me if it would be all right for Him to stay overnight in the presidential bedroom. I told him, "Mr. President, I won't say yes and I won't say no." He took Him to the second floor and told me to pick Him up in fifteen or twenty minutes. I was glad. I went up at 11:00 P.M., but the President had changed his mind again and said the beagle was staying overnight. Seven-thirty the next morning Him was brought downstairs.

It was the start of something new—dogs sleeping with Presidents, or to quote a cliché, "Politics makes strange bedfellows."

5/3/65 6:00 P.M. The President returned in his car. He called Him and Blanco to C-9 Post. Luci arrived shortly after that. She hugged the President. The President slapped her three times on her buttocks so hard it could be heard at C-11 Post. The Prez told Luci, "Let's see who the beagle goes to." Him ran behind C-9 Post into some bushes. Him is too smart to get into family competition. The President left his office at 9:00 P.M. and took Him to the second floor. Luci said it wouldn't be protocol or regular but for me to teach Him to shake paws with his left paw as she had at one time closed a car door on his right paw.

120

My favorite picture of Harry Truman is this one, taken in November, 1961 when he returned to the White House and played piano in the East Room for President and Mrs. Kennedy, seated in the front row.

President Eisenhower has a greeting for his weimaraner Heidi, as she pokes her nose through the White House fence. Ike was walking home from his news conference in the Executive Office Building nearby. (*Wide World Photos*)

Heidi was three years old when this picture was taken in 1958, as she surveyed the world from the White House grounds. (*Wide World Photos*)

I never saw a more expressive face than Eisenhower's. One always knew his exact mood, which could change from calm to stormy in a few seconds. Here he calls an amused remark to someone off-camera as he prepares to address the nation on TV. Behind him, standing nervously by, are Press Secretary James Hagerty and Hollywood actor Robert Montgomery, his make-up and lighting advisor.

Ike and Mamie were relaxed hosts at a party for the White House staff, held on the lawn of their farmhouse at Gettysburg. Here Ike is reading the card that accompanied the gift we gave them—table trays for dining while watching TV.

Hollywood's Robert Montgomery (left) was around the White House a lot in Ike's time, and he would go over the President's speeches. Here Eisenhower and Jim Hagerty are going over some points in a speech Ike is going to make.

For those who wonder what I did at the White House, the answer is a little of everything. I took care of dogs, strung electric cables, decorated Christmas trees, helped TV men at news conference time, and even sat in for the President—as shown here—to help the photographers figure out their lighting. The date is January 17, 1961, and I am the stand-in for Ike before his farewell address to the nation.

Jacqueline Kennedy with yours truly before she had her ill-fated baby, Patrick Bouvier. The picture was taken August 2, 1963; the baby was born prematurely five days later. We are standing in the garden of the rented house where Jackie had planned to spend the summer at Squaw Island, Hyannis Port.

This photo was taken shortly after the death of the Kennedys' baby, Patrick Bouvier, when Jackie was still grieving. She had gone, with her sister Princess Radziwill, to relax and recuperate on Aristotle Onassis' yacht in the Mediterranean. President Kennedy continued to entertain foreign dignitaries with his sister, Jean Smith, standing in for Jackie.

This is the famous Pushinka, daughter of the Russian space dog Strelka, a gift to the Kennedys from Khrushchev. The Secret Service made sure she was not "bugged" internally as a "spy dog" before Caroline and John-John were introduced to her. Another White House introduction resulted in the birth of these puppies—Caroline's dog Charlie fell madly in love with the Russian beauty on sight.

I taught Pushinka a trick that delighted the President. Jack Kennedy laughed as he watched her climb the ladder herself and slide down Caroline's and John-John's White House playground slide. He said a picture of that was worth six million votes, and asked how I had trained her. My answer is in this book.

Everyone had fun with the Kennedy dogs at Hyannis Port—even the Kennedys' photographer, Cecil Stoughton, who is holding Shannon, a cocker spaniel that was the gift of Irish President Eamon DeValera, and Wolf, the wolfhound, a gift from an Irishman named Kennedy. I am on the left holding Caroline's Welsh terrier Charlie, while on my lap are Pushinka's pups—Blackie, White Tip, Butterfly, and Streaker—sired by Charlie. Pushinka had been sent back to Washington because the neighbors in a nearby house complained that she barked too much, but Clipper, the German shepherd (left), given to Jacqueline by Ambassador Kennedy, was big enough to make up for Pushinka's absence, and loud enough, too. As I said, everyone had fun with the Kennedy dogs—except the neighbors.

Here, Nehru visits Kennedy at the White House. I remember when Nehru's daughter, Indira Gandhi, visited Nixon years later in 1971. Behind them is the White House "Official Greeter," Dave Powers, a Kennedy friend and aide.

My favorite Kennedy picture is of the President in bedroom slippers, feeding his pet buck at the Kennedys' new home in Atoka. He had fenced in a small area to tame the deer so that Caroline and John-John could enjoy it. But he enjoyed it most.

This was the last time I saw Jacqueline Kennedy at the White House—December 6, 1963. A few of us staff members—behind me are an upholsterer and a carpenter—had stopped by to say goodbye to the bereaved former First Lady, who was finishing her packing. I admired Mrs. Kennedy for making the farewells cheerful.

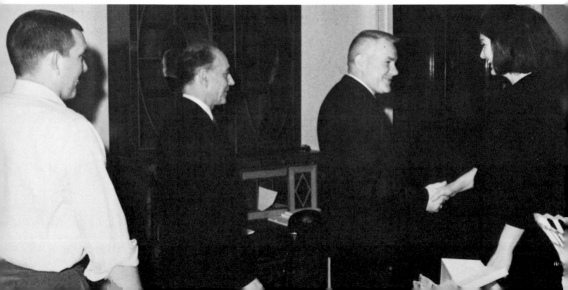

Jacqueline Kennedy was just as friendly as ever when I saw her again. This photo was taken at the launching of the aircraft carrier *John F. Kennedy* at Newport News, Virginia, during the Johnson administration. In the starring role was Caroline, who finally broke the champagne bottle after several valiant attempts.

Caroline at Newport News with her brother John-John, whose hair was a lot trimmer than it had been at the White House.

(RIGHT) The Johnsons arrived at the White House as a simple two-dog family. Little did I dream that eventually the White House would be overflowing with dogs. LBJ is petting Him, while Her cringes under the attentions of Lynda Bird and society writer Hazel Markel.

(ABOVE) Soon after LBJ became President, a little schoolgirl in Illinois sent him a white collie to keep the two beagles company. Afraid that he would be deluged with gift dogs, the President announced that he was accepting the collie as representing all the children of America. Blanco turned out to be nervous and temperamental, but LBJ loved him anyway. Here Jack Valenti, LBJ's aide, watches from the south side Diplomatic Entrance.

(ABOVE) Luci was a true dog lover, like her father. The rest of the Johnson family—Lady Bird and Lynda—merely tolerated the antics of the dogs, and sometimes not even that. But Luci went into raptures over every dog, as if they were children, and tried to hold school for them. (LEFT) LBJ and Blanco had a special relationship: very formal. The President would shake Blanco's paw very gravely on all occasions. The press loved it but Him was very jealous. In this picture, reporter Merriman Smith of the UPI is just behind the President's head. Before Merriman's tragic death, he had agreed to help me write my book.

LBJ didn't like to be photographed in his hat and he rarely wore one, but when he did he preferred a modified cowboy hat. He claimed that the tiny-brimmed hats that other men wore made them look like Robin Hood or Peter Pan. Here, Lynda Bird (in white) and Luci (in black) are behind him at the Diplomatic Entrance. Helping me with the dogs is John Pustka, who was a groundskeeper when he wasn't busy with the kennels.

(LEFT) I don't know how much credit LBJ's dogs received for his reelection to the Presidency, but I believe they deserved a lot. I slapped "LBJ for the USA" buttons on every dog that came through the White House gate, but Him and Her were the best campaigners as they greeted the long lines of tourists. (BELOW) The first thing I learned, when Johnson took over, was that he wanted to continue the Kennedy tradition of having the dogs out to meet his helicopter whenever he arrived and to see him off when he left.

There is no way to describe how much dogs loved Lyndon Baines Johnson; maybe they sensed how much he loved them. Here he greets Him and Her, who have just come to call on him at the Oval Office.

The President walks with aides and a few newsmen along the Colonnade near his office. The door beside him leads to the swimming pool. Behind me (holding dog) at the extreme right is Assistant Press Secretary Mac Kilduff, who sprang to fame as the first man to call Johnson "Mr. President" after Kennedy's assassination. Marvin Watson, the presidential assistant who later became Postmaster General, walks beside Kilduff.

The press had a field day photographing LBJ and his dogs. It was while trying to give the photographers something different that he tried to lift the dogs by the ears, and started the world-wide controversy that some people haven't forgotten even today.

After the 1964 election, tragedy struck the White House when LBJ's beloved Her died as a result of swallowing a stone. LBJ became more attached to Him and both of them seemed to be sorrowing together. Here Him is leading the President on one of his press hikes around the grounds. That's Helen Thomas of UPI walking abreast of me.

Long after Her was dead, LBJ
continued to send out the same
picture to children that he had
before—a photo of himself with
both beagles. I finally came right
out and told him he had to pose for
a new picture and he did, much like
an obedient little boy. This is the
picture that resulted, and I put
Blanco's and Him's autographs on it
to go along with the President's.

This was the scene on January 20,
1965, as the President and First
Lady walked out to the Inaugural
Stands to watch the parade. It looks
as if LBJ is talking to Lady Bird, but
I was right behind them and the
President was talking to his
beagle—telling him he'd better not
try to steal the show when he got to
the stands or he'd ship him back to
Texas.

Blanco   Him

... and their Master.

LBJ loved all animals—horses, cows, deer, antelope—and he kept little treats for them in his pockets. The angriest he ever got at the dogs was when they chased his sheep. Some people thought he loved limousines, but I know for a fact that he was happiest on a horse.

At one time, the famous Washington watercolorist Lily Spandorf was around the White House a lot. Her paintings were sometimes given to foreign dignitaries as gifts. Here I'm helping to pose Blanco and Him.

5/4/65 The President walked the south roadway with reporters and photographers. After the first lap the President told me to let the dogs loose. The Prez unleashed the beagle. Blanco was so nervous he ran toward a tree, then came running back and almost knocked me down. He was very excited. A picture was made of the Prez with Him drinking out of the drinking fountain on the White House grounds.

5/6/65 Blanco attacked Him and caused an abrasion on Him's right eye. I got a limousine and took Him to Fort Myer, where Him was treated about 3:15 P.M.

I explained what happened to the President. The President said not a bad word against Blanco. LBJ said, "You take good care of Him."

5/8/65 The President wanted to take Him to Camp David. He was upset because Him was still at the vet's. The Prez still not angry at Blanco.

5/9/65 Colonel Chadwick called me at the White House and told me Him was very fortunate—that he almost lost his sight. Him was attended by an eye specialist and then watched round the clock. He may return tomorrow.

5/10/65 I took Him to the President's office at 2:00 P.M. LBJ wanted to know all about Him's eye trouble. Still not a word against Blanco. The President took Him to the second floor at 3:30 P.M. Him wet on a chair while Lynda had tea for Princess Benedikte of Denmark.

5/12/65 The President took the dogs to the second floor at 9:55. He said I should take better care of the dogs so they won't nip at each other. "Yes, sir, Mr. President." 11:05 P.M. I went up to the President's bedroom. He was talking on the phone. Mrs. Johnson was in the President's bed. Him had spit grass on the center of the bedroom rug. I wiped it up with a cloth. Mrs. Johnson thanked me and said I was sweet to take such good care of the dogs.

Mrs. J came to the elevator hall as I was leaving with the dogs. I told her I was afraid that Blanco would harm the beagle. I suggested that Blanco be sent to the ranch and learn to herd cattle, but she said everyone was so busy at the ranch no one would have time to tend to Blanco. Meanwhile, she was tenderly rubbing Him's back with her bare foot.

When you got them away from the public, the Johnsons were just home folks, I noticed.

5/13/65 I took the dogs to the President's sitting room outside of his office. I told him I was talking to Mrs. J and suggested that Him get a girlfriend. The President had one off-record man in his office [someone whose presence is hidden from the press]. He was in a great humor. The

President told me to tell Colonel Chadwick to talk to someone in the Beagle Breeders Association and to breed Him with the best damn small beagle bitch that they could find. President Johnson said, "How come the dogs haven't come to see me? Maybe they don't approve of my politics? Maybe Him has heard something." Then they both laughed.

5/14/65 Tony Catella, an Associated Press reporter, called me at 4:30 P.M., wanting an interview. I told him it had to be cleared by the White House Press Information Office. He said it was okay with Willie Day Taylor. I told him I would have to call and get an okay. I called Mrs. Taylor, and she said George Reedy said no. I called Tony and informed him. The press people have many tricks, but so does the White House.

5/15/65 Him and Blanco went to Camp David.

5/16/65 Luci came in with her boyfriend. I told her the President would fly in by chopper at 4:00 P.M., as he had stopped at Berryville. Luci said, "Where in the hell is that?" I told her the air control officer could tell her. The President was visiting Harry Byrd, but I never tell!

Looking back, her boyfriend may have been Paul Betz. It was about this time she was breaking up with Betz and falling in love with Pat Nugent.

The Prez returned. He said Him almost got into a fight with Senator Byrd's cocker spaniel, but Him went into a corner. Blanco has gotten Him so terrorized Him is afraid to fight anyone. Blanco came back by car from Camp David with a Secret Service man. Him returned with the President and Mrs. J, because Him attended the party.

I took a hundred feet of 16 mm. film of the President's chopper and of the President walking off with Him. Lady Bird felt the top of Blanco's head and wondered what was wrong. I told her nothing, the lump was a small bone. Luci and her boyfriend went to the pool and played with the dogs in the Bouquet Room. Lynda petted the dogs at 8:00 P.M.

5/17/65 President Chung Hee Park of South Korea walked Him on a leash, and President Johnson walked Blanco on South Lawn. Like two schoolboys with their pets.

The Presidents both sat in wicker chairs in the West Rose Garden, talking. President Johnson asked me how come Him got wet. I told him he got in the South Fountain pool to cool off. Photographers came out. The President told photographers they had "Eighty seconds. And, Bryant, you can take the dogs." The dogs and I retreated to a flowerbed behind the President.

5/19/65   Him has wet on two chairs on the second floor in the past two weeks. I have learned that two New York reporters who want to do a book on the dogs are being investigated by the FBI.

From two to six photographer George Tames took pictures of the dogs with me as "watchdog."

4:00 P.M. A photographer had to leave the South Grounds for a few minutes as an off-record guest was coming in the grounds. Tames made pictures of a small boy with a baseball glove leaning against the south fence and petting the dogs; he also made pictures of the dogs in their quarters. He photographed Him in the South Fountain pool and Him drinking from a drinking fountain; Blanco chasing a squirrel; and all the dogs playing with my cowboy boots.

These boots of mine were the bane of the White House staff. Everyone had been told not to wear cowboy boots or Western hats as it would look as if we were copying the President—or trying to get in good with him. The word was he hated to see Easterners wearing them. I said I was from West Virginia, wore them before he was in office, and would be wearing them after he was out.

President Johnson is going to visit friends and left the White House at 9:15. He asked me if the dogs wanted to go; I told him yes, so he took Blanco and Him in the rear seat of his limousine. The dogs were still out with the President at 11:30 P.M.

5/20/65   Blanco and Him had their picture taken with Mr. and Mrs. Valenti and their little girl Courtney. Courtney squealed when Blanco chased the squirrels.

Courtney was the most special child to come to the White House. She absolutely ruled the President and could make him "fetch and carry" any time she wanted to. The President gave orders to be informed any time she came to see her daddy, LBJ's special assistant, which was often.

Courtney's mother, Mary Margaret, started out as LBJ's receptionist in his Texas office when he was U.S. senator and then came to Washington as his personal secretary. She was the real beauty of the LBJ gang, and when she came to visit the White House, she rated extra kisses and a real fuss was made over her by the President. The President liked to relax in his office just sitting around talking to Mary Margaret.

Everyone was amazed when Mary Margaret—who was Mary

123

Margaret Wiley—suddenly married Jack Valenti. Except those who say LBJ engineered the marriage. Maybe he wanted to keep her in the family. To him, Mary Margaret and Courtney were a family.

Time and time again LBJ would tell me to look out for Courtney. To be good to Courtney. To protect Courtney. To keep Blanco away from Courtney. Once he said, "You let anything happen to Courtney and I'll hang your hide on the barn door." In other words, the President liked that child.

5/21/65   9:50 P.M. Blanco and Him were taken to Camp David for three nights. The word is that Camp David agents have a hard time running Blanco down; some are afraid they may get bitten.

5/24/65   President Johnson took some Italian dignitaries, dogs, reporters, and photographers for walk. President Johnson tried to shake hands with Blanco and said he took his dogs on trips. Italian Foreign Minister Amintore Fanfani said, "This is more liberal than your immigration law." 8:00 P.M. The dogs and I went out for a walk. We met President Johnson in front of the Bouquet Room. He asked me why Him was whining. Then he asked me if Him was jealous because he was getting Blanco to shake hands. I said, "Yes, Mr. President." The Prez knows these things but likes to hear them from me.

5/26/65   Military reception 6:30 P.M. Some admirals and other high-ranking officers and their wives petted dogs. Prez and Lady Bird, Vice President Humphrey and his wife, and Secretary of Defense Robert McNamara stood on a red carpet on the roadway with a military guard, shaking hands with guests. The President would hold up the line time after time to call for the dogs and pet them; then he would resume the hand-shaking. Some of the guests looked annoyed, some amused. The dogs were served from a silver tray by Jeff. The President mingled with the guests, then again called for dogs. He shook hands with Blanco and had Him jumping up and down playing with a paper napkin.

5/27/65   Congressional aides' reception at 7:30 P.M. The Prez came out of the Oval Office and called for Him as he walked toward the lawn party to greet guests. Blanco, Him, and I were on the grass just outside his office. After his speech the President went into the White House for a moment, probably to remove his contact lenses.

It's a presidential secret that he wears contacts. He hates them.

When he was getting into his car he missed the dogs. The Prez called out, saying he wanted both dogs to go to Texas. I put them in the rear seat with him and they drove to the Ellipse, where they took off in a chopper. Before the President appeared [at the lawn party], the dogs were chief attraction. People introduced themselves and told me about their own dogs. The dogs and I were close to one of the tents where they served sandwiches and punch. I asked for a drink without alcohol. House-keeper Anne Lincoln was standing next to us. She turned up her nose. Her drinks were of another color. I gave Willie Day Taylor a yellow rose from the Bouquet Room. She said it reminded her too much of the song. She has been with the Johnsons for many years and is like family. She works in Press Information Office.

6/1/65   President Johnson had an off-record dinner with former President Eisenhower. After dinner the President came out to the South Portico and told Ike, whom he called "General," to look at his dog Him. Vice President Humphrey was also present.

As General Eisenhower and his party were leaving, the Prez again called Him over and had Him stand on hind legs. Him stood up and then got down. President said "Damn it, stand up! Stand up and salute!" Ike laughed. Senator Byrd said, "Him and my dog got into a hell of a fight in Berryville," and laughed.

The President told me Blanco should be put back on tranquilizers. He said Blanco cannot go back to Texas, as he is too scared.

There was a story about the dogs and some pictures of them on the front page of the *Evening Star*.

I showed the dogs to Mrs. John M. McCormack. She was in her limousine while her husband was attending President Johnson's dinner. Him and Blanco got into her car. Blanco laid down at her feet, all ready for a ride. She was delighted and petted both dogs.

Mrs. McCormack, wife of the Speaker of the House, was in poor health and often waited for her husband in the car. He was very loving and tender and took her with him as much as he could to give her a little fresh air. She told me that sometimes they would drive to church and she would wait in the car while he went in. She hoped he was lighting a candle for her.

In June I was writing:

Luci just graduated from National Cathedral School. Daddy's gift is a green Sting Ray. She acts delirious. I talked to Rex Scouten in Usher's Office, asking his advice on sending the dogs to Walter Reed instead of Fort Myer. He told me to see Jack Valenti. Five minutes later I met Mr. Valenti on his way to see the President in the mansion. He told me to send the dogs where I thought best.

The problem with Fort Myer was that Colonel Ralph Chadwick was in danger of being transferred and LBJ didn't know anyone else there he could trust to keep his mouth shut about taking care of the presidential dogs. Every time the dogs yawned they made news if reporters saw it.

Since the ear-pulling incident, President Johnson had always been afraid of adverse dog publicity. He also dreaded doing anything that smacked of trying to take advantage of his position. Yet when he got a bill one month for $89 from a private veterinarian, LBJ said, "Mr. Bryant, you are breaking me with those vet bills." The vet was on call to the White House and actually came over fairly often, so the bill wasn't padded, but LBJ was determined to cut down the cost of veterinary care.

In self-defense I looked into the matter of veterinarians and discovered that we could send the dogs to Fort Myer, where good veterinarians were taking care of the horses that participate at funerals in Arlington Cemetery. I suggested that to him. He thought it over and asked me if he would have trouble sending the dogs over to Fort Myer for vet care. I said, "Mr. President, you are Commander in Chief. You rate it. It won't cost you a penny."

Lady Bird flew off to the Virgin Islands June 2, and I wrote:

NBC called me up to connect a TV truck for a TV pool on the four-day space trip—supposed to start tomorrow. I had the dogs in Juanita Roberts' office. Wearing a sports coat, President Johnson walked in all smiles, teasing his secretary—Juanita—about a date for tonight. 7:20 P.M. President Johnson took Him for a boat ride on the Potomac. As it had been raining, I wiped Him's feet off and put Him in the front seat of the President's car with agent Youngblood. For consolation I took Blanco with me to wait for the NBC-TV truck to hook up electricity.

6/3/65 Blanco has hookworms. The vet gave him a shot. George Tames took more pictures, more shots of me tossing Him into the South Fountain three times. Blanco got jealous and bit Him on his right rear quarter. Jealousy. Tames wanted to stop taking pictures, but I checked Him and found out that mostly his feelings were hurt. Tames got a nice shot of Him on the low branches in two different trees. A shot of Him and Blanco chasing squirrels. A shot of Luci kissing Him on top of his head as she and her boyfriend [Editor's note: probably her new boyfriend, Pat Nugent, who had come from Milwaukee to see her graduate] were heading for the helicopter. A nice shot of President Johnson as he was going to get aboard the chopper. Monday he will make shots of John Pustka feeding and washing the dogs.

The two men have been in space today for four days. I took the dogs to the North and South Grounds for the tourists to take pictures of them.

6/4/65 The President came out of his office and called for and petted Him and Blanco. LBJ was on his way to Howard University to make a speech at 6:30. Lynda went with the President. He also took his pretty colored secretary, Geraldine Whittington, whom he calls Gerry. The President said to Him, "I'll see you later."

While Lynda was at Howard University, her boyfriend, David LeFeve, arrived at the White House. The airport cabbie unloaded three bags at the South Portico and the cab bill came to three dollars. A White House policeman told me LeFeve gave the cabbie three one-dollar bills plus a tip of one dime and five pennies. The cabbie disgustedly told the White House policeman that when he picked up his fare at the airport and LeFeve said, "To the White House" he was sure he would get at least a two-dollar tip, as his previous fare, a little old lady going to a reunion, had given him a tip of $2.75.

Waiting for the President, the dogs and I wandered into Mrs. Kennedy's East Flower Garden. Watercolor artist Lily Spandorf was painting the garden. She wanted to paint a portrait of Him. So I let her make some sketches of Him and made an appointment for next Monday for Him to sit and pose.

When the President returned from his Howard University speech, the dogs and I were at C-11 South Portico. The President's car stopped at C-9. He called for Him. I let both dogs loose. When Him had almost reached the President, Blanco snapped at Him. Him turned away from the President in pain and started to chase Blanco over the putting green. The President scolded Blanco and Him went to the President. Hurray, at least the President now knows that Blanco is dangerous.

Later, the President came out to the South Portico and asked Him if he wanted to go on a boat ride. Him was eager. I gave the President the leash and asked him if he wanted Him in the front or rear seat. The Prez put Him in the rear seat.

The President's chauffeur said earlier he was going to report light bulbs out so I'd be busy and couldn't have the dogs out when the President makes a trip. He laughed when he came back from Howard University, saying he didn't have to take Him on that trip. So just for that I let the chauffeur take Him on the boat ride.

All the chauffeurs and agents would get teed off about the dogs hogging the car and getting better treatment from the President than they did.

127

My wife said that I had received a mysterious long-distance call from a man in Texas. He would not leave a message.

6/5/65   Him went on another boat ride with the President. The Secret Service agents were disgusted. They didn't sign on to protect dogs. The Prez returned at 11:00 P.M. and Him slept in the President's room all night.

At 6:15 P.M. I received a call from the Texas mystery man, who may be a nut or a legitimate treasure hunter onto a hidden fortune. He wants me to get the President to help him get a permit to get on the White Sands missile range to hunt for treasure. A mountain is supposed to have a gold treasure worth possibly two hundred million dollars. I told the guy to write to the presidential secretary, Juanita Roberts, giving all facts. Later I called Secret Service agent Milton to tell him about it, and later agent Caldwell called me for more information. When I talked to Juanita about it, she said, "Well, he's human. I'll contact him. He deserves some response." Juanita is a beautiful woman with a soul.

6/6/65   Him and the President left for a boat ride at 2:30. Lynda's boyfriend, David LeFeve, was leaving. He asked me if Blanco was still nervous. Lynda petted Blanco. The Secret Service called the Usher's Office from the boat and said that the President wanted Him to go back to Fort Myer as his eye didn't look very good. I called Colonel Chadwick and gave him the information.

6/7/65   Lily Spandorf drew sketches of Him until Him went on another boat ride with the President, who returned at 10:45. Blanco was sketched. The two dogs have another sitting tomorrow at 4:00 P.M. Lily Spandorf also sketched some entertainers while they were rehearsing for tomorrow. I did her a favor and got her an autograph from one of the authors, John Updike, whom Blanco and I watched read excerpts from three of his novels *The Poorhouse Fair*, *The Centaur*, and *Rabbit, Run.*

Lily showed me a beautiful painting she did of the South Fountain and the Washington Monument. She said not to tell anyone but she worked over a holiday at the White House and once stayed until one o'clock in the morning, and nobody knew she was there. I cannot believe the Secret Service men didn't know exactly what she was up to.

8:45 P.M. I had Blanco at the South Portico when Mrs. Johnson arrived home from the Virgin Islands. I told her, "Welcome home." She said that she had a wonderful time but was glad to be home. She hugged Blanco around the neck. Mrs. Johnson asked me if the President took Him on the boat ride. I answered, "Yes, ma'am." She had a bad moment, no doubt, wishing her husband was there to greet her. She greeted one of the girls who climbed down off the light scaffold. We are working on the flood-lights for the entertainment on Tuesday.

6/6/65 I received another call from the guy we now call "The Gold Bug." I told him I had called Mrs. Roberts and she had told me to give him her exact message, which was, "I don't want to waste your time and money." I feel sorry for him. He really feels frustrated and is sure there is gold in them thar hills.

Colonel Glenn, the "space man," shook hands with me and autographed a picture of the President, Blanco, and Him. Luci was playing with the dogs. I gave Colonel Glenn some copies of the picture of the President with the dogs for his children. Several scholars petted the dogs and had their pictures made with the dogs.

Later Mr. Hare came running to C-9 Post and whispered that the President was going on an off-record boat ride and wanted Him to go.

11:05 President Johnson and Mrs. J and their company returned from the boat ride. The President shook hands with Blanco. I made Him stand up and told his company that Him was jealous of Blanco. Mrs. J petted both dogs. I took the dogs for a walk. I gave Blanco a tranquilizer and put them to bed. A busy day!

6/9/65 National Rural Electric Youth Day. 5:30 P.M. Hundreds of youths circled the dogs and me, petting the dogs, taking pictures, and asking questions. The President shook hands with as many as he could as he walked along the edge of the roadway. The President took Him to a party on the second floor. Later a military aide called me and asked me to pick up the "mutt."

In June, 1965, the President was at the height of his light-switch kick. He horrified the ladies of the press by reaching into their ladies' room and switching off the light. He was trying to give them a message. George Reedy was with him when it happened and didn't blink an eyelash.

During June, also, the White House lawns looked like a local junkyard—sheet metal all over the place. It was called the White House Festival of the Arts. The dogs were going crazy. No wonder. It looked like fire-hydrant row. There was one thing called *Male Presence* made of auto bumpers and a car grill. The lucky artist was Jason Seley. I don't know what his prices jumped to after he had exhibited at the White House. It's better than the Good Housekeeping seal of approval. Blanco was so excited that I had to double his dose of tranquilizers.

129

The tranquilizers helped some, but they still failed to prevent one of the most shocking wettings to take place at the White House. My diary records the historic event.

6/15/65 A White House policeman greeted me with "So that's what Blanco thinks of that art piece." He was pointing. I looked and cringed. Blanco had vigorously watered down *Whale II* by Alexander Calder, a piece of sculpture lent by the Museum of Modern Art, New York.

Meanwhile, I see by my notes that the day before, early in the morning, I received a third call at home from my friend, the Texas gold bug. I called Juanita Roberts and told her to expect a call from him, and I thought, Wouldn't it be funny if the man is right and has spotted a fantastic fortune that everyone else is passing by.

And Blanco was causing plenty of excitement at Camp David. A Secret Service man told me that on June 20 Blanco stayed up all night chasing chipmunks and squirrels. A Marine shouted "Halt, who goes there?" Blanco barked back at the excited Marine. Just in time, too. He was getting ready to shoot.

As a husband, LBJ was one of the most loving and affectionate men I have ever known. He could also get utterly impatient with Lady Bird, and I used to give her high marks for balancing his deficiency with her own gentleness and patience. If Lady Bird was not ready the moment the President got itchy feet, off he went without her. Fortunately there usually were other cars, so she could catch up with him. Here is a perfect illustration:

6/23/65 The President and his party plus Blanco and Him went for a boat ride. Miss Marie Fehmer came out of the President's office with the President. She got in the rear seat. Blanco jumped in with her. Marie switched to another car. I put Him in the front seat. I told President Johnson I didn't have a leash for Blanco with me. He said, "You go get his leash." So I ran to the Bouquet Room and got Blanco's leash. When I got back the President was greeting some guests outside of his car. I put Blanco up front. The President said, "Where is Lady Bird? I am disgusted with her. Let's go." So they left without her at 8:13.

Now let me tell you what Lady Bird was doing that made her late and why I think she was the greatest wife any President ever had. For one thing, she was delayed because Mary Lasker, her friend and a member of the White House Committee for Fine Arts, was a guest in the Queen's Room and she was changing dresses for the boat ride. So the First Lady was waiting for her.

And for a second thing, Usher Pierce had run upstairs after the President's clothes for the boat ride:

Pierce asked Mrs. Johnson which shirt he should send. Mrs. Johnson asked him what kind of suit President had on. Usher said he only saw the President at a distance from C-11 to C-9. Mrs. Johnson said to take them both and they would be sure.

I was amazed at how Lady Bird Johnson always solved little problems so easily and sensibly and kept things going smoothly. Eventually she hurried down, jumped into still another car, and got to the dock on time.

A few days after that happened, LBJ, his humor restored, commented that he knew of only one time a President had been kept waiting, and that was when the great singer, Enrico Caruso, was three hours late for a meeting with Teddy Roosevelt. When Roosevelt was asked why he'd put up with it and hadn't lost his temper, LBJ said that Teddy gave a very modest reply—"America has had many Presidents, but it has had only one Caruso."

During 1965 and the following years, LBJ made his brother stay at the White House for long periods so he could keep an eye on him. LBJ admitted to friends that that was why his brother was always around. Sam Houston Johnson didn't mind too much being incarcerated in the White House as long as he had something to do. So— as several insiders, including me, knew—to make him feel important, the President let him listen in on phone conversations to "make sure" security was not being violated—"monitoring," the President called it. Once I got a look at his room and saw his small telephone switchboard.

You could see that Sam Houston was kept busy, busy. But he may have done good work in telling the President things other people were afraid to say. I remember once he was not too impressed with the President's electric light economy program and he expressed his reservations very vividly. He turned off all the lights on the second floor while the President and First Lady were out one evening attending an official gathering. When they returned, there was brother Sam Houston working away on some papers by the light of *one* candle.

Sam had a great sense of humor and LBJ actually loved him very much. The most fun they had together was when they played dominoes. Even then the Prez was very competitive. He hated to have anyone get ahead of him, even his brother.

When they played dominoes in a foursome, LBJ would team up with another player against his brother. The President's favorite partner was Congressman Jake Pickle, with whom he had a special relationship. They cheated. I mean, cheated like crazy. A typical match might pit Congressman Jack Brooks and Sam Houston against Jake Pickle and Lyndon Baines, and Jack and Sam didn't stand a chance.

Afterwards LBJ would chortle away about how he and Jake "whomped the opposition—whomped 'em and swamped 'em and tromped 'em till they cried for mercy." LBJ and Jake had a set of signals to let each other know what they had. Or what they wanted done.

Code words stood for numbers. LBJ might say he'd heard some talk about a new bridge. Bridge would mean some number, say, three for a three-span bridge. And if he said he heard about a water bill, that might mean number one, for the one finger raised in grade school. And if he talked about the age of a buck deer on the ranch that would tie in with the number of points on the antlers. And there was some clue for a double six.

I really never knew too much about it. But I was impressed with how fiendishly clever LBJ could be in dreaming up his signals. If he said his dog hurt its leg, that could mean three. If he said his eyeglasses were bothering him, that could mean four for "four-eyes."

After LBJ left office we heard a report from the ranch that he was furious and deeply hurt by Sam's unflattering book. It was said that LBJ felt his brother had done him wrong. And I read in the newspapers that when LBJ died, with something like $25 million in his estate, he left his brother only a token gift—$5,000.

That's only a little more than he left Mary Margaret Valenti, mother of his beloved little Courtney, or than he left his trusted secretary Mary Rather. And he left his ranch foreman five times as much as he left Sam Houston—$25,000.

Time and again, LBJ had commented that for some reason having a relative or friend for President brought out the worst in people. Once when Sam Houston arrived at the White House and showed signs he had been hitting the bottle pretty heavily, LBJ commented to me sadly, "I just don't know about him. He studied law, women, and booze and hasn't made a success of any of them."

Though Sam Houston was not supposed to be served any liquor in the White House, on orders of the President, he was such a charmer that he was able to convince a certain member of the household staff to slip him a libation in his room on the third floor of the mansion, which he called "Cell 326" after the guest-room number.

The President acted a little worried when Sam Houston was around. Several times I recall him saying that if a President had one friend he could count on, he was lucky. "That's why I choose dogs," he would say. Then one time he added something that I thought was a great bit of philosophy and copied down: "The fact that dogs haven't given up on humans completely and still make people their friends shows there must be some hope for the human race."

12

July 1965 was a rough month. The Prez was testy. For one thing a woman had sued because a big wind from the President's helicopter had flung a chair against her leg when the Prez came to inspect the site of a proposed San Francisco Bay Area Rapid Transit System. She won her case, to the tune of $6,240. I don't know if it came out of LBJ's pocket or the government's. Either way, I'll bet he didn't let his helicopter pilot ever hear the last of it.

Then the President had discovered an opening for a new economy binge and was going after it with a vengeance. He ordered all unnecessary subscriptions to newspapers canceled. A number of papers from Texas, New York, and other parts of the country were being distributed free to his staff. This free service was costing over $10,000 a year, and somehow it came to his attention. "Hell, I'm tired of being a sucker," he told me, petting Him. "Only a dog can really appreciate everything you do for him."

The executive staff people were all griping about buying their own papers from the new automatic newspaper vending machines.

And poor Luci was limping around with a sore toe and being mysterious about it. The story making the rounds was that she had cut a toenail too deep while giving herself a pedicure. That was the kind of thing the President would call "plain ox stupid."

On the other hand, the President was very proud of Luci when she took a job as assistant to an optometrist, Dr. Robert A. Kraskin.

"She's finally learning responsibility," LBJ told me as he watched her get out of her car in her neat white uniform. "Some day I'll be saying, 'My daughter the nurse.'" Then in the next breath he yelled, "Here comes my daughter the nurse." Luci was planning to enter Georgetown University Nursing School.

Once I asked Luci what she did for the doctor. She told me she checked the children's eyes, shining a little light into them. Then she asked them to name toys and other objects at a distance of eight feet. Then she checked reading patterns. If a child's eyes fought

each other for dominance while reading, she helped the child overcome this handicap. She said her own grades in school had been
atrocious— she'd never learned to read properly because her eyes
were always fighting for dominance. Dr. Kraskin, her idol, discovered her problem of eye focus, cured it, and changed her life. That's
what inspired her to be a nurse.

7/1/65 The President took a brisk walk around the White House
grounds. The press had a good laugh because one reporter was so busy
taking notes while chasing the President that he bumped his head hard
on a tree.

Busy day. Everybody is arriving home at once. Luci got out of a chauffeur-driven car and petted the dogs. I told her Him had gotten a drink
out of the upright fountain. She asked Him if he was coming to her
eighteenth birthday party tomorrow night. I answered for him: "Yes."
She kissed the dogs good night and went into the White House.

8:00 P.M. Mrs. J returned from a trip. Him and I greeted her at the
South Portico. She was so surprised that she thought the Prez was going
out. I said I didn't think so.

Lynda returned from an archeological dig out west. The dogs were at
the South Portico on the grass. She looked out the rear window at the
dogs but rushed to C-9 Post to the President's office. That's where Luci
and Lynda are different. Luci would have petted the dogs and then
rushed to her father's office.

Later I heard a better explanation for Lynda's excitement—she'd
just uncovered a 600-year-old Indian skeleton, and wanted to tell
her daddy all about it.

Though it was time for Luci's birthday party, the family was again
being separated, some going to New York and Texas, some staying
in Washington.

7/2/65 The President took Him to New York for a speech, then flew to
Texas for the Fourth of July holiday. The President and Luci had pictures taken with Blanco. Luci had her eighteenth birthday party. I was
walking Blanco on the South Grounds when I got a call that Luci wanted
me to get some blue or green light bulbs for decorating the Solarium on
the third floor. I went to Usher's Office. Usher Pierce said for me to
buy them.

The dogs' air conditioner in their locker room and Bouquet Room
quarters has gone haywire. I fixed it. Then I called the garage for a car.
Went to two drugstores before I found blue lights. All I could find were

25-watt bulbs. I took them to the Solarium and Luci's party was in full swing. Young friends of Luci's were dancing and drinking beer out of enormous mugs. Luci said the blue lights were all right.

7/7/65 Agent Johns asked me about breeding Blanco with his collie "Princess." I told him to leave a note with Juanita Roberts with a picture of his dog for the President to see.

The dogs got a new air conditioner today for their room.

7/8/65 Lily Spandorf called and said the White House wouldn't let her in any more to paint the dogs' pictures. I told her to call Liz Carpenter's office, and I would call to straighten it out. Liz is in Texas with Mrs. J.

Toward the middle of the month, we had a first-class White House mystery. Someone had poisoned the dog belonging to a White House chauffeur. Morgan Guys called me from the garage wanting someone to be a sleuth and find out what kind of poison had been used. I recommended Colonel Chadwick. To my knowledge the culprit was never found.

7/12/65 Willie Day Taylor proudly showed me a telegram from Luci inviting her to a 1:30 P.M. dinner at Blackie's Beef House. Luci said in the telegram, "to my Number One Chaperone."

I had learned right after the Johnsons moved into the White House that when you couldn't find Luci, she was probably with Willie Day. Early in Luci's life, Willie had been her substitute mother, staying with her and Lynda when Lady Bird was away politicking with Lyndon or building her own TV fortune.

The story around the White House was that it had been rough on the girls to have such an ambitious set of parents and the girls themselves admitted that as kids they had resented it very much. Luci had taken out her resentment by tormenting her mother— playing the piano loudly while she was trying to entertain or coming barefooted into a room full of guests. Lynda had expressed herself by overeating and becoming a butterball. But by the White House days both girls had forgiven their parents and become happy members of the family team.

What remained from the past, however, was a special tenderness that Luci always exhibited toward Willie Day. Luci, in turn, was the apple of Willie Day's eye.

7/14/65 Talk of the White House is UN Ambassador Adlai Stevenson falling dead on the street [in London] while with female friend.

President took a walk around the grounds with Henry Cabot Lodge, Blanco, and Him. The photographers went back in after making some pictures. Then agent Youngblood told the Secret Service agent walking beside me to stay behind out of listening distance. The President looked very grave. Later he was not in a good mood. He complained, "You have been taking care of Him for a year and you haven't taught Him to stand up. What have you been doing?" I told the Prez, "Him is hard to teach but I never have any trouble with Blanco."

Luci is being a spoiled brat. She wanted to see the movie *What's New, Pussycat?* last night. Fischer was with the Prez, so a helicopter landing radio man was ordered to show the movie. Halfway through the movie he had to quit to go help the President's chopper land. Press aide Joe Laitin told me today that Luci stopped three electricians from working in the theater on a rush job needed in an hour's time so she could see the rest of her movie. They tried to explain but Luci didn't care.

Later talk was circulating the White House that the discussion between the Prez and Lodge concerned all the secrets Ambassador Stevenson knows and is taking to the grave—secrets about world leaders and agreements with other nations. Also, who to trust to replace him. LBJ likes Lodge even though he is a Republican with the Eisenhower brand on him.

7/15/65 5:20 P.M. The Prez took Him on the helicopter to Andrews Field to meet the plane that brought in Adlai Stevenson's body. Him got confused. When the helicopter returned, the President came out alone and Him came out of the baggage side.

7/17/65 I had a moment of panic. Little Courtney Valenti and another small girl had run under a temporary stage on the South East Grounds as the President's helicopter was coming in to pick him up. A White House policeman alerted us to get the children, who were chasing the Valenti dog, Beagle. I can't have anything happen to Courtney.

7/20/65 Rex Scouten, on the warpath, told me Blanco took a leak on one of the large tablecloths that cover the tables for serving the food at a reception for the White House Education Conference under the tent canopy. Someone on the Truman Balcony saw Blanco in action. I said I cannot be everywhere at the same time.

I'll never forget the day LBJ went on an economy kick, petwise. My diary records the date as July 22, 1965. It was the day the President discovered what dog food costs. It had been a day like so many others—the President gave a speech in the Rose Garden and afterwards took Him and Blanco to the south fence where tourists took pictures, shook hands, and formed quite a crowd.

But at 9:00 P.M., the President suddenly blew his stack. He had just found out his monthly dog-food bill was $80. "Goddamn it," he said, "I'd be laughed out of Johnson City if anyone knew what I'm paying to feed a couple of dogs. Christ, a family could live on it."

I told the President I would leave word for the ushers to stop buying hamburger. I did and Usher Carter asked me if the dogs were getting too fat. I said, "No, the President's pocketbook is getting too lean."

Later the President got friendly again and asked me if the dogs liked anyone better than they liked Luci. I told the President that they chose him.

7/25/65 Lynda returned at 11:00 P.M. from her Western camping trip. She got out of the car and played with Blanco. At midnight President Johnson, Lady Bird, and Luci returned by helicopter from Camp David. All three patted Blanco before going into the White House. Blanco growled at Him as usual. The Prez grumbled they could have stayed at Camp David if Lynda would have agreed to go to Camp David.

I made a note that the family tried to humor Lynda because her daddy was worried about her future. He told me he hoped Lynda married first but wouldn't want to bet on it.

Another note in my diary reports the President having a good laugh when someone reminded him of a visit he'd paid the White House as a young man, to see FDR. A second guest—a man from Tennessee—was so proud of having sat in the President's chair, he later cut out the seat of his pants and had it framed. "It takes a Southerner or a Westerner to know how to properly mark an occasion," said LBJ. "He probably had a plaque made saying, 'These pants knew FDR's chair.'"

7/26/65 I saw housekeeper Anne Lincoln and told her when someone buys anything for the dogs to have the ushers or me okay it. She acted much annoyed and told *me* to tell them. So I guess she doesn't give a damn how the President's money is spent. Engineer Nolan bought two new choker collars for the dogs. John Pustka showed me the bill—$5.93. I told John to let Nolan collect the money himself, as too many people are buying what they think the dogs should have, but it's the President's money.

Agent Johns and Juanita Roberts called and told me the President said it was okay to breed Blanco. The President is anxious to see what those white collie pups will look like.

Frederic March (the movie star), his wife, and his grandson were getting into a car to leave the South Portico, and Mr. March wanted to see Him. Him jumped into the back seat with Mrs. March and the grandson. The star and his wife acted delighted.

I told Zephyr Wright that we were cutting hamburger out of the dogs' expenses. Zephyr said, "If he can't afford to feed his dogs, don't ask me for any handouts."

The Prez came out of his office forty minutes late for a dinner party on second floor. He clapped for the dogs. The Prez said I had the dogs looking good. I told him we had cut out hamburger. It had been ground steak, $1.08 a pound, three and a half pounds a day. Regular hamburger is about three pounds for a dollar.

The President was going to the Mansion. I opened the door and Blanco ran in before the President. I told Blanco to come back, but he got in the elevator. President said, "Blanco, you had better mind, as Mr. Bryant will get after you." I pulled Blanco off the elevator. The President said, "They want to come upstairs." Some of the dinner guests were on the balcony; they waved to us as we walked by below. I took the dogs to the south fence for the line of tourists. Him barked furiously at a Manchester dog.

The President was starting to cheer up. About this time he had a houseguest who tickled his fancy, Dame Mabel Brooks from Australia. She had been kind to him during the war when he was stationed there more than twenty years earlier, around 1943. He came to her house, played cards with her three daughters, and ate her food almost every night for three months. Then he just disappeared.

She never knew what happened to him until she saw his picture in the papers as the new American President. She said, "Gracious sakes, here's the boy who used to be here—Lyndon Johnson. I always wondered what happened to him."

Word of this got to the Australian Prime Minister Menzies, who told LBJ, who immediately picked up the telephone and invited her to visit him. LBJ was delighted with the lady, according to backstairs talk, except for one thing: she kept saying how much LBJ had "fleshed out" and how "handsome and slim he *used to be.*"

7/29/65   The state governors arrived for a meeting. The dogs and I were on the South Lawn when the helicopters came in. A few governors came up and petted the dogs.

After the meeting Governor George Wallace walked over and spoke to

139

me and petted Him. He laughed when Him tore my shirt pocket. I had put Him on tree limb and Him was looking for a squirrel but he'd given up and was jumping down. As he jumped I caught him, but one of his paws caught in my shirt pocket.

7/30/65   Him went to Missouri and then to Texas with the Prez. John Pustka complained that his stock of dog food was down to two cans. He said housekeeper Anne Lincoln wouldn't give the storeroom buyer any money for dog food, using what I had said to her as her excuse.

I took John to the housekeeper and told her to let John buy dog food and treats any time he needed to; I explained that I was interested in cutting out only nonessentials, especially ground steak at $1.08 a pound, three and a half pounds per day.

13

August 1965 was economy month again. LBJ really stretched himself to think of new ways to cut costs.

First the President asked me if I could find a cheaper way to get Unipets—the dog candy that he kept in his pocket for Him and Blanco. I found a cut-rate drugstore that sold them for less, and bought some more from a private vet who gave me a reduced price as a favor.

Then the President came up with a way he could save 94¢ on every pen he handed out when he signed bills into law. The guests at such ceremonies had been getting $1.11 pens, marked down from $1.75, but even with this discount, LBJ calculated that it had cost $651.57 one day just to sign five bills into law. So he ordered a switch to 17¢ pens, marked down from 25¢. Since the pens usually got framed and hung on a wall anyway, he said, what difference did it make? To *him* it made quite a big difference.

Finally, the President had a brainstorm about file cabinets. He declared a moratorium on buying any for the government. Instead of adding new cabinets, he asked, why not throw out the stuff in the old ones? As a result, 35,000 file cabinets were emptied by a simple housecleaning. In half a year LBJ saved the government a little over two million dollars.

On August 5 the President took a break from economizing and staged his version of a Hollywood stunt. He had Blanco and Him put their pawprints in new concrete outside the West Executive Entrance of the White House. When reporters praised Blanco's pawprint as being better, LBJ acted just like a doting father and said yes, but Him had given a more polished acting performance while doing it.

And about the same time LBJ played a game with his dinner guests. Each guest drew a slip of paper from a cigar box. Those who came up with a slip that said "speaker" had to get up and give a three-to-five-minute talk on any subject they chose which would increase the knowledge of the other guests in any way. He liked the results so well that he vowed he'd have similar meetings frequently. But that was about the last I heard of it.

8/5/65 A farewell party was given for Mr. Reedy in the Jacqueline Kennedy Garden. The President came out of his office and told me to let Him go. I was at the JFK Garden. Him ran to the President and followed the Prez to the garden. I shook hands with Reedy, who told me to take good care of the dogs, with Pierre Salinger, and with Mac Kilduff, who was the first man after the Dallas tragedy to call LBJ "Mr. President." Salinger told me that he saw I had changed dogs.

Martin Luther King was here to see the President.

The following day, Reverend King and his wife Coretta attended the signing of the voting rights bill in the President's Room of the Senate. Luci took her mother's place and went marching in with her father arm in arm, wearing white gloves. She came back to the White House clutching two of the pens that had been used in the signing. She said, "Daddy gave out nearly a hundred pens." So he *saved* about $94, the way I figure it.

8/10/65 I talked to Helen Ganns of the Press Information Office. She wants to know if Luci's hamster Natasha is pregnant. She said Dr. Young thought so, but he wasn't a vet. I said the hamster looks a little broadbeamed and I'd guess yes.

11:10 P.M. The President and his party returned from a boat ride. The President told his guests good night and then he played with the dogs. The President said, "You are taking good care of the dogs, and I want you to know that I appreciate it very much."

8/11/65 Marie Fehmer came to the Bouquet Room and told me the President was in front of his office and wanted the dogs. The President held up Valenti's little girl, Courtney, and told her, "Look honey, here comes Bryant, Blanco, and Him." She wanted to play with the dogs. She led Blanco on a leash while I kept an eye on him. I made Blanco sit, and she petted Him. Then she hugged Blanco and called him "Blink." Her Daddy pointed to the beagle and she said, "Him." Valenti then pointed to the President and Courtney said, "Prez." LBJ beamed ear to ear and kissed her nose.

They went into the President's office and the dogs and I went toward C-9 Post. The President came out and said Courtney was still wanting the dogs. The President told me to come into his office with the dogs so

142

Courtney could play with them. The President and Mr. and Mrs. Valenti and Virginia Thrift went into the President's sitting room.

I was watching over Courtney and making trips from the Oval Office to the sitting room with Blanco. Marie came into the President's office and said Mr. Watson's secretary's typewriter wouldn't work. So I put in a breaker and started back through the President's office. The President called out, "How are the dogs doing?" Valenti said the dogs were behaving but the medicine cabinet wasn't and the lights wouldn't come on. So I installed a new toggle switch. Then as I was finishing, another aide found me and said, "Here you are. Mr. Watson's secretary says the President wants you to get Him and Blanco." The President was reading the ticker-tape news. Him growled at Blanco as I was lifting Him off the davenport. The President said, "What is the matter with Him?" I said that Him couldn't stand Blanco. The President said, "He shouldn't do that." He probably is going to tell the dogs to "Come, let us reason together."

8/12/65   The President took Him on a boat ride with the foreign ambassadors. I talked to the ambassador from Nicaragua, Sevilla-Sacasa. He has known five Presidents. He remembered President Roosevelt's dog, Fala, especially fondly. I had Blanco on a leash. He asked me if Blanco would attack. I said I hoped not.

We had a great talk about the White House dogs during the Franklin D. Roosevelt days, and how a big police dog named Major had the frightening habit of grabbing a visitor by the arm and not letting go until he had satisfied himself that the person was a friend.

It was a nice trick until Major grabbed a lady senator's leg instead of her arm and wouldn't let go—he must have been a leg dog.

First Lady Eleanor Roosevelt loved that dog and wouldn't get rid of him until he bit the hand of a tourist who was reaching in through the iron fence to pet him.

The ambassador said LBJ reminded him of FDR when FDR rode around with his Scottie, Fala, beside him. I was glad I could tell the dean of Washington's Diplomatic Corps something he didn't know—that during World War II, Fala had become an honorary "Army private" by contributing a dollar to the war effort, whereupon hundreds of thousands of dogs across the country became Army privates too.

How times change. Earlier that day TV newscaster Nancy Dickerson was in for a TV shot of Luci coming out of the South Portico petting Blanco and leaving in a car with Pat Nugent and friends. My diary shows:

Mr. Nugent arrived at the grounds in Luci's Sting Ray. Luci and photog-

143

rapher George Sobel were waiting. Nugent hopped out of the car in his shirt sleeves and went to Luci, and then she said something, frowning at him. He came back to the Sting Ray, got his coat, and put it on. He said, "I'm catching hell already," and grinned at me.

8/22/65   A White House policeman stamped his feet and scared Blanco as we were walking by his post. I told the White House policeman if he ever did that again he would be the second White House policeman to be reported to his lieutenant.

8/24/65   UPI reporter Helen Thomas is trying to find out where Him is and is following up a lead he is romancing some dog in Texas. I'm avoiding the question until the story is cleared by Liz Carpenter. I told Helen that until it was cleared I couldn't comment and then Joe Laitin of the Press Information Office came up with the perfect answer for her. I gave Helen his message: we won't ask her about her sex life if she won't ask about Him's sex life.

Liz called me on the phone and I told her what is going on in Texas.

The Prez left the South Portico about 8:15 with pretty reporter Marianne Means in his car. Luci and Mr. Nugent left earlier in her car. Marianne Means told me it had come over the wire that Him was having a love affair. I told her I didn't know. A policeman asked me the same thing. He got the same answer.

8/25/65   Well, the cat's out of the bag: Him got a write-up on the front page of the Washington *Post*. "Him has found a her." And the story tells how President Johnson's pet male beagle has gotten his mate "in a family way." The story said that the Chief Executive had been the blabbermouth, confiding to reporters yesterday that Him is having a love affair. The story then quoted Liz Carpenter, the First Lady's press secretary, as saying, "Him's mate, whose name is Bridget, is a charming young beagle with handsome markings," and that "the affair" had been conducted discreetly at a veterinary clinic in Austin, Texas.

Finally, the story credited Willard Deason of Austin, the friend of the President who raises beagles, for making the introductions.

8/26/65   The President is supposed to leave today for Texas for his birthday tomorrow but a storm is coming our way. So the Secret Service said no.

August 27 was the President's fifty-seventh birthday. The weather cleared and his plane got off in the afternoon in time for him to attend a surprise party on the ranch. He was surprised by a twenty-pound cake decorated with symbols of legislation he had pushed and the words, "You *can* have your cake and eat it, too."

8/29/65 Now we know if Luci's hamster was pregnant. Usher Carter asked me to check the hamster's six new babies. I gave them food and water and provided the mother with some scraps of newspaper to keep her babies warm. The mother covered her brood with the scraps. If one crawled away, she would carry it back to the nest. The hamsters have been given Russian names, like Natasha, Jr., and Boris, Jr. Nugent dropped the male on the floor. Luci cussed and was disgusted with Pat. I quickly checked and said it was not hurt, it had fallen on a soft rug. Luci is rough on poor Pat.

8/30/65 Before I went on duty, Mr. Scouten told me to call agent Johns to put Princess in the south playpen. I brought Blanco and let the two white collies get acquainted, as they could probably breed Wednesday or Thursday this week. They seemed to get along together. I let Princess stay in the pen from 4:00 to 8:10. Agent Johns drove his car in and picked up his dog for tonight.

President Johnson escorted "General" Eisenhower to his car at C-9 Post. President Johnson told Ike that Blanco was one of only twelve white collie dogs in the country. I'm sure there are more than that, but I don't correct a President.

Dogwise, the romantic month of September started on a sour note.

9/1/65 Agent Johns and his wife drove Princess in for a try-out with Blanco. No luck. The vet gave Blanco a hormone shot so he can try tomorrow. I say it will take more than hormones.

Him has the croup. He was x-rayed today just in case he has swallowed a bone. I told the President to leave Him here this week and not to take him to Texas so the vets can continue treating him. A guest said that all the dogs in her kennel caught the same disease and that it was highly contagious to humans. President said he sure didn't want Him to give it to him.

The public didn't know it but LBJ was a great pill-taker. You didn't have to remind him to take his pills. And he always dosed himself with nose drops at the first sniffle.

9/5/65 Blanco is still a dud, romantically speaking. Mrs. Johns said we can't blame her dog—she has been taking Princess to Fort Myer for her checkups and the bitch is in A-1 condition and rarin' to go. Blanco had better get started soon.

A few days later my wife and I left town for a three-week vacation. We drove to Myrtle Beach, South Carolina, and camped out on the beach with our tent.

9/27/65   I returned from my nice vacation. At 8:15 P.M. Luci played with the dogs before she went out for dinner. The dogs were glad to see me.

9/29/65   The President came out on his way to Sargent Shriver's home in Rockville, Maryland. President asked me if Him wanted to go. I told the President he did. Him pulled the President into the car.

10/5/65   I helped Cleave Ryan with the lights for the President's talk. The President is going to have his gall-bladder operation on Friday. I hope and pray the operation is a success.

10/9/65   The word is that the President wants to see his dogs before leaving the hospital. Even the newspapers carried the story.

10/10/65   Luci and Pat Nugent played with the dogs. Luci said her father would like to see the dogs at the hospital. She said the other time LBJ was in the hospital the doctors didn't want the dogs in the hospital visiting. But Luci said the President's room is isolated now, so there wouldn't be any trouble.

Pat said to Him, "You are a mess, just like Luci." Nugent has taken lessons from LBJ in how to handle Luci, I see. She loves it!

10/11/65   I saw Mrs. Johnson at about 3:00 P.M. as she was leaving the White House for the hospital. She petted the dogs and said that the President would like to see the dogs most any day now.

10/12/65   I took the dogs to meet the new housekeeper, Mary Kaltman. She said she would send me a copy of the dogs' monthly food bill. She played with the dogs and said she was interested in saving money for the President, herself, and anyone else. She seems very nice. She suggested I take Him to hospital to cheer the Prez.

10/14/65   Mr. Watson's secretary, Mrs. Cook, said the President has some pain, so the dogs can't see the President for a while. She said soon they'll go to hospital.

Juanita Roberts said that the President was getting a haircut and watching the final World Series baseball game between Minnesota and the Dodgers. She laughed and said, "Tonight's the night." She told me to go into the Press Information Office with the dogs and if a light on the phone selector came on I should push a button which would carry the President's voice over a speaker. Then he could hear the dogs bark back. We waited, but it was the light that failed. I guess the President fell asleep.

10/19/65   Everybody is concerned about the President wanting to see his dogs. It is really amusing how everyone discusses the pros and cons of it—whether dogs belong in a hospital.

The dogs' teeth were cleaned. Life goes on. Dog life.

10/20/65   LBJ's Secret Service man, Youngblood, said he seriously thought that the dogs won't get to visit the President, to prevent any chance of infection.

10/21/65   Ring bells! Him's mate, Bridget, gave birth to five puppies, all females.

About 2:00 P.M. policeman Shearon told me to bring the dogs to the South Portico where the White House photographers were, because the President was arriving from the hospital. The first thing the President did as he got out of his car was motion to me for the dogs. I picked up Him for President to pet. "Mr. President, the dogs sure missed you," I said and meant it. The President said, "I hear you have been writing poems." The reporters and we were on TV so I couldn't correct him and tell him it was engineer Nolan's handiwork. So I got the credit for Nolan's big effort. Now I'm one up on the Engineer's Office.

The President flew to Texas to recuperate from his operation, taking Blanco and Him along.

10/27/65   An agent told me in Texas Blanco hid out in some tall field grass. They had to use a small helicopter to flush him out so he could be caught.

Dean Rusk and his wife returned from Texas on the Johnsons' *Jet Star*, bringing Blanco with them. I went on and got Blanco off the plane.

10/28/65   I took Blanco to the third-floor Solarium. Luci had a surprise birthday party for Willie Day Taylor, her "substitute mother." It was very touching.

Yolanda Boozer's son, Valenti's daughter Courtney, and a little Chinese girl who was visiting had their pictures made with Blanco when I took Blanco to surprise Mrs. Taylor. I called the vet and told him to send me some more tranquilizers because they didn't bring back his medicine from Texas. I hear Blanco also chased some sheep into a fence in Texas.

10/29/65   The White House is buzzing with the rumor that Luci flew to Texas for permission to marry Patrick Nugent.

A White House officer at the South East Gate was telling how tourists often gather at the gate where they could see me with the President's dogs. They point at me, he said, and ask if that is the President with the dogs. He merely says he "doesn't think so." A woman tourist said, "I know that is the President. Look how he is petting the dogs. I know you officers won't tell us anything about the President, so I'm sure it's the President!"

I told the officer I hoped no fanatic would mistake me for the President and take a shot at me. The officer said if a nut thought I was the President I would be the President as far as the nut was concerned, which didn't make me feel any better. But I guess I would rather he shot at me than the President, as I am a smaller target. Besides, a lot of people can run dogs and electric cables, but there aren't many around who can run a country.

About this time I had a little fun with White House engineer Jenkins. After a State Dinner, when the gold service was returned to the pantry by Johnny Johnson, I picked out choice leftovers for the dogs. Engineer Jenkins, seeing the heaped plate, stopped greedily, saying the food was too good for the dogs. So I let him have his choice of the pieces of beef. He was chomping away happily till I said, "Well, Pearl Wiggins gathered this up from the dinner plates. I didn't know you wanted it for yourself." I thought he would gag.

I was one up on him. But to fix me, he complained to the Usher's Office that I had a color TV set in my electrical shop. The next day the Signal Corps yanked it out and left a black and white set. I couldn't win them all.

10/31/65   Luci and Pat Nugent returned from Texas about 1:30 P.M. I was in the basement and I wanted to go to the ground floor. Someone was holding the elevator in locked position. I kicked once on the door. It came to the basement immediately, and I was surprised to find Luci aboard with an ice cream scoop in her hand. I apologized to her for pulling the car to the basement. She said she was hunting for some ice cream.

I told her I couldn't help her, that the engineers had put Blanco in the outside runway and I was on my way to take Blanco for his exercise. Luci said, "You are sweet." She looked a little sad and wistful. I don't believe that the President wants her to marry for a while. Pat looked gloomy too.

11/1/65   I had Blanco out for his exercise. Willie Day Taylor came to the South Portico in a small car. She had turned her ankle and had been to the doctor. She asked me to help her up the stairs. I helped her into the Oval Room in the family quarters. She sat on a small chair with rollers and I pushed her to the elevator and then to the second floor to the Queen's Room. She sat on the bed; she's staying overnight. Later she called me on the phone to come fix her TV antenna. Luci and Pat were with her. Luci said, "Bryant, my clock in the Solarium is four hours

148

slow." I disconnected the clock and left it in our electrical shop for replacement.

11/3/65 Luci and Pat came in about dusk with a strange young man and tried to play with Blanco. Blanco didn't like their friend and shied away from them. I tried to bring Blanco back. Luci stopped me. "Mr. Bryant, leave him alone! I want to overcome Blanco's shyness myself." Yep, she's a lot like her Dad.

11/8/65 I received a letter from Clarence Johnson, my former chief electrician boss at the Navy Department fourteen years ago, talking about what would make his mother most happy in her last days on earth—a birthday wish from the President. November 17 she will be a hundred and three years old. I gave the letter to Juanita Roberts, and I am sure that she will give it to the President with a birthday card to sign.

Mary van Rensselaer Thayer sent me an autographed copy of the book she wrote, *Jacqueline Bouvier Kennedy*. It was thoughtful of her. She interviewed me when she was working on it. I gave her no secrets since I was saving them for myself.

11/14/65 I had Blanco at the South Portico waiting for the President and Mrs. Johnson to land at 11:00 P.M. Luci and Mr. Nugent came over and petted Blanco as the helicopter landed. They were as nervous as kittens. Mrs. Johnson ran to Luci, hugged her, and greeted Pat warmly. She even shook hands with Blanco. The President got off and hugged Luci. Then the President patted Blanco. He was only medium cordial to Pat. Looks to me like Lady Bird is all for Luci getting married and LBJ is not.

The President said he was going to take Blanco to second floor and for me to come up after Blanco in ten minutes. I did. Him is still playing father in Texas.

According to a story that made the rounds at the White House a few months later, this was the big night when Pat finally got to talk to Luci's daddy about his honorable intentions. It didn't happen at all the way Luci had planned it, and it was slightly hilarious. When the couple had gone to the ranch to speak to him about marriage a few weeks before, he hadn't given them a chance to do it. But he knew perfectly well what was going on—he was just up to his old trick of keeping people with a problem waiting until he was ready to face it himself. The President bided his time until they were all back in Washington together.

But at last he was ready. Pretending great innocence, he asked Luci to go get Pat and bring him to the presidential bedroom. Then

149

the Prez said in a tough voice, "What's this I read in the papers about you two coming to Texas to ask me something?" And he huffed and puffed to show his confusion about what was going on.

The story was that Luci had filled Pat Nugent in on how to handle her father, but he was still scared half to death because it was so unexpected and sudden and because he had to give his little speech in front of Luci and her mother as well as the President.

As any other father might have done, the President asked those hard questions such as how are you going to support my daughter, and don't you think she's a little too young. And what about her schooling?

Pat talked about the money he had saved up and how he would not stand in Luci's way of finishing her education. And of course how much he loved her and would take care of her.

Luci jumped in to play her trump card. She said she might take up typing and shorthand. Later Luci said she knew she couldn't go wrong if she mentioned typing and shorthand "because Daddy always says those are the two greatest virtues a woman can have."

11/15/65   8:30 P.M. The President and Mrs. Johnson were coming out of Juanita Roberts' office. The President called to Blanco and said he was too nervous. Also, LBJ said that Him had worms. I told the President that I would like to see Him's babies (pups). The President and Mrs. Johnson were on their way to a White House reception.

I asked Juanita Roberts if she had taken care of the card for the hundred-and-three-year-old lady, Clarence Johnson's mother. She said she had. I told her it was nice of her.

11/17/65   Blanco is a nervous wreck. Blanco and Him's room is being painted. This is the second day of painting.

Now I know LBJ can be a jealous husband. I got a call to get an extension cord for Mrs. Johnson. The outlet was behind and under a dresser in Mrs. Johnson's room. She was sitting there. As I plugged the cord in I was lying on the floor almost under her to insert the plug. Just as I was getting up off the floor the President walked into the bedroom, his mouth wide-open. I couldn't believe my eyes. The look on his face before he realized who it was, was the look of a jealous husband. I said, "Mr. President, I was just putting in an extension cord for Mrs. Johnson's manicure table." I could see Lady Bird enjoyed seeing he cared that much.

LBJ and Lady Bird flew to Texas again.

11/23/65 An agent told me Him was having fun in Texas chasing cats up trees and under cars, but Him slows down when he corners a cat.

11/26/65 Here we go again. Dog hotel. Mr. Valenti's secretary called me at home and said Mr. Valenti asked if I would look after his dog for two or three days. I told her okay, to bring the dog in and we would try to give him good care.

I don't know whether it was the President or Lady Bird who had decided that we must get rid of the starlings that were giving the White House grounds and the official limousines a design in droppings that was, as Lady Bird said, "mighty embarrassing." They certainly were not part of the beautification program. But getting rid of them was easier said than done, my diary shows:

11/29/65 Now we're at war—with starlings. I played a tape recording of the sounds of a starling in distress; a speaker is in the magnolia tree at C-11 Post. The birds don't pay much attention to it. Chief Usher West says the trees will be sprayed tomorrow to keep starlings away.

11/30/65 Mrs. Johnson returned from Texas at 9:55 P.M. She petted and shook hands with Blanco. She said Him was getting skinny, as he ran around too much in Texas.

She asked how the starlings liked the spray. I said they liked it very much; it was like cream in their coffee.

12/2/65 The starlings hit two cars today. A little fancy cussing among the drivers.

12/9/65 Starlings do not stay overnight at the White House. I turn the tape recorder on and clap my hands while one of Mr. Williams' grounds men uses a paddle to hit a cardboard box. It works, but it's a one-hour chore each evening. I just hope my friends don't see me. And especially Helen Thomas of UPI.

12/12/65 The Prez is back from Texas. He arrived at 2:00 A.M. with Him. He said he had to punish Him for chasing sheep. Luci played with the dogs and told me Texans would shoot a dog chasing sheep as they wouldn't know the owner of the dog. They would shoot first and then check afterwards.

12/16/65 I had the dogs in the West Lobby. Prime Minister Wilson came in, pointed at Him, and laughed at recognition. The President was escorting Mr. Wilson to the Oval Office. I accidentally stepped on Him's foot and Him yelped. Someone said, "Thank goodness it was not the President who did it, or it would be flashed around the world."

151

12/17/65   I had florist Jimmy Nelson make big Christmas bows for the dogs just in time. The President was in his car with Luci, the First Lady, and Prime Minister Wilson. The President called for the dogs, shook hands with Blanco, and took only Him along to help light the Christmas tree on the Ellipse behind the White House. After coming back, Luci said, "Thanks for the run." Him had put a run in her stocking. But he was the star at the tree-lighting ceremony.

Valet Paul Glynn said the President punished Him with a belt for chasing sheep. The poor assistant who was holding Him for the President also received a couple of sharp licks from the belt. The President's aim with his tongue is better than his aim with his hand.

12/20/65   President had a dinner for West German Chancellor Ludwig Erhard. The engineers were lighting a fire in the Red Room fireplace. I was holding back a curtain. The window was raised so the fire could get a good draft. A butler came back and asked us to close the window, as the dinner guests in the State Dining Room were cold. We ignored him. Then LBJ's special assistant McGeorge Bundy walked in and said the guests were freezing. I explained we were trying to get a fire going without smoking the guests out. I told Bundy it was either smoke or frost. He said the guests would rather have the smoke than freeze to death. We ignored him, too, and the window was closed as soon as the fire started roaring.

12/21/65   The President and his family left by helicopter for Texas. Luci wished me a Merry Christmas, and she looked so happy—LBJ must have said yes. Mrs. Johnson thanked me for caring for the dogs. Lynda praised Him's red bow and Blanco's green bow ribbon. I couldn't move, because with one hand I was holding Blanco by his leash and with the other I was holding onto one of the South Portico Christmas trees to keep the chopper from blowing it over. A policeman was holding the other tree with both hands. I glanced at the chopper as the jet was gunning for a takeoff and the President had Him on his lap looking towards Blanco and me waving. He was letting Him get a last look at us. Him was happy to be aboard.

12/25/65   Now the world knows Luci's daddy said yes, and the Christmas Day newspapers carry the story of Luci's engagement to Pat. Joe Laitin made the announcement to the press at the historic Driskill Hotel in Austin. It's a very Merry Christmas.

14

1966 was the year beagle puppies were coming out of my ears. So were weddings—Luci and Pat Nugent's that did happen and Lynda Bird and George Hamilton's that didn't.

And 1966 was the year that broke Lyndon Johnson's heart—not to speak of my own and Luci's—when the President's favorite beagle, Him, was run over and killed on the White House grounds.

But that was later in the year. At the beginning of the year, how happy it all seemed when everyone was going around the White House saying, "The way to start a happy New Year is with a basketful of fresh wiggly puppies." Him's mate in Texas had had five of them, all female. They were delivered to the White House from the airport by a rented truck. Him looked at his puppies with fatherly tolerance, but Blanco transferred some of his jealousy of Him to them. Thereafter I had to protect the pups from Blanco as well as from the photographers, who couldn't get enough pictures.

Luci took a fancy to one of them, a puppy with a freckle on its nose, and made my life harder by giving her a tough name for me to handle—"Pecosa," Spanish for a single freckle. Eventually Luci gave up, but at first she was adamant that we use only the Spanish moniker.

Pecosa was supposed to become a television star by appearing on a TV interview with NBC-TV commentator Tony Sylvester. Sylvester had gone through a lot of trouble to arrange a special taping at the White House, it had been cleared by Liz Carpenter, and I came in early to do Pecosa's talking for her. But Pecosa seemed destined to be known as a hard-luck pup. First the interview had to be postponed because of the President's State of the Union speech. The entries in my diary struggle on:

1/13/66 No interview today. It was hailing golf balls at 3 P.M. We'll try for tomorrow.

1/14/66 Sylvester was left cooling his heels while his cameraman and

153

sound technician went to the Capitol by mistake. So we will try for tomorrow.

And it was not until January 18 that Tony Sylvester finally made it, arriving with his cameraman and entourage. By then I'd changed my mind about having Pecosa interviewed all by herself, so I met Sylvester's entourage on the South Lawn with an entourage of my own made up of dogs big and small.

The interview was finished at last but Pecosa's hard luck continued. When LBJ's adored Courtney Valenti stepped into a dog mess, whose mess was it? Pecosa's. And when a press information gal's ire was raised because one of the pups redesigned her blouse by nipping off a button, who was the little nipper? Naturally, Pecosa. I was glad the blouse wasn't low-cut. She had razor-sharp teeth and would bite anything.

LBJ asked for the pups frequently, and every time they visited, they left their calling card or a puddle. With all I had to do, inside the White House and out, I simply did not have time to housebreak them. And when I had time, the dogs were elsewhere, bringing cheer around the White House or flying off with Luci or the President.

A sample day is enough to tell the story:

1/19/66 Mary Kaltman, the new White House housekeeper, asked me to bring the new pups to her office yesterday. I finally got there today with two pups. She got down on the rug in her office and played with them. Pups were frisky and ran all over the place. Suddenly one pup stopped running and squatted behind her desk and let go. It was a mess. I offered to clean up, but Mrs. Kaltman was very polite and said she would clean up. End of visit. Sorry about that.

But it wasn't just the pups. Their father, who knew better and should have set a good example, was just as bad:

1/20/66 The President returned from an Independence, Missouri, ceremony at the Truman Library marking the establishment of a Harry S Truman Center for the Advancement of Peace in Israel and an annual $50,000 Peace Award named for Truman. I had Him and Blanco out on the lawn for the landing of the helicopter. The Prez motioned for Him. He shook hands with Blanco, then he took Him to his office on a leash. Him left a "present."

The next day a top presidential aide got the floor treatment:

154

1/21/66   One of the pups wet the rug in assistant press secretary Laitin's office. Later I got a call from Mr. Valenti's office to bring the pups over. Little Courtney played with the pups on a leash. She took one of the pups into Marvin Watson's office and the pup wet the rug. Mr. Valenti told me to get someone to clean the spot. Instead, I cleaned the rug myself and left word for the night cleaners to go over the spot—a streak about four feet long. As I was taking the pups into the Bouquet Room, President Johnson stopped and petted the pups. I told the President Courtney was playing with the pups but she had just left. The President was furious. "Why didn't they let me know Courtney was here?"

He was really upset. "Damn it, I'm supposed to be notified." The President loved Courtney just as much as his own Luci and Lynda Bird—he once called her, "my little girl, my little heartbeat"— and certainly spent more time with her when she was around than with his big, busy daughters.

On almost any excuse, the President had Valenti or his wife bring Courtney to the White House and the President thoroughly relaxed as he played with the child, catering to her every whim.

1/23/66   President Johnson called for the two pups in the second-floor Oval Room. Freckles' friend wet the rug. Mrs. Johnson told the butler to get some corn meal to put on the damp spot.

The President seemed to pay no attention to such problems as rug-wetting, but dogs were frequently a frame of reference for his colorful language. It came as no surprise to me when he said to a reporter, "I'll leak to you like a dog on a fire hydrant."

I was relieved when the President finally brought himself to part with two of the dogs, one going to his Texas friend, Willard Deason, whom he had appointed to the ICC; the other went to the Ted Reardons. Luci decided Pecosa was her dog, and to keep the freckle-face company, she decided to keep a second dog as well. The President, who never seemed to have gotten around to naming a dog in the past, decided that he was going to name the second pup himself.

Meanwhile I was referring to the second one as "Freckles' Friend." One day word spread that the President had finally found a name for Freckles' Friend, and it was a great name. Something every bit as good as Pecosa. But I never could find out what it was.

Eventually Luci named the pup Kim as a temporary thing until the President could remember what his choice was. But the President never mentioned it again, and Kim—for Kimberly—stuck. My wife, Doris, commented, "Any President who will go for years calling his dogs Him and Her is not going to waste his brain cells naming dogs."

As January drew to an end, the White House was snowbound, but that didn't stop me from my appointed rounds or from observing the playful activities of the lovebirds.

1/30/66 A big snow and blizzard. I walked over eight miles to get to work and worked a double shift Monday.

I am staying a second night at the White House. Luci was lying on a snowdrift face down and told me to go get Pat. He saw her and laughed and gave her some spanks. They played with Him and Blanco.

As it turned out, I stayed over snowbound a third night at the White House. During those days I was worrying about an old problem, the lack of space for the pups.

A few days before the storm our great plan to improve the dogs' quarters had flopped:

1/25/66 Workmen started drilling on the wall of the Bouquet Room to enlarge it for the doghouse, but Jim Jones said it would cost too much, as the White House walls are three feet thick and the President has an economy drive on. Mr. Deason called me and said his pup and Ted Reardon's pup have mange. He asked me to examine the President's pups. I told him I had informed everyone that the pups must have some fresh air.

As a cheaper way to get the pups some sunlight and fresh air, I suggested to Jim Jones that we install glass in the wallboard and a clear glass window in the door. Charles Rotchford of GSA (General Services Administration) brought his chief carpenter over to make an estimate. I really stirred up a hornet's nest—everybody was consulting everybody but nothing was being done.

2/3/66 The vets met with Mr. Rotchford and Mr. Moore concerning the dogs' window. The vet called me and said he was on my side. So where is the window?

But there was plenty of other action around the White House.

2/4/66 Mrs. Johnson received a portrait of Eleanor Roosevelt for the White House—the one with many hands.

The President wanted the pups at his office. I took them over, and President Johnson took the leashes and played with Courtney. Her mother was also there. The President watched the TV news on Vietnam. LBJ asked Mary Margaret Valenti if she was going to let Jack go to Hawaii. She said he might get shot. The President bent over and kissed her. Mr. Valenti entered later from the President's secretary's office. Courtney pulled the pups by their leashes and gave them a piece of firewood kindling to play with. She started to hit one of the pups with a piece of wood, and I told her not to hit the pup.

2/5/66   President Johnson went to Hawaii.

Dr. Fox called me and said that the President has heard that people handling the dogs seemed to have an itch! I told him I was using flea powder. He told me to stop using that brand and see if that is the trouble.

2/17/66   Mr. Ketchum, the White House Curator, introduced me to Zsa Zsa Gabor. She petted the pups and Him and Blanco. She was very beautiful. She made a face when she saw Blanco. She said white collies weren't much good for pets. They were too timid. "And they are not even good lovers, dahlink, ven they are mating, so vat are they good for?"

2/23/66   I had Him and his two pups at C-11 Post when Vice President Humphrey returned from his Asian trip. The President greeted the Veep. Valenti's secretary told Courtney to go see Daddy, who was on the helicopter. Courtney didn't see her daddy as she ran toward the President, who lifted her up.

A reporter told me she saw Zsa Zsa Gabor on Johnny Carson's TV show. She said that all she could talk about was the President's dogs.

The President and his guests went into the kitchen. The President said they had him on a diet and he came back with a huge dish of ice cream, ate it, and sent Luci back for a second helping. Freckles jumped up on a table where the President had put his ice cream and I ran over and pulled the pup's leash as it started to lick the ice cream.

The President was talking to Lynda on the phone. He asked her when she was going to leave Hollywood and come home. Her present boyfriend is George Hamilton, the actor. The President said, "Oh, Luci is here with an ugly boyfriend." It was Pat Nugent. Luci took the phone and said, "Did you hear what he said about your future brother-in-law?" The President asked me which pup I liked best. I told him I liked them both the same.

The President was always checking his family's reaction to everything—and mine as well.

2/27/66   Luci and Pat played with the dogs. I went to the second floor and picked up four dogs. The President asked me when the pups were going to be bathed. He's on a self-improvement kick for family and dogs. He wants a fenced-in runway for the dogs.

3/1/66   The President said, "Mr. Bryant, Him isn't getting enough exercise. Him is almost as fat as you are." I told the President I would let Him run loose as soon as Capital Parks finished fencing. The President wanted to know when it would be finished. I told him I would get after Mr. Williams and get it started.

I told the President I wanted some new pictures made of the President and the dogs, because we were still passing out his pictures with Him and Her, and Her is dead. So he called his night secretary, Vicky, and kidded her and told her she was getting fat like Bryant before he told her to call the photographer. She got photographer Wolfe. He snapped quite a few shots. The President told him, "If you don't have any good pictures with all that snapping, you don't deserve any."

I saw Jim Jones and told him the President has asked me twice about the fence, so I think someone had better get on the ball.

3/2/66   Today a Capital Parks crew put up two rolls of fencing. Courtney and the pups had their picture made. The President never gets tired of posing with Courtney. I told Mrs. Valenti that I wanted a picture of Courtney, the President, and pups. She said she would get me one.

3/10/66   I had Blanco and agent Johns' female dog Princess on the South Grounds to try again to breed Blanco with Princess. President Johnson walked around the roadway and wanted to know if that was Blanco's mate. I told him it was. He asked how it was going. I told the President we were working on it.

3/11/66   Blanco didn't breed. The vet said he wasn't developed sexually, that he wasn't very fertile. The President was disgusted. He says Blanco's a eunuch.

3/16/66   The President walked the dogs; he is picking on Valenti through Valenti's dog. He told him that Beagle was too fat. The Prez told Jimmy Nelson to put the dogs away and said, "Don't put that mutt—Valenti's dog—with my thoroughbreds." Beagle is staying at the White House while the Valenti family is moving to Georgetown.

3/18/66   I saw a funny sight. Luci and Pat ran Him around and around the South Grounds about three times in her Sting Ray while Jack Valenti also ran around the South Grounds but under his own steam and with his dog. Beagle was jumping around and following him: Jack says LBJ tells him he has to keep in shape.

3/21/66 I sent Him to Fort Myer vets because his right eye was blood-shot and closed. The vets are keeping Him overnight. Luci wants a trampoline from Camp David installed. Mr. Williams told me we now have to relocate the dog pen because Luci wants her trampoline in that same spot where it's very private and hidden away.

LBJ liked to needle me in front of an audience:

3/22/66 President took a walk around the South Grounds with his admirers including secretaries, aides, Luci, and Pat. I was in front with Blanco, Freckles, and Kim. LBJ picked me as his victim, first complaining that I wasn't keeping in touch with the vets. Then when that didn't work he spotted a suspicious bulge on me. "Mr. Bryant, what is that in your hip pocket?" I lifted up the end of my coat and showed him my flashlight, pliers, and screwdrivers. I said, "Mr. President, it gets kind of dark around here at night." I walked on a little farther; then the President said, "Mr. Bryant, you have a hole in your coat." I had torn it closing the pups' room Sunday night. I was afraid to tell him or we'd be in another hassle over who pays for it.

3/29/66 The South West Gate was open for the presidential cars to exit for the reception given him at the Indian embassy by Her Excellency Indira Gandhi, prime minister of India. Everyone was waiting impatiently. The President came out of his office and leisurely petted the dogs on his way to his car. I guess Presidents get pretty jaded. If Indira Gandhi were giving a party for me I wouldn't be standing around petting dogs.

4/1/66 The Prez came out of his office and played with Courtney. Then he took her back in. One of the pups gave her a kiss; she wiped it off with her coat. The President gave the dogs some dog candy in his office. Courtney got jealous, closed the candy drawer on the President's desk, and said, "That's all." She didn't want the pups getting the Prez's attention.

Luci and Mr. Nugent left and went to jump on the new trampoline. They are like two puppies themselves.

4/4/66 Luci was playing with the dogs on her way to the trampoline. The President called for the dogs in his office. I had the pups. The President wanted Luci to greet the Vice President and some legislators.

Luci declined and apologized to her father and said she had on her jumping clothes. Also she was missing a slipper—it came off and one of the dogs got it. The President fed the dogs some candy.

4/6/66 I left word slipped into President Johnson's night reading to see if he wants any of the dogs to go to Texas for the Easter holiday.

159

4/7/66 I got back word that President *isn't taking any dogs.* Luci and Pat came out to C-11 Post and Luci said she wanted Him to go to Texas. I told her the Prez had said *no dogs.* She made a face and she and Pat went over to the President's office. Shortly afterward, as the President walked from his office toward the helicopter, Jack Valenti ran to me and said the President wanted Him and his pups to go to Texas. He didn't surprise me. I already had the dogs ready.

4/19/66 Mayhem at the White House. Some Democratic committee-women had their pictures made with Kim and Pecosa. Some of the women said they didn't get to kiss the President, so they kissed the two pups. The ladies got so excited they broke a candle lamp stand in the Red Room and two ashtrays. The Prez came out of his office and clapped his hands, and I took the pups to him. He walked to the South Portico and up the spiral marble steps to the first floor. The women mobbed him. He loved it. He was covered with so much lipstick, he looked like he'd been attacked by hornets.

4/26/66 The Prez was feeling a little blue today for some reason. He made me and dogs his entourage again so he won't be alone a minute. I trailed along at his request after he spotted me in the hall. I was on my way to answer a request to show the dogs to some children on the first floor. The Prez, the dogs, and I went into his office. Prez looked at ticker-tape news for about ten minutes. He said, "Follow me." He walked to the elevator with us following. He was muttering something about a President can never count on his friends. I didn't answer and I never got over to see the children.

The Prez said, "Come on." The dogs and I got on the elevator with the President and ended up at the barbershop and stayed while Prez got a haircut and a manicure. The Vice President and several other men came in and talked to Prez while the manicurist worked. We rode the elevator again to first floor, and one dog, Kim, squatted to water Marvin Watson's rug. I lifted up on the leash and tried to leave the President unannounced. The Prez was totally unconcerned about the mess, stopped me. Soon he was feeling better, joking again and asking me if I liked the pups better than I liked Him. And if the dogs liked Luci. I told the Prez that the dogs liked to ride in the car with Luci—they either like *her* or the *car.* He liked that and laughed. Then the President asked what it was the dogs liked in the Unipets. I said I didn't know as I hadn't tasted them, but they probably had put something sweet in to mask the flavor of the vitamins.

5/9/66 Willie Day Taylor asked me if I wanted to see *President Johnson's Hill Country,* a one-hour color TV program. I said sure, it beats working. Luci had ordered fried chicken for her and Pat from the local Hot Shoppe. We watched the program in the President's bedroom. Luci said Texas ranchers are proud of their cattle, so they only have one or two breeds of cattle, Herefords and Black Angus. I liked the ranch life I saw in the film. Someday I'd like some of the same.

5/11/66 Pat Nugent walked by as I was putting in a 300-watt streetlight at C-9 Post. He called Luci and went into the White House, taking Him with him to see Luci. Nugent has the run of the White House now. The wedding is getting closer.

Looking back I knew Luci was a big girl and ready for marriage when she gave her six hamsters away. She did it in a cute way, reminding me of how Jackie Kennedy had given away Pushinka's pups. She sent several to individual children who had written her about them. But she saved one for a class of retarded children in Battle Creek, Michigan, and she sent another to the children in a kindergarten class in Philadelphia who had written saying they had saved their money for a white mouse but when they read of Luci and her hamsters, they decided that hamsters were "even nicer than mice."

5/13/66 I took the pups over to the President's office. Courtney and Mary Margaret Valenti were in his sitting room. The Prez told Courtney to feed the pups some candy. I asked the President if he tried out the chocolate malt candy balls that I gave Juanita Roberts for them. He said he hadn't seen them. I went to his secretary, who said the Prez keeps her so busy she never even had a moment to put the candy in his desk. I took the candy in and gave it to the President. He let the pups jump in the air for their treat.

He asked me where I got the candy. I told him at Peoples Drug Store. The President started to eat the candy balls, saying, "They're starving me." Luci and Pat came in with Him and Blanco and Willie Day Taylor. Luci told the President to watch out, that Lynda had eaten too many of the candy balls while she was on a diet. The President paid no attention and kept eating absent-mindedly. Later, Luci, Pat, Courtney, and Mr. and Mrs. Valenti came out and sat on the grass outside the President's office.

Earlier while I was in the office I asked Mary Margaret if Mr. Valenti needed a good dog man now that he could afford it. The President turned around and gave me a dirty look, but he never said anything. Valenti laughed. Valenti now has a $175,000-a-year salary for heading the Motion Picture Association. A step up from his $30,000 at the White House.

161

Henry Cabot Lodge was leaving the South Portico. He saw the pups and said, "Hi, dogs."

5/7/66 John Pustka and I had an interview and our pictures made with the dogs by the Washington *Post*. John told the reporter that college kids sometimes climbed the fence at night undetected and slipped up toward the White House. I firmly told the reporter to cancel that statement, as that had no connection with the dog story. I don't want to get in bad with the White House police and the Secret Service.

5/19/66 I received a call from Wally Siegel, Goodson-Todman Producers, New York, and I agreed to go on *To Tell the Truth* if he cleared it through Mrs. Carpenter's office.

The Prez had a group of people out in the West Garden and called for dogs. The President squatted to pet the pups and Freckles quickly kissed the President. Then Kim squatted and took a leak in front of the Prez, with cameras grinding.

The Prez was annoyed by a funny story in the papers on Blanco being demoted as the President's Number Two dog. The Prez cornered me and wanted to know why I let Blanco lose his tag #2. I told the President it was the man who relieved me with the dogs on Saturday night. He told me to set the reporters straight, that he didn't want his White House dogs bumping someone else's dog for a lower number. I told the Prez that he rated the lowest numbers for all his dogs. He said goddamn it, he didn't care a four-letter word if the dogs' number was #81.

What had happened was that a front-page headline of the Washington Evening Star had blared: LBJ DOWNGRADES BLANCO— IS BLANCO OUT OF FAVOR AT THE WHITE HOUSE? The story told how Blanco had been bumped from his #2 tag down to #4, to make way for Him's offspring, Freckles and Kim.

LBJ was annoyed that Blanco was being upstaged, but what really infuriated him was to read that the two cairn terriers of his good friend, J. Edgar Hoover—G-Boy and Cindy—and the chihuahua of World War II General Omar Bradley—Ginger Boy—had also been demoted by two notches in the list of Top Ten Dogs of the Nation's Capital, simply to make room for the two White House puppies.

I rushed over to the License Bureau and was able to report in my diary the next day:

New White House dog licenses are going to make everyone happy, including the President. Mr. Nelson at the License Bureau changed Freckles to #208, Kim to #209. Him is now #1 and Blanco #2. I gave Juanita Roberts the list for the Prez's night reading.

162

I was in Juanita Roberts' office with all the dogs and the President came in on his way to the Cabinet Room. I told him I got the licenses. That I got twelve dollars from petty cash and walked over and got tags personally. He said it looked like I was having a dog show. I didn't charge the three and a half hours of my time to the government, as it was worth it to get the license numbers fixed correctly. If you want anything done right, do it yourself.

Dog tags were a familiar headache around the White House. Someone was always dissatisfied with the protocol of which dog outranked which dog. Once LBJ came at me with "Now you've got me in trouble with those damned equal-rights women."

I said, "How do you figure that, Mr. President?"

He said, "The press dames are complaining that I let Him have tag number one and Her only got number two."

Liz Carpenter and the Prez were always hassling about the dogs, too, and once the President asked her, "Liz, why don't you just stay out of my dogs' life?"

She retorted, "I'd like to if only the reporters would let me."

Liz especially had trouble with Blanco, the gift of a little girl in Illinois, because the Illinois reporters were always asking about him. They would ask her and she would ask me. Sometimes they tried to get around her by asking me, but I knew Liz was a powerful gal and I didn't upstage her. I would refer them to her.

One day I knew she would explode, and as soon as it happened the press room was laughing about the snappy retort Liz had given Mary Pakenham, reporter for the Chicago *Tribune*. Mary had asked the usual questions of how Blanco was doing and where did he stay and was he happy?

Liz tried to get rid of it all in one breath and said Blanco was fine and living in his doghouse, and very happy.

Mary said, "How do you know?"

Liz said, "Because I'm in the doghouse with him most of the time."

Dog tags continued to be a pain in the neck after LBJ was gone. Whether King Timahoe, a latecomer, outranked Vicky, who had come to the White House with the Nixons, became a burning issue in Nixon's time—for about two days. An even subtler question was whether Vicky, who belonged to the married Nixon daughter, Julie, and who was therefore an Eisenhower dog and only a *visitor* at the White House, outranked Tricia's dog Pasha. Tricia was not married when the Nixons moved into the White House, so Pasha could claim to be the more authentic Nixon dog.

I got a good laugh when President Ford was presented with his golden retriever, Liberty, and the first thing the newspapers did was to headline the news that TOP DOG ISN'T NO. 1 and that the female puppy would have to settle for a mere number 9 on her dog tag— at least until renewal time came up.

5/20/66 Liz Carpenter said that the President frowned on White House personnel being on TV shows. I told her that the President had said it would be all right for me to be on *To Tell the Truth*. She said it was all right if he said so.

5/21/66 The presidential helicopter with four dogs and some people aboard was about ready to leave for Camp David. The helicopter caught fire, so they turned the dogs loose and the people got off. They took another helicopter.

5/23/66 Luci came out and petted the dogs; she said the big dog write-ups in the Sunday Washington *Post* and *Evening Star* were very good. Even Mrs. Johnson complimented me. The Secret Service called, distressed, and said they were getting calls about John Pustka saying to the reporter from the *Post* that sometimes people came over the fence and got halfway to the White House before the police discovered it. I told the Secret Service John just had a slip of the tongue.

None of the Johnson family mentioned the people coming in over the fence—they let the Secret Service worry about security. What they were amused about and quoted to each other was the papers' account of how the pups had chewed away two large hunks of the wall of the Bouquet Room, and also one reporter's misconception that the room was named for the way it smelled with dogs in it. The articles also explained that Monday was wash day around the White House—the day the dogs got washed—and that Friday was check-a-pet-at-the-vet day, when the dogs got a weekly checkup. They also mentioned my practice of feeding each dog a tablespoon of bacon drippings once a week to keep their coats nice and shiny.

5/29/66 The President had to go to the bathroom during a movie in the White House theater. The agents couldn't turn on the lights in the toilet in the china room, so the agent told the President the lights were burned out. The switches were turned off at the main breaker by some stupid dumdum who didn't know what he was doing. I caught hell.

On June 6 I became involved in a security incident. A private company's panel truck was leaving the White House grounds when out of the blue one of the men in it started yelling nutty comments and insults at me. I'd never seen him before. I told the policeman at the gate to stop the truck so I could talk to the man. I got his name, badge number, and the name of the company he worked for. Turned out that he was an outside electrical technician and had been at the White House doing some work. Before I even turned in a full report, an order was given that the man was not to return. A few days later I was told that the man was found to have a police record, and had no clearance for working at the White House.

I knew the Secret Service was careful, but I was still surprised at the number of times they interviewed me about the matter and how detailed a report I had to sign.

6/7/66   Officer Wells called me and asked me to check dog at B-4 Post. Someone had found Mr. Valenti's dog on the street eating garbage. A Mr. Ray Harwell of Takoma Park, Maryland, picked up Beagle and brought the dog to the White House at 8:15 P.M.

6/9/66   New York. We were taped by Bud Collins for the *To Tell the Truth* program. The two imposters did a good job posing as the President's dog man. Only one guess was for me, so we won a hundred dollars apiece. The panelists were Kitty Carlisle, Peggy Cass, and Orson Bean. Kitty talked about seeing Lynda recently.

6/10/66   A policeman told me Mr. and Mrs. Johnson came out the South Portico and asked for his car. It wasn't there. The President went in to a phone and blessed someone out. The other person said a White House car was available, but the President said goddamn it, he wanted his car and only *his* car, not *a* car. The President told the C-11 Post policeman that when *his* car came to tell the driver that he and Mrs. Johnson were *walking*. They walked out the South West Gate; there was still no car.

6/12/66   Lynda, a girlfriend, and two male friends played with the dogs. I told Lynda that Kitty Carlisle said she was pretty. Lynda said coldly she was at a party with Kitty. She didn't seem to appreciate the report a bit.

6/14/66   Ambassador and Mrs. Averell Harriman petted the dogs. Mrs. Harriman said she had a poodle. Some United Nations people came out on the first-floor balcony and watched the dogs. Officer Hill, a lieutenant, tried to ream me out for having Blanco and Beagle out without a leash. I

165

told Lieutenant Hill I was getting sick of people telling me how to take care of the dogs. I said, "Every time I turn around, some son of a bitch is trying to tell me how to take care of the dogs." He apologized, then said he was only afraid one of the dogs would go out the South West Gate. I told him that the dogs would stay with me. Luci had Him. The dogs enjoyed the roast beef.

Mrs. John W. McCormack, the wife of House Speaker, petted the pups in her car. She often comes with her husband and waits for him. She is not well enough to come in. A sweet woman and a great love story, those two.

6/15/66 My God, what a day! Poor Him is dead. Him was chasing a squirrel and Luci's driver, Mr. Dunn, coming in the South West Gate, ran over Him, crushing his rib cage and puncturing his lungs. I went to the south roadway with the pups on a leash and carried Him to the Bouquet Room. Carl Beam put Him on a flower table, cleaned up the blood, and covered Him's body with tissue paper.

That day, LBJ was the saddest I've ever seen him, and the angriest. Luci was about to jump off the Truman Balcony about it. And she swore she was unable to go on with her wedding plans. The President was in an important meeting in the Treaty Room. He screamed at me on the phone: "Can't you make those guys control their speed?"

I knew he was screaming to keep from crying. I will never cease being grateful to Lynda Bird, who was a sane and sensible presence in the midst of chaos. She was kindness itself and understanding. She also was afraid I was going to have a heart attack and got a White House doctor. Then it was my turn to be on tranquilizers.

Him was cremated, and for a long time afterwards the President grieved for his unusual friend. I didn't think he could ever care again about a dog to such a degree. But then it happened, as if by a miracle, and appropriately on Thanksgiving Day at the LBJ ranch—the President had himself another dog.

This one was not a beagle or even a distinguishable breed, but a tiny, funny-looking white mongrel named Yuki, which means "snow" in Japanese. Luci had given the dog a Japanese name for some obscure reason—she said at the time that "Yuki" meant "white." She had the right to name it in any language she chose because she'd saved the dog from the dog pound when she picked it up whimpering at a filling station on her way to dinner at the ranch.

166

Before LBJ found Yuki and Yuki found LBJ, a lot of things happened that concerned us. Good things and bad. Three men were killed on June 19 in the President's Regatta on the Potomac, for example. And to add to my own worries, an agent returning from Camp David said the way Blanco roams around there, it will be a miracle if he doesn't end up shot by the military guards.

Day by day Luci's wedding came closer. Mrs. Johnson was perhaps the happiest of anyone. The President ribbed her about how she'd been happy herself with a simple $2.50 ring from Sears, Roebuck, but now seemed intent on breaking him with the most expensive wedding in history for her daughter.

A watering ban had been proclaimed but the gardeners watered the White House lawns after midnight so the public wouldn't know. They were determined to have green grass for Luci's wedding and reception.

7/29/66 Mrs. Johnson is on cloud nine over Luci's happiness. Lady Bird walked around the South Grounds looking at the shrubbery and flowers. She came back close to C-11 Post, lay down on the grass, and played with Kim and Freckles. She laughed like a young girl. One time Freckles was on top of her romping playfully. I told Mrs. Johnson that I missed Him very much. She said, "I do too, Mr. Bryant, Him had a special personality." She is thrilled for Luci.

A small cloud of another kind hung over the wedding—sort of an atomic cloud, left over from World War II. The Friends of Japan, an organization of Japanese and Americans, was giving the White House a hard time because the wedding was scheduled for August 6, the twenty-first anniversary of the day the Americans dropped an atomic bomb on Hiroshima in World War II.

Luci was upset about it but explained that the choice of the date had been a personal matter. She hadn't been born when the bomb was dropped and hadn't thought about that tragedy when she planned her wedding. The White House refused to move the wedding to another day.

I felt sorry for both sides. Luci was also hurt that another group was up in arms because her wedding would be held in the National Catholic Shrine, a privilege denied other brides.

Most of the time, though, Luci was in a happy and carefree mood, like everyone else.

167

7/31/66 I went out to C-11 Post just as Luci and Pat drove up in his beat-up Pontiac convertible. Luci had the two pups on her lap and said, "There is Mr. Bryant. Go to your daddy." I took the dogs. Pat said, "Mr. Bryant, I am going to send you a bill if these dogs scratch my car." He sure learns from the master. I told him I would get their toenails clipped and send *him* the bill. They ran into the White House, and a little later Pat came out carrying Luci on his shoulders piggyback. They left by car, yelling and laughing.

Then it was the Prez's turn to be on cloud nine.

8/5/66 The Prez is floating on air. He rolled down his limousine window when he spotted me and said, "Come on, Mr. Bryant. You and the dogs are riding with me to Luci's reception." I was amazed. The pups and I jumped in the car. We went out B-4 gate and the President said, "Stop." He shook hands with people from both sides of the car. He wanted the chauffeur to back up the car, but the Secret Service car was behind us. The White House police were trying to push the people back.

The President said, "Stop pushing the people back." Then he turned to his agent in front—"Tell those goons to stop." The President wanted to shake hands with a little boy, but the little boy was pushed back. We rode to the reception and another White House car brought us back to the White House.

8/6/66 Toot horns, throw rice! Luci's wedding day! I took the three dogs to Luci and Pat as they posed for their official photos. They petted the dogs. One of the pups started chewing Luci's bouquet. She had laid it on the ground. They both grabbed me and thanked me for everything. It's a pity they bothered to water the grass. No one can see the grass for the thousands of guests. It was a beautiful wedding reception and about everyone was worn out. I worked seven days this week. Luci yelled at me above the noise: "This all happened because I wanted just my immediate family and friends. My parents invited only the immediate nation."

Some mighty funny things happened at the wedding, but the picketing conducted in front of the White House by the Friends of Japan wasn't one of them. They had been there all through the night in what they called the Hiroshima Day Fast, Penance, and Vigil. Another group of picketers, this time war protesters, showed up for the wedding ceremony at the National Shrine of the Immaculate Conception carrying two open coffins and a sign, WEDDING RICE FOR STARVING VIETNAMESE—DEPOSIT HERE. I didn't see this group myself, as I was on duty at the White House, awaiting the reception guests.

168

The reception had its tense moments, too. First and foremost were the problems with the wedding cake, which stood in the East Room and was eight feet high. By mistake the cake had thirteen tiers. So to prevent bad luck, they called the flowers on top the fourteenth tier, and poor Liz Carpenter, who was in charge of press relations for the cake and the bride, wanted all the reporters to be sure to call it fourteen and not thirteen. Then in the crush, the cake almost toppled over and the President had to steady it. And the bride couldn't cut through the hard crust which the chef had put on the frosting to keep it beautiful, and the bridegroom tried to help her by pressing down on top of her hand.

Still the cake wouldn't yield, and all the guests were waiting. Once again the Prez saved the day, this time by putting his strong mitt over both their hands and applying heavy pressure, finally getting the knife through the iron icing.

Some whispering went on backstairs that Barbara Howar was trying to repay the Johnson family for the humiliation of being dropped from the prenuptial plans. She showed up for the wedding in a "bridelike" gown of white.

On the lighter side, too, was Justice William O. Douglas introducing his own twenty-three-year-old bride, a beautiful girl named Cathy, who seemed to delight the President.

Toward the end of Luci's reception the President got a little wistful because it was almost time for his daughter to leave on her honeymoon. The Prez stood with a bemused look on his face on the Truman Balcony, with little Courtney in his arms, surveying the mob below.

That is the scene I'll always remember when I think of Luci's wedding. That and the big to-do over those damn flowers on top of the wedding cake—the same ones that were called tier number fourteen.

Out of the blue, the Agriculture Department had called the White House to say that the lilies of the valley that were going to be on top of the cake were poisonous, or at least could cause hallucinations and speeding up of the heart if tiny bits of them got on the cake.

This problem was Bess Abell's baby, as social secretary, and she did some quick reseach. Then she had the flowers sprayed with a clear plastic coating that wouldn't kill them or the guests.

Happiness about Luci's marriage must have eased the pain still in the President's heart about the death of his pet dog, Him.

8/7/66 The President told me to go out to Mr. Deason's on Kennedy Drive (of all names) and pick up the new beagle, a gift from J. Edgar Hoover to replace Him. Deason showed me his dogs, including a Russian wolfhound. He had invited me and all the dogs to his sitting room on the ground floor. A cousin of the President, with the Johnson name, had been staying with the Deasons during the wedding festivities and we drove her to the White House to say goodbye and then to the airport to catch her plane for Texas. She definitely seems to think Lynda Bird will soon be marrying her movie star. She said Lynda told her that she positively will not have a big wedding like Luci's.

The Prez is still busy with wedding guests, including late-arriving George Hamilton, and he showed off his new dog to them and to Lady Bird. LBJ said he is calling it "J. Edgar," as J. Edgar Hoover, his good friend, gave it to him. He said the dog's father was sold for a fantastic amount of money. Lynda Bird started teasing her father for having, for once, come up with a name on his own for his dog. And everyone laughed and kidded him about his "originality."

Lynda and George Hamilton took the dogs for a late walk on the South Grounds and gave me the dogs at 11:40 P.M. I gave Mr. Hamilton his billfold that he had misplaced earlier. I found it and I didn't count the money. I just checked for his name. He was mildly surprised. He acted like he didn't know it was missing; he said, "Oh, thanks," in an offhand way as if money meant nothing, but he offered no reward.

8/10/66 The Prez wanted to know if the dogs missed Luci. I said, "I'm sure they do." There he goes again. I think he means *he* misses Luci, who's off on her honeymoon. He hates to show how soft and sentimental he is. *He* loves Luci.

8/11/66 Lynda was talking to honeymooner Luci on the telephone. After Lynda left, I went into the Usher's Office and Mr. Hare was telling a secretary, Barbara Keene, "You know, Luci said she and Pat were reading." Miss Keene burst out laughing. "So that's what newlyweds do."

In August the President had a special treat. He took Courtney and her family to the ranch.

8/15/66 The Prez returned from Texas. He held Courtney at the window while they were landing so she could see Blanco and Beagle. The President carried her off the helicopter.

8/18/66 Luci and Pat Nugent returned at 9:00 P.M. from their honeymoon. They got out of the White House car and started calling for the beagles and Blanco, just like Luci's daddy. I told Luci Freckles was in heat. Pat told Luci, "Freckles will be a mother before you are." Luci said, "I should hope so." Luci told the pups she sure missed them. I told Luci that the dogs had missed Luci.

The ushers ordered the dogs' tags. They got #74, #75, and #76. I told them I had to have #208, #209, and #1 for Edgar, the new top dog of the country.

The Prez had scored only 50 percent with his name. We had to drop the J. Who could yell, "Here, J. Edgar, here, J. Edgar"?

8/21/66   Mr. Valenti sent me a fancy box of cigars from the Philippines. The card said, "With my compliments, Jack." It was a nice surprise.

On August 27, Doris and I set out on a camping trip to California. We were back in Washington exactly one month later.

9/30/66   Prez saw me and asked me if my vacation was over. He told me to call Mr. Woodward, president of American Airlines, and arrange for Edgar to fly to Austin to breed with Luci's dog, Kim. He said Luci called him and said Kim was in heat. He asked me why Edgar didn't breed with Freckles. I told the President that Edgar was more interested in Mr. Deason and beagle field trials. He can't be bothered with females.

10/12/66   I know Lynda is thinking of marriage. She brought out her bicycle and rode around the driveway of the south roadway a few times. She petted Blanco and Freckles. She said she thought Freckles was bred too soon. I explained that the President wanted Freckles to have pups. She said maybe when she got married she would get a pup. She mentioned that she took the dogs for a walk last night. An agent said she got teed off at her mother after an argument and took the dogs for a walk to cool off.

10/14/66   Mrs. Johnson met the press in the Jacqueline Kennedy Garden. I told her Freckles was expecting a blessed event about October 23, when she and the President will be on a trip to the Philippines. The only thing she wanted to know is if they would arrive in time to be Christmas presents. No wonder her husband calls her "a very practical lady."

10/21/66   I see in the paper today that Lady Bird has had her picture taken with a kangaroo in Canberra, Australia. She made a little beautification history even in Australia, planting an Arizona cypress tree overlooking a lake.

Freckles went to Fort Myer to have her pups.

10/25/66   I visited Freckles at Fort Myer. A young vet came to the White House to fetch her puppy doghouse so she could get used to it

171

before the pups come. A vet stays near her twenty-four hours a day. Last night she tried to get in the vet's cot, which is in the same room. She has been trying to build a nest, so it can't be long.

10/26/66 Freckles' pups were born at 6:30 to 10:30 A.M.—five of them. I got a call at 10:40 A.M. She had three females and two males. The President was notified immediately. Usher Pierce phoned the news to Willie Day Taylor in Manila to relay to LBJ.

Usher Pierce also called Luci in Austin. Pat Nugent then called me and told me Kim too was going to be a mother about December 17. I asked him about Luci and he said, "Here she is." It was so nice to hear her voice. She said, "Hello, grandfather," and laughed. She said that she missed the dogs and also me. They may get up here before Christmas. I told Luci that Blanco missed her very much.

11/2/66 I went to Fort Myer and brought Freckles and her pups home. The President held one of the pups before entering the elevator. He said he received my telegram about the pups. I told the President he couldn't keep the announcement of the pups' birth from the press much longer. He said it was up to Liz Carpenter.

11/3/66 Frank, the White House photographer, made some pictures of Freckles and the pups. I ordered three pounds of beef and two pounds of liver for Freckles. She deserves it.

11/4/66 Walking out of his office with Marvin Watson on his way to the helicopter to fly to Texas, President Johnson motioned to me with his hands cupped as if a person was dipping water out of a stream. I told the Prez the dogs were too little to go to Texas. He said, like a hurt little boy, "I just want my picture made with the dogs." He took the three dogs and walked to the East Steps by the South Portico and sat down and waited humbly—most unusual for him. Two doormen rushed out with the five pups, so I removed the older dogs from the camera range.

12/11/66 Lynda and her Secret Service agent came into the pups' room and played with them. She said she took one of the pups over to the President's office—the pup tore her hose and wet the President's rug. Lynda said the Henry Duponts want a female pup, but we would keep one male named "Bo" for Beauregard and one female named "Chinkapen" after Luci, as when she was a child she called Luci "Chinkapen." She said Kim was expecting this month. Lynda had on a long robe. I had to pry the pups' teeth from her hemline a couple of times, as their teeth are like needles.

12/12/66 I showed Mrs. Johnson the new pictures of the pups. She made a face, liking them. One pup was inside my boot, two were wrestling, and the rest were in their puphouse.

12/13/66   Luci's Kim had four pups. Luci delivered them herself. What a footnote for history! She's probably the only President's daughter to be a midwife.

12/15/66   President Johnson called for me to take all five pups to the Oval Family Sitting Room, on the second floor; he played with the pups and Lynda picked out two pups to keep. Lynda told the President that Luci had promised all four of Kim's pups. Very hurt, the President said, "She should have saved me one." Mrs. Johnson said, "Now, now, Lyndon, you have two beagles and a collie and two pups."

I told the President he shouldn't let the pups run on the floor as they might damage the rug. He did it anyway, so they did it anyway. What a mess!

Later that evening he told Mr. Fleming to get me on the *Today* TV program, as he said I did a good job on the other TV shows, like *To Tell the Truth*. I didn't know he saw it, as that was the day of Him's tragic death. Then the Prez called for Joe Califano to come to the second floor and told him he could have his pick of the pups for his boys.

Lady Bird said I could have my pick of the dogs too, but I said no, thanks, I live in an apartment and have a free-flying bird that might get nervous with a frisky puppy.

12/16/66   The Prez brought Mr. and Mrs. Califano and their two boys over and they picked out a male pup. One pup went over and wet on the paper—by lucky chance. The Prez said, "See, Mr. Bryant has them trained already." The two boys were very happy.

In the years to come I'm sure Califano was sorry he ever saw the pups, and I know the President was sorry he'd been so generous. They started a tug of war that caught me in the middle, as you will see in the diary to come.

As the year was coming to a close I knew that Lynda was desperate to have her situation with her movie star boyfriend resolved one way or another. As Lyndon put it bluntly, "No girl wants to be the older sister of a younger sister who is married and pregnant."

Some insiders at the White House said that Lynda would just die of mortification if Georgie didn't marry her. But others said Georgie would never propose because he was afraid of being under the thumb of Lyndon and having to account to him for any time he spent away from his daughter.

The word was that Lynda Bird was panicky about not spending Christmas with George and even offered to go to Germany, where he was making a movie. Hamilton told her it wouldn't be a good idea.

173

"Poor girl," they said of her around the White House, "she's trying too hard. How will she ever keep up with him after marriage?"

LBJ, who had served in World War II, let slip in an unguarded moment while playing with the dogs that he "just couldn't understand" a well-fixed man who wriggled out of going into the service of his country "because his mother needed him." He said he understood George had a couple of other brothers and wondered what was wrong with them.

"I just can't see him on the ranch," said Lyndon. "I don't understand him. I don't know if he can be home folks. Pat is home folks. Why can't Lynda ever attract herself a young fellow like that?" And a little later he added, "She's the smartest one and the one I worry about most. That doesn't make sense, does it?"

I said it did, if you thought about it.

Another time he burst out with the information that George Hamilton changed clothes three times a day—"How does he have time for anything else?" he demanded. It turned out Hamilton had given an interview to *This Week* magazine, and Johnson had had the misfortune of reading it with his Sunday paper. In it, Hamilton had told how he felt about American women—how he thought of them as drum majorettes and cheer leaders and how it was such a "drag" and that they made you feel you had to marry them.

Lyndon had been more than generous with Lynda Bird. For her graduation from the University of Texas he had given her a gift of a two-month trip to all the romantic places of Europe. It meant that she lost out on a lot of the partying and wedding planning of her little sister. That was part of Lyndon's reasoning, and he didn't mind telling me, "I don't want her to feel too bad about her little sister getting ahead of her like this. Shucks now, she might even come back with that slick Hollywood boy out of her hair."

Of course, Lynda Bird came back in time for Luci's wedding. But George Hamilton did not make the scene to be a charming member of the wedding party until everyone was already seated in the church. And Lynda was not as happy as she should have been, even if she did catch the wedding bouquet. But Lyndon was a sly man and he knew what he was doing. To tell the truth, I had a feeling that Lyndon, loving kids the way he did, wasn't going to let Lynda cheat him out of grandchildren, even if he had to round up some "home folks" fellow himself.

174

15

1967 was really wild. It was "The Year of Lynda," and "The Year of the Baby." Or babies. It was "The Year of Yuki." It was "The Year of the Fighting Catbird." And it was the year LBJ was on the warpath, frequently exclaiming, "Everybody's taking advantage of my good nature," as the White House became more and more the dog dumping ground for all and sundry.

If LBJ was good-natured about it, he didn't let it show—he made it hard on the people who dumped their dogs on him. But while the Prez was hurting, the staffers around him got many a laugh out of the situation, and behind his back we renamed the White House "The Dog Hotel."

It all started pleasantly enough with Luci phoning from Texas on January 2 to tell me she was sending me a puppy for her daddy and for me to save one of Freckles' pups for her. But Lyndon was not happy because at the same time Lynda Bird had announced she was definitely keeping two puppies—a male and a female—and that she had promised another puppy to the Duponts. In fact, Lynda directed me to hide her pups when the Duponts came so they wouldn't try to get either of the two she had picked for herself.

Lyndon was upset. "Where are my dogs?" he asked. "Everybody is taking my dogs." He went through the list—"Luci took Him to Texas. Now she has four pups. Lynda picked out two pups. Luci and Lynda don't have any business keeping the pups." He sounded hurt.

I said, "Right, Mr. President, they are your dogs."

My diary for that day, January 8, shows other dog business as well:

Mr. Deason called me at 11:00 P.M. and said he showed the President a screened cart for taking pups out in the sunshine. He said the Prez told him to get Bryant to show the White House carpenters how to make one.

Me pushing a dog baby carriage is all the press needs to see. This is one I hope the Prez forgets.

175

1/10/67 Blanco bit Edgar now that he doesn't have Him to push around. I sent him to Fort Myer, where they put a stitch in his foot. The President gave his State of the Union speech to Congress and returned to the White House. I told the President he made a good speech. He thanked me and said, surprised, "Mr. Bryant, did you listen to it?" I said, "I keep pretty good track of you, Mr. President."

When Mrs. Dupont came with her twenty-seven-year-old son, Lynda wasn't there, as far as I know, but they did get a pup—the one whose picture had been made standing in my boot.

Then it was Luci's turn to be generous and give one of the pups to Dr. Kraskin, the optometrist who had taught her to coordinate her eyes for reading and given her a job.

It took weeks for me to corner LBJ to get his okay to let another puppy go. He was furious with Luci and cussed her and Pat out over the long-distance phone. Luci soothed him by promising to send one of Kim's pups immediately as a trade, and Lady Bird chimed in to help, telling him he would still have three pups plus his grown dogs. But he wasn't buying it. He avoided me for days to delay his decision after I sent him a note in his night reading.

The innocent Dr. Kraskin, who showed up so cheerfully with his sons to pick out a pup, may learn here for the first time about the hell Luci and I went through to make their happiness possible.

As a matter of fact, the President, after putting a "See me" on my request, never did finish fighting it, and eventually I'd just gone ahead and told Kraskin to come get the pup. With LBJ, I'd learned, silence sometimes meant consent.

LBJ punished me for "trying to steal" his puppies by reaming me out for letting Edgar get too fat and decreed that he must be kept "in a room by himself so he can't eat the other dogs' food." I moved Edgar into the Bouquet Room, where the dogs had never been welcome to begin with. My diary records the result.

1/17/67 I left Edgar in a corner of the working area of the Bouquet Room and the flower people—Rusty and Jimmy and Carl—are shocked and angry at me. I told them it would be only temporary and it's presidential orders. Someone said, "Then let the President order the dogs to make the bouquets. There's no room here for humans to work."

On the day Dr. Kraskin came for his dog, the President sent for me to complain that Edgar had "vomited up grass" on the rug in his Oval Office.

1/24/67 I told the Prez that Edgar's food was cut down and he has started to eat some grass, and I explained dogs do that if their stomach is upset. Edgar's not happy.

The President isn't happy either. The Hill didn't like the requests he sent up today.

The President was also driving everyone slightly nuts about his dog run.

2/1/67 Mr. Deason, Mr. Nash Castro, Mr. Williams, and a couple of Capital Parks men came in to survey for a dog run outside President Johnson's office. Also Lieutenant Starkoff, a White House policeman. Mr. Castro told me later that it was too large; he was going to talk to Mrs. Johnson and see if she would go along with him. I called Mr. Deason and he said he didn't want to make it small, since this time next year I would probably have more dogs. Heaven forbid. Usher Pierce was worried about security. I told him I had notified the Secret Service. Also I asked Mr. West about a sign on doors leading to the North Grounds so the dogs wouldn't be let into the North Grounds by people passing through. Chief Usher West turned request down.

2/2/67 Lady Bird saw the light on in the Bouquet Room. She opened the door. All the dogs started to bark and howl and run to the door. I called them back. Mrs. Johnson said, "Oh! My goodness," and slammed the door.

2/3/67 Deason returned to the White House for another conference on the dog runway. It will now be L-shaped. Edgar went home with Mr. Deason.

Mr. Williams is ordering some shrubbery and trees to hide the dog run. It's part of Mrs. Johnson's beautification program to screen unsightly things. I told the Press Information Office and Mrs. Carpenter's to keep the news of the dog run quiet for the present time.

Usher Hare complained to me that when I wasn't there he had to take the small pup Little Chap to the second floor for the President and the pup wet on him on the way. I said cheerfully, "You have all the luck."

2/13/67 Simone Poulain had me come in early and I took two pups to the President's office for a picture with Vicky Solomonson, the darling little blond granddaughter (age six) of the Vice President. Mrs. Humphrey takes Vicky around the country showing what retarded children can do with proper schooling.

2/15/67 Christine Anderson called me and said Mrs. Johnson's hairdresser saw Freckles in a tree this morning and thought she was going out of her mind. She couldn't believe it. I said, "Believe it." I took Christine to the paulownia tree that Freckles climbs when she is following a squirrel that races up that tree. Freckles goes about ten feet up and leaves all the other dogs down on the ground barking furiously and trying to do the same thing. Once Lady Bird phoned to see if Freckles needed help to get down; she told me that everyone was worried about a dog in a tree. I told her not to worry, that Freckles can jump up *and* down.

I mentioned that 1967 was the year of the babies. The first one almost made history by being born in a White House reception room. During a reception for a group of congressmen, Mrs. Richard S. Schweiker—now a senator's wife, but whose husband then represented Philadelphia in the House—started having severe labor pains. She didn't even dare take time to say goodbye to her hostess, Lady Bird, or to the President, but just flew out of there with her husband and rushed down the street directly to George Washington Hospital. They made it just in time.

Before February was over, Mrs. Johnson managed to get rid of another dog by offering a pup to her Secret Service agent Jerry Kivett, for his son. Jerry got Beauregard, and he took the dog home muttering that he sure as hell hoped Bo could manage to get along with his cat, because weight-wise they'd be evenly matched in any fight.

Early in March, the First Lady revealed at a Capitol Hill luncheon that she was going to become a grandmother; Luci was pregnant. Scores of reporters started calling the White House to confirm the big news so Liz Carpenter's office made it official. And Luci finally admitted it in Texas, when reporters caught up with her outside St. Francis Xavier Catholic Church, near the ranch, where she had gone to 9:00 A.M. Mass.

Luci was in great form, giggling when someone asked her if she might have twins and saying she didn't care what she had as long as it was a boy or a girl.

About this time construction was finished on a proper doghouse and new dog runs. A certain amount of peace returned to the White House, but it wasn't to last for very long.

3/3/67 The dog pen outside of the President's office now has shrubbery all the way around the fence.

3/7/67 The Prez asked which dog I like best. I told him I like them all the same, all equally. He's happy again because he has something to

178

complain about besides his shower. The new doghouse isn't good enough. He has shown it to all his friends and each one has a different idea. LBJ says the doghouse gets only a C— rating. He said the doghouse is too small and too cold and asked me if it is heated. I told him we could get it enlarged and have it wired to heat it with electricity. He nodded his head.

I went to the Usher's Office and Nash Castro of Capital Parks Service was there drinking coffee. I told him what was needed. He looked at me strangely, and asked me to show him the doghouse.

3/8/67 Mr. Deason called me. Capital Parks is going to make the doghouse two feet longer and put in electric heat.

The President was still fussing and fuming. It wasn't good enough.

3/9/67 Freckles and Blanco jumped the new dog fence when the Ellipse cannons were fired during a formal arrival ceremony at 1:30 P.M. Freckles' pup, Dumpling, hurt her right rear leg. Usher Scouten said they would put an L-angle barrier on top of the fence if Mr. Deason agreed. I called Mr. Deason. He didn't like the idea.

3/10/67 Freckles jumped the fence. I called Deason again. He said I should have called him three minutes earlier, as he had just told Rex Scouten to forget it. He came in and took Edgar out for a hunt in the woods about twenty-five miles from his home. He said he called Scouten back and told him to proceed with the angle on top of the fence.

3/12/67 Now the dogs have *two* doghouses with electric heat and a floodlight. The Prez showed it all to little Courtney. Courtney liked it. LBJ liked it.

3/13/67 Califano's secretary, Peggy Hoxie, called and said the Prez okayed Califano's dog George to stay at the White House. I went over and got George, who had just messed on Califano's rug. I asked Peggy, "Where is the dog's food?" She looked amazed. I told her that I tried to keep the President's dog-food bill down. She said she would notify Mr. Califano.

LBJ zoomed off on another trip, this time to Guam.

3/21/67 What a reunion! President Johnson returned from Guam at 7:15 P.M. It was sprinkling rain. Including Califano's, I had six dogs to meet him. The Prez went down the doggie receiving line, patted each dog on the head, and shook a few paws. Earlier, Mrs. Carpenter was in the Usher's Office. She was concerned that the President would return alone with no one to greet him, so she wanted a log fire in the Diplomatic Reception Room. Mr. Pierce objected, but the fire was built.

179

Hell, I'd say he had greeting enough.

Mrs. Gonella said her dog is lonely. She wants to bring her Honey in to play with our dogs a few days. I told her to get permission from the President of the United States; these decisions are too big for me.

3/24/67   Mr. Califano's dog, George, was escorted to his home. Good riddance!

3/30/67   Valenti's secretary called me and said Mr. Valenti was in the Virgin Isles and Beagle almost landed in the pound for running away from home. So I took a deep breath and told her, okay, send Mr. Valenti's dog to the White House and be sure to send some dog food.

Luci arrived from Texas with more dogs—Kim and Astro.

4/4/67   Luci called for her dogs last night. J. B. West and a doorman went to get the dogs. They couldn't find the light switch. The doorman was laughing because Mr. West was under the influence of too much bubbly. So I told the doorman about the time Pushinka and I got high on eggnog at one of the Kennedys' parties. No one told me it was spiked. Pushinka lapped up almost as much of it as I did and ate a whole bowl of shrimp as well. The next day she had a hangover, and so did I.

4/5/67   Luci called for her dogs after 1:00 A.M. I was gone. The engineers didn't know which dogs were hers. She finally had to come and get her own dogs and she was mighty upset. She wanted to know where Bryant was.

Chief Engineer Chester Burkette got excited today and told Usher Pierce to put Luci's name on the collars. Mr. Williams and Mr. Ruback talked to me about it. I told them not to bother and just to put a note on the door: "Kim and Astro have beaded collars, in the room with Blanco and Edgar."

An agent told me that not long before, during a visit to the ranch. LBJ got furious because Luci's dogs, Kim and Astro, were chasing his sheep. He called Luci at her home in Austin and told her to come get her dogs or he would have the Secret Service agent shoot them dead. I'll bet he meant it—almost. Anyway, she came a-running.

4/18/67   LBJ and his family returned from Texas about 12:30 P.M. I told the President that Blanco had bit Edgar on the head. The President said, "Did you whip him?" I told him no, that I took Edgar to Fort Myer immediately, and they put some wire stitches in his head.

I'll never forget the first time I learned to recognize Joseph Califano, the President's chief legal counsel, who later became chief counsel of the Democratic party:

4/20/67 President Johnson and two other gentlemen walked over to the dog pen. I walked to the other gate and all the beagles left the President and ran to me. The President complained mournfully, "You are getting the dogs away from me." Then he said, "Who are all these dogs?"

I told the President that Mr. Califano brought his dog, George, in for ten days and didn't bring any food for him. I said I had asked his secretary about the food and she'd said to bill them. The two gentlemen were standing with the President at the gate. The President said, "You know Mr. Califano is rough." I said, "Maybe, but he's Number Two man."

They laughed and circled around the south driveway once. Meanwhile I asked an agent if one of the two men was Mr. Califano. He said he didn't know; he was a new agent. So I asked a regular agent. He said yes and pointed Califano out—a dark-haired, good-looking man.

They circled back and the Prez said, "What about the dog barking in the pen, whose is that?"

I told him it was Mrs. Gonella's beagle, Honey. I said, half kidding, that she never brought any food either, so that dog wasn't eating too well.

The Prez still acted confused and asked me how come little Honey was in the pen? I told the President that I told Mrs. Gonella long ago to get permission from the President or Mrs. Johnson before bringing her dog in, so I assumed somebody gave her permission. And if not, I added, a little huffy myself by this time, we could haul her off to jail right now—dog and owner both.

I could see the President was very pleased with the answer. But he wasn't through yet. He said, "You know, Mr. Califano is a rough fellow. He has a lot of people afraid of him around here."

I said I could get along with anybody who supplies his own dog food. Mr. Califano smiled sheepish-like and said, "We get along all right."

Ashton Gonella called me about 6:40 P.M. very humble and asked if her dog could stay overnight. She said that the President was giving her a hard time and asked her who gave her permission to bring her dog. She said she would bring in three cans of Ken-L Ration.

The simple truth is, the President was back on the warpath about his dog-food bills. He had complained before during his early White House days, when he merely fed two, three, or four dogs of his own a little fancy hamburger. But that bill was nothing compared with what it cost to buy dog food when the dogs began to have puppies, and the puppies grew up and had puppies, and one hell of a dog explosion was underway.

The Prez might have put up with the higher bill, but what he couldn't stand was that people were taking his puppies away from him and then reserving the right to bring them back at a moment's notice to be left a day, a week, a month, or even longer.

Secretaries who were traveling with the President or who were just going off on their own vacations left their dogs at the White House. Jack Valenti left his dog on nearly permanent loan. Luci was running a dog shuttle service between Austin, Texas, and the White House, and the White House carpenter's shop had even made her special shipping crates.

But what seemed to get the President's dander up most and bring out his fighting spirit was that his top aide, Joe Califano, dumped his dog off at the White House kennel and seemed to forget him completely.

The President harassed me steadily about all the unwanted dogs and the food bills. So I decreed that everyone who parked a dog there had to leave dog food as well. Now and then a few cans of dog food would trickle in, but mostly the hotel we ran stayed a free one. Still, I think the President got his money's worth in the needling he was entitled to when the culprits were around. It was his favorite form of relaxation. That, and the trick he tried to play on poor Ashton Gonella, Lady Bird's secretary.

Ashton was one of the sweetest women in the White House and one of the prettiest. She was a favorite with everyone around the place, including the President. But she was one of the most blatant dog parkers. In a gentle, helpless little voice, she was forever talking about taking Honey, a cute beagle, home, but there was always some reason she couldn't. The neighbors complained about the barking. Or the yard needed a fence, or she was going to be away. Company was coming. A hundred and one excuses, each supposedly temporary.

But when she came up with the reason that she was afraid Honey would get pregnant and she must keep her there at the White House for security, it gave LBJ the perfect opening for a fiendish trick. I must admit his sense of humor was about like mine because I cooperated fully. He came to me and said, "Why don't you just go ahead and see if you can get her dog pregnant?"

We both thought it was hilariously funny to pay her back for keeping the dog endlessly at the White House. The little joke between us was a gem. LBJ and I almost doubled up with laughter when Mrs. Gonella would thank us profusely in her gentle voice for taking care of Honey until her yard could be fenced in to protect her virginity.

When the fence was finished and Mrs. Gonella finally dared take Honey home, I told her the fence wasn't going to hold a dog like that, she'd just burrow under it, and that's exactly what happened. Soon Honey was back at the White House. And LBJ and I were back at our old tricks.

There was only one catch to it. For some reason Mother Nature was stepping in and not letting little Honeybun get pregnant.

Here are just a few of the entries in my diary on the subject:

10/19/67 Yuki crapped in the second-floor dining room. 11:00 P.M. I took Yuki to the President's bedroom. LBJ was dressed in evening clothes. He told me I should let Yuki mount Mrs. Gonella's dog. I told him Yuki mounted Mrs. Gonella's dog tonight after dark but didn't get hung up. He smiled. I said "Good night, Mr. President." He said good night.

10/20/67 Yuki mounted Honey, Mrs. Gonella's dog again. Mr. Watson saw me and said the President wanted Yuki. I took Yuki to the President's office door on the West Garden side and released him as the President called to him.

10/22/67 9:30 P.M. I took Yuki to the West Hall. President and Mrs. Johnson had company. The President said he put Yuki in the pen with Mrs. Gonella's dog. I told him I put Yuki with Honey too and this time he got hung up. Mrs. Johnson said, "Oh, don't start on that again."

10/23/67 I took Yuki to the second-floor dining room for the President and his guest Jim Jones. The President asked me if Yuki got with Honey. I told him twice. The President, pleased, asked if I saw them and how long. I told him I had seen and it lasted two minutes each time.

10/26/67 The ushers told me that the President had had Yuki with him all day. I went to his secretary's office and Marie Fehmer called the President on the phone and said, "Mr. Bryant says it's time for Yuki to eat." The President said to send me in. The President told me Yuki was too thin. "He needs a woman." He told me to let Yuki see Mrs. Gonella's dog. I took Yuki to the pen. He got hung up on Honey again.

183

On December 18, 1967, Joseph Califano and Ashton Gonella were both at the Johnson dinner table. The President had sent for me to bring him a few dogs. By this time Califano had finally taken his dog home, but Honey was freeloading as before. Very deliberately, so his guests would get the point, LBJ started asking me about the dogs in residence and the money situation. Was it still costing so much to feed the canine corps, he wanted to know. Then he turned the conversation to Mrs. Gonella's dog—was she still there? I told the President Honey was still aboard, and added that I thought maybe Mrs. Gonella had given him the dog. He asked me if she had brought any dog food. I told him if she had, I hadn't received it.

I could see the President was relishing these answers as poor Mrs. Gonella squirmed. The President was getting ready for a trip to Australia—it was the time Prime Minister Holt was discovered to be missing as he swam in the ocean. I said, "Have a nice trip, Mr. President," and started to leave.

But LBJ was not through yet—he called me back. Now it was Califano's turn. He asked me if Califano had settled up on his dog-food bill. I answered, "Mr. President, you will have to ask Mr. Califano. I understand he has that office adjoining yours."

Poor Califano looked sheepish. LBJ had had his fun, so he was through with the subject. I took the dogs and headed for the door. I had, of course, pretended I didn't know Califano or Mrs. Gonella were there.

That kind of horseplay helped to make the time speed by at the White House in the year of 1967. That and other moments that seemed important then. Little things, when you look back.

Like the day Lassie came to the White House. It was meant to be a big day for Blanco, and I could see the headlines, WHITE COLLIE GREETS GOLDEN COLLIE CELEBRITY AT THE WHITE HOUSE. But it didn't work out that way.

5/3/67 TV dog star Lassie came to the White House. Blanco and I met Lassie coming up the East Garden. Lassie growled. Blanco growled menacingly. TV cameras were rolling, so I had to pull Blanco away fast and the dogs didn't have time to get used to each other. Lassie picked up a piece of paper and deposited it in a trash basket. He posed with Mrs. Johnson; Blanco and I were shown on TV as we left the East Garden. I put a Lassie promotional poster on the beagles' doghouse.

Five days earlier a great Hollywood figure from an earlier time had paid us a visit.

4/28/67 I had the dogs on the South Grounds. Martha Raye and another woman walked out on the grass and petted the dogs. Martha let Dumpling kiss her. Then she made a face and everyone laughed. Same big mouth. I stayed out on the grounds until General William C. Westmoreland arrived for a White House luncheon.

Lynda Bird had been nervous as a kitten and touchy that April. The word was things were not going well in her love life—George Hamilton was just never there when she wanted him. My diary shows how restless and impatient she had become.

4/20/67 I went to the theater to see the movie *Eldorado*. It had run two minutes when Lynda got up and yelled, "Fischer, damn it, I have seen this movie." So there was no movie for anyone.

But Lady Bird was in particularly good spirits those days.

4/24/67 Mrs. Johnson's car drove up to the South Portico. She got out, looked over the roof of the car, and laughed. "It looks like a beagle hunt," she called to me. I had five beagles on leashes. I told her I was escorting the family in to dinner. She laughed again. Later I took the dogs to see Willie Day Taylor. She was talking on the phone. When she saw me, she said, "Here is someone to talk to you." It was Luci in Texas. We talked about her dogs. I had two of Freckles' pups, Little Chap and Dumpling, with me. I asked Luci if she knew where my two dog shipping crates were. She said she gave one to her mother for storing things. She said she would tell Pat to call me about them.

And he did call. I was forever fighting to get my government-property crates back and never making it.

LBJ flew in and out in April, as usual.

4/26/67 President Johnson returned from Germany. He was walking toward the dogs and me but he saw Mrs. Johnson under the canopy at the South Portico. He went to her, kissed her, and then left her immediately to come over and pet Freckles, Dumpling, and Little Chap.

A nasty moment in May had all the backstairs help at the White House snickering.

5/12/67 Mrs. Eisenhower, a former First Lady, attended a Senate wives' dinner. Mrs. Humphrey arrived and petted the beagles. A lady asked her if she would like a dog. She said no. Someone in the background muttered, loud enough for everyone around to hear, that she already had a dog—named Hubert.

I thought at the time that if the Vice President had heard the remark, he would have laughed the loudest of all. He was a pretty nice guy. He had fallen out of favor with some people in the administration because of his views on the war in Vietnam.

Then there was a great moment when my wife and I received an invitation to go to Newport News for the launching of the aircraft carrier to be christened by Caroline Kennedy. All my favorite people were there—Jackie Kennedy, her brother-in-law Robert, and President Lyndon Baines Johnson.

5/27/67 Before the ceremony Mrs. Kennedy was walking toward the platform and I spoke to her. She turned her head, smiled in surprise, and said "Oh, Bryant." I held my breath for poor Caroline when it took her two swings to break the champagne bottle for the christening of the ship. Then President Johnson came by, saw me, and winked and smiled. As Jackie Kennedy was leaving the platform, she saw me and walked over and shook hands with me, my wife, and several other White House people.

A nun behind me asked me to call Robert Kennedy over. I called, "Hey, Bobbie," and he recognized me and came over. I whispered in his ear, "I want you to run for President someday." He smiled, thanked me, and said he might not fight it. He shook hands with my wife and with the nun.

In June our boarder, Honey, had a bit of bad luck. Ashton Gonella was so concerned she took a drastic step.

6/12/67 Emergency: I took Honey to the Fort Myer vets. A bug or bee or several caused a bad lump on her lower right jaw. The vets gave her an antibiotic shot and some pills. Mrs. Gonella was so shocked at Honey's appearance, she took her home, saying that her dog looks like the U.S. ship that the Israeli torpedos hit.

A few days later the White House was stunned to learn that Ferdinand, the pastry cook, had cancer and would probably have to have his leg amputated the next week. I quickly sent a picture of Freckles and her pups to brighten up his hospital room.

6/19/67 Ferdinand's leg amputated today.

But then the mood at the White House took a radical change for the better. LBJ was ecstatic.

186

6/21/67 Luci had a baby boy born this morning. The President let the dogs out of the pen before he celebrated by taking a party out for a boat ride.

Lynda Bird gave me the inside story:

6/23/67 Luci is something else again. Lynda Bird was getting ready for Texas when I told her to tell Luci "Congratulations from Bryant and the beagles." She laughed and started to tell me how Luci surprised the doctors at the hospital. She said some women curse and scream when they are having a baby, but Luci just talked a blue streak about the dogs while she was giving birth.

About this time the President criticized my haircuts, and—nothing new—my weight. "With your G.I. haircut, Mr. Bryant," he said, "you look just like an overweight kewpie doll. And you are feeding my dogs so much they are all going to end up as kewpie dolls."

7/20/67 The Prez had a four-year-old boy in to see him today after arrangements were made on the spot by a White House guide, taking tourists through. The little boy can name all of the Presidents by memory and LBJ is fascinated. He predicted the four-year-old might be including his own name some day if he keeps it up and goes to school.

I was having my usual hassle with people wanting this and that. Joseph Califano wanted a doghouse made for his dog George. If he was hinting that the government might do it, he didn't get very far—several people jumped in and suggested he try Sears, Roebuck or Hechingers. Jack Valenti wanted me to come to his house and help him with some electrical work, but I turned him down politely, saying I had all the overtime I could handle.

Blanco was getting worse rather than better, in spite of tranquilzers. He was totally unimpressed with the honor of living at the White House. I asked Deason to intercede with the President to move him to the ranch, using the precedent of Eisenhower's Heidi for a persuader. But LBJ was like a wall when he didn't want to hear something. I realized I was stuck with Blanco and that I would have to protect everyone from the dog, especially Lyndon's beloved Courtney. Luckily, little Courtney somehow had gotten through to Blanco, and she was about the only one besides Luci who could lead him around by the nose. I think Blanco liked Courtney almost as much as the President did. But I still watched the two pretty

187

carefully as they romped about, remembering Lyndon's warning that if anything happened to that little girl, he'd have my hide on the barn door. He would have, too.

And the President was still looking for a bargain in Unipet vitamin dog candy.

8/8/67   I got the Prez a bottle of Unipets for $2.00 from Friendship Animal Hospital and I called Fort Myer to order some more for $1.19.

Then suddenly we had a freakish situation. A catbird declared war on the White House dogs, especially Blanco and Yuki. The bird was really vicious in its aerial attacks:

8/10/67   I called Dr. Bradford E. Buell, at Fort Myer, and told him to check Yuki's right front paw and ears and Blanco's ear tips, as a catbird has made them raw, and while he was at it to clip all the dogs' toenails.

And then old married Luci was back. And so was the presidential temper.

8/13/67   Luci and Pat returned this evening. She hugged and kissed her dogs. She asked Usher Pierce if I was here.
The President is on a light-turn-off binge in the west basement, blaming me. He said, "Damn it, Bryant, I'm going to have to get someone else to turn off these lights." I told the President I just turned them off in the snack bar and someone else turned them right back on.

In spite of his bark, President Johnson was really happy, and so was I. It was becoming clear that Lynda Bird was in love again. This time LBJ felt he'd been in on things from the start, and highly approved her choice. As he petted his dogs one day, he commented to me with self-satisfaction. "Yes, sir, right at the White House, I provided my daughter with a home-folks fellow." He mulled it over, chuckled to himself, and continued, "I guess you can find anything you need here, Mr. Bryant, right around the White House." And he walked away, looking smug as a bug.

In bits and pieces I learned what there was about Chuck Robb— Marine Captain Charles S. Robb—a White House social aide, that made him the President's kind of choice for his daughter. Lynda couldn't have pleased her father more if she had drawn up a blueprint and put him together or had let Lyndon do it.

Chuck, first of all, knew nothing about Hollywood, and that was in his favor.

Secondly, Chuck was tight with his money, and Lyndon liked that. He had saved every cent and had about $1,500 in the bank, and he had been Lyndon's kind of "poor boy." As LBJ bragged, Chuck "had sold newspapers as a little shaver to help pay for an eye operation for his mother." That really made him a winner.

Then he had a farm background. The farm was in Ohio, but the President forgave him that mistake of locale because he had learned to ride a horse out west in Phoenix, Arizona. And Chuck's father had grown up in Milwaukee, "with an American flag flown every day in the front yard."

"Yeah," said LBJ, "he's a fine young man. Good stock there." But maybe what impressed LBJ most was that Chuck was no high school dropout—something that had distressed LBJ very much about George Hamilton. Chuck had, in fact, won a four-year scholarship at Cornell. His college ROTC and his good record as a Marine were what got him in line to be a social aide at the White House.

I realized that Captain Robb, who was attached to the Marine barracks in Washington as an adjutant, was staying overtime a lot at the White House in the summer of '67, playing bridge with Lynda and her friends. I thought at first he just felt sorry for her because of George Hamilton's absence.

Maybe that's how it started, but by the middle of June I noticed that Lynda was blossoming out again and was all smiles when she was around him. She was no longer suffering. By the end of July it was clear she was in love and they were talking banteringly of marriage.

Lynda Bird herself later let the country know how one night early in August she crawled into bed with Lady Bird and LBJ at 3:00 A.M. She'd done the same thing as a child when she felt lonely, but this time it was to wake them up to tell them that Chuck had popped the question.

Lynda Bird told her sister Luci and her best friend Warrie Lynn Smith on August 15, swearing them to secrecy, and after that I started to get little clues of what was going on. But the engagement wasn't officially announced until September 3, the month before the wedding.

As for how Lynda got rid of George Hamilton, it was easy. The situation had climaxed in July. She was tired of waiting. She was really starting to like Chuck and his brand of good treatment of her

189

and she decided to check out George Hamilton just one more time. The word around the White House was that she wanted to see if she could live without him. So she flew to London in July, and George joined her there, flying in from a movie location in Spain. Lynda compared the two men, and in spite of the spell George had cast over her in the past, she later told her friends she missed Chuck a lot while she was away.

That trip helped Lynda realize, to her own surprise, that there was something to what her daddy had been saying. Maybe she did need a man who treated her like a queen. Chuck made her feel like a star, whereas with George she would always be competing with other stars. Besides, she could never count on him to be there when she needed him. Even with Luci's wedding, she'd had to attend with a White House aide for an escort, Captain Michael Phenner, because George was late in arriving.

Looking back, I'd say Lynda proved again she was a careful shopper. To show you just how careful she could be, here's a story that made the rounds at the White House after the engagement was announced. When Lynda flew back to the States after her final break with George, she brought along a tie she had picked up in London as a gift for Chuck. But on thinking the matter over during the long transatlantic flight, she decided that for an outsider who might or might not propose, the tie was too expensive—$12.00. So she gave it to her daddy instead.

16

I can tell you exactly when I realized LBJ had a new love. Or put another way, that Yuki had taken over the President:

8/21/67   I was bringing some bacon-fat drippings in a coffee can for the dogs. As I opened the door from the house toward the Bouquet Room, the President came by. The President went through the door and turned around and said, "Mr. Bryant, have Yuki washed and combed." He said, "That dog sleeps with me. The dog keeps me warmer than a woman." I had to laugh at his statement. I said "Yes, sir, Mr. President." I washed Yuki.

All kinds of stories had started circulating backstairs about Yuki and how Yuki meant more to the President than any mere human. And how he'd said he'd rather sleep with Yuki than anybody. Several clashes occurred between the White House help and the President during the mornings before I came on duty, and soon everyone was convinced Yuki had to be given top priority. I recorded two characteristic incidents in my diary.

Last week the President told a policeman at C-9 to get Yuki. The policeman, Officer Gibson, thought the President said to tell Bryant to get the dog. The officer dialed the phone. The President said, "Goddamn it, get Yuki." The officer went to the other gate, picked up Yuki and carried him to the President. Now *any* policeman who is told to get the dog has to immediately carry out the President's order.

Last night after I left, the President wanted Yuki again. Doorman General was the lucky guy who got to do the honors, and he rushed upstairs with Yuki. Doorman General—yes, that's really his name—said he got his suit muddy when he carried the dog to the President. He said he put the dog down as he knocked on the President's door. Yuki then leaped on the President's bed. Yuki acted like he owned the place.

Yuki treated royalty and commoners alike.

8/22/67   I had Freckles, Dumpling, and Yuki at C-11 South Portico on the iron bench for the ceremony for the arrival of His Imperial Majesty

191

Rezashah Pahlavi Shahanshah of Iran. The President pointed at the dogs as he was taking the Shah to his office. Marvin Watson told me to let Yuki loose. The two beagles were on a Y leash and they wrapped it around the President's ankles, so I freed the leash. The President took Yuki and the Shah into his office. About half an hour later the President tossed Yuki out, disgusted. Yuki had taken a leak in front of the Shah.

8/27/67 6:00 P.M. A chauffeur brought Yuki to me. The President and his party walked out of the South West Gate to go to the bowling alley. He asked me where Yuki was. I told him I had the dog in the Bouquet Room so he would stay clean.

About 9:30 P.M. Usher Hare called and said the President wanted a Secret Service man to bring Yuki. I told Mr. Hare to get one. He said, "No, you better do it." The President yelled, "Yuki!" Yuki jumped on his lap. The President leaned back and howled. Yuki also threw his head back and sounded a few musical notes. I swear it. Mrs. Johnson walked down the hall. I told her that the President and Yuki were singing. Mrs. Johnson said, "No one would believe it unless they saw it." She shook her head and rolled her eyes toward heaven, as if to say, give me strength. The President told me Yuki was spending the night, so I left.

Eventually Yuki's dulcet tones were even recorded for TV. It was during an interview with Marty Duprey of Greenville, South Carolina. Duprey had called me and asked me for an interview by telephone. I said that if Liz Carpenter's office gave permission for the telephone interview I would even get Yuki to sing a few words on the air if Duprey would *promise* to send me a tape of it.

I did and he did. He sent a seven-inch reel of our whole conversation. Including Yuki singing.

I knew the President would get a big bang out of hearing Yuki sing over the air because I had told him about my deal. LBJ wanted to hear that historic first. I had the Signal Corps make a duplicate of my tape and put it in their file to be ready any time the President wanted to hear it. Then I left word with one of LBJ's secretaries that if I was not around when the President wanted to listen to the tape, the secretary could phone the Signal Corps and they were prepared to play it for the President over the telephone.

8/28/67 Usher Hare called and said that the President wanted Yuki on the second floor. I took the dog up and the President was already in his dining room. I had Yuki on my lap outside the President's rooms. I leaned back to rest my head and Yuki thought I was going to howl like the

President does. Yuki howled so loudly the Prez left the table, came out to West Hall, and yelled for Yuki. I left and went back to my shop, as I was going to work on Lynda's hair drier.

In a minute Lady Bird was on telephone asking me to come back—something was wrong with Yuki. I went directly to their private dining room. The Prez said that Yuki had swallowed a bone without chewing it. He handed me a steakbone and said, "It was just like this one." Johnny, a butler, politely gave me a cloth napkin for the bone. I told them I didn't think it was serious but I would call the vets and let them know. I called Dr. B. E. Buell, who said I should bring the dog to Fort Myer immediately for an x-ray. I went back and told Mrs. J. The Prez was on the phone with Luci. Califano was eating with them. As I was waiting to get on the elevator with Yuki, the President ran out to tell Yuki goodbye. Three x-rays were made. The bone had a sharp point. They gave Yuki some special canned food and poured mineral oil all over it and said he would pass it. I returned and showed the First Lady, Lynda, and her boyfriend the x-rays.

8/29/67 The President personally called Fort Myer this morning and inquired about Yuki. I called Dr. Buell about 3:00 P.M., and he also left me a letter. I gave a copy to Mrs. Roberts and told her to give it to the President before he went to lunch. She didn't but consigned it to his night reading mail. The usher called and said the President wanted to see me immediately. I asked Mrs. Roberts for the letter from Dr. Buell and she called Mr. Watson in the President's office to tell them I was on my way. I gave the President the letter and explained that the dog would be all right. The President said sternly, "Get another x-ray made."

In a day or so, everything was back to normal and the President was off on another kick.

8/31/67 As the President was going to the White House theater, he said he wants Yuki brushed every day. I told Usher Hare, as I am going to be away on a two-week vacation starting Saturday.

9/1/67 5:00 P.M. Usher Carter called and I took Yuki to the President's office. Yuki ran to the President howling. Yuki really loves the President.

9/18/67 I have just returned from my vacation. I shot a Russian wild boar in Tennessee—between 180 and 190 pounds—with a .35-caliber carbine.

10:00 P.M. The President phoned me at home. He is worried about Yuki; he says Yuki doesn't have much pep and should weigh more.

I told the Prez I had been on vacation for two weeks and that I had

193

gone wild boar hunting. He said for me to tell Juanita Roberts how he could get on my payroll so he could take a vacation. He said he would like to go hunting wild boar. He said, "Here comes Yuki." Yuki yelped. Then the President said Yuki had bit him. I told him I would call the vets to find out why Yuki was so cranky.

9/20/67   7:00 A.M. Prez called me at home and said he hated to bother me this early in the morning, but Yuki is listless and almost paralyzed and would I quickly please come right over and take the dog to the vet's or to an expert on dogs. I took Yuki to Fort Myer. My wife drove the car so I could hold Yuki. I told the captain on duty that the President of the United States is very concerned and they have got to save that dog, I don't care how they do it, just do it!

Later that day Yuki was taken from Fort Myer to Friendship Animal Hospital for a series of tests. Then he was brought back to the White House for at least a day or two while the vets arranged for him to enter Benson Animal Hospital. The Prez told Mr. Pierce, an usher, that "Yuki meant more to him than anything in the White House." Even Mrs. Johnson petted Yuki tenderly that day.

9/24/67   10:00 P.M. I took Yuki to the second-floor kitchen and washed his paws. Then I took him to the Prez's bedroom and put him in the middle of the bed between Mrs. Johnson and President Johnson.

The Prez asked me if I was personally taking the dog to Benson Animal Hospital at 7:00 A.M. tomorrow morning. I told him Usher Pierce was sending the dog over as I have an 8:45 dental appointment.

A few days later I went searching for the President. I had some good news and some bad.

9/26/67   Yuki is back. He does not have heartworms, but he does have a parasite, *Dipetalonema.* Also a ligament in one of his rear legs is torn, which causes the kneecap to jump out. Yuki will have to be operated on soon. I took Yuki to the President's bedroom at 11:30 P.M. Here I found the pajama-clad Prez in a happy domestic scene, reading some personal mail in bed. He asked me kindly to turn out the ceiling light as he turned on his fluorescent bedlamp. I said "Good night, Mr. President."

9/28/67   The President took Yuki to Texas with him. I told Pat to send my two dog crates back to the White House.

9/29/67   I worked on the electric heaters in the two doghouses.

10/1/67   Blanco bit George on the right front leg last night. I took George to Fort Myer at 4:00 P.M. It took three stitches to patch him up. I asked the vet about some rough spots on George's ears. He scraped a particle off onto a glass slide and examined it under microscope. He said George had ringworm, contagious to humans and other animals. He asked me if I wanted some treatment. I said no as George was leaving the White House as soon as I can make arrangements. I called Califano at home and told him that Blanco had bitten his dog and that he should take him to a private vet to be treated for ringworm. He said he would come get him in the morning. He said if George had it he got it from our dogs, and that was where George got bronchitis. I got a little hot. I told him we gave our dogs pills three times a day for three weeks after George left the White House.

I didn't tell Califano everything I wanted to say but I was so burned up, I let off a little steam that day in my diary:

Some people are as inconsiderate as hell. That S.O.B. should be grateful his kids didn't get ringworm. The dog has been here for over a month. If he doesn't want the dog he should give it away.

The President, Lynda, and Yuki returned from Texas about one o'clock in the morning on October 1, and I was there to meet them with Freckles and Dumpling. LBJ came right over to see us and I told him about about Blanco biting George and about George's ringworm.

10/2/67 This is "Take your dog to the vet of your choice" day. Joe Califano's secretary, Peggy, called me at home and said a White House chauffeur would drive Califano's dog, George, home at 2:45 as he has a 3:30 date with the vet. I called Mrs. Gonella and told her to take her dog to the vet for a checkup. Then at 10:30 P.M. I took Yuki to the second-floor private dining room. Califano and Marie Fehmer were dinner guests. The President said Mr. Califano had quoted his private vet as saying that his dog did not have ringworm. I decided not to argue. Lynda, who was also at the table, said she had a message for me from Luci and her vet. Luci wants me to feed Yuki a dry cereal, Purina, for his health.

The next day I picked up Califano's challenge.

10/3/67 I called Fort Myer and they verified that Mr. Califano's dog has ringworm.

10/4/67 I called Mrs. Gonella and told her that Honey is in the pen with Blanco and Little Chap and that her dog might get bit. She pleaded with me to keep her dog at the White House because she is having problems. Her neighbors complain about her dog's barking. She sounded so pathetic I told her I'd try to save the dog from the others. I let Yuki play in the pen with Honey and Little Chap until dark because Lynda says Yuki likes to play with the beagles. I call Yuki the "poor little rich dog" because he spends so much time in the presence of the President he loses out on getting to play with his own species.

11:10 P.M. Mr. Hare called and said that the President wanted Yuki. The door to the President's bedroom was partially open. I said, "Mr. President?" He answered and walked out of his bathroom wearing only his pajama top. "Hold Yuki until I get my bottoms on," he said, and walked bare-assed into his bedroom. Vice President Humphrey was in the room for a conference. Well, that's show business.

LBJ loved to parade around nude in his bedroom. He was proud of his physique, and he had a lot to be proud of. He was a big man—6 foot 3 and well-proportioned. Somehow he stayed in condition, and it was amazing how slim and strong he looked without clothes. And all man.

I guess Lady Bird's diet control deserved a lot of credit even though he was always falling off the diet whenever he found a dish of ice cream to fall into. And he loved that combination of nuts and popcorn and caramel called Fiddle-Faddle. At a White House reception, when Lady Bird wasn't watching, he'd reach behind him and snitch a chunk of Fiddle-Faddle.

10/5/67   Ashton Gonella picked up Honey about 7:00 P.M. She said she owed me some dog food. Then she noticed that one of our dogs had chewed up the leather handstrap of her chain leash. I said I do the best I can. Usher Hare told me that Mrs. Gonella told him that Bryant had raised so much hell that she was taking her dog home. I told Usher Hare that she gave me a dirty look about her leash. I said to Hare, "This isn't a public kennel. It's only for the President's dogs. We've got enough problems of our own." Freckles is in heat, and twice today Yuki jumped over the gate to the dog pen. I left a request for a higher block over the two gates. I hope Lady Bird doesn't have to have her beautification people okay it. I fed the dogs meatballs and spaghetti for a treat. They went wild over it.

10:30 P.M. I took Yuki to the West Hall. President Johnson, Lady B, and Lynda had company. The Prez was saying they might get Chuck Robb, Lynda's future husband, a gold watch. I told the President Mrs. Gonella took her dog home tonight. He said, "What's that dog doing here?" He asked me if Mr. Califano ever brought in any dog food. Because the First Lady looked disapproving, I changed the subject: I told him Yuki jumped the fence. Mrs. J said in Texas, Luci has a four-foot fence with no toe holds and Yuki jumps that with ease. Lady Bird said I shouldn't have to take care of other people's dogs. She asked me about the Purina. I told her I would put all the dogs on Purina when we depleted our other stock.

I told the President Freckles was in heat and that Mr. Deason suggested Edgar unless the President had another dog in mind. The President said not Edgar, as he looked like a dachshund. I relayed the message to Mr. Deason.

10/6/67   I took Yuki to the second floor. Luci yelled for Yuki. The dog ran to Luci and she picked up Yuki and hugged him. She says she would like to take Yuki home but can't break the President's heart. She said that I should remember Yuki is still her dog.

10/9/67   Mr. Deason came in to check Freckles, who is in heat. We were walking from the pen with Freckles and Yuki. He said, "Let's see if Yuki will try Freckles." Yuki got hung up with Freckles. Still hung up, he rolled over on the ground on his back, and he was yelping. Mr. Deason said, "Let's carry them out of sight of the White House window into the shrubbery." We had to wait about ten minutes. Later I got a White House car and took Freckles to Deason's home. We bred Freckles with Mr. Deason's male dog. They also got hung up. 10:30 P.M. Usher Carter called and said the President wanted Yuki. I took him up. The President was naked. He was on the phone prior to getting a rubdown. He asked me if Yuki pulled me toward his room. I told him he did. I told him Freckles was bred this evening. I left the room and the doctor called me back. The President said he wanted Yuki bathed and perfumed.

I was to hear that order frequently from then on. I remember one night I had just gotten through spraying the hell out of Yuki with a perfume bottle when I stopped at the Usher's Office on my way to the President's bedroom.

Usher Hare sniffed the air and exploded, "Christ, Yuki smells like a New York whore going to church on Sunday morning."

10/10/67   Usher Carter called. I took Yuki to the second floor, rapped on the door, and walked into the President's private dining room. Lady B, the Prez, and Marie Fehmer were just starting dinner. The President said Yuki had fleas. I told him I sprayed him. Mrs. Johnson asked if he had had a bath. I told her he had. The President said Mr. Califano had said we were down on his dog. I told the President that George was like the runt of a litter. The President laughed and told me good night. I left the room. Everyone was laughing about Califano and his unlucky dog.

10/11/67   Mr. Deason picked up Edgar and Little Chap for beagle training. He said he would bring Jezebel, a female beagle of his, to the White House. Edgar has had his rabies shot. All dogs were washed in a solution to prevent ringworm.

11:00 I took Yuki to the President's bedroom. He was getting a rubdown. He said, "Don't let him jump up here on the table." He talked to Yuki: "I saw some food in a bowl here for you." The Prez asked me if Freckles got hung up when she was bred. I told him she did. Then I asked him if he had talked to Mr. Deason lately. He said no.

I gave Yuki a rubdown while the President had his rubdown. Even a President loses a little wind during a hard rubdown. At first I thought it was Yuki. Yuki didn't like it either and went under the bed, and I left as the President was watching the news in color on three TV channels.

Lynda had a dinner-dance for Princess Alexandra of England.

The President never worried about his own welfare—only Yuki's.

10/13/67   The Prez and George Christian, his press man, came out of the White House for a walk. I let Yuki loose. He ran to the President with Blanco chasing him. The President picked Yuki up and held him high over his head with Blanco jumping up, snarling. For once I was afraid Blanco would bite the President. As the President put Yuki down, Blanco chased Yuki, snapping at him. Prez said, "You had better watch Blanco or Yuki will be back in the hospital."

10:00 P.M. I took Yuki to the West Hall for the President and his company. The President held Yuki and leaned back and got Yuki to yowl his song.

10/15/67   I had Freckles on a leash as the President and Mrs. Johnson came out to their car on the way to church. Yuki was with the President. The President saw Blanco and said to Yuki, "Sic 'em." Mrs. Johnson said she had on a black dress and didn't want Yuki to ride in the back of the car. Yuki came over to sniff Freckles, as she is in heat. The President said, "Let Yuki have some fun. Let him mount Freckles." Mrs. Johnson was sitting in the car. I told the President we could walk around the corner out of sight. We did. I told the President Yuki was more interested in the car. Yuki sniffed and that was all. Agent Johns told me to give him Yuki and he could ride in the front with him.

10/16/67   The President walked out of his office with Ashton Gonella. He called, "Where are you going?" I told him I had just fed Blanco; he

198

said, "Come along." We walked up the roadway and cut through the West Rose Garden.

I told Ashton that Honeybun was still in heat while the Prez stood by, relishing our little secret. He winked at me. Then in front of her LBJ acted real concerned; he said Blanco was out with all the female dogs Saturday, and he hoped nothing had happened. So for her benefit, I told the President I was off Saturday and I had told Capital Parks men to keep the dogs separated. I told Mrs. Gonella that Blanco was too large for her dog. She said she certainly hoped so. She said she didn't need any puppies to take care of. The Prez winked at me again. The President asked me which dog I liked best, Blanco or Yuki. I said Yuki.

10:30 P.M. I took Yuki to the second-floor dining room. The President, the First Lady, and Marie Fehmer were dining. The President asked me in an aside if Blanco could breed with Ashton Gonella's dog. I was shocked that he would even think of putting that monster with dainty little Honey. I told him no, Blanco was severely underdeveloped and not interested in sex. He asked Marie if she had seen Freckles and Yuki the other day. She said no. The President said, "Yuki has to have more than one bath a week as he sleeps with me." I felt sorry for Lady Bird. She doesn't appreciate his sexy Yuki humor. To help Lady Bird get him on another subject, I went into the pantry and told one of the butlers to give Yuki a piece of meat—to give it to the President and let him give it to Yuki. The butler brought it in on a paper plate and I handed it to the President, who walked to the closet door and laid it on the floor. The President said the dog was starved. He said to the other butler, "You people should save the choice leftovers. Let Yuki have some meat each night." Mrs. Johnson said, "He is eating the same meat as I'm eating."

10/25/67 Edgar placed fifth out of thirty-five beagles in field trials.

10/30/67 Blanco made the Prez laugh when we met his copter. The Prez, carrying Luci's baby, returned from Texas at 9:30 P.M. Blanco had a Halloween mask on representing a tramp with a stubby cigar. What a crazy family scene that was. Too bad the public couldn't see the Prez holding the baby with one hand and the masked marvel with the other.

11/1/67 The Prez is still in a rare funning mood. On the dance floor some woman was showing some breastworks with a low-cut evening dress. The President asked Chief Knudsen if he got a picture. Then the President went over to the woman and stood taking a closer look as Chief took a close-up. She didn't know what was going on.

11/3/67 Dumpling came back today. I soldered a belt buckle for Luci. She and her husband were dressed and ready to go to City Tavern in

Georgetown for the first prenuptial party for Lynda when it broke. It was a pretty evening gown of chartreuse with a jeweled top. She and Pat thanked me. They left the electric shop, but then Luci came running back. She had forgotten her mink stole. She had borrowed it in New York from Rebekah Harkness. Earlier Marvin Watson called up Usher Hare and said he wanted someone to carry some chairs for a presidential meeting. Hare said he didn't have anyone as everyone had gone home. Mr. Watson told him he didn't care what their job description called for, just get some chairs. Hare called two engineers and told them to put them on the elevator but to stay out of sight, and "let them put the damn chairs up themselves." I was working on a fluorescent light outside of Watson's office and got a good laugh at the presidential aide's frustration.

11/5/67   Usher Hare said that Luci had sent the mink stole back to New York by way of American Airlines, with an American Airline employee or representative escort to hand-carry the mink and in New York to take a cab to Rebekah Harkness. Hare said this administration doesn't care how much money it spends.

On November 10, the President flew off to visit military installations in the West and South. Everyone agreed it was no place for a dog, and Yuki was not scheduled to go. Marvin Watson tried to keep Yuki from jumping on the helicopter, and Bruce, a doorman, tried to pick him up and hold him back. The President said, "Leave him alone," so Yuki climbed aboard with a couple of jumps. The results were predictable.

11/14/67   Word has arrived that Yuki leaked on the admiral's rug aboard the *Enterprise,* an aircraft carrier. The scuttlebutt was passed happily through the crew's quarters—Yuki is their "naval hero" now.

When the President got back, one of the first things he wanted was a good rubdown from his masseur, Mr. King. LBJ was a very sensuous man. He loved walking around in the nude and he loved a rubdown. And he loved to have company while it was going on. My notes for this day show he didn't have his massage till half an hour after midnight:

When Yuki and I arrived, the President was stripped to the nude as he was getting ready to have a rubdown. I told the President I was going to take two weeks off. He said, "You take off more than any one I know of —you work a week and then take off two." Then he asked, "Who is going to take care of the dogs?" I told him I had made arrangements for the engineers to do it as they were on duty twenty-four hours a day. The President told me that Marianne Means' beagle had had pups. I told him Freckles was going to have pups in December. The President asked me if Yuki had been in my shop. I told him he had been, and when he heard the telephone ring he was ready to go. He knew the call. I soldered an LBJ-for-the-USA tieclasp on Yuki's collar.

12/3/67 My vacation is over. I let six deer go by. Too many trees, I couldn't see.

Wedding gifts were piling up for Lynda Bird. I gave my own gift for her to Ashton Gonella so it wouldn't get lost in the shuffle.

A few days before the wedding I got my first hint that the President would not be running for reelection.

12/3/67 The President said he was going to cut down on the number of dogs he had so when they left the White House they wouldn't have too many. So maybe he won't run for reelection next year, or why would he be talking about it? Only a guess now. The President said he was keeping Blanco and Edgar. Mrs. Johnson said, "Oh, not Blanco!" The Prez asked me how many he had; I said he had six—four beagles and one collie and Yuki. Luci said she had some friends she would like to give them to. Mrs. Johnson said she was surprised he would choose Blanco. The Prez asked me to name one more dog I liked. I said Freckles. I told the Prez I had called Dr. Buell and he had x-rayed Freckles and found out she was only going to have one pup.

The First Lady, for some strange reason, asked me if I was still wearing cowboy boots. I was. I said when people kid me about them I always say, "All the way with LBJ." They looked at each other. I got the feeling the campaign slogans were over.

12/5/67 I took Yuki to the President's bedroom and knocked on the door. Mrs. Johnson told me to come in. She and the President were reading newspapers in bed. Yuki jumped up on the bed to sniff the President and then went to the foot of the bed and curled up.

Even though LBJ was busy with parties the last few nights before the wedding, he never neglected Yuki. The night before the wedding, I wrote:

12/8/67 The President was late as he came to the Mansion to dress for the party. He spoke to Yuki and told me to keep him, since he was leaving for the party. I had just replaced a light in the ground-floor Oval Room. He said, "You feed that dog." I told him he was fed at 7:30 P.M. Freckles

201

went to Fort Myer to deliver her pup. Yuki had a checkup. Tomorrow is Lynda's and Chuck's wedding.

12/9/67   Lynda's a Mrs., at last! Topping Luci for her part in history—eighth daughter of a President to be married while her father is in the White House; sixth daughter of a President to be married in the White House. And LBJ is the second President to give two daughters away in marriage while in office. The other one is Woodrow Wilson. And I'm sure she's the first in history to have a dog dressed up in red socks as a member of the wedding party—until he got thrown out of the wedding party.

I had Sam bathe Blanco and Yuki. I dressed Yuki in a dog Santa Claus coat Doris bought for me. Sandy Fox in the Social Office had one of his men write *Congratulations* in silver glitter on the coat. On Yuki's feet I put two pairs of red thirty-nine-cent baby socks. Blanco, Yuki, and I walked to the east side where the wedding guests were to enter, and Yuki was a sensation. Reporters grabbed us and cameramen took pictures. I was also interviewed on radio and TV. Later I had to go to the second-floor family quarters to stand by in case a breaker went out during the official family wedding pictures. Before I even got near, Liz's assistant Marcia Maddox grabbed me and said to get Yuki out of sight, as the First Lady didn't want the President to take Yuki in the room. So we went into the President's bedroom and watched football on color TV until the President went into the Oval Room. Then we came out of the bedroom. Pat Nugent saw me and told me to let Yuki go with him. I told him what Marcia said. He said, "The hell with her!" He walked Yuki over to the President, who then insisted that Yuki be in the picture. Mrs. Johnson said *No!* She was blazing mad, so an aide brought Yuki back to me. After the pictures were made, the President went into the West Hall and said, "Yuki, I'm sorry, but Lady Bird wouldn't let you in the picture." He went to his chair in the West Sitting Room and called for Yuki and ignored what was going on.

I congratulated Lynda and turned Yuki around so she could read his congratulations on his coat. She half smiled, coolly, and said she had seen it. Later the President had me bring Yuki to his bedroom while he and Mrs. J and some aides watched a tape of the wedding in color. An instant replay. Mrs. Johnson said to him, "We had better go to the reception downstairs." The President told me to call up recording and tell them to tape the events in full so he could see it later when he had time. Yuki danced a few rounds with the President on the dance floor under a tent covering. Then I took Yuki to my shop to await developments. Yuki was asleep on the couch in my shop when I got a call saying that the President was waiting for Yuki at his helicopter. I grabbed Yuki and ran up the back stairs. Gaddis the valet was on his way to the Oval Room. The

President was coming through the Oval Room toward his elevator. He said, "Why in the hell didn't you have that dog out there?" I said, "Mr. President, I didn't know you were leaving." He took the leash off Yuki, picked him up and walked to the helicopter.

I think he is mad at Lady Bird for spoiling his wedding. I mean, his wedding fun. I guess Lynda Bird's wedding could be called "The Day of the Revolt of Lady Bird."

After it was all over, the backstairs talk centered on Hollywood star George Hamilton and how he'd had the guts to put in an appearance at the wedding, even escorting the glamorous star, Merle Oberon. And for once everyone was loyal and no one stole the show from Lynda on her day—not the President, not the Hollywood stars, and not even Yuki.

12/13/67   I received a message to contact presidential assistant Jim Jones. I went to his office and he said that he was worried about the President's order that he wants Yuki "washed every day, combed, brushed, and perfumed." He said he thought that was bathing a dog too often. I agreed, but pointed out that LBJ is my boss and what can I do?

11:00 P.M. I received a call from Usher Carter to take "the campaign manager," as he calls Yuki, to the second-floor dining room. LBJ's night secretary, Vicky, and her husband were having dinner with the President. The Prez asked about Freckles' puppy and told me to bring the pup up. I brought Freckles and her pup, and I made Yuki keep away.

12/15/67   Yuki wore the Santa Claus suit with white whiskers to accompany the Prez to the tree-lighting ceremony on the Ellipse. The reporters later told me Yuki stole the show as he trotted on stage behind the President.

12/20/67   Yuki and the First Lady have kissed and made up. The Prez is still on a trip around the world. Lady Bird spotted Yuki in his Santa suit, so she came over to pet him and admire his coat. She said nothing about the wedding incident and neither did I. I was out of the doghouse.

Just as 1967 seemed on its way to a happy ending, a sour note crept in.

12/28/67   11:00 P.M. I received a call from Jim Jones at the Texas ranch. Earlier, press aide Tom Johnson had called and asked me several strange questions about the dogs' expenses and about where they go for treatment. I knew it had to mean trouble. Jim Jones asked if we got any vet bills from Fort Myer. I told him we had better not, as the President was entitled to free vet care since he was Commander in Chief. By pretending to be a member of the White House staff, a reporter had tricked some green young flunky at Fort Myer and he had let slip all kinds of information about presidential dogs coming and going there. I called the ranch, but Tom was out. Later he returned my call. I told him I had called Major Robinson and said to find out for sure that the President ·is eligible for free vet care.

The Prez was upset about the bad publicity, but Tom said everything was all right as long as he and I stayed on the same wavelength.

It would be farewell to Fort Myer, I was sure. It would be a new year with a new dog hospital, a new set of people to cope with. And with a President who slept with a dog, and gloried in it, I didn't know what to expect next.

17

The year 1968 started on a sour note, too—how quickly things change at the White House!

1/4/68   8:00 P.M. Lynda and Chuck returned from Austin, Texas. Usher Carter told them he hadn't gotten word that they would arrive, so he didn't have any cooks or butlers, but they would be here in the morning. Mike, Lynda's Secret Service man, told Mr. Carter that someone had better get some cooks from home to the White House or someone would hear about it. Carter told Mike he wasn't calling in any cooks or butlers at 9 P.M. and for Mike to look after his own job and Carter would run the house. Lynda and Chuck have waited over forty-five minutes for the Signal Corps to bring in a portable color TV set. The doorman took up some fire logs.

Less than a month ago Lynda and Chuck had a feast on their wedding day, and tonight they can't even get a hot dog.

1/6/68   When the family was away, we tried to check all the electrical systems. But Lynda's unexpected presence complicated everything. There was a temporary blackout at the White House. I had to come in at 12:30 P.M. to help two other electricians run a power line from the emergency generators from the east end of the White House over the roof of the theater to the second-floor East Hall, and then to the Queen's Room, so Lynda and Chuck would have one table light and an electric heater during the blackout. Also, so Lynda didn't have to give up her three-hour movie. It was off for five minutes one time. She was furious and told someone, "Wait till I see Mr. Bryant!"

1/10/68   Poor Lynda is not Luci in the kitchen. Usher Pierce told me Lynda burned up two TV dinners she was fixing for herself and Chuck this week.

Earlier I went up on the President's elevator with Lynda and Chuck. I showed them how to turn on the electric heater and light the stove.

On January 14, the President said he might like to keep Freckles' pup because it reminded him of the old dog he used to have before he came to the White House. He surprised even me when he asked me to get my wife to make some boots for little Yuki to wear when the weather was wet. Doris had made some coats for Yuki, and they had delighted the President. In fact, he had come up with his new idea after bragging about Yuki's red wedding outfit *with socks* that the dog had worn at Lynda's wedding reception. The Prez scratched his head and said he didn't know how she could make the boots, but he was sure she could figure it out somehow.

She did, too, even though she had to make several pairs before she got them right. Anyone who can figure out computers eventually can figure out dog booties.

My diary shows the President also discussed something more serious than boots, which was where to send the dogs for free vet service.

1/14/68   The Prez talked to me about the news leak from Fort Myer. He now wants a leak-proof place. I told him I would like to send the dogs to Walter Reed. I told the President that Mrs. Kennedy sent Pushinka to Walter Reed until there was a leak to the press. I told him it was traced to a White House chauffeur.

We walked into his doctor's office, and LBJ asked the attendant if there was a difference between a horse doctor and a veterinarian. The President told me to see Major Robinson.

1/16/68   Major Robinson called me to his office and made the proper arrangements. He took my word for it that the President would prefer the Walter Reed vets.

1/17/68   At 3:00 P.M. Robinson introduced me to the Walter Reed vets in his office, and we talked about the need for absolute secrecy. Later I showed them the dog runway and the pups' room.

The Prez was returning from the theater, where he'd been rehearsing the State of the Union speech he'd give that night. He told me to go up with him and Yuki. He told his valet, Paul Glynn, kiddingly, "Why don't you stay until after the speech, and about eleven-thirty or twelve, after we get drunk, bring Yuki up to the buffet dinner?" I saw Glynn didn't want to stay. I said, "Give him a break, as I will be here until 11:30."

1/21/68   Usher Carter died today: a heart attack. I bathed Yuki and let the President take him upstairs at 5:00 P.M. The President told me to bring the pup to his room. As I entered he was putting on his pajamas. Yuki jumped up on the bed and crawled under the covers to the foot of the bed. The President and Yuki took a nap.

1/23/68   At 8:45 I took Yuki to the second floor to see the Prez and his guests. For the first time Yuki wore the boots my wife made for him.

The President told Yuki, "You have got some mighty fine boots." Lady Bird asked where he got them. Mrs. J told the President that they would have to have Freckles' pup spend some time with them so the pup would get used to them. The Prez ignored the suggestion. He wasn't interested in anything but Yuki. He told me I was a good public relations man to get Yuki so much publicity. Yuki and I ate some filet of beef tenderloin ($2.20 a pound). It beats hamburger at 60¢.

1/30/68   The Walter Reed vets came in and checked the dogs. They also brought in a medicine locker and stocked it. I took Yuki to the second-floor private dining room. Earlier, Usher Hare had called and said for me to brush the dog first. The President told me that Yuki had been in his office and Yuki had gotten hairs on his suit. I told him I had brushed Yuki and I could brush him every hour on the hour and he will still shed hairs on LBJ's suit. The President was talking to Mrs. Johnson, who was at the ranch. As I left he was letting Yuki howl over the telephone. Earlier, when I had gone to the East Wing—I was waiting for the vets to come in—cute secretary Cynthia Wilson kneeled down and petted Yuki. She suddenly said, "Fresh, stop that." A young man at the desk asked her what was wrong. She said Yuki had tried to get his nose under her dress. She left. I don't know where he learns these things.

From this day forward, the President was on the warpath about Yuki's white hair and showed me again and again the hairs on his dark suits. All my brushing of Yuki couldn't get rid of the last few loose fluffy white hairs.

2/1/68   Marie Fehmer said the President wanted to see me. Prez said sternly Yuki was still shedding hair. I told him Yuki would have to be outside more. He told me to ask Luci if she wanted Freckles' pup. If she didn't, then I was to give the pup to Mr. Deason. Luci said her dog had ringworm. I called Mr. Deason and asked him when he was going to pick up his new pup. He said he would pick it up this week.

9:00 Usher Hare called and said the President said to brush Yuki and bring him to the West Hall. I did and put a coat on Yuki. The President had company. He picked up Yuki and let him howl, and then he said to me, "Come here and look at the sleeves on my coat." He showed me the hairs and acted like I had put them there. Someone asked me where Yuki had gotten his coat. I told them my wife had made him three coats.

2/4/68   A policeman said he almost shot Yuki after dark when he moved some bushes near the President's office. I told him he had better think before shooting. The Prez asked me if I had seen *Look* magazine. I told him Juanita Roberts let me see a copy. He said, "You are getting more publicity than I am." He seemed to relish the thought and repeated it. "You're getting more press coverage than the President." I said "Mr. President, we are for you."

2/5/68   Marvin Watson called me and said for me to do what I could to keep Yuki from shedding his hair on the President's suit.

10:45 P.M. I took Yuki to the President's bedroom. He was in the buff, getting a rubdown from Mr. King. Mrs. Johnson was in bed reading. I told the President I had washed Yuki. Yuki jumped on the bed. Mrs. Johnson laughed as he went to President Johnson.

2/6/68   I went to the President's office at 1:30 P.M. What a homey scene. The President was reading the news ticker tape. Yuki was asleep on the divan. Joe Califano came over and whispered that the President wanted me to brush Yuki. Califano! That was the last straw. The Prez must be complaining to the world about his dog hairs. I was about to whisper back, "Tell him to wear white suits."

2/7/68   I came in at 1:30 P.M. and had Blanco and Yuki at the South Portico when wounded vets from Walter Reed came for a party at White House. One young black had both legs off. A few petted the dogs. Big housekeeping news! Lynda's chauffeur told the ushers that Lynda asked him how to fix hot dogs. She boiled them for lunch. She put some frozen unbaked rolls in a *broiler* and they only browned on top; they were raw dough inside. Chief Usher West said she broiled some steaks in an oven without a pan.

The chauffeur said he told her next time to put the ready-to-bake frozen rolls in the *oven*. No wonder Mr. Robb is going to Vietnam.

2/9/68   The vets came in today and treated Blanco. He had a bruised place below his eyes. Yuki got a gland treatment—a cleaning of the anal gland.

Tom Miller, who works in the doctor's office, said everyone carried a towel at the ranch to wipe the mud off Yuki. He said he had personally cleaned up after Yuki messed in the President's bedroom. He laughed and said, "That's how I made Lieutenant J. G." It's like a Gilbert and Sullivan operetta. Incidentally, Major Robinson is now *Lieutenant Colonel* Robinson.

Hare called: "Take Yuki to President's bedroom." I went in. The lights came on and I announced, "Yuki is here." I wiped Yuki's feet with a damp rag. The President called for him and Yuki jumped between the President and Lady Bird. The President was so tired he didn't even talk a minute.

He turned out his lights before I could get out of the room. The darkness had me completely blind and groping for the door. Mrs. Johnson asked him to turn on his bed light so I could at least get out of the room. The President and Mrs. Johnson said, "Good night," and then the President, tired as he was, said, "Turn out the lights in the hallway." I left it dark.

Several girls in the Correspondence Room were assigned the important job of social secretaries to the LBJ Canine Corps. You wouldn't believe some of the invitations the dogs got by mail and phone.

Yuki hit the jackpot with an "invite" that naturally included me—a party for the stripteaser Gypsy Rose Lee. It was really tempting, but we didn't go. It wasn't because I was afraid a stripper could steal the show from Yuki, because I knew she couldn't. Nobody could.

It was just that our hosts were touting some brand of dog food, and Yuki was not *that* kind of dog and had not gone commercial.

2/11/68 I took Yuki to the President's bedroom. He asked me where Yuki had been. I told him in my shop. The President said, "Damn it, you must have the dirtiest shop in the White House." Yuki jumped in bed with the President after I wiped Yuki's footpads.

The President got Yuki howling as I left the room, so I guess he gets his mind off the war and other problems for a while.

The war in Vietnam became more and more unpopular in 1968 and everyone was saying that LBJ's credibility had slipped. About this time a credibility joke made the rounds, which the President heard and suffered over. But true to his way of easing pain, he was soon telling it himself as an illustration of how mean people could be. Especially the press.

The joke was in the form of a riddle: How can you tell when Lyndon Johnson is not telling the truth?

Answer: Well, you have to watch him. If he scratches his face, he's telling the truth. And if he rubs his nose, he's telling the truth. And if he wipes his eyes, he's telling the truth. But if he starts moving his lips, he's not telling the truth.

2/12/68 What a day. I almost got into a fistfight with John Pelkey, one of the White House electricians. He objects to my bringing Yuki into the White House electric shop. I told him that I would slug him if he ever harmed Yuki. He said Yuki got on his pillow on the couch. I went to the

Usher's Office and told Ushers Hare, West, and Pierce, so they know my problem. Hare decreed Pelkey must put his pillow in his locker. I hope he remembered to tell him.

11:25 P.M. I took Yuki to the second floor, the President's bedroom. The Prez said, "Yuki crapped in the Queen's Room last night." I said, "And that's not all." I told the President I almost had a scrap with White House electrician Pelkey. I told the Prez that I'd told Pelkey the President gave me permission to take Yuki to my shop so he would have company. Prez said, "That's right," and he and Lady Bird had a hearty laugh. They were in bed reading. The President said, "Much obliged."

Suddenly I had a new worry.

2/12/68   Liz Carpenter called me at home and asked me if I had received any requests from anyone trying to claim Yuki. I told her I had not, but I wouldn't be surprised after the pictures in *Look*. I don't know what the Prez would do if anyone claimed ownership.

2/14/68   I took Yuki to see Willie Day Taylor. She got me a copy of the *Wall Street Journal* to show me a picture of Yuki and me on the front page. The President was just leaving Willie's office. He turned around when he heard Yuki. I told the President we had a nice story in the *Wall Street Journal*. He said, "Did you get some more publicity?" I said, "Mr. President, *you* are in it, too." He gave me a dirty look, but he loved it— my patronizing him. The Prez read the story and said it was a good one. He showed the paper to Yuki, putting it right in front of Yuki's nose. The Prez said "Yuki, here is your picture. I have a famous friend."

2/15/68   11:00 P.M. I took Yuki to the President's bedroom. He was in bed reading and watching the news on three televisions. He asked me how the other dogs were doing. He also asked me if Yuki jumped when the telephone rang for me to bring Yuki. I said, "Jumps like a bullet." The other electricians—including Martin, my boss—are pouting and giving me the cold shoulder because of Yuki in the shop and because I blew the whistle on Pelkey. Paul Glynn, the valet, said, "The hell with them."

9:45 P.M. I took Yuki to the Prez in the second-floor dining room. Mr. Deason was a dinner guest. Yuki jumped on LBJ's lap and I left them singing. Deason was laughing, amazed.

2/18/68   The President returned from a trip to California where he saw some troops off for Vietnam. His helicopter landed about 1:20 A.M. I had Yuki in the Diplomatic Room to greet him. He howled when he heard the chopper. The President came into the room and called for Yuki. He lifted him up and let Yuki howl and told me to bring Yuki to his room. We rode in the elevator with the President. The President pulled off his shirt and read the newspapers on his bed, leaning over the bed reading. He let out two of his infamous gas bombs and kept on reading. Someone said one day they should send him to Vietnam and he'd end the war himself, gassing them to death. After he finished reading, he put on his pajamas and called for Yuki. Yuki ran to the Prez and then jumped on the President's pillow on his bed. The President, puzzled, said "Where are you going, Yuki?" I told the President Yuki wanted him to come to bed. He was showing him his pillow. The President said, "Now the dog is giving the orders. How did I get in this position?" He looked Yuki in the eye, nose to nose. He said suddenly that Yuki's eye was getting better. I told him we had expert vets and then told him about Yuki howling when he heard the chopper landing. The Prez said he was complimented.

3/5/68   I had Yuki in the second-floor kitchen. Lynda petted Yuki. Chuck Robb came in and said the President was in the West Hall with some company and wanted Yuki, so I took the dog to him. Yuki jumped on the President's lap and the Prez got Yuki singing and howling.

I stayed and told the Prez I needed to feed Yuki. Mrs. J wanted to know if I would be around for an hour or so. I told her I would leave Yuki if she needed him. The President said no, for me to take Yuki to dinner. I had a time catching Yuki, as he wanted to stay. Just when I caught Yuki the President walked behind me and got Yuki to howl as I was holding him up over my shoulder.

3/10/68   A Secret Service agent called and said that the President wanted Yuki—quick. The Prez was practicing on the golf green. He had already turned Blanco and the beagles Edgar, Dumpling, and Honey loose. Honey started a fight with Yuki. I was shocked at LBJ's violence. The President threw his golf club and almost hit Honey. He was extremely angry.

I told him that the offending dog was not one of ours but belonged to Ashton Gonella and that it had been at the White House about six months. I told the President that he is feeding Honey for free. Later, Lady Bird came out and said she was going to the bowling alley. The President called me over and asked me in front of Mrs. Johnson about Honey fighting with his dogs. He wanted her to hear it from me. The President said we should breed Blanco with a collie. He asked me if it was okay to take Yuki to the bowling alley. I said okay, but I found out I was wrong. Later I got a call to come over to the bowling alley and pick up Yuki. I went over and he was tied up outside with two handkerchiefs and a piece of wire.

I talked to Mr. Turner later, and he said Yuki followed the ball below

211

where the machinery was operating. Mrs. Johnson yelled to him to cut off the electricity. The machinery continues to operate about forty seconds after the power is cut off. They had a bad scare. Luckily Yuki wasn't hurt.

Later on I took Yuki to the second-floor bedroom. The President was in bed with his pajamas on and some pads over his eyes. I was wiping Yuki's feet off and he broke away, chain, leash, and all, and jumped over the President to the other pillow. The President reached for him and said it was all right. I leaned over and took the leash off, and left them there.

3/19/68   Pat, Luci, Luci's baby Lyn, Kim, Astro, and one pup arrived at the South Portico about 10:30 P.M. Pat is going in the air service tomorrow. He asked me to take care of their dogs. I asked him if any dog is in heat. He said, "I hope not." I put the pup in the puppy room with Yuki, Kim in with Freckles and Dumpling, Astro with the others. A total of eleven dogs at the White House now.

I was trying to help the President thin down his dog population. I started with his wife's secretary.

3/19/68   I asked Gonella if she wants to give Honey away, that Marcia Maddox wanted a dog. I told her that the President was cutting down on the number of his dogs. She said winter was over, so she might take Honey home—whatever that means.

Mr. Deason called. He said Marie Fehmer wants a dog for her kinfolks in Texas. Luci is calling her pup Norman. What a name! I took him out to the dog run for a while today—very peppy, like his mama, Kim.

3/24/68   I took Yuki to the second-floor kitchen. Luci was feeding baby Lyn spinach. She tried to force-feed him, but the baby cried. He slapped Yuki hard on the head playing with him. Yuki took it.

I told Luci her baby tried to ride my back the other night as I was connecting some buzzer wires under the dining-room table on the second floor.

I asked her if she had decided on the pup giveaways. She said she couldn't locate her friend yet but to save Little Chap. She said her mother had considered a contest. Mrs. Johnson came into the kitchen. I asked her about it and she said she would let me know in the morning. I'm not saying or asking any more; let them decide, as I am dizzy enough just taking care of eleven dogs.

3/28/68   I got a call from the Secret Service that the dogs were loose. I went to C-11. Luci, Pat, and two friends were sitting on the grass on the South Lawn. I heard pup Norman yelping pathetically. An agent grabbed the pup. Luci ran over very much concerned. Blanco had bitten the pup on top of its head with a hard blow. The pup's eyes were glazed and it couldn't hold its head erect. I carried the pup to the Bouquet Room and called the military assistant on duty, who sent for the vets, Captain Moreman and Dr. Goodwin. I told Luci they should get rid of Blanco, as he had also bitten me four times; luckily I know he doesn't have rabies. Luci held the pup tenderly on her lap until the vets arrived. Meanwhile, Pat took care of their sick baby; he went to the second floor and walked Lyn, who is running a temperature. Pat called to ask how the pup was doing. The vets treated the dog. Luci thanked us all for caring for it. She said when Him was killed she felt like jumping off the second-floor balcony and almost delayed her wedding. I said I remembered.

3/31/68 An historic day. President Johnson gave a TV broadcast stating he would *not* be a candidate for the "awesome office of the President of the people." The White House is like a morgue!

April 1968 was a terrible month, unlike any other I had seen. The White House aides were in a state of shock over LBJ's announcement.

4/1/68 Most of the Johnson people are very sad today, shaking their heads and asking each other "But why?" Health is my guess.

4/2/68 I asked Ashton how her dog was doing. She said Honey barked and woke them up at 4:00 A.M.
Martin Luther King was killed at 7:00 P.M. today. "Terrible times are upon us" is the word at the White House. I agree.

4/5/68 There were Negro riots and burnings in Washington, D.C. At 8:45 P.M. I took Yuki into the President's office. He was on the telephone. Yuki ran to him, and the President bent down and petted him. I knew that the President needed a little diversion. He was very upset. He said, "I love my city of Washington and my country and people. They are trying to destroy each other."

4/7/68 The President waved for Yuki before he and General Westmoreland took off in a helicopter to inspect the burned-out parts of Washington, D.C. Then they flew to Andrews Field. When the Prez returned he held Yuki up to the helicopter window to look at Blanco and me. Yuki ran to us after the helicopter landed. The Prez is sad about what is happening to the national capital—looting and burning. "I can't believe I'm in America," he said.

4/8/68 Yuki and I waited for the Prez to come to the helicopter. Earlier I took Yuki to the second-floor dining room. Ashton Gonella was one of the guests. The Prez asked me if I got rid of Mrs. Gonella's mean dog. I told him, "Yes, sir, Mr. President." He asked me which dog was the meanest. I told him Joe Califano's George. Ashton Gonella said if Mr. Califano was at the table I would say her dog was the meanest. I left before the President could involve me any further. He likes to be in the middle and get something started.

4/9/68   Dr. Martin Luther King was buried today. A very long funeral.

The Prez said that Yuki shed on his suit at the dinner table so much that his suit looked like the baking-powder biscuits ready for the oven that his mother used to make.

Mr. Deason called and said he was going to bring two pups over for ten days. Great. That's all I need—more dogs.

4/18/68   Mr. and Mrs. Clifton Daniel—President Truman's son-in-law and daughter—and their children came to the East Room and Margaret unveiled a picture of her mother, Bess Truman. Later Margaret's children came out on the first-floor balcony underneath the Truman Balcony. I took Yuki up the steps and let the children pet him.

4/22/68   Yuki and I were waiting for the President to return from Texas. (Yuki couldn't go because of his cold.) Taylor, a Secret Service man, said we couldn't stay on the landing site. I told him the President always wants to see his dog as he lands after a trip. I asked him if we could stay at F-1; he said Yuki could and I couldn't. So I said we both go.

Later, as the Prez, Mrs. J and Lynda were having dinner, I took Yuki up to President's private dining room. I told him Yuki wanted to see him so much that I had to bring him up. He petted Yuki and got him to sing a little. Yuki coughed once. The President said "He still has it." He asked me why I hadn't had Yuki out to meet him. I explained about the Secret Service orders. He said they shouldn't have done that. He asked me what I thought the reason was. I told him I presumed that he had some company that they didn't want us to see. LBJ always likes to hear how people figure things out. Later Taylor told me he was acting on orders from Jim Jones' office.

4/29/68   The Prez was grumbling to guests that Yuki got hairs all over his suit and nobody on his staff cares. Later he said that Yuki was starting to look good as he is picking up weight. I asked Mr. Deason how his dogs were. He said fine. The President's valet, Glynn, said that the President wants Yuki "white" tomorrow, so I left Sam a note for a wash-up. I gave Ashton Gonella some capsules for her dog's cough.

5/3/68   The Prez returned from visiting Harry S Truman at Independence. He played with Yuki after he got off helicopter. The vets came in but didn't have to do anything today. Ashton Gonella was in the carpenter shop asking in her poor-soul voice for some short lengths of wire fencing a foot high, supposedly to keep Honey from watering the plants and shrubbery. Or digging. She wants to know where to buy the scent spray that keeps dogs away from shrubbery.

5/5/68   The President took Yuki to the second floor. Yuki wet the family sitting room rug. So what else is new? I never have dogs long enough to really train them. There are just too many masters at White House. But Prez doesn't care—Yuki can do no wrong. And as long as the President is happy . . .

5/6/68   The Prez is in a playful mood. He returned in his car and clapped his hands as he passed the South Portico. He got out at C-9 Post. Agent Hill hollered, "Turn him loose." Yuki ran to the President; the President then sicked the dog on Okie, his photographer. Yuki nipped at him. Later I got a call from the President's secretary that the bite hadn't been funny. Yuki really bites.

5/8/68   11:30 P.M. I was carrying two electric heaters that had been on the Truman Balcony to warm the Thailand dinner guests watching the military march and the fireworks display. I was walking toward the President's elevator when he came up on his way to his bedroom. I told the Prez Yuki was helping me. He said Yuki's harness was chewed up. I told him I had sent it to a shoeshop to be repaired. He took Yuki with him to his bedroom. I told the President Yuki was crazy about him. He looked like he needed cheering up.

5/9/68   The Secret Service is giving me a hard time, keeping me from taking Yuki to the Prez. They told me the President would call for the dog if he wanted Yuki. We fooled them via the Vice President. HHH arrived and petted Yuki. I told him Yuki wanted to see the President. He said, "Come on, Yuki, we will see the President." He took him by the leash and walked him to the President at a table in the West Garden. Ho, ho, ho.

5/11/68   Yuki went to Texas after a press dinner honoring the President. They gave LBJ a silver collar for Yuki. One of the press had called me earlier about the size.
  The doctor's office called and asked me if Yuki could take the trip to Texas.

5/13/68   Jim Jones called and said that I would get the Civil Service Grade 13 I requested. As LBJ says, "Them what asks, gits. If they're lucky." It's taken me a long time to git lucky.

5/15/68   I took Yuki to the second floor for the President. Mr. Fleming told me the President loves the silver collar and will have it refitted if needed after a test wearing, he likes it so much. The dogs ate steak tonight. Lynda Bird said *everyone* is having a baby. So that means she's going to make LBJ a grandfather again. Hard to remember how worried he was about her finding the right man.

5/15/68   After the Tunisian State Dinner, LBJ called for Yuki at 12:15 midnight. I knocked on the door. He was in bed talking to someone on the telephone. He told me to clean Yuki's paws good, which I was doing with a wet rag. Yuki jumped on his bed and sat on the right pillow. I left them growling at each other.

Then there was a sinister incident.

5/19/68   I was at C-11 South Portico talking to officer Plutto about guns and so forth. A second officer came up to us on his way to another post. He pulled out a pocket knife, opened it, and showed us the blade. He said, "How long do you think it would take me to skin this dog alive?" I said, "Not long." I didn't know if he was kidding. The dogs obviously thought he meant it. Blanco growled at him. Yuki jumped and bit him in the groin right on the penis. The officer kicked Yuki hard and said, "I'll kill him if he bites me again." I said, "You do and the President will have your job." I told him I would have to report the incident to the captain's desk. I called Lieutenant Freeman and talked to him. He asked me if the officer was injured. I let the officer talk to Freeman on the phone. I went to the captain's desk and talked to Freeman. Then I gave a report to Usher Pierce. Captain Starkoff called me on the phone while I was in the Usher's Office. He told me to cool it and to cooperate with the police. Then I notified a Secret Service man in his office in the west basement.

5/20/68   I never received a call from Major Lanier, so I made an appointment with Mr. Jim Jones for a three-thirty talk. While I was waiting, Secret Service man Taylor called and asked me if I was waiting to see the President. I told him no, that I was going to talk to Mr. Jones about it. He suggested that I talk to Major Lanier and see if he couldn't work out something. I canceled the appointment with Mr. Jones' secretary and I went to the major's office. He had a report in front of him. I asked him if it said anything about the officer asking us how long it would take him to skin Yuki alive and stating that he would kill Yuki if he bit him again. He said no. I told him I didn't think that he had a complete report. He said he'd been busy about plans concerning the Poor People's March, that he hadn't had time to go into the report very deeply. He said that he would work out something for the police not to touch or pet the dog. He

216

Here's a view of the White House the tourist seldom sees. In the foreground is the Jacqueline Kennedy Garden; behind it is the canopy under which Tricia Nixon was married.

Pat Nugent looks rather puppylike
here as the press, at the left, strains
at the ropes to get to the poor young
couple. Spoiled as she was, Luci
was my pet of the White House
brats.

My favorite photos of the Johnson
girls' weddings. First was Luci's, in
August, 1966. Although the
wedding didn't take place at the
White House, the reception did.
This scene on the first floor South
Portico looks like anyone else's
wedding shot with all the in-laws,
and the expression on Pat Nugent's
mother's face seems to be saying,
"What am I doing here?"

My favorite wedding picture of Lynda Bird, showing the dramatic crossed-sword ceremony in the East Room where bridegroom Chuck Robb's Marine colleagues did him proud. Lynda never glowed so beautifully as she did that day in December, 1967, and I was amused that LBJ claimed a lot of credit for supplying his daughter with a fine young husband (Chuck had been assigned as a military aide at the White House).

When Him had pups with a Texas charmer named Bridgit (October 1965), Luci took such delight in the pup with a single freckle—upper right—that she named it 'Pecosa,' Spanish for "freckle," and made my life miserable demanding I use the right name. I defied her and put the name 'Freckles' on the puppies' box. Eventually she gave up trying to teach people the Spanish name and "Freckles" stuck. LBJ was so fond of Him's little family that he autographed this picture for me after I had 'Papa' Him "autograph" it, too.

FRECKLES

LBJ would be most amused when I would dump one of the pups into my Texas boot. This one was Kim, who distinguished herself one day by wetting the rug in the second floor Oval Room. (Undaunted, Lady Bird told the butler to get some corn meal to put on the spot.) It was frowned upon for anyone working at the White House to copy the President by wearing cowboy boots or a western hat, but as I told the Usher's Office, who were issuing one of their warnings, I had been wearing both before LBJ got there and I would be wearing them after he left.

Party time at the Oval Office would find Freckles, Kim and Him jumping up for dog candy, which LBJ was forever economizing on by ordering me to look for a bargain price. He was always chewing me out because of his dogfood bills, but he loved his dogs and it was more bark than bite.

Freckles, Kim and Him get treats on the White House lawn—steak bones that I had brought from home. Poor Blanco was always served last. This was taken in the spring of the year Luci got married but already Pat Nugent looks like one of the family.

This is the famous Courtney Valenti, whom LBJ adored above all other children except those of his own family. He had a standing order that any time Courtney came to the White House to see her father or to visit someone with her mother, Mary Margaret (who had been LBJ's private secretary), he was to be notified. About the angriest I'd seen him was once when Courtney had been there and he had not been informed. Courtney returned his affection and here she is paying more attention to "The Prez," as she called him, than she is to Freckles' pups.

After Him was killed by a car on the White House grounds, I thought LBJ could never give his heart so completely to a dog again, but I was wrong. Yuki, a little white mutt Luci had found wandering around lost, became his closest friend and the apple of his eye during his last few years at the White House. Yuki and the Prez sang duets and traveled everywhere together. Here they are at the LBJ Ranch in Texas.

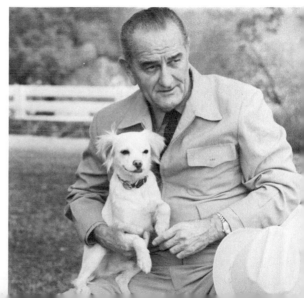

LBJ and Yuki, the inseparables, sing a duet on the White House lawn during a party for young people in September, 1967. Lady Bird looks amused, but sometimes she got a little fed up with the hoopla over LBJ's canine corps.

Lyndon loved Yuki so much that he even told me to have my wife make costumes—including booties—for Yuki to wear. Here is what the Best Dressed Canine was wearing for Christmas, 1967. Yuki sounded like Jingle Bells when he walked because Doris, my wife, had decorated the costume with little bells.

One of the fun days at the White House was when TV star Lassie came to call and showed the First Lady how not to be a litterbug. Lassie picked up a piece of paper and deposited it in a trash can. I tried to bring our white collie, Blanco, on the scene but he and Lassie hated each other on sight.

One of my all-time favorite LBJ photos, this was taken August 10, 1967 and shows Baby Lyn and Granddad Lyndon "eyeballing" each other, as LBJ would put it.

Sharing a secret—LBJ and Lady Bird were the closest presidential couple during my years at the White House.

On January 20, 1969, I went to Andrews airfield to pick up President-elect Nixon's dogs. Yuki, who would be leaving the White House later in the day with outgoing LBJ, came along as a welcoming committee. The Johnson and Nixon dogs hated each other on sight and we had trouble keeping them apart. But even worse, Fina Sanchez—Pat Nixon's maid—didn't believe I was really from the White House, and she was not going to part with the dogs. The airplane noise was deafening and we were screaming at each other, but the loudest screech came from Pasha, the tiny Yorkshire terrier, who was hiding behind Vicky the poodle but talking big.

Because Nixon had known and loved an Irish setter when he was a boy, the staff presented him with King Timahoe on January 28, 1969. For a long time the President seemed shy and even timid with the dog, and to a great extent I helped him win Timahoe over. Standing by beaming are Press Secretary Ron Ziegler, Presidential Assistant H. R. Haldeman, and Private Secretary Rose Mary Woods.

The Nixon girls, looking young and carefree in a painting which was, I believe, done before they came to the White House and learned the rougher side of politics.

Julie was my favorite Eisenhower, married to a really nice man—Ike's grandson David, whom I had watched chase golf balls for his grandfather many years before. This photo was made at the White House on April 18, 1971, after David, a Naval officer, had been assigned to the *Albany*.

On the Nixons' first Christmas at the White House, I had a little fun with the dogs, posing Pasha, Vicky and King Timahoe with their own Santa, their own decorated tree, and their own stockings of doggie toys and goodies.

Christmas was a special family time for the Nixons and they did not have the mobs of people upstairs—as had the Johnsons—to help them celebrate. This was a small family party to decorate the tree in the second floor residence: the David Eisenhowers and the Edward Coxes are showing the President some of the old tree decorations and recalling when they were bought. There was a special ball, with his or her name on it, for each member of the family. The girls' ornaments dated back to their babyhoods.

Miss Patricia Nixon

Mr. and Mrs. Dwight David Eisenhower II

request the pleasure of your company

at a supper dance to be held at

The White House

on Friday evening, July 17, 1970

at nine o'clock

Black Tie

Miss Patricia Nixon

Mr. and Mrs. Dwight David Eisenhower II

request the pleasure of your company

at a picnic to be held at

Camp David

on Thursday evening, July 16, 1970

at six o'clock

Miss Patricia Nixon

Mr. and Mrs. Dwight David Eisenhower II

request the pleasure of your company

at luncheon

aboard the Presidential Yacht Sequoia

on Friday, July 17, 1970

at twelve o'clock

These are the invitations that went out when Prince Charles of England was coming to visit, and when, backstairs, the White House was buzzing with the rumor of a possible romance between Tricia and the prince. Nowhere on the invitation does it show that the prince would be the guest of honor. But everyone *knew*—they certainly knew.

Manolo Sanchez, President Nixon's valet, in dinner jacket, steps into the kitchen to see how the serving is progressing during a State dinner.

When Prime Minister Lynch of Ireland visited Nixon, I wore an Irish flag and joined the festivities with King Timahoe.

Until things got too tense around the White House, the President would frequently signal me over when foreign dignitaries were his guests. Here Emperor Haile Selassie of Ethiopia takes a fancy to Pasha and tells about his own little dog. The Protocol Chief, Ambassador Emil Mosbacher, Jr., is at the right of the photo.

When Indian Prime Minister Indira Gandhi arrived in November, 1971, I waited in the background, as you can see above the car door; but the dogs and I got no signals.

At the White House, Nixon would sometimes give Timahoe a dog biscuit that I had suggested he keep in his desk. Here John D. Ehrlichman, Henry Kissinger, and H. R. Haldeman talk with the President in August, 1969, long before Kissinger was appointed Secretary of State.

Timahoe loved to ride in golf carts—but the President had to use a leash because the dog would run away as soon as it stopped.

Tricia was not quite as active as her sister Julie, but she did look as cute as I'd ever seen her the day she helped the 4-H Club break ground for a building addition in Washington. The fellow on the right looks like her brother-in-law David Eisenhower, but he is Chris Peterson, a 4-H member from Pennsylvania. The other man is Howard Harder, Chairman of the 4-H Advisory Council.

This is the famous, or infamous, wedding cake that brought great embarrassment to the White House—especially to Chef Henri Haller—when newspaper food editors tried the same recipe and said the cake came out more like pudding than pastry.

This is my favorite photo of the White House—tulips blooming at the South Fountain, the breeze blowing King Timahoe's hair, and the waters of the fountain dancing happily. I wish I could relive that perfect day.

Now here's a man who's at ease with his dog, and a dog who's at ease with his man! I was relieved when President Gerald Ford's daughter Susan and his photographer David Kennerly put their heads together and decided to follow tradition by getting the President a dog. Here Liberty, a golden retriever, makes the President's work more pleasant in the Oval Office. Looking at this picture I almost feel I'm back at the White House, entering the office to retrieve the retriever.

said it would be awful if the newspapers got hold of it. I agreed. He said he has some men that are afraid of dogs. He was very nice about the incident.

5/22/68   The President called me over; he's in wonderful spirits—he has not yet heard about Yuki and the threat. He said Yuki was looking good. He called up Ashton Gonella and made a big thing of inviting her for an outside luncheon. He told her, "Mr. Bryant is here and says your dog is almost as mean as Mr. Califano's." I left before she arrived.

I called Mr. Deason and told him about Yuki biting the policeman. He said he would tell the President the story after he leaves the White House and retires in Texas, as he would be furious and upset if he knew now, and no telling what he would do to the policeman. I'm glad I won't be there when Prez learns of it!

Dumpling had her pups Monday. Everybody's having trouble. Marcia Maddox said the police came to her door and told her they would pick up Freckles if she continued to bark. She said she may bring Freckles back to White House as a guest. I told her to get permission from Mrs. Johnson.

5/24/68   Unbelievable scene. It was lucky no press was present. The President was at his luncheon table in the West Rose Garden. I walked Yuki to him and let him go. He jumped into LBJ's lap. The President said to Christian, his press secretary, "Come here and wipe these damn hairs off my coat." George Christian and I crouched beside Lyndon Johnson picking dog hairs off his coat with our hands, hair by hair. It reminded me of a bunch of monkeys grooming each other. That was one for the history books.

Later, I told Christian about the White House policeman that Yuki bit in the groin. I told him it was just for his own information. He thanked me. For me, the incident was now closed.

217

18

As June rolled around, everyone was wondering who LBJ's successor would be and if he'd finally give the nod to Bobby Kennedy.

6/5/68   Robert Kennedy is shot. I am shocked, but I was afraid something terrible would happen to him.

I sent Yuki to Walter Reed at 7:30 P.M. as he is scratching again. Captain Moreman took him.

6/6/68   Senator Kennedy is dead. I feel sick about it. This is turning into a year of death and destruction. I remember when I asked him to run for the Presidency when I saw him at launching of the aircraft carrier *John F. Kennedy* at Newport News (May 27, 1967). He looked so happy at the thought. Now he'll never have a chance. Maybe history is poorer.

6/7/68   I was in Juanita Roberts' office with Yuki pawprinting a picture for the President to sign. I had just made Yuki's print. LBJ picked up a pen and growled, "How come Yuki signed first?" Joking, deadpan. Yuki had chiggers, not fleas, from his Texas trip.

6/8/68   Senator Kennedy was buried in Arlington Cemetery. *Sad!*

6/10/68   Luci asked me to put her dogs in the lower pen so she could bring them to her room at night. Her baby turned over a half gallon of bacon-fat drippings that the cook saves for the dogs in the second-floor kitchen. Luci called her mother in to laugh at the mess. They had to take the baby's clothes off and bathe him. Luci said he felt and looked like a greased pig.

The black mood of the year was continuing.

6/17/68   A Capital Parks man emptied some ashtrays into a plastic garbage can. This set fire to some old tennis shoes and the smoke clouded the swimming pool. I'm glad Yuki was in Texas, as his room adjoins the locker room. I'll be glad when 1968 is over—what a year!

6/21/68   I took Yuki to the West Garden where Luci's baby Lyn was celebrating his first birthday. Yuki kissed the baby.

6/26/68   I was in the second-floor kitchen with Yuki, about 5 P.M. Luci came in and asked Chef Haller to do her a favor, if he wouldn't mind.

He nodded. He was busy and hardly listening. She asked him to change the baby's diaper while she was out visiting. He nodded his head yes. After Luci left he asked one of the pantry men what she had said to him; he said couldn't hear her because the exhaust fan was running. I think he half heard Luci, but it didn't register at first. When he found out what he'd promised to do he was in a state of shock. His dignity is suffering. Not only is he the Head Chef but he already had his hands full cooking family dinner for the First Family tonight, since Zephyr Wright is off. And it has to be flexible cooking when you cook for the Johnsons. You never know how many you are cooking for.

7/25/68 I had Yuki in the family quarters. Zephyr Wright was cooking a hamburger for Yuki. The telephone rang. Zephyr picked up the phone and no one answered. She hung up. Then the phone rang again. She said, "I am going to teach someone a lesson." The phone rang and rang. When she picked it up she snarled into the phone. Then she looked stunned. It was Mrs. Johnson. Zephyr hurried over to the West Hall, PDQ.

7/30/68 The Prez was up to his old tricks. The phone rang—the President calling me on my shop phone at 10:00 P.M. I had a feeling he was going to be putting me on and that we were on conference call. He asked me how Yuki was doing. He said he wanted Yuki to visit him after I got him to quit shedding and put some weight on him. He wanted to know which one of his dogs was bitten by Mr. Califano's dog last Saturday. I told him that I hadn't heard about the incident. He said I *should* know. I said, "Well, as you know, I'm off duty on Saturdays, Mr. President." Then he wanted to know how "that mean old beagle George" behaved while he was left here by Mr. Califano. I told him George did all right. He couldn't get a rise out of me, but he wasn't giving up. He asked if Mr. Califano brought any food in. I figured Joe Califano was listening to our conversation. I told the President I'd asked his secretary about the food bill and maybe he'd be getting a check from somebody. He said he'd like for me to check that. I said, "You know, Mr. President, he has that office right next to yours." Then he asked about Mrs. Gonella's dog, and if Ashton had brought in any dog food. I told him she had at first but not for the last six months. I tried to change the subject. I told the President that I took Yuki to the second floor at 7:30 P.M. every night and Zephyr fed Yuki. But the Prez was still at it. The President said, "You and Zephyr make a good salary. You all should put some weight on Yuki." I said we were working on it. The President said, "Well, you better take good care of Yuk." I looked at my watch. The President must have been talking for eight or ten minutes. I thought he was through, but then he had to bring in my home state—I guess to show his company how he knows everything about everything. He said maybe I was confused about his wanting to put some weight on Yuki but to take the fat *off* the beagles. The President said, "In West Virginia don't they say 'skinny as a hound dog' when they refer to a thin object?" I sighed and said, "Yes, they do, Mr. President. I understand your desires perfectly." And I certainly did. It was to have a little entertainment with his dinner.

It seemed that everyone was after me about that time. The carpenter shop was moving a lot of junk into Yuki's room and I was fighting to get the stuff out of there before a heavy locker or something fell on Yuki and crushed him to death.

Then Ashton Gonella sent her little boy to tell me that Honey had done a job on the floor of their living room and had chewed up some rugs. I told him to go back and tell his mother, "He's just behaving like a White House dog."

Then Marcia Maddox called and said she desperately needed to leave her dog, Freckles, at the White House for just a few days while she goes to Texas. I groaned and gave her the okay. I see by my diary that there was even bigger news in the land that day:

8/7/68 It looks like Nixon will get the Republican nomination tonight.

He got it and immediately went to see the President in Texas.

8/10/68 I have just heard the inside story. As candidate Nixon was leaving the LBJ ranch after being briefed on the war, Yuki jumped aboard the helicopter and got under Mr. Nixon's seat. President Johnson came aboard after Yuki. He said to Mr. Nixon, "Look, you've got my helicopter, you're after my job, and now you want my dog."

Later I told the Prez, "I guess Yuki would rather switch than fight." He gave me a dirty look.

8/12/68 Califano's dog, George, came in for a visit today. Freckles is still a guest.

8/13/68 I received my picture of the mockingbird chasing Yuki, autographed by President Johnson. It beats everything. It's one of my favorite pictures.

Then Usher James West got after me.

8/16/68 J. B. West said some dog had messed in the Red Room recently. I told him it wasn't our dogs, as they haven't been in the house lately. Probably some dog with someone on a private tour as there are many private tours when the President is out of town that the First Family knows nothing about. Staff people take their friends and families through the family living quarters. I remember how everyone was laughing during the Kennedy administration—that is, the servants and backstairs people—when one pretty staffer showed her family the President's bedroom and pretended she didn't know where it was and had never seen it before.

8/20/68   Colonel Asbill, the top vet at Walter Reed, and his fifteen-year-old niece Kristie MacDougal, who was visiting from California, came to the White House on tour. I showed them the dogs and they made pictures posing with the dogs. They saw Luci. That's one day a vet was a celebrity at the White House.

8/21/68   Zephyr is not worried about budget. She fried Yuki a couple of lamb chops as she didn't have any other food prepared. I took Yuki over to Jim Jones' office. He soon had Yuki howling. I told him if Vice President Humphrey didn't get in high gear that I would be taking care of poodles for Mr. Nixon. He laughed. I saw Ashton Gonella getting a highball in the second floor family quarters. I told her that I never knew she was expecting a baby until I read it in a newspaper. She said that she didn't like it being in the papers. I told her that reporters would make news out of anything that was connected with the White House. She was a little upset over the news story.

When I heard later that Barbara Howar labeled Ashton "the resident lamb among wolves," I thought how true that seemed and how sweet and vulnerable she always appeared.

8/22/68   The President said Luci was going to write a book about the dogs and he told me to help her out on any good information I could give her. I have my diary notebooks in the bank vault, and this one will join them before long for future reference. But she'll have to read my memoirs with the rest of the public. If she asks questions, I will answer them, but I won't volunteer.

8/30/68   Hubert Humphrey won the nomination. It was a wild three-ring circus.

9/7/68   My wife and I attended the commissioning of the aircraft carrier *John F. Kennedy* in Newport News, Virginia. Robert McNamara started to give a nice speech about the late President Kennedy. He got very emotional. He broke down before he finished his speech, and couldn't go on. Everyone was choked up. Caroline presented the ship with a sword. John received the pen used in signing. We watched the cake-cutting ceremony. Jackie Kennedy and little John shook hands with me and then with my wife. They were very nice to us. It was worth the trip just to see Mrs. Kennedy, who is still so beautiful.

9/8/68   I had Yuki in his striped coat to let the children see and pet him at the White House Country Fair for underprivileged children, one thousand of them. Yuki and I rode in a 1922 Model T Ford. Yuki and I met Mayor Washington of Washington, D.C.

9/9/68   The Country Fair is continuing today for two thousand of our own White House staff and families. Yuki in a red coat rode the Ferris wheel and didn't mind a bit, as I was holding him and talking to him. Lady Bird complimented my wife on the cute coats she has sewn for Yuki. Then an artist painted Yuki as I was holding him on my lap. The lights went out—an overloaded breaker. The other electricians reset the breaker. The painter kept on painting. The President stopped and came over to the platform and patted Yuki. Then the Prez headed for the cooked spareribs. Lynda hollered out to me that the painting was better-looking than the dog. I introduced my wife to Liz Carpenter and George Reedy, and we met some friends we hadn't seen since the Eisenhower party for White House staff at Gettysburg. Doris took the painting home. The officer Yuki bit some time ago in a delicate place was there and fed Yuki a piece of spareribs. He said he and Yuki were friends now. His wife was with him and said she didn't appreciate Yuki biting him. I played it cool and didn't say much about it.

9/13/68   I went to the Vice President's office in the Executive Office Building and asked the girls in the outer office if they were giving out any HHH tieclasps, pens, or other things. They said that the Vice President liked to give them out as presents himself. I said, "Thank you. Then let Mr. Humphrey give out the campaign buttons himself too," and walked out of the office. If his campaign is run as haughtily as his office staff he may be a loser. I asked one of the girls in Jim Jones' office what's going on. She said that one of the HHH girls gave her a tieclasp and it seemed as if it came out of Fort Knox the way she gave it. So I told her I believed I would get a Nixon pin.

Mr. Califano's secretary complained that George lost his dog tags while he was a guest at the White House. Ashton Gonella says her dog is now ruined and unfit for civilized house living. I wonder if they're trying to tell me something.

Yuki went to Camp David with the President. An agent told me that the President had Yuki in a convertible at night hunting for a rabbit for Yuki to chase.

Mrs. Johnson was on the Truman Balcony. She asked me where Blanco was. I told her in the pen. I asked if she wanted him out. She said yes. I let Blanco out. A TV crew made pictures of Blanco and Yuki to be shown in December. They were making a film of Mrs. Johnson narrating about the White House.

LBJ flew to Texas for a short visit.

9/24/68   The President and Yuki returned from Texas at 1:30 P.M. As the President got off his helicopter he was looking around and then he pointed toward me and motioned for me to follow him. I walked beside him into the Diplomatic Room. He said that Yuki had ticks and something was wrong with one of his paws. I told him I would check him. I sprayed Yuki. Later an agent told me that Yuki was playing with a burr and he got part of it in his paw. Yuki and I went to Lynda's movie, John Wayne in *Red River*. About a half-hour before the movie was over, she received a phone call. She said, "I have to go upstairs and show the President how to operate the damn tape recorder."

About this time, the scuttlebutt was that the President was working on his memoirs. He had a pretty girl he hired to help him at the White House and ranch. Luci was having a go at writing, too.

LBJ's helper was named Doris Kearns. She had caught the President's eye when she kept him waiting when the President was meeting a group of young scholars. She was one of the scholars and had actually written a nasty article about dumping LBJ in 1968 for the *New Republic*. But the President didn't know it at the time. He just saw an attractive gal and probably said, "You're the prettiest thing here," as he liked to say when he met a new female who struck his fancy.

9/26/68   Willie Day Taylor said she wished Luci would have let her check her writing before she sent it to New York. She said Luci wasn't too good at spelling. She said Luci wants to write a book or article showing the good side of LBJ.

9/28/68   I am going to Wyoming to hunt antelopes and mule deer with three other hunters in my Alaskan truck camper. (We should have a nice time whatever the result.) Alice Longworth petted Yuki. I wanted to talk to her about the pony her brothers smuggled up to the second floor of the White House in Teddy Roosevelt's day, but I didn't. She is a lovely lady.

10/10/68   I just returned from my hunt. I shot a nice antelope from over three hundred yards and I also saw a mule deer fawn that came running through the aspens.

10/20/68 The President was at Camp David. He sent for Yuki. The dog jumped in the car and sat in the rear seat like he owned it, said engineer Simmons. That night they returned on the helicopter. I had Blanco out to meet them. The President shook hands with Blanco.

Mrs. Kennedy married the man from Greece, Aristotle Onassis. Good luck to her, but I wish she had married an American. The rumor around the White House is that Caroline and John are taking it hard and are just miserable about the marriage.

10/24/68 Luci brought Lyn into the second-floor kitchen and told the maid to change his diaper and feed him. Maybe she couldn't find Chef Haller. Ha-ha. Lynda went to the hospital to have her baby.

10/25/68 12:03 A.M. Lynda had her baby, a girl, in Bethesda Naval Hospital. President Johnson gave out cigars. Lyn played with Yuki tonight. Everybody is grinning from ear to ear. The Prez said to me, "My brainy daughter finally made it. Luci will probably give birth to a future Miss America, but Lynda's baby will be the first lady President of the United States."

An inside story was that Lynda was so determined that her baby be born on Texas soil that she had a jar of Texas dirt from the LBJ ranch under her hospital bed. She had the baby—Lucinda "Cindy" Desha—in Maryland at Bethesda Naval Hospital, since she was living at the White House while waiting for her husband Chuck Robb to come back from Vietnam.

10/27/68 The Prez and Mrs. J, Luci and Lyn returned from New York. The President let Lyn walk off the helicopter. Yuki wore his blue and white coat with the HHH badge pinned on top. Prez saw it and said, "HHH." That was all. No smile. The President told Yuki, "Come on." Mrs. Johnson said that there were two hams, Lyn and Yuki. The Yuki ham stayed with the President overnight.

10/28/68 Yuki caught a squirrel. He held it by the back of the neck and the squirrel bit Yuki's left rear leg and ran up the tree. What a scene! I'm sure Yuki wanted the squirrel as a present for the Prez.

10/31/68 Lynda brought her baby home from the hospital. Luci came into the kitchen with Lyn. Baby Lyn had a Halloween suit on. She asked me where the Yuki mask was—the tramp with the cigar. I told her it was in my locker. Share and share alike, Yuki always says.

President Johnson stopped the bombing in Vietnam. I doubt the war will be settled in this administration.

11/1/68   LBJ waved for me to board Yuki on the helicopter. He let Lyn walk up the helicopter steps and had pictures made by White House photographers. Everyone in the family left for Texas but Lynda and her baby.

Luci told me while she was here she was not wasting time but had finished a short story about Yuki. She said she would give me an autographed copy. I heard from the best inside sources it is thirty pages long and she is getting $30,000—pretty good wages for a girl who can't spell.

11/5/68   I voted for Mr. Nixon, as I believe it's time for a change. I just didn't feel Johnson was heart and soul for Humphrey. If he'd said one word for him to me, I'd have voted for Humphrey. He didn't look a bit enthusiastic when Yuki wore the HHH badge. So I took my cue from that.

I could see the President was getting nostalgic as his remaining days at the White House dwindled down, as the song says, "to a precious few."

11/6/68   Returning from Texas, the President shook hands with Blanco as usual after the helicopter landed; then suddenly he held out his hand to me and shook my hand and held it a long moment.

It was very warm and personal and a moment that brings tears to my eyes whenever I think of it now and realize he is gone forever.

11/12/68   An historic moment. The President introduced me to the President-elect, Richard Nixon. This is the first time this has happened to me in seventeen years at the White House. Yuki and I were out earlier to see Nixon arrive, but press people Simone Poulain and Tom Johnson said it wouldn't be appropriate for Yuki to be seen at the arrival. But Yuki was with me when we were introduced and the President-elect asked President Johnson if that was the dog who boarded his helicopter at the ranch. The President said yes. Nixon looked around like he owned the place already.

11/16/68   Lynda's agent, Mike, told me that Yuki killed a squirrel at Camp David a couple of weeks ago. He quoted Lynda as saying "I'd kill that S.O.B. if he belonged to me." I think humans around the President are jealous of Yuki's position.

11/23/68   President Johnson said he would talk to Mr. Nixon and see if he wants Blanco. If Nixon has good sense he'll say no, thanks. I can't understand LBJ's offer. Is he being kind or paying him back for making the country go Republican?

225

11/28/68 Yuki was on TV at the ranch. Prez said they would call this Yuki's birthday. No one knows his age for sure, but he first came to the Prez at Thanksgiving.

I let Blanco out for squirrel chase. Blanco got excited, bit the back of a Capital Parks man who was leaning over working.

12/9/68 I was in Treaty Room setting up lights for a signing. Mrs. J walked in a few minutes before the signing. She said the President had sent Lois Wilson a letter explaining how Blanco reacts at the ranch. Negative. She told me I could ask someone if they wanted the dog. I told her I had a couple of people who wanted the dog. She told me not to say anything to the President, just give the dog away. That means she's desperate at last. As the President left the room after the ceremony he again shook hands with me. I think he wants me to know that our friendship did mean something special to him. To lighten the mood, I told him I was helping Cleave Ryan, the photographic electrician. The President looked at Cleave and said, "It looks to me like Mr. Bryant is working and Cleave is helping."

Luci was concerned about her dogs' welfare. I told her they were in a heated kennel.

It was "all systems go" at LBJ's party for the astronauts, who won't be home for Christmas because they'll be orbiting the moon aboard *Apollo 8*. William Anders, Frank Borman, and James Lovell, Jr., all danced with their wives as the Marine Band played everything moonie—"Moon River," "Moon over Miami," "Fly Me to the Moon." Former NASA Chief James Webb was there too.

12/12/68 The Prez and Mr. Christian were going to the Mansion from the Oval Office. He said Yuki was putting on weight nicely and asked me if Yuki was ready to go to Texas to become a gentleman dog rancher. The President asked me how many dogs he had. I told him that I had the names of three people who wanted Blanco. He said, "I didn't ask you that. I asked how many dogs I have."

I said, "Three—Blanco, Edgar, and Yuki." He looked surprised. I said the other three beagles belong to Luci. He walked away muttering about everyone being out to take his dogs away.

12/13/68 Yuki went to Texas with the President and Mrs. Johnson. Luci stayed at the White House with Lyn and Lynda and the baby.

12/15/68 Blanco bit Edgar on the foot. Dr. Moreman from Walter Reed took him back to Walter Reed. The President and Mrs. J returned about midnight from Texas. Yuki ran off the helicopter to me. I picked him up and walked into the Oval Room with Lady Bird. The President was behind us. I told her about Blanco biting and I advised her not to give Blanco to a family that had small children. I knew better than to walk in front of the President, but I had to let her know. I guess now I'm conspiring with her to get Blanco away.

12/16/68   I wasn't at the White House so Yuki didn't get to go to the tree-lighting with the President. Last year he stole the show. I saw on TV that this year it was baby Lyn who was the star.

12/17/68   I put Blanco back on tranquilizers. Lois Wilson wrote to the President and said they would take Blanco back only if the President couldn't find a home. They suggested that the President give the dog to me. However, I live in an apartment and no dogs are allowed—at least that's what I said. It's my policy not to take White House dogs.

8:30 P.M. I took an electric heater to the President's room to heat a flannel cloth to put on the President's chest. He has a chest cold. LBJ still likes those old-fashioned remedies of his mother's, he says.

12/18/68   President Johnson went to Bethesda Naval Hospital. They think he has a case of the flu. The old-fashioned remedy didn't work.

UPI reporter Merriman Smith and his wife stopped and talked with me as they left the reporters' Christmas party. I told him I would like to get my dog book written when I retire. He said, "Do it and you will get rich."

12/19/68   Yuki kissed Luci. She told Yuki, "Granddaddy is sick in the hospital." Mrs. Johnson showed Yuki to a young boy and girl at the ground-floor elevator.

12/22/68   The President returned from the hospital. He carried Lyn into the Oval Room as it was raining outside. Yuki was dressed in his new red Christmas coat with three red bells. Mrs. Johnson said he was in "a pretty outfit." She said, "I don't guess anyone has given you the bad news, but the President's sister is bringing her dog in as they will be our house guests for Christmas." The President had already told me about the dog, a miniature schnauzer. Lynda also called me later; she said it was her cousin's dog. Later on Mrs. Johnson called and said she was grateful that I was going to look after the dog.

I'll never forget LBJ's last Christmas at the White House:

12/23/68   I took Yuki all dressed up to the Usher's Office. Bess Abell found me and asked me to take Yuki in to see the children in the State Dining Room. Lynda and Luci came by. Lynda said, "I might have known it was Bryant and Yuki." She was disgusted that the children had gathered around us and we were more popular than Santa, who was standing there fat and jolly, saying, "Ho, ho, ho," to himself.

12/24/68 I helped the White House photographers with the lights as they made pictures of President Johnson and his family opening Christmas presents. I had Yuki in his red coat and he posed with the family. Lyn was fascinated most with a plastic telephone he received. The President asked me why Blanco couldn't go to Texas instead of Kentucky. I told the President that Blanco would kill sheep. The President said, "I don't have any sheep now." He told his secretary to hold up on giving Blanco away for a while. He's really grieving about giving up that dog. I distributed the presents and Marie Fehmer opened most of the President's presents. She asked me to gather up the wrapping paper and bows so they wouldn't clutter up the picture. The President said to Yuki, "Mr. Bryant's sweet wife made you a pretty coat. I hope you're grateful." That was as close as the President could come to saying thanks.

12/26/68 Yuki's guest dog left this evening.

12/27/68 The President and Lady B came out of the Diplomatic Entrance to board the helicopter. I had Yuki in his red coat. The Prez said, "Aren't you going to let him go?" I told him yes, and handed the Prez the leash. Yuki gave a lunge and practically pulled the President across the grass and aboard the helicopter.

1/6/69 I asked Mary Lasker if the President has decided about Blanco. He hasn't.

I took Yuki to the second-floor dining room. Tom Johnson and George Christian were dinner guests. The Prez was concerned about my getting laryngitis as I was so hoarse.

The Prez asked me what I was going to do with Yuki. I told him I wanted Yuki and Edgar to go to Texas. I told him I would give Blanco away to anyone he chose. I suggested the doctor in Corbin, Kentucky, who wants him and has a lot of land, the brother-in-law of Secret Service man James Mitchell. LBJ said what about Deason? I said he wants a beagle.

The Prez gave Yuki a lamb-chop bone. I grabbed it and held it and let Yuki bite off a little at a time, as I reminded Mrs. J of the steakbone incident that landed him in the hospital. She smiled and gave me her napkin to wipe the grease off my hands. LBJ thanked me for bringing the dog. He said he thought that Mr. Nixon had Checkers for me to take care of. I told him I thought that Checkers was dead, as that was eight years ago. I thought that he now had a terrier.

228

1/7/69   I took Yuki to Liz Carpenter's office. Yuki posed with her for several pictures. I held Yuki as she was at her desk talking on the phone. The photographer said it was a shot of Yuki bidding her goodbye. I will miss Liz—a great gal, with a great brain. Whenever LBJ needed great humor in a speech the inside story is he didn't trust anyone but Liz.

Rex Scouten was in the Usher's Office. I asked him if they were leaving the dog fence up. He said it was coming down at 12:00 noon on January 20. I told him to hold on, he might have to put it back up. He laughed and said he knew, but he just couldn't wait to take it down.

1/13/69   Mary Rather told me that President agrees with me and is giving Blanco to Dr. W. T. Daniel of Corbin, Kentucky. He owns a nice big house set on twenty-eight acres of land. I will contact agent James Mitchell tomorrow. I'm glad Blanco will have a good home.

I had Colonel Smith call Luci and tell her *Air Force One* will be too crowded for dogs on January 20—other than the President's Yuki.

1/14/69   I asked Head Usher James West to have the pups' room painted for the Nixons. He told me to see Whitey Williams. Now he has to see Rex Scouten. So that's the extent of my preparations for the Nixons.

Blanco will leave for Kentucky Friday morning. Luci's beagles and Edgar will leave here Wednesday to fly to Texas.

Colonel Robinson called me. He said his replacement is Colonel Coffey. I showed him the puppy room. He agreed it should be painted. I also showed him the two dog kennels. He said the Nixon dogs might arrive here Sunday. We were on the ground floor walking toward the theater. The President walked up behind us and told me to keep Yuki at the White House until the twentieth and give him a list of things concerning Yuki. I asked him if it was all right if Edgar went with Luci's dogs ahead of time. He said yes. The Prez was on his way to the theater to tape his Capitol Hill speech. They taped it and then reran it so LBJ could hear how his delivery was doing.

I called Rex Scouten at his home and asked him if he could get Capital Parks Service to paint the puppy room. He said he wouldn't waste the taxpayers' money until he was sure the Nixons would have dogs. I told him I wanted it painted. He said, "*You* do?"

I told him one of the Nixon people had said to have it painted. He asked me for Mr. Coffey's name. I told him I didn't remember the name. He said, "You find out the name and give it to the Usher's Office." I don't want to give out any names until the Nixon people are actually in charge. So I will have to pull some more strings tomorrow. President's last State of the Union address is tonight. Ashton Gonella told me that Honey tore up the rugs and furniture so much that she is now exiled out on a farm learning to hunt. So that's the sad ending to Honey, White House drop-out. When the President returned from Capitol Hill he said, "Hello, Yuki," but didn't take him. Mrs. Johnson waved to us. They went upstairs to listen to the TV comments. This is hard on the Prez.

An inside story around the White House at this time was that what finally tipped the scale in helping LBJ decide not to run again is that Lynda Bird made her Daddy feel so bad when in the middle of the night she returned in tears from seeing Chuck off to war and asked *why* her husband had to go to Vietnam. The Prez realized he had no answer.

1/15/69 I called Colonel Asbill and asked him to do me a favor, to call Colonel Coffey and request a paint job for the doghouses as a sanitary measure. Colonel Coffey told me that he received a call from Colonel Asbill.

I saw Scouten. He asked me for the name of the Nixon person. I told him Colonel Coffey.

Luci's beagles and Edgar left for Texas. I helped Sam Page load them in a White House car. I hated to see the dogs leave, but I can't hold back the clock. I will miss the dogs.

1/16/69 The painters painted the ceiling in the pups' room. Tomorrow they will finish the walls. Liz Carpenter's office called and I gave them the information for a press release on Blanco.

1/19/69 A White House driver in a station wagon took me to Andrews field. Yuki went with me. As President-elect Nixon's plane landed we drove up to the plane. Yuki and I went to Mrs. Nixon's personal maid, Fina Sanchez, and I told her I was there to take the Nixons' dogs to the White House. She was not going to let go of her dogs and acted like I was going to steal them. The airplane noise was deafening, so we were leaning towards each other screaming. Her husband came and introduced himself as Nixon's valet and he told his wife it was okay. Yuki was barking up a storm at the Nixon dogs, like he didn't think they belonged in his territory, so I let the chauffeur take him to the station wagon and I told him to keep Yuki up front. I took the Nixon dogs—a poodle named Vicky and a Yorkshire terrier named Pasha—and got in back with them. As we drove up to the South Portico, Luci and baby Lyn were playing on the lawn. Luci excitedly asked me if those two were the Nixons' dogs. I told her they were. She asked if she could take some pictures of Lyn playing with the Nixon dogs, for history. She took the pictures and said she would send me my autographed picture. So Luci took her pictures of the real changing of the guard, from one set of dogs to another. Lynda thanked me for my services during their stay at the White House. I said I hoped she would not be a stranger now that it was about over.

I asked the President what time he wanted Yuki to leave the White House on January 20. He said, "Have Yuk at Andrews by three on Monday."

1/20/69 I took Yuki, Pasha, and Vicky to the North Portico for the arrival of the Nixons. I dressed Yuki in a green coat and Vicky in a red, white, and blue coat. I had nothing that fit Pasha. LBJ spoke to all the dogs just before the Nixons arrived.

When the Nixons drove up President Johnson told the Nixons that their dog was greeting them. They walked over and petted Vicky, ignoring Yuki. A bad sign.

As President Nixon and his family were on their way to the stand to watch the parade they stopped and petted the dogs. I had Pasha under my coat, as it was cold. Tricia said she was pleased that I was taking good care of the dogs. I told the President that my wife made Vicky's coat. They said it was pretty, but said it without much warmth. I hope it will get a little warmer later. At least Lady Bird and the Prez had showed warmth to the Nixons' dogs earlier.

When the Nixons arrived at the White House before going to the Capitol Inaugural, LBJ kissed Pat Nixon on the cheek. Then Lady Bird hugged her. And the men talked about the weather four years ago at Johnson's Inaugural.

Then Nixon asked LBJ if he remembered Yuki's jumping into the helicopter with the wrong man, and both men laughed. Nixon said, "Well, I told you I wanted your job, not your dog." Yuki was sitting there looking up at both men and trying to figure them out.

Then Lady Bird wanted the Nixons to come inside the White House. She said, "Won't you go ahead?" But Pat said, laughing, "Not until noon." So the two ladies walked in side by side. Tomorrow Mrs. Nixon would go in first, according to protocol.

An interesting footnote to history is the treatment Luci Nugent got from the Secret Service men on her last day. I heard about it the next day. The way the story came back to the White House, on the morning of January 20, Luci was in Austin, giving orders as usual. She was telling the Secret Service men something about her luggage and possessions from her room at the White House, just exactly where she wanted it all placed.

231

Suddenly at noon the Secret Service men plopped the rest of her luggage down outside her house.

"You can put all this on the porch," she told them.

"I'm sorry," said one, "our time is up. We have to go back to the White House now."

Pat Nugent wanted one of the Secret Service men to carry his golf clubs, and the Secret Service man said, "You carry them yourself." And walked away.

Thus ended power. I feel sorry for White House kids when they have their rude awakening, which they all do.

After the Johnsons were all gone, I found a quiet corner and read the note that LBJ had left for me, and I'm afraid I blinked a little:

Jan. 18-69

Dear Mr. Bryant,

The companionship of my dogs has brought comfort through all my time in the White House. I am grateful to you for making that companionship possible, at whatever hour of the day or night you were called upon, and for caring for the dogs so devotedly.

You have been their faithful friend and their master as well.

Sincerely,
(signed) Lyndon Johnson

It was over. It was really over. It was a relief. It was not a relief. It was as if someone told me I would never see a member of my family again. I had known LBJ and felt closer than a brother. And now if we met again, we would be almost like strangers. I felt lost. Then free, as I realized I wouldn't have to take his guff any more. Then I felt lost again as I realized I would miss his teasing and making me participate in his jokes on other people.

I went home and told my wife that after the Presidency, the hardest job at the White House was dogkeeping. And, like LBJ, I felt sorry for myself. A few days later, I could stand it no longer. I had to communicate with the friend who was gone forever from my life.

What I wanted to say I couldn't say. But I had to say something. I put it in the form of a telegram, addressed to Stonewall, Texas, Box 213. The box-number code would get it "to the eyes of the President":

Mr. Lyndon Johnson

The departure of the members of your family from the White House is very evident. Best wishes for continued happiness to all the family and Yuki. Miss you all. Please give Yuki a pat for me. You have done more for the good of the country than anyone since the days of Franklin Roosevelt.

TRAPHES L. BRYANT

It was over.

III
Richard M. Nixon

19

I never met a President I couldn't like—in some way or other. And I started out ready to like Richard Nixon very much and to make a real friend. After all, I'd voted for the man.

Maybe I wouldn't have as personal a relationship as with LBJ— how often does such a thing happen? But at least I'd work on developing something warm and genial. *Right from the start*—to borrow a phrase from him—it was hard to do, and it got harder and harder. Something seemed a little cold and unyielding from the very beginning, and eventually there was even a sinister note—like you could get into real trouble if you didn't toe the line.

Eventually, I felt I had to get away. I almost asked to retire a little early. I just couldn't take it at the White House any more.

My timing was perfect. A few weeks after I left, the news of the Watergate burglary crashed in upon our surprised nation. But I wasn't surprised. I had seen strange work going on. Much wiring and strengthening of cables. I didn't know exactly what it was for and I wasn't supposed to know anything about it.

Secrecy started from the very beginning. Suddenly everything was off-limits to everyone but a few intimates—those who were close to the throne. And more and more Nixon struck me as acting like a monarch of all he surveyed.

In true royal style, the word around the White House was, "Don't contradict *the Boss*—it infuriates him." Well, I thought, that certainly is a change from Lyndon Johnson. LBJ—or *the Prez*, as he was familiarly called behind his back—liked to fight around with the people around him. LBJ seemed to be waiting, hoping you would say something he could challenge so he could argue with you. He baited people so he could prolong it.

The royal feeling, strangely enough, started with the name the new President gave to a dog presented to him by his staff. Rose Mary Woods, his personal secretary, had been ringleader in choosing a suitable pup, and I remember being happy when I heard that they were planning to give Mr. Nixon a presidential-size dog—an Irish setter. The story was that Nixon had once had an Irish setter who had been his constant companion and had kept him from feeling lonely during terrible times of illness and money problems in the Nixon family.

So it was quite appropriate that Rose Mary Woods, who felt great sympathy for the Boss, should want him to have a duplicate of that noble beast. He cost two hundred dollars. Nobody had come to me to contribute, but I would have, and I was prepared to make that dog feel really welcome.

I remember the day the beautiful, six-month-old, red-coated creature arrived by station wagon, driven by E. Irving Eldredge of Tirvelda Farms late in January 1969. Mrs. Nixon took time to get acquainted with him on the lawn. The dog knocked her down three times. He was so friendly, he would jump up and put his paws on the First Lady's shoulders.

Each time she fell, she just laughed—and got up without letting anyone help her.

President Nixon was so thrilled, he even knelt down and hugged the dog, and he knighted him "King Timahoe," explaining that the name was for "the little village in Ireland where my mother's Quaker ancestors came from."

So that was our *first* king in residence at the White House— King Timahoe. The President said, "If he's the presidential dog he will be treated like a king around here, won't he? Even a President's dog gets the royal treatment."

I said, "Mr. President, every dog at the White House gets treated like royalty."

At first the President called his dog King Timahoe. But when everyone chopped off the King to make it easier, the President went along with it and usually called him Tim or Timahoe.

The second king in residence was the President himself, who acquired the nickname of King Richard for the regal way he swept in and out of the White House in his limousine and the grand way he did just about everything. The way he lived. The way he treated his staff. The way *he* wanted to be treated. The way he seemed to be trying to build an empire by hand-picking men and training them at the White House and then sending them out to take over some government agency.

Every time I turned around, there was a new expression of royal grandeur. Like having a $100,000 sauna installed. And using two helicopters instead of one. Or, much later, having a lowly photographer banished from the White House for daring to get into the background of a picture in which the President was being sworn in for his second term of office. The fact that the White House photographer was dressed in casual clothes was a second high crime.

And speaking of clothes, the signal was there at the first Inaugural when Richard Nixon insisted on going back to striped trousers and a cutaway coat after LBJ had taken the oath of office at his Inaugural in a plain business suit.

Things got more and more regal from that day on. Soon President Nixon decreed that even workers like me had to get all prettied up for official functions. The White House had suits tailored for any electrician or carpenter who might be around during a party or official function. Several times I had to go to a Georgetown haberdasher to be measured and fitted for my black suit, which looked almost like a tuxedo. With it, I always had to wear a white shirt and black bow tie.

It wasn't just clothes, of course. The mentality of the new administration showed through in countless ways. In the middle of a heat wave, for example, with the temperatures soaring to ninety-five degrees, Nixon had his valet, Manolo, call the engineers to light the fireplace in his little study in the Lincoln sitting room. Then he had them turn the air conditioner down to the lowest point they could get—close to forty-degree air.

People backstairs shook their heads about a man who would have a log fire roaring in the middle of July, when New York and other cities were having brown-outs and trying to get people not to use too much electricity. Here at the White House, we had the fire blazing in the fireplace and the air conditioning going full blast to pour in the manufactured cold air.

As a maintenance man at the White House, I got used to the strange behavior of its inhabitants, but I often thought how amazed the public would be to see highly paid engineers running around performing their assignment—tending the "royal" fireplaces of the President and his "Ins" among the presidential aides such as Haldeman—carrying logs, stoking the fire, adding wood, and hauling out ashes.

Watching it all, I kept thinking, This White House is now a

castle—everybody's royalty now. And when there was a ghost of a chance of a romance with British royalty—Tricia and Prince Charles—the President almost danced around with anticipation, mentioning it at every opportunity.

Tricia was called "The Little Princess." She liked it, even when she protested she didn't like it. The First Lady acted remote and mysterious, like a languishing queen. The only one who showed she wanted to be a commoner was Julie. Julie loved all people and demonstrated it.

Backstairs, the White House staff chuckled at the President's ambitions for his daughters and said it was a good thing Julie happened to fall in love with David, a grandson of a President, or she would have had a hard time getting his consent for the wedding.

But the irony was that David Eisenhower was the most old-shoe member of the family. The story was, he used to hitchhike to Julie's college to court her until his grandmother, Mamie Eisenhower, heard of it and gave him an old car to do his courting in, because she was afraid someone would kidnap him and hold him for ransom.

The member of the presidential family I felt sorry for was Pat. She was withering away at the White House because she was sort of shut out of the President's life. Clubwomen were thrilled about the Dick-and-Pat act and said that a vote for Dick was a vote for Pat; they even had signs that said "Pat for President." But Pat and Dick were not the strong, always-together team they seemed to be. They were good friends, you might say, but they had separate rooms.

Of course, all Presidents have their own bedroom suites and all First Ladies have their private suites. But that doesn't mean that Madame First Lady has to sleep in her own bedroom. Hell, I remember when the White House had a good laugh because Harry Truman and his wife Bess had broken a slat of the presidential bed and it couldn't have happened from lying there like a log. Everybody knew they always slept together. Harry was all man and everyone at the White House knew it, even if he was stuck with wearing his sissy-looking glasses in the swimming pool. Maybe because of these glasses, he was feistier and cussed more, acted tougher, and drank more bourbon than he needed to.

And I'd be in and out of LBJ's bedroom night after night finding Lady Bird there tucked into bed reading and waiting for her husband to get off the phone or quit playing with the dogs. He, too, was very turned on by women and showed it.

First Lady Betty Ford frankly said she'd slept in the same bed with her husband all the pre-presidential years and wasn't going to change now that she was in the White House.

Pat Nixon, however, hadn't been sleeping in the same bed and explained, "No one could sleep in the same bed with Dick. He's too nervous." And she told how he got up in the middle of the night and turned on the light to read or work, then turned it off, then back on again.

President Nixon seemed to keep women at arm's length, even his wife. I never saw him grab her and just kiss her or hug her as LBJ would do spontaneously with Lady Bird. Nixon seemed to prefer the company of men. He was more comfortable with them. He liked to sit and talk with them and drink with them. And of all men, the most important to him seemed to be Bebe Rebozo. They had been friends for many years and the story was told to me that after he lost the race in 1962 for the governorship of California, and bitterly told the press they wouldn't have Richard Nixon to kick around any more, he and Bebe sat around a friend's office and held hands and pledged eternal friendship no matter what happened. They vowed they'd stick together. And so they did. Even in the White House.

Backstairs the story was told of how lonely Pat had become in New York because her husband spent more time with Bebe and in his business and political pursuits than with her. Eventually she made new friends and achieved her own kind of happiness that didn't depend much on her husband, though she still would perform her social duties and go anywhere Dick needed her. But according to a source close to the First Lady, when Richard Nixon decided to run for the Presidency again, in 1968, some of his backers went to Pat and told her that she would have to give up her new friends and concentrate full time on helping her husband if he was ever to win.

She did make the sacrifice, though she knew that Nixon had no intention of giving up his own friend Bebe Rebozo. And I noticed at the White House that as Nixon blossomed in the early good times and seemed to get happier and happier, Pat was more and more subdued and quiet; she seemed to be fading away to a shadow of herself. Some of the women reporters commented on how thin Pat looked and wondered if she was ill or something. But they were told by the Press Information Office that she wanted to look that way and was dieting.

I used to wish there was something I could say or do when I would see her smiling, smiling, always smiling whenever people were around, and carrying out her job, as she saw it, of backing her husband in anything he did. I was sorry she didn't come on strong like Lady Bird did with her beautification program—that would have given her something to be excited about and would have kept her busy.

What can I say about Rebozo? If Rose Mary Woods, the President's private secretary, was the fifth member of the Nixon family, Bebe was surely the sixth. He seemed to live only to be near the President, to make Nixon's life happier, to be a friend. He ran errands for the President, took care of anything the President asked him to do, and stayed in the background. Eventually, stories came out about his connection with money given by Howard Hughes some time in 1969 or 1970 and kept in a safety deposit box by him and later returned. This all came to light after my time in the White House. I never heard of it there.

It's easy to see why it took the press so long to notice that Rebozo was around. He was so quiet at parties, you might mistake him for someone on the staff, like a Secret Service man. He was so modest at all times, you might think he was a poor relative. But the word was he was very well-heeled, the top man in some bank, involved in several businesses, and had helped the President up the financial ladder. To Julie and Tricia he was a sort of Uncle Bebe. And President Nixon tried to please his friend whenever he could. Here's a characteristic incident mentioned in my diary:

6/5/70 The President's car stopped before reaching the West Gate exit. Bebe asked the President if Tim could go with them on a boat ride. (I didn't want Timahoe to go.) I told Bebe that Tim wanted to chase a squirrel on the White House grounds. The President said that Tim *could* go.

According to insiders, Nixon first met Rebozo in 1950 after he'd just been elected to the Senate from California and had gone to Florida for a rest. He brought with him a letter of introduction to

Rebozo from Florida's Senator George Smathers. They struck up a friendship immediately and Rebozo was never out of his life after that.

In 1960, the story goes, Rebozo was the only outsider in Nixon's hotel suite in the Ambassador Hotel in Los Angeles, after Dick Nixon lost the Presidency to Kennedy. In every crisis, Rebozo was there to share victory or defeat. Bebe shared a three-day holiday with the President-elect after the 1968 triumph. And when Nixon bought a home in Key Biscayne, it was a $127,700 house two doors down from the bachelor house of Bebe, which was worth about the same amount. In the middle was, of all things, Senator Smathers' house.

Even before President Nixon moved into the White House, the Secret Service was supervising the planting of a gigantic twelve-foot-high hedge around all three houses, making them into a compound. The story was that Rebozo had been married for a few years, but was estranged from his wife and had gotten a divorce in 1950, just before he met Nixon.

Rebozo was pretty good-looking. I heard a White House secretary say she could forgive him his paunch because he had the most beautiful eyes in Washington. Another told me Rebozo had been voted the best-looking boy in his high school class in Miami. As far as I know, he didn't look twice at any girl in the White House, but he always was friendly and nice, giving them a mysterious little smile if they tried to talk to him.

For a while there was a story making the rounds that a pretty woman named Jane Lucke was Rebozo's girlfriend, and I do believe I saw her at the White House on the evening Johnny Cash entertained the President. The big talk the following day was that Rebozo's girlfriend, Jane Lucke, had been seated at the right side of the President, apparently to honor Rebozo. But when the press interviewed Miss Lucke in Florida she said it was a strictly nonromantic relationship and that they had known each other a long time and played bridge together, and things like that.

Pat Nixon's relationship with her husband wasn't romantic, either, but she was a good soldier and did all the things she was asked to do. She helped him present the picture of a perfect couple, happy and content together. After his election in 1968, she put in appearances for many a good cause. In October 1969, for example, she

243

sold her handshake to make money for a day-care center which was part of the Child Development and Diagnostic Center in Georgetown. At $10 a shake, Pat Nixon quickly earned $750 for the center plus the original $3,750 that two hundred and fifty members of the D.C. National Council of Jewish Women paid to attend the charity luncheon.

How well she played the game is shown by the fact that on September 27, 1969, she received a citation from the National Federation of Republican Women signed by the fifty state presidents for her "memorable contribution to international understanding through her gracious warmth and friendliness."

But many people remarked about Pat's thin, pinched look. She was certainly a much thinner version of the candidate's wife who had helped him campaign against Kennedy in 1960.

I read after my retirement that President Nixon became so agitated during a public appearance that he shoved Ron Ziegler, his press secretary, off the path in annoyance. That was perhaps the first time the public really became aware of the high tension inside the little group at the top in the Nixon administration. Ron Ziegler was always fighting for power and so was everyone else. I remember once the other aides played a trick on him, sending him a copy of a note supposedly from the President, telling someone else to bring press problems directly to the President and not to Ziegler. Ziegler, I heard, was really in a cold sweat for a few hours, thinking he was out of favor. The game, or the "game plan," as they called it around the White House in those days, was "get him before he gets you," and Ziegler must have figured he'd been gotten.

As the Watergate story unfolded, the world learned how well President Nixon had come to know his aide Chuck Colson—too well for the comfort of either. Colson had come a long way—in the earlier Nixon years he once went through the receiving line at one of the President's White House church services, and the President shook his hand without even recognizing him, as if he were a stranger. At least I can say this about my own face, the President did know it, even when he saw me in unaccustomed surroundings. When my wife and I were invited to the White House for a religious service, he recognized me and held up the line to chat about his dogs.

Just as Bebe Rebozo and President Nixon went together as a team on the social and personal side, H. R. "Bob" Haldeman and the President were a team on the work side. Haldeman was really the top man around the White House, at least for as long as I was there, and he was known for his temper. He was always threatening to fire a man if he didn't jump to do something. He'd say, "Grab this ball or we'll find someone else to carry it."

And he was famous for giving people assignments that he wanted finished in a couple of hours. He'd say, "Let me have a memo by two o'clock." So naturally there were a lot of missed lunches around the White House. All he had to say was, "The President is waiting for it." And if the fellow started to try to explain something, Haldeman would wave him away with, "This is not a question, it's an order."

If Haldeman didn't like the way someone was talking about the administration he would say, "We'll expose him." There was all kinds of talk about exposing this person and that. Everyone seemed at least potentially an enemy. You had to be "loyal." I got sick of hearing that word—so-and-so did not appear to be loyal to the Boss. And, Who was loyal to Richard Nixon, and who wasn't? I almost started worrying about my own loyalty.

Lyndon Johnson had complained to me that you couldn't tell who your friends were and that a President *loses* his friends. And he felt sorry for himself. But this President, if I could believe what I heard, actually *feared* his friends, and a lot of other people, too. Some said his obsessive distrust and fear of people bordered on the paranoic. I'm not a psychiatrist, but I do know his own dog, Timahoe, was a little worried about him, preferring to be where the people and the atmosphere were not so nervous.

Nervous was a good word for Nixon. As the youth of today would say, he was uptight—that is, part of the time, because he seemed to fluctuate. One day he would be elated and talking fast and excitedly. The next time I'd see him, he'd be sort of silent and sullen and not to be disturbed.

Sometimes the President was so nervous, he couldn't hold onto things. I remember once, when he was trying to sign a congressional bill, he had gotten so nervous, he had put the cover on the pen and tried to sign the bill with the cover on. And then he had dropped the pen and cover on the floor.

And he would have a terrible time with the dog's leash. He would get Timahoe's leash all wadded up in his hands and I would stand there wanting to help him out but not wanting to draw attention to it. And sometimes, in his nervousness, he would just chuck the wadded-up mess to me.

There was something else that struck me as strange: everybody tried to flatter Nixon—I mean his aides. I never saw anything like it. I'm not saying staffers in other administrations didn't do it, but it just wasn't taken that seriously.

I remember in Johnson's day, the men would butter him up but there would be some humor about it. As an aide praised some action of the Prez, he might add something funny under his breath to the other aides. And if he seemed to be too sincere in his praise of LBJ, the others would accuse him of being a brown-nose the moment LBJ was out of the room. In some cases, LBJ himself would be embarrassed by the flattery—as when Jack Valenti said he slept better knowing LBJ was in the White House.

But with Nixon, it was different. His aides weren't half kidding when they praised him. They almost seemed to think he was a savior, or headed a cult. I recall that John Ehrlichman earned brownie points by copying down something Nixon had said and having it made into a big sign that he hung on his office wall with Nixon's name under it. The quote was: "Let us not fall into the dreary rut of just managing chaos a little better. Let us use the great power of this place to do something for the nation."

20

I think Pat felt that whatever happened, her fate was bound up with Dick Nixon's. In September 1969 she visited the home where she grew up in Cerritos, California, and said some striking things about her childhood. Her father and the President's father, Frank Nixon, had lived about eight miles apart in the Cerritos area; by chance, though they didn't know each other, they owned adjoining cemetery plots. "So I think we were meant to be together," Pat said. There were tears in her eyes.

Other people thought Pat had a rough childhood because her mother had died and she had to cook for her father and brothers, but she didn't see it that way. "The sad things that happened were character-building," she said. "And we had the support of friends." All in all, her childhood had been a happy time. "We had all the fun anyone could ever have in the whole wide world. I took care of this home, made the curtains, really loved it, rode bareback, played 'run, sheep, run' and had a wonderful time." And she added, "I had a gorgeous garden."

Then she added wistfully, and I think she was talking of her own life too, "It's changed a lot—progress, I guess."

Pat's visit to Cerritos was somewhat marred by war dissenters. Signs outside were held aloft: "CHILDREN PLAY IN THE USA, BABIES BURN IN VIETNAM and AMERICAN PARADOX: CHILDREN'S PARKS IN THE USA—CHILDREN'S GRAVES IN VIETNAM." The First Lady kept smiling and pretending not to notice. Many other times it came to me how well she had learned not to notice. Around the White House it was said she was smart as a tack and knew much more than she let on, but she was determined not to make waves.

Pat liked happy colors—orange, pink, red, and yellow. At a quilting exhibition in Kentucky she once fell in love with a particular quilt that had these colors combined. Its price was $350, so she didn't buy it for herself, even though she had just accepted a gift quilt for the President's bedroom, and could have figured she was getting two for the price of one. The gift quilt was a beauty, and very patriotic, showing a blue eagle surrounded by red stars in a sea of white. Pat promised that before it was put on his bed, it would hang in a place of honor at the White House for everyone to see.

Pat always knew what to say to bring a lot of people into the act. "While it is being displayed," she told the quilters, "I shall see it often and be appreciative of all my good friends from Kentucky."

As I saw her, Pat still had something of the schoolteacher about her, liking to explain things, always interested in how things were made, always learning. I remember when she was curious about how puppets are made with styrofoam balls molded on top with cheesecloth soaked in paste. She was interested in everything.

Some people said that when Pat Nixon got away from the White House, she started to feel at home. That's when she seemed to relax, spread out, and come into her own. Around the White House, everything centered around Richard Nixon and she had to play her careful role as queen. One nickname for her was Lady Patricia.

If Pat ever had the urge as First Lady to act like a commoner, she lost it in a hurry. Almost the first day the Nixons were in the White House, they entertained all the campaign workers who were in town for the Inaugural. Pat got on the East Room stage and began a little speech, saying that from now on the White House would be open to the little people. She said, "We're going to invite our *friends* here and *not* all those big shots."

Nixon interrupted her quickly, saying, "Of course, *all* our friends are big shots."

Pat clammed up and rarely tried to make another pronouncement on her own.

The Nixon White House was clammed up in every way. The Johnsons had stuck around after official parties, and sometimes you couldn't get LBJ to quit dancing as long as there was any music. The Nixons made a beeline for the elevator the moment they could, and the guests were left to their own devices. One Christmas, the Nixons had a party for the press and didn't show up at all. The press was plenty peeved.

The Nixons showed little warmth toward the entertainers at their parties. Lady Bird and LBJ had kissed dozens of entertainers after their performances. When Israeli Premier Golda Meir was a guest of the Nixons, Isaac Stern and Leonard Bernstein performed following the State Dinner in her behalf. Golda went up on the stage and congratulated both of them with a kiss. Pat Nixon merely shook their hands. Later, when Golda Meir was leaving, Pat did give Mrs. Meir a little hug before she got into the limousine for the ride across the street to Blair House.

Pat had a suppressed warmness but was shy. And President Nixon certainly didn't help her overcome her shyness—he was shy himself. I don't think I ever did see the President kiss anyone other than his daughter Tricia at her wedding. It was a complete departure from the LBJ style, as everyone agreed around the White House.

When Pat would go places without the President and people would ask her why, she would always defend him, saying, "Oh, Dick can't come, he works eighteen hours a day." We would smile about that at the White House, because we would know that the President was off on the presidential yacht with Rebozo, relaxing. But to my knowledge, no one around the White House ever heard Pat say a word of complaint about sharing her husband's time with Rebozo.

Pat had not always been a completely placid individual. One person who knew them back in the vice presidential days happened to come to their home in Spring Valley at the worst possible time, when Pat was blowing her stack over something, as she and her husband sat at the table. Seeing her always the same, always reserved and in control, I was glad to know that once, at least, she had blown off steam.

The only other time I ever heard of her getting a little heated was when the ladies of the press cornered her at a social event to ask her about Watergate. She felt they had gone too far in questioning her about it at such a time and told them so.

Pat was modest and repressed, but she was First Lady and everyone at the White House tried to please her. In attempting to live up to her husband's standard of perfection she occasionally got a little finicky herself, as you will see by my diary.

The President seemed to have a thing about perfection. Whatever he did, he liked to brag about it. He once made a hole in one in golf and liked to talk about it. He tried bowling with Pat and on

249

his fifth try got a 204—"five strikes and two spares," he gloated, "that's pretty good, isn't it?"

Pat, he added, scored 110. And Pat jumped in to say, "Yes, I can't beat him. Dick is a good bowler." It turned out that his other scores that night were around 150.

Every President I've known had some particular point of pride. With LBJ, it was personal freedom. LBJ was always mentioning a pillow he had on the ranch which said, HERE I DO WHAT I DAMN PLEASE. He was proud of his pillow—and his freedom. Lady B understood his feelings about his freedom, and that's why they got along so well.

Truman's point of pride was never to duck responsibility. Everybody has heard of the sign on his desk that said, THE BUCK STOPS HERE. He could take the heat. He made decisions. That was Truman's greatest pride.

Kennedy's vanity concerned his seamanship on his sailboat. I think it was as important to him to be good sailor as to be a good President. Maybe there was even a connection.

Nixon's point of pride was that he could make a speech off the cuff. For the longest time he didn't want anyone to know he had help with his speeches, and all the aides around the White House went around saying that Nixon was his own speechwriter, even though it was ridiculous to think one man could do it all. Insiders knew his top speechwriter was Pat Buchanan.

Nixon's perfectionism may be why he wanted his reelection to be the greatest landslide in history, topping LBJ's victory. If he could have been satisfied with just a smashing victory, there might never have been any Plumber's Unit, or CREEP, or Watergate.

Not only was Richard Nixon a perfectionist himself, but he surrounded himself in the White House with others who thought the same way. Insiders called Henry Kissinger the worst perfectionist of all and said it made it well nigh impossible to work for him. Take the matter of his correspondence. Kissinger hated the word "sincerely" because he thought it sounded insincere. If an aide dictated that word in closing a letter the whole thing had to be retyped. He wanted the closing of his letters to read "With warm regards" if it was going to someone he knew and liked or "Best regards" to people he scarcely knew or didn't particularly like.

Haldeman was another perfectionist. He wanted everything

down on paper and he even tried to have a complete pictorial record of the Nixon days at the White House. It amused the White House gang that Haldeman was taking his own pictures of the President. As if the White House photographers weren't doing it well enough themselves. Sometimes new or foreign lensmen, seeing Haldeman with his camera, would mistake him for one of them and would grumble to him that Nixon was a lousy subject because he wouldn't do this or that for the camera.

One of Haldeman's main jobs was to get a lot of people to write memos and "position papers" on this or that for "the Boss." LBJ had wanted a man to sit down and tell him face to face about something and defend the recommendation he was making. Nixon seemed to need nothing but the memo or a bunch of memos; he would then go into seclusion to think it over. Haldeman, however, frequently shared in the President's thinking of this kind and some said the two men were like one man with two heads—sort of a two-headed President.

Rose Mary Woods, the President's top secretary, was a third perfectionist. Insiders warned you not to cross "Rosie," as they called her, because she had a fierce Irish temper and could tell the high and mighty to "go to the devil" if she thought they let the Boss down. After Nixon's election defeat in 1960, she wanted to tell the whole Republican party to go to the devil. The White House crowd said, a little enviously, that Rose Mary had risen far in life, starting as a factory worker in a little town in Ohio—Sebring. But she came from a talented family. Her brother, Joe Woods, had done well for himself, too, becoming the sheriff of Cook County, Illinois.

The atmosphere at the White House was thick with distrust. The word was "Watch out for this one and that one." Haldeman was jealous that the press liked Kissinger better than the President, and wrote nicer stories about him. Later he became annoyed that the White House dogs were taking attention away from the President.

Eventually even Fina Sanchez, the wife of the President's valet and the First Lady's maid, was infected with suspicion. She thought someone was out to get her. I never did figure it out completely. Did she mean the men around her husband were against her because her husband was so close to the President? Because he really was close. Never had I seen a presidential valet a guest at so many White House parties and receptions. In China, Manolo was the

President's food-taster. Manolo hero-worshiped the President and frankly said he would do anything for him.

On the side, Manolo was Richard Nixon's Spanish teacher. They practiced their Spanish on Timahoe, and I think with Fina and Manolo talking Spanish to him by day and me talking English by night, poor Timahoe didn't want to follow orders in any language.

When I saw how nervous Nixon was, I felt sorry for him and decided I wouldn't want to be President if they gave me the job. Some people didn't notice the President's nervousness because he really loved crowds. He liked a group where he could walk around and shake a hand here and a hand there, and make some quick comment, "Yes, I know your town, I once ate at the such-and-such restaurant there. Say hello to your mayor for me." That kind of thing. But his nervousness came out when he had to sit around and talk to just one person. Unless the person was someone on his staff and they were discussing politics or a government program, he was just stiff and silent. He really had nothing else to talk about.

At first I tried to get on a footing with President Nixon something like the one I'd been on with LBJ. To open things up a little, I'd say, "Well, I see by the papers such and such." But he cut me off once or twice and I just gave up. If he had something to talk to me about, I answered. He never kidded me as LBJ had done.

The way I figured it, President Nixon felt he was on stage all the time and didn't know you could just sit around and say nothing and have a nice friendly feeling. Lots of times I'd been around LBJ for hours and he hadn't said a word to me but knew I was there and just wanted me around. If I tried to leave, he'd call me back.

Nothing like this ever developed with me and Nixon. Or even with any of his advisors. The White House talked about how Nixon seemed to have a shell around him. That no one could get through to him. And the newspapers talked about a "wall" that had been thrown up between the President and the outside world.

Only with Bebe Rebozo did he relax. And I was glad he had at least one such friend.

I also got used to seeing Billy Graham around. Graham was there most often, but the President gave many other ministers a turn at leading the religious services in the East Room. Terence Cardinal Cooke came up from New York one time and based his sermon on a line from St. Augustine: "I shall work as if everything depended on me; I shall pray as if everything depended on God." Later Nixon repeated the statement several times and commented, "That's the whole thing in a nutshell."

When Nixon was campaigning he deplored the bad language that people like Lyndon Johnson and Harry Truman had used and he said if he got in the White House, that kind of talk would end. He also condemned the four-letter words used in the movie *Love Story*.

Once installed in the White House, President Nixon's language was little better than that of his predecessors. Only the words had changed. Nixon introduced some new phrases I hadn't heard before. For example, if he thought someone was soft on the Vietnam war he'd call him a "sweet-ass." Once I heard the President use that expression as he walked along with Haldeman and another staffer. Nixon was saying, "I'm telling you to keep that sweet-ass away from me." And Haldeman replied, "We'll cut him off at the ankles at his first move."

I don't know who they were talking about, and in a moment they were out of earshot. Other times he liked to refer to this group or that as "jackass people" and he was not above saying so-and-so had the "balls of a brass monkey."

This reminds me that Nixon was not the kind of man to make leisurely tours of the White House grounds shaking tourists' hands and playing for a while with his dog. No, he seemed all business around the White House. Always in a hurry to get somewhere. And frequently talking business en route.

President Nixon was always completely dressed when I saw him. Never did I bring Timahoe to his bedroom. He was a very formal person. And so was Pat. No one was permitted to photograph her on the beach in swim clothes, or the President in shorts or swim trunks. The only beach picture I ever saw of the President and First Lady showed them walking away from the camera into the mist with their arms around each other—his arm around Pat's shoulder, her arm around his waist. Both are fully dressed and Pat is even wearing a scarf around her head. The picture was made by Ollie Atkins, the official White House photographer.

One Nixon staffer I really liked was Herb Klein. During the campaign he had been the person closest to candidate Nixon and I was told he had given up his own career as a newspaperman to

253

help him. So I figured he would be top dog at the White House. He was a pleasant fellow. I liked him, but what was more to the point, the whole press corps seemed to like him. He had a great sense of humor. Soon after the new President was in the White House, some reporters asked Herb about the White House swimming pool and whether Nixon was using it much. He replied, "No, he's not using it. He tested it and found you could put instant coffee in the pool water and drink it. The Boss doesn't like hot water and Coffee Mate for swimming."

It turned out that Herb Klein's days were numbered and so were the pool's. Pretty soon the President had it covered over and made into a press room so the hated correspondents would be out of his wing of the White House altogether. Klein himself was a little harder to get rid of. He was assigned to deal with high-level editors and such, and kicked upstairs—or out the door, since he was moved across the street to the Executive Office Building.

The man who took his place at the White House was Ron Ziegler, a handsome young fellow who'd been a Disneyland guide before becoming a high-level PR man with the J. Walter Thompson advertising agency. The press was forever saying Ron could go back to Disneyland when he got through trying to interpret President Nixon, and some wished he would.

The word was that President Nixon liked to surround himself with young-men-in-a-hurry types. Easygoing, salt-and-pepper-haired Herb Klein didn't fit that description—or even try to fit it. The people the President picked for jobs in the White House or for political assignments were nearly all clean-cut, tall, dark, and handsome fellows. Herbert "Bart" Porter, Bob Odle, Gordon Strachan, Jeb Magruder, Ron Ziegler, Dwight Chapin, and Stephen Bull fit the pattern—a man could hardly tell one from the other. John Dean was dark and handsome and fitted the bill, too, except that he was a little sawed-off-looking—"small, dark, and handsome," we called him.

Peter Flanigan was certainly handsome enough. They called him "Mr. Fixit" at the White House because he was supposed to come up with answers to people like Ralph Nader who were attacking the President—saying that no one but the inner circle had access to the President and that the President was not concerned about the high prices people were paying for groceries.

The word around the White House was watch out. These people are nobody to fool around with. They don't trust anybody. If they don't like you, too bad. When a friend came to visit one aide in the White House, he was warned not to say anything derogatory about the Boss that could be overheard. "Some of my colleagues can be ruthless," the aide said in a quiet voice. "Be careful not to cross any of them."

Kissinger at first seemed to be the clown around the White House. No one took him seriously except the President and his own aides, who complained because they had to work fantastic hours. But the truth was, he was the LBJ of the Nixon White House, the man with the whip.

He had to be. If he was going to pursue all the females he did, he had to have someone back at the office keeping up with things. He and President Nixon seemed to have an agreement. Kissinger would be the girl-chaser for both of them. That way the White House maintained its reputation as a sexy place to work. Barbara Howar was among the many women he dated. He also dated Jill St. John and every starlet who came to town. And he had all the right telephone numbers when he happened to find himself in Los Angeles.

Kissinger also occasionally took a married woman to lunch—if she would go. Once someone from the White House happened upon Kissinger dining with Cristina Ford, wife of the auto magnate, who, incidentally, resembled Nancy Maginnes, his New York girl-friend whom he married in 1974. Kissinger asked the White House man not to say a thing. But he needn't have bothered. By the time he got back to the White House the press already knew he had eaten with Mrs. Ford. The restaurant owners themselves, he was told, called the press to tell them he was there.

The backstairs story was that Kissinger was President Nixon's humorist, just as Powers had been Kennedy's. Kissinger would tell the President what the press had asked him and repeat back his own humorous replies, and this tickled the presidential funnybone. Once he told Nixon that he had told the press, "There cannot be a crisis next week, my schedule is already filled." When the President asked him how it felt to be so famous, he commented that it was a great relief: "now when I'm boring at parties, people think it's their fault."

When Nixon asked him which movie star was the lucky girl this week, Kissinger said, "A gentleman of the press just asked me if it's true I am seeing Liz Taylor, now that she is estranged from her husband. I told him Liz Taylor is not now and has never been my girlfriend. But I am not discouraged."

Kissinger made one quip in 1971 that must have brought a pang of pain to Nixon if he thought of it during his troubled Watergate days: "This job has done wonders for my paranoia. Now I really do have enemies."

The nickname for Kissinger was Dr. Strangelove. And someone once said he wouldn't be surprised to look up and find Peter Sellers at the White House "studying our Dr. Kissinger." Kissinger didn't seem to care what was said about him in the papers as long as they spelled his name right. I heard talk backstairs at the White House that it was all right for President Nixon to lean on Dr. Strangelove for advice and help on foreign affairs but he would never make him Secretary of State because of his strong German accent. Which just goes to show that backstairs stories can be wrong.

There were many people the President couldn't stand, but Martha Mitchell, the Attorney General's wife, was the most newsworthy of them. The President wanted Martha kept off his plane. His exact words were, "Keep her out of my hair." She was more in demand than any other lady of the administration just before Watergate broke, and she kept trying to hitch a ride to her speaking engagements on *Air Force One*. Once when she actually was aboard the President's plane, she was determined to break into his private compartment and talk to him because she had some things she thought he ought to hear. Others on the plane had to restrain her.

The word was that Attorney General Mitchell was left off the White House guest list many times because Martha would have come too. Naturally, what went for Dick was good for Pat, too, so she was not inviting Martha to ladies' doings and whenever the press asked her about it, she dodged the question, always saying she liked Martha.

But the one time Martha had to be included in the White House scene was for Tricia's wedding. Pat Nixon cringed when she saw Martha arrive in a costume right out of *Gone With the Wind*, complete with parasol. And she stole the show. The photographers gave her more coverage than anyone but the bride. I'll never forget her arrival at the East Gate, throwing kisses at the crowd, with the photographers going wild.

Martha sometimes said things that other people in the administration wanted to say but didn't dare. She and her husband attended the banquet when President Nixon gave Freedom Medals to the founders of the *Reader's Digest*. Entertainment was provided by the Ray Conniff singers, and right in the middle of the performance, Carole Feraci, one of the singers, suddenly reached into her blouse, pulled out a flag that said STOP THE KILLING, and started giving an antiwar speech directed right at the President, who was sitting in the front row. Bill Cliber, the electrician who was spotlighting the singers, let out a loud laugh. The poor President was speechless and just kept smiling a sickly smile. But Martha Mitchell did more than laugh or smile; she hotly declared, "I think she ought to be torn limb from limb." Most Americans now admit the war was wrong, but at the time Martha expressed the sentiment of many people in the room. John Mitchell grabbed Martha by the arm and steered her right out of the room and out of the White House. But not before she had managed to repeat her opinion to the press.

The Attorney General always seemed to be simply amused when Martha scolded him in public or made remarks that would have embarrassed anyone else. He would say, "That's just Martha." But the story around the White House was that he was really very hurt and disappointed in her behavior and wished he knew how to control her. Also there was much talk that Martha didn't trust anyone and thought that someone was going to assassinate either the Attorney General or her—or both of them.

It didn't make for easy relationships. Bebe Rebozo was the one who dealt with the Mitchells for the President, one time getting a house for them to stay in, shortly before I retired from the White House.

People who meet me these days always want to know one thing— did I know the President's Oval Office was bugged?

Not exactly, but I did know something was going on. I knew stronger cables were being installed. I knew the President didn't like certain conversations to be carried on there and that he took people to his hideaway in the Executive Office Building for secret discussions. And I knew he sometimes talked to people in a low voice over in the corner of his office—probably so that it couldn't be recorded or understood, when taped.

And what was most peculiar, I knew he held conferences standing out in the ocean so that he could not be overheard or recorded at all. The story coming back from the winter White House in Florida was that Nixon would walk far out into the water with a group of aides and advisors and hold a conference there in swim trunks.

All along I'd heard bits and pieces about how it was possible to bug someone from a good distance with a directional device. And people were telling each other around the White House, "Listen, watch what you say. This administration doesn't brook any disloyalty. They'll have you investigated if you say you don't like Nixon's tie." This was part of the loyalty kick I mentioned earlier, but the worry about being overheard is significant.

With nothing much happening on the *surface* in the Nixon administration, the doings backstairs got more attention. Every bit of information was naturally passed along. One day the story making the rounds was that someone from the White House staff had made a homosexual approach to an electrician and was quickly told off. The next day it was something else.

Everybody seemed to be feuding. The kitchen staff was feuding. Fina Sanchez's problems with the rest of the White House help were a steady source of speculation. She feuded with the maids. As for me, I feuded a lot with Manolo, who was undercutting me where the dogs were concerned and competing with me for the glory of taking the dogs into the President's office.

Looking back, it does seem a little ridiculous, but so do a lot of things.

21

My first job with the Nixons was cut out for me—teach Tim not to jump up on people.

My second job came when President Nixon called me to his office and asked me if I could teach King Timahoe a few things, like how to board a helicopter. I said I thought Tim could learn that —after all, I'd even taught Pushinka, the Kennedy dog, to climb a ladder to a tree house.

The Boss didn't look too impressed. Or interested. So I didn't go on to tell him what Freckles, LBJ's dog, had learned to do.

Later that day, according to my diary notes, Tim's need of training came to my attention again.

1/30/69   After I left the President's office, I took Tim to my basement office. I went up to talk to the usher about a lamp in the President's bedroom. When I returned, my raincoat, pouch of tools, and hat were scattered over the room. He ruined my new fifteen-dollar hat. I scolded Tim but didn't punish him, as I realize he is still a six-month-old pup.

In the early Nixon days, I would be called to bring King Timahoe to President Nixon's Oval Office in the West Wing, where he would stay about an hour before I would be called to come and get him. And often at the Mansion—the main portion of the White House— I would take the dog upstairs to the second-floor living quarters and turn him over to the President personally, just as I had done for previous Presidents.

I used to laugh when I would read that President Nixon didn't read the newspapers, "he just reads the morning report that his press office puts together for him—the news highlights excerpted by the staff."

I'm not saying he didn't read the twenty-page condensation of news they produced for him first thing every morning, but I do know what I saw. Once I took Tim to the President in his West Hall sitting room. There was the President, sitting in an easy chair, like millions of other men around the country, reading a newspaper, with a cocktail beside him, sipping as he read. Nixon continued sipping his drink as I put King Tim through his paces, ordering him to "sit," "stay," and "lie down."

When Tim had settled down comfortably at the President's feet, the President said, "That's good," and turned his full attention back to the newspaper. After a few minutes, I took the hint, leaving Tim in a holding position.

Gradually I noticed that I was being kept away from the President and that Manolo or Fina Sanchez would take the dogs from me. It hurt to realize that I was not as close to the new President as I had been to the past one. But what I was to LBJ, Manolo Sanchez was to President Nixon. I doubt that any other President's valet had been such a close friend or had been present at so many White House parties and receptions. At the time, I took this as a sign that the President wanted to be warm and friendly. But looking back, I'm not sure. Maybe he just had trouble getting close to many people, or he didn't trust them, or both. His closest aides, sensing this and being jealous of their own positions, kept other people away.

At first the President was even shy with King Timahoe, and didn't know how to handle him. I could see he wanted very much for the dog to love him best, and be a real companion, but when the presidential chopper would arrive and King Tim would be there to greet the President, Tim would go to everyone else first, and finally come up to the President. The President would look a bit sheepish.

I did my best to help the President win Tim over. I took goodies along when I brought the dog to his office, and President Nixon would feed them to him. And I would tell the President what new tricks Tim had learned—like roll over, sit, stay, and shake hands— and the President would put him through his paces.

It was in Camp David that man and dog had the best chance to become good friends. President Nixon loved nothing better than to get away to Camp David in the mountains of Maryland, where it is really rustic. But even there Tim wasn't 100 percent converted. He was always running away from Nixon, and a few times the President left without him. He just climbed aboard his chopper and let the Secret Service cope with King Timahoe.

The President asked me about veterinary care right at the beginning and I explained that the Johnsons had sent their dogs to the vets at Walter Reed and that every President had the same privilege as Commander in Chief. President Nixon was concerned that he not have the kind of bad publicity about dogs that Johnson sometimes suffered. He said he thought it would be all right to send the dogs to Walter Reed for medical attention, but he added that Vicky, a French poodle, needed to be clipped correctly, and he didn't think it would look proper to have that done by government vets.

Here are some of my early Nixon entries.

1/24/69 I turned the electric heat on in the doghouses as Sam Page put new straw in them yesterday. I took the vets from Walter Reed—Moreman and Linn—to visit President Nixon's doctor, Walter Tkach. Also to visit Jay Wilkinson, who is staff assistant to Haldeman, and Lieutenant Colonel Coffey. The vets checked Vicky and Pasha. Vicky is seven and Pasha is two. Both were given the full array of shots as a protective measure. Jay is a former All-American quarterback like his famous dad, Bud Wilkinson.

1/31/69 I took King Timahoe to Dwight Chapin's office. He took Tim into the Oval Office, where Tim stayed for over an hour.

2/2/69 I took King Tim to the West Hall in the Mansion and gave him to President Nixon. He told me to come get him in thirty minutes. When I returned the President was studying Tim's contours. He said that Tim had a nice head. I agreed. I gave him some goodies and he fed Tim some. I tried to strike up a conversation with the President but failed.

Two things were developing, to my embarrassment. First, the Irish setter was making me his hero instead of the President. There was nothing I could do about it unless the President spent more time with Tim and made more of a fuss over him. And secondly, some people around the President, including Manolo, were acting as if I were trying to steal the affections of the President's dog. I could see that trouble was brewing.

Just then I received a personal letter from LBJ. It made me feel better and worse at the same time.

January 30, 1969

Dear Mr. Bryant:
We gave Yuki a pat and read your telegram to him.

261

I am sure he understood; and by the wistful look in his eyes, I am also sure that he misses you very much.

But he is having a pretty easy life, if you ask me, sitting in an upholstered chair in my office, and as much as possible avoiding Edgar, whom we don't let in the house if we can help it.

I know you miss Yuki the most, but we all appreciate your generous remarks about us. They made us proud and we thank you for your kindness. Our very best wishes to you,

Sincerely,
(signed) Lyndon Johnson

2/3/69   I took Tim to the President's office.

2/4/69   President Nixon was on his way to his car at C-9. I had the three dogs out. He spoke to Tim and asked me if Pasha was cold. I told him that we were out for a walk and were fixing to go back to the pups' room. Later I took Tim into the President's office.

Fina and Manolo returned from New York with Mrs. Nixon. I took Pasha and Vicky to the second floor and left them with Fina. Later Manolo took them in for the family.

2/5/69   I took Tim to the President's office for forty-five minutes. I told the President Tim has learned to shake hands, in two fifteen-minute night sessions. The President was showing Tim to a crippled child, the "March of Dimes Boy," who was answering questions from the press, and someone said he sure is smart. The President thought the person was talking about his dog, Tim.

2/6/69   I asked Mr. Chapin if the President was going to take the dogs to *Texas*. He laughed when I made this error from habit. I meant Florida. It's a whole new ball game.

I washed Pasha and Vicky. Fina asked me if she could let the dogs sleep with her tonight. I told her yes, but not to take them outside tonight, because I had bathed them and they might catch cold. Mrs. Peggy Michael has been answering my fan mail. Most people seem to think that Yuki was left at the White House, on account of a reporter's mistake in a story.

I took the dog to the President's office. I opened his door and let Tim in. Tim is six months old. Tomorrow is my fifty-fifth birthday.

2/7/69   President Nixon petted Tim's head before he boarded his helicopter for Florida.

The vets treated the dogs' eyes and took stool samples. Pasha weighed 5 pounds, Vicky 20.5, Tim 54.0.

2/9/69   Tricia and a boyfriend came out to the South Portico to walk around the grounds. Tim jumped up on her white jacket. She asked me to teach Tim not to jump up.

2/10/69   President Nixon returned from Florida. When he got off the helicopter he motioned for me to bring the dog to him. He took Tim by his leash and took him to his office. Later I had to pick him up. Tim now shakes hands very nicely and sits down on order.

2/11/69   Manolo Sanchez took Tim to see the President on the second floor. I see he wants to be dogkeeper as well as valet.

2/13/69   I had Tim with me on the east end of the second floor visiting the girls who answer dog letters. Tricia saw the dog and she came to Tim and shook hands with him. I told her that Tim still jumped up on me. I showed her my mud-streaked raincoat. She laughed.

Mrs. Nixon also came over and Tim shook hands with her. She was pleased. She said, "I think Dick likes you very much." Unfortunately, she was saying it to the dog.

2/14/69   Julie told the President she would like to see the swimming pool. Later, as they started to go upstairs, Julie asked the President if he wanted Tim to go upstairs. He said yes, so I put Tim in the elevator and told him to sit. Then Mrs. Nixon got on as I got off. Tim stayed in the Mansion for about forty-five minutes. Manolo brought the dog down to me and said he thought Tim wanted to go outside. I took Tim out on the South Lawn and let him run. When I tried to call him back he just avoided me and kept running. A White House policeman was on his way past C-9 to the post on the hill behind the President's office.

He kept distracting Timahoe, whistling for the dog to come to him, as I was trying to call the dog to me. Any idiot could see I had the dog on a long training leash and was training Tim to obey the command, "Tim, come."

I told him to stop whistling. He wouldn't stop. I said, "Why, you silly bastard." The policeman on the post said, "You shouldn't have called that poor dog a silly bastard."

2/17/69   President Nixon waved to Tim as he left in his limousine. Later I took Tim into his office. I also fed Tim some asparagus and Spanish rice. He liked it. The Nixons love Mexican and Spanish food so their dogs are going to have to get used to it.

2/20/69   The vets returned Pasha and Vicky from Walter Reed where they had their teeth cleaned yesterday. I saw Major Lanier and asked him about ordering the policemen to stop calling the dogs while I am training them. He said they discussed it at a meeting, but he would put out an order. I took Tim to the President's office. He stayed thirty minutes. I received a new "psychosonic" conditioning device tonight. I studied the book. Tomorrow we start training.

2/23/69   President Nixon left for his European trip. Before he left he told me, while he was gone, to give Tim his helicopter-boarding lessons. Fina Sanchez said that Mrs. Nixon told her to ask me about a discreet salon where Vicky could get a poodlecut.

2/24/69   Colonel Asbill of Walter Reed suggested that I check Margaret Smith, who has a beauty shop for dogs out in Arlington, Virginia. I called Margaret Smith and made an appointment for March 3 at 9:00 A.M. I asked Mrs. Lucy Winchester, Pat Nixon's social secretary, to check with Mrs. Nixon and see how she wants to pay the bill—cash or check. She will let me know soon.

2/25/69   President Nixon was telling some people in England about the dogs. He paused for a moment, then told them he had a special link with England—a Yorkshire terrier, Pasha. I'm sure they were thrilled.

2/26/69   Tim and I rode practice helicopter landings for four landings. I had to carry Tim aboard three of the times, and he will probably still have to get used to it. Washington is beautiful at night from a bird's-eye view.

3/1/69   J. B. West, Head Usher, retired yesterday. Rex Scouten is the new Head Usher. J.B. brought his wife, Zella, in and Chef Haller fixed them a gourmet meal that they ate in the kitchen. It was mighty democratic of West, hardly his style.

3/2/69   10:30 P.M. President Nixon returned from Europe. Tricia asked Tim to shake hands. He did, and his wet paw got her white glove wet. She took the glove off and shook his paw again. President Nixon came over and shook hands, and he said Tim knows who is in command. I said, "Yes, sir, Mr. President." He didn't know it, but I had told Tim to shake.

3/3/69   Vicky went to the grooming shop today. She looks good.

3/13/69   I showed Tim to Julie Eisenhower and her friends. She said, "I was told that you had all three dogs out when the President came in on a helicopter." I said that was one of the prerogatives of being Chief Executive—you get a dog's welcome at the White House. She didn't know whether to laugh. One of her girlfriends said she should take Tim back to college with her. Julie said that she didn't want to separate the dogs, so she won't take her own dog, Vicky the poodle, either. She is a nice person.

How strange it seemed to have David Eisenhower returning to the White House a grown man and the President's son-in-law! I remembered him as a lovable brat, the apple of his grandfather's eye. Countless times he'd kept Ike company on the putting green while Ike practiced his golf swing.

Keeping little David company on those visits was a little mutt named Spunky, who was always hungry. David would take Spunky to the chef, François Rysavy, and Rysavy, busy with some State Dinner, would excitedly chase them both out of the kitchen, scolding them in his rich Czech accent.

And here David was, back again. His face looked about the same and still had that boyish grin, but he was a lot taller. And he was kidding his bride a lot about her cooking. When he went with Julie to a Republican ladies' dinner at the Washington Hilton, he told them, "Julie made her best dinner the other night, curried hot dogs—with sour cream." He made a face. Then seeing her face, he added, "Oh, it was *good*. I really *liked* it."

3/14/69   I told Lucy Winchester that I had been to the housekeeper three times for an accounting on the dogs' monthly bill. Before I could get back to my shop, Usher Carter said that he had a letter for me. It was a bill for two months' food. Quick service when you know the right people. Lucy Winchester is the person to know in this administration.

The vets came in today. Captain Woods said they would have to wear identification badges.

Usher Hare called me and said that the President wanted all three dogs in the State Dining Room. I walked the dogs into the State Dining Room toward the President, who was sitting at the head of the horseshoe table. Some man was giving a speech; he was surprised and stopped speaking for a short time. The President asked him if he would lift up one of the dogs by the ears. The guests at the table roared with laughter. The President motioned me then to take the dogs out of the room. Pasha was on a leash also, but she broke loose and ran out of the room, which caused more laughter.

3/17/69   The Boss had Tim visiting him on the second floor for half an hour. Rose Mary Woods was visiting the Nixons. I could see that Rose Mary was not just a secretary but a close friend, the Ashton Gonella and Juanita Roberts of the Nixon family.

3/18/69   As I had done with the Johnsons, I turned in a picture of the Inauguration for the President to autograph. Rose Mary Woods seemed reluctant and said it might take quite a while, as they were behind in work. I said I'm in no hurry. She said Pasha and Tim had a time last night. I put Vicky's and Pasha's pawprints on the picture. Vicky's grooming bill was fourteen dollars.

Eventually I did get my autographed picture of the President back, but I was lucky. As I wrote in my diary on August 1, 1969: "Rex Scouten put out an order starting that anyone asking the First Family for autographs or favors would be immediately dismissed from his job." It was just another sign of the royal air around the White House.

I heard through the grapevine that the President was annoyed that White House staff and "underlings" were trying to get close to him—and so was Haldeman, and so was Ehrlichman, his "Little Sir Echoes," as they were called when they weren't called the "German Mafia."

Mamie Eisenhower had come to the White House for a visit. She divided her time between her Nixon in-laws and Walter Reed Hospital, where her husband was lying gravely ill from his heart attack. We were concerned about Ike, but it still seemed like old times to have Mamie there.

Mamie always tried to give Julie and David things for their honeymoon apartment off campus, and one story Mamie told at the White House was that she had tried to give Julie a nine-by-twelve rug for her bedroom. Julie had gasped, "A nine-by-twelve! That would never fit our bedroom. The whole room is only six by nine."

I recalled how David and Julie were laughing about an incident that showed Mamie's stubbornness. "Mimi," as they called her, had been scheduled to receive an honorary degree at Wilson College in Chambersburg, Pennsylvania, and when she got there she was most annoyed to find that Vietnam war protesters had piled skulls and shrouds in front of the outdoor speaker's platform. "Mimi" flatly refused to go on stage to accept her degree, and the whole faculty was in a tizzy. The university would be disgraced if their honorary degree were turned down. But then Someone-Up-There who liked her passed a miracle and gave the university an easy out—it started to rain. Grabbing everything but the skulls, they rushed inside where Mamie could receive her degree with proper dignity.

3/28/69   General Eisenhower died today.

3/30/69   President Nixon and Mrs. Nixon returned from the Capitol, where General Eisenhower's body was at rest.

Mrs. Nixon got out of the car and told me she wanted Tim. I gave her the leash and she and the President walked the dog to the elevator and then took him up to the second floor, where Tim stayed for one hour. President Nixon looks very sad.

4/3/69 The President's office called me and said someone wants to ship paid freight or express one Lhasa apso—and what is it? I said I would check and call back. I called Walter Reed and a colonel later called me back and said it was a small Tibetan dog, something like a terrier with a feathered tail curving over its back. I doubt that it will be accepted.

4/6/69 The President and his family returned from Florida with Pasha and Vicky. When they got off the helicopter they all came over and petted Tim. I gave Tricia a goody that she gave to Tim. Mrs. Nixon hugged Tim.

I always had the feeling that Mrs. Nixon was starved for affection and just eager to grab something to hug. I felt sorry for her. She was so painfully thin. I never saw her grab the President and hug him. He seemed to need it, too. She just grabbed Timahoe.

4/12/69 Timahoe had to be carried aboard the helicopter for Camp David. Well, I tried.

4/13/69 President Nixon walked Tim off the helicopter on a leash. Tim was pulling the President toward me. I asked the President how Tim behaved. He said that he was a little nervous.

4/14/69 I took Vicky and Pasha to see Rose Mary Woods. She said the dog pictures I showed her should be in a magazine.

4/19/69 At last! Tim walked aboard the helicopter. All the dogs went to Camp David.

4/20/69 One chopper is not enough for the comfort of the new President. The dogs returned from Camp David aboard the second helicopter that landed. Manolo told me that last weekend Tim got lost in the woods. The guards could have shot him by mistake.

22

President Nixon was the interior decorator of the family.

At least, the President was the one who was most interested in everything about the décor of the White House. When he went through it with Pat the first time after they had moved in, the staff was amazed that it was he who asked all the questions. Pat said everything was fine and she guessed she'd leave it all the way it was except for fixing up Tricia's room.

The President made the big decorating decisions for Pat. He was the one who decided to banish the swimming pool, even though there were whispers that some members of his family were not very happy about it. And then he ordered a sumptuous $100,000 sauna installed for his use in another building.

He also wanted the best help he could get in his interior decorating efforts. At first Pat brought in her female interior decorator from New York. But the President wanted his own expert. So he borrowed a top man, very knowledgeable in the field—Clem Conger, who had worked on the State Department's historic reception rooms. Conger became a great fund-raiser as Curator of the White House.

I sighed and thought, "Here we go again," as Nixon made his first move to erase the memory of Lyndon B. Johnson—he ordered the multi-nozzled shower spray taken out of his bathroom. And after LBJ had gone to the trouble of showing it to him!

"If bigmouth Lyndon had kept his trap shut," my backstairs informer commented, "I'll bet Nixon would have used it and bragged about his super bath."

President Nixon had his own bathtub quirk. Out came the multi-nozzled shower, out came the glass enclosure etched with the presidential seal, and in went a new whirlpool bathtub at the small cost of $1,500. The new tub was intended to relax him. Finding ways to relax in general seemed to occupy much of the President's time at the White House.

If Johnson heard what happened to his pet shower, he must have muttered, "You sure know how to hurt a man."

The bath was just the beginning. Soon people were buzzing that Nixon was intent on getting rid of everything that reminded him of previous tenants.

So out went the plaque that said that in this room President John Fitzgerald Kennedy lived with his wife, Jacqueline, for a thousand plus days. The whole emotion-fraught mantel that meant so much to Jacqueline Kennedy went with it.

And out went the Monet painting that had been given in the name of the dead President, and that had hung so proudly in the Green Room with the plaque mentioning the Kennedy family.

And out went the Catlin paintings of Indians that had been Lady Bird's pride and joy as well as Jacqueline's.

And out went the large TV set that Johnson had used in the living quarters.

President Nixon personally decided how the East Room should look for church services on Sundays and chose which set of chairs his personal "congregation" would sit on. He ordered that the Jacqueline Kennedy Garden be renamed "The First Lady's Garden." And, oh yes, there was something else President Nixon knew he wanted—a red, white, and blue bedroom. The White House was now his own.

My diary records just a bit of what was going on.

4/22/69 Now it begins. I can just see the White House getting torn up again. I had just finished rewiring a table lamp beside the President's bed. Mrs. Nixon walked in with Head Usher Rex Scouten and a lady. Mrs. Nixon shook hands with me and said to the lady that I was the person who always had Tim out to greet the President when he came in by helicopter. Then Mrs. Nixon introduced me to the lady—Sarah Doyle, a New York interior decorator.

It turned out that she was the only person the First Lady introduced me to during the whole administration. But this was the "honeymoon stage."

4/24/69 Funny, funny! At 2:00 A.M. Mrs. Nixon's bathtub ran over on the second floor and the water streamed down the chandelier in the State Dining Room on the first floor. We used electric heaters to dry the large rug in the State Dining Room. Well, she's finally making a little White House history.

4/25/69 Mr. Wright, Zephyr's husband, died today. I'm very sorry. I gave President Nixon Tim on the leash as he boarded his helicopter for Camp David.

5/1/69 Mrs. Nixon and Rose Mary Woods' niece were in the West Flower Garden. The niece was the "Cerebral Palsy Child." Tim shook hands with her.

5/2/69 The President told me to bring Tim to him as he and another man were being photographed in the West Garden, outside the Oval Office. The President was holding a pair of wooden Dutch shoes. Tim then went over to a cameraman who was squatting down with his movie camera. Tim licked his lens. The whole scene was very funny. The cameraman had to stop and clean the glass.

5/4/69 The President and his family returned by helicopter from the home of Senator Harry Byrd, Jr. The Boss motioned for me to approach him with Tim. He petted Tim. Young Mr. Barry Goldwater, the senator's son, was with him. Barry asked me if Tim liked the water. I told him I would put Tim in the pool of the South Fountain this summer and find out. He said he had a Labrador retriever that liked the water.

Later on I had to take Tim out to the golf green. Julie and her husband David were there with the President and Pat. I told the President that Tim ate vegetables besides his regular meal. I told Julie that Tim would roll over. She told him to roll over and Tim obeyed.

I turned Tim loose. He pointed at a bird and the family, fascinated, watched Tim point.

For daily relaxation, the new President really got his biggest kick out of watching King Tim—especially, watching him point. I will never forget this particular day because Nixon stood absolutely motionless for fully ten minutes as Tim stood riveted, pointing at a bird in a tree—nose stretched outwards, one paw raised off the ground, tail straight out and body leaning forward. It was the bird that finally tired of the game and flew away.

In the early days of his administration, President Nixon seemed to enjoy having the dogs out on the lawn when foreign dignitaries were guests, just as President Johnson had.

5/7/69 President Nixon and Prime Minister Gorton from Australia were on their way from the President's office to C-9 Post to Prime Minister Gorton's car. The President nodded his head and Tim and I approached them. The President told the prime minister to shake hands with Tim, which he did. The President told him that Tim had just learned this trick recently and he told him Tim's weight—sixty-two pounds.

But as the President got more and more distracted, the dogs gradually lost prestige and he beckoned for them less and less often at historic moments around the White House. I turned in other directions for my amusement. Especially the White House kitchens.

Poor Chef Haller—actually I felt sorry for him. He was always getting the short end of the stick. He was very proud of his fine French cooking, so he was a natural target for needling.

Frankie Blair, the kitchen helper who cut up food for Haller and served as pan washer, aspired to be a chef some day. So I would come through the kitchen and say, "Frankie, how did everything go at Camp David? Did you fix the President a pretty good meal?" Haller would look at me and grit his teeth.

One day the President, on impulse, came into the kitchen to bestow a good word on the cook. Nixon, who was gaining a reputation backstairs for not being able to tell one White House helper from another, saw Blair standing there with a look of surprise on his face, marched over to him, and grandly asked who had cooked the meal. Caught off guard that way, Frankie gave the first name that came to his mind—Julia Farrow, the cook who was helping Haller that day, but whose job was cooking for the servants down on the basement mezzanine, in the servant's kitchen. The President said, "The family enjoyed the dinner," and walked out.

Chef Haller heard this exchange, and his chin dropped about a foot. After the President had left, he poured himself a glass of wine and paced up and down the kitchen mumbling to himself.

5/8/69   Fina Sanchez, wife of the President's valet, called me on the phone and said that she wanted to talk to me. I told her to meet me in the ground-floor kitchen. She said someone is trying to undercut her. She wondered if it was because of her broken English. I told her that I could understand her okay, even with her Spanish accent. I told her that she wouldn't be in the White House very long before she found out that certain people—I ran my finger over my throat—would try to make their point on her neck. She was very upset and said she would find out who it is. I told her I had no idea who it could be as I was on the night shift and am not in contact with the day people very much.

By May 1969, the intrigue around the White House was already thick. Nobody trusted anybody on any level. It was much worse than in LBJ's time.

Nowadays, when I read my diary for kicks in the safety of retirement, I see it with new eyes because of everything that has come out in the Watergate hearings and trials. I shake my head with disbelief as I look at some innocent comment in my diary and realize what was going on behind the scenes that same day in the Oval Office or in Kissinger's office when he worked for the Boss as top foreign policy advisor.

For example, the next entry in my diary, for May 9, is so unsinister it's jovial. But on that very day the wiretapping of Henry Kissinger's aides began—the tappings that Kissinger later said were done to help his aides prove their loyalty.

5/9/69   Tim and I went to a movie. Mrs. Nixon and Tricia saw *Mackenna's Gold,* a Western. I told Tricia that Tim slept through all the good parts.

5/11/69   Mrs. Nixon was at the South Lawn with the dogs. Tim jumped up and knocked her down twice. Mrs. Nixon told me about it and wanted to know if he could be trained not to. I showed her how to knock his paws off her shoulders to discourage his bad habit. Julie said he wasn't as bad as he seemed. I told Mrs. Nixon that Tim weighs sixty-two pounds. She said that the President had a setter once that weighed over a hundred pounds.

The President later returned from Florida; he came over and shook hands with Tim and patted him. Rose Mary Woods also petted Tim. She said the weather was good, and Manolo fished.

I was starting to realize how important Manolo Sanchez was. He was more than a valet. He was a trusted confidant and friend like Rose Mary Woods. He had the run of the White House and attended parties and formal receptions.

5/13/69   I was on the second floor checking the lights. President Nixon went into his room. I told him I was checking the lights. He smiled. How different from LBJ: no teasing or sharing of his thoughts; no orders to watch those lights.

5/14/69   I had an interview with Bonnie Angelo of *Time* magazine. Their photographer took pictures. We had to delay the interview for an hour as Vicky was on her way to the White House from a beauty treatment at another dog-grooming salon in Wheaton, Maryland. I was putting a light in a chandelier outside the President's bedroom. He came out on his way to the Lincoln Sitting Room. He smiled and said, "You are putting in lights." I said "Yes, sir, Mr. President." Fina and I were on the South Lawn with the dogs, and we saved a couple of baby birds from them. The birds had fallen out of their nest. It took a ladder to put them back.

5/16/69 President Nixon petted Tim before departing for a boat ride.

The new President was like the old President. He wasn't taking his wife out on the yacht much either. But the atmosphere on the boat now was masculine, and frequently his special guest was Bebe Rebozo. Other guests, though less regular, included Kissinger, Haldeman, and Ehrlichman.

5/21/69 I took the three dogs into the President's office today. Tonight on television the President appointed a new Supreme Court Chief Justice, Warren E. Burger—7:00 P.M. Mr. Rockefeller talked about the dogs on the South Portico. I had all three dogs out as the guests arrived to witness the swearing in.

5/23/69 President and Mrs. Nixon took the three dogs to Camp David at 3:30 P.M. Tim will chase the deer. One time a deer cut off sharply and Tim rammed a tree head-on. The vet brought a Miss Moyer with him to the White House today. The police at A-1 wouldn't clear her. However, she was finally admitted and she went on a private tour with some other guests. I gave her a picture of President Nixon and a picture of the three dogs. I suspect she will be the last one admitted to the White House. Word is the White House security is stricter than ever. No one is to get in unless invited by the President or unless he has business in the White House. Fina and Manolo had the three dogs out on the South Grounds, and Pasha was almost run over by a taxi bringing someone in, in a hurry.

5/24/69 Senator Warren G. Magnuson stopped to pet the dogs and talked with me as he was on his way to the South Portico to go to a stag party at the White House. He told me his family had lost a dog who was about ten years old. He said it hurt them almost as much as losing a child.

5/27/69 President Nixon was having his picture made with Normandy war correspondents. He looked toward the dogs and me and he told them Tim was nine months old. Later he walked over and he told the reporters that "we are fortunate in having Mr. Bryant to train and look after the dogs." One of the reporters said, "Mr. Bryant must have the rank of a general." The President laughed.

Colonel Coffey told me all three dogs would leave for Florida tomorrow at 1:00. Sanchez will pick them up.

5/28/69 I had all three dogs at C-9 Post as the President and his two guests, the prime minister and foreign minister of the Netherlands, were walking to their car. The President told them to shake hands with Tim. The foreign minister, Joseph Luns, offered his hand. Tim didn't oblige. Then the prime minister shook with Tim. The foreign minister told the prime minister, "You must have a better reputation than I have." Nixon asked me Tim's weight. I told him sixty-two pounds. The President asked me if he would reach a hundred pounds. I told him about eighty pounds.

6/6/69   Some drillers came and drilled two hundred-foot-deep holes nine inches in diameter—they said to test the soil—in Tim's lower pen and three holes outside of his fence. I don't know what's going on. Are we drilling for oil? I let Tim sleep in the Bouquet Room for the night.

6/9/69   The joke's on me! I left the Treasury Building after having lunch and I saw a red setter running down Fourteenth Street. I took off yelling "Tim!" A White House policeman, Officer Williamson, got out of his car and held the setter for me. As the officer got in his car, I said "This isn't Tim." The dog belonged to a Mr. Swindler of Foxhall Road, District of Columbia. I took the dog to the North West Gate and told the officer to contact the owner. Mary Kaltman, the housekeeper, hugged and petted the dog and said "Oh, Tim, you have gained some weight." I told her, "That's not Tim." She dropped his paw like a hot potato and said "You shouldn't have let me pet the dog, knowing it wasn't Tim." Someone said, "Talk about class consciousness!" The owner came after the dog and offered me a five-dollar reward, but I didn't take the money. I told him I was glad to protect the dog to keep the cars from hitting him.

6/13/69   President Nixon took the three dogs to Camp David. Fina Sanchez cried because Pasha went. She is a very emotional woman.

6/14/69   A *beagle* bit Pasha at Camp David. The President and the dogs returned to the White House. Shades of LBJ!

6/15/69   Tricia had her picture in the Sunday newspaper holding her Yorkshire terrier with a cute and funny-looking bandage around its head. The President had Pasha sent to him on the second floor. The dog that bit Pasha was a beagle named "Wiggles." The owner is Commander Dunn of Camp David. Manolo was feeding the dogs and Pasha tried to eat first. Pasha was bitten at the base of the right ear and on the stomach.

6/16/69   I saw Colonel Coffey and he called Camp David for me, telling them that Commander Dunn should keep his dog in a pen while the President's dogs are in residence.

6/19/69   Mrs. Nixon and Julie returned from trip out west. Had the three dogs out to greet them. Pat petted Tim while Julie petted other two dogs. Later the President petted Tim before entering his car for the Washington-Baltimore baseball game with David and Julie.

6/24/69   Trouble. W. Martin, Chief Electrician, told me Rex Scouten wanted to see me. I went to his office. He said he had a report that instead of fixing it myself, I was telling the police to report a light out in their day book so the day electricians would put a new bulb in. I told him that I always tell them to call their captain and have him put it in their book. I told Scouten that the ruling came from Walter Martin. Scouten called Martin and he came to the office. Martin verified my statement, explaining that it was more *dangerous* to change streetlights at night. During the day the power is off.

I took Tim to the President's office at 10:30 P.M. Manolo was angry because I didn't let him take the dog to the President. I can't understand his broken English, but I sure got his message.

7/1/69   I heard the President was displeased at a story that appeared about Vicky being groomed at the dog emporium in Wheaton, Maryland. I met Mrs. Nixon in the ground-floor hallway. She laughed and said that a policeman told Fina of a place in Georgetown to groom the dog that is absolutely off-limits to reporters. I told her it would be better if Vicky were taken out in a station wagon—like in "a plain brown wrapper." So that's what we may do! She said that the President enjoyed watching the dogs swim in Florida. I told her I show the dogs to the Fourth of July crowds that come into the White House grounds to watch the fireworks. She told me that Julie takes visitors to the dog kennel when she leads a tour.

Mr. Scouten told me he was going to let Fina go to Georgetown with Vicky and explain to them how to trim Vicky, since it's not being done right. He said Fina is taking a trip to her native Spain soon.

7/6/69   The dogs returned from Florida. Tim did a lot of swimming and chasing of birds, a Secret Service man told me. Tim was ravenous. I fed him two cans of dog food. He and the other dogs were glad to see me.

7/7/69   Fred Blumenthal, the Washington editor of *Parade*, interviewed me about the dogs. I showed him the dog kennels and the fish pond the Johnsons dedicated to the White House. We walked around the grounds. I took him to the press office so he can arrange to get some dog pictures.

As part of her beautification program, Lady Bird Johnson had installed a small fish pond in the South Grounds near Jackie Kennedy's trampoline. Vicky was delighted with the fish pond that the

275

Nixon family was totally neglecting, and spent many a happy day getting herself a goldfish dinner.

But she didn't share. And Pasha, who was too small to go it alone, watched jealously and barked in frustration.

7/8/69   Emperor Haile Selassie asked to see the dogs today.

7/10/69   I showed the dogs to Haile Selassie as President Nixon was escorting him to his car. He petted Pasha and Tim and smiled at me.

The emperor was such a tiny man and so fine-featured. It was hard to think of him as the Lion of Judah. More the Mouse that Roared.

The emperor talked about his own dog, Lulu, who he said was famous as the only male dog in all of Africa to have a girl's name. I saw that Selassie was another dog lover on the order of LBJ, and maybe had LBJ beat. He said that Lulu, a chihuahua, was his complete secretary and told him when it was time to do everything, each step of the day.

7/10/69   Manolo and Fina flew to Spain.

7/11/69   Vicky and Pasha returned from the beauty shop in Georgetown. I took them to Tricia's room after the vet checked them. She thanked me and said they looked good. The inside rumor is her parents are worried about Tricia. She spends too much time alone in her room.

7/14/69   Usher Hare told me to pick up two dogs on the third floor. I asked David and he said they went downstairs. I went to Tricia's room on the second floor to get the dogs. Mrs. Nixon came out of her room and told me that the picture of the three dogs all looking in one direction was a masterpiece. I showed her my Hi Fido chain with a tuning fork that I had used to attract the dogs' attention. She said that Tim had scratched Julie by jumping up on her. I told her I would work some more on Tim. I thought he had improved. She said that the two dogs missed Fina. I told her I am giving the dogs special attention. I also told her that I take the dogs out for the last time about 11:15 P.M. She was surprised I was there so late.

The next day Julie brought a tour to the dog kennel. She caught me inside playing with the dogs, to keep them from being so lonely for Fina.

7/17/69   Paul Fischer took the three dogs to Camp David in an air-conditioned White House car. They rate better than a lot of people around the White House.

7/21/69   I let some blind children pet the dogs today.

7/22/69   All dogs are out on display as President Nixon gave a speech to the foreign students. After the speech, students almost pulled him off the platform trying to shake his hand. Later tonight President and Mrs. Nixon left on their around-the-world trip.

While they were away Tricia was trying her best to please her parents by dating young Congressman Barry Goldwater, Jr., of California. The day he was supposed to take Trish to a ball game, the game was rained out and they went to dinner together instead, to the Georgetown Inn in Georgetown.

Eventually the romance got rained out, too. The word around the White House was that Tricia was in love with a New York student named Ed Cox, who came from a fine old family. But the family wasn't fine enough for the President, the word went, because he wanted his elder daughter to do at least as well as her little sister, who had made off with a President's grandson. Young Barry Goldwater, the son of the nation's top Republican, would have suited the President just fine.

Meanwhile, out in Honolulu, Pat Nixon was said to be enjoying Hawaii while the President went off to the aircraft carrier *Hornet* to greet the astronauts who had been walking on the moon. She was entranced with some hula dancers who entertained her and confessed she had taken one hula lesson once.

7/30/69   Julie, acting as a tour guide for four children, stopped me and showed the children Vicky and Pasha, who were with me in the hallway next to the Gold Room. She told the children that the dogs were on their way to Walter Reed to get their teeth cleaned. She stressed to the children how important it was to clean their teeth and to visit their dentist regularly a couple of times a year. "If dogs can do it, so can you," she said!

Several years later I read in the newspapers that President Nixon had tried to get a tax break for the work his daughter was doing as a guide.

8/3/69   President and Mrs. Nixon returned from their round-the-world trip at 11:30 P.M. I had Vicky, Pasha, and Tim at the Diplomatic Entrance. They greeted the dogs and petted them and the President said bring the dogs upstairs.

8/4/69   The President took the three dogs and Manolo to Camp David for a rest.

8/6/69   The President returned from Camp David with the three dogs.

8/8/69   The three dogs left at 6:00 P.M. for California. Fina and Manolo took them to the airport in a station wagon.

In September, I thought, Here we go again:

9/2/69   Mrs. Haldeman called and asked me if I would take care of their dogs until Sunday. They arrive at Dulles at 8:00 P.M. tonight .
The dogs, a Dalmatian named Pokie and three pugs, Amy, Dottie, and Patsy, arrived. The chauffeur helped me to put the crates away and to get the dogs in the outside dog pen. It was raining.

9/3/69   Mr. Higby from San Clemente, the Western White House, called me and wanted to know how the dogs were doing. I called Charlie Rotchford of General Services Administration, who sent a couple of men to put a heavy wire screen over a fan near the dog pen so the dogs can't get hurt.

9/7/69   Mrs. Haldeman and her mother came in the North West Gate in their station wagon to pick up their dogs. She said Pokie was eleven. They were very nice and thanked me. They went out to the pen and helped me. She showed her mother "Mr. Haldeman's patio" under a tree outside his office. She said that, being from California, her husband had wanted a patio here, too.

Haldeman really rated, but even he didn't impose his dogs on the President again.

9/8/69   Tim, Pasha, and Vicky arrived about 7:45 P.M. Timahoe was glad to see me. He tore off my clip-on tie. Pasha and Vicky were glad to see me. I took them for a walk and fed them.
10:30 P.M. Tricia, Julie, and David came in by helicopter. They stopped and petted the dogs. I told them welcome back. Julie thanked me.
President and Mrs. Nixon came off the chopper and petted and shook hands with Tim. I said, "Welcome back." They thanked me and smiled, and the President shook my hand.

9/9/69   Usher Hare called and said since Tim was crying, Julie had let him out of his runway, and she couldn't get him to come to her. He asked me to round up Tim. Tim came to me when I called. I saw Secret Service agent Robert Foster tonight; he said that he had to give away Jackie Kennedy's Charlie, the terrier who was Caroline's favorite. Charlie chewed furniture and Foster said the dog had cost him a small fortune in damages. I said I felt Caroline should have been permitted to keep Charlie. I think Charlie felt deserted. He never chewed furniture at the White House.

9/12/69   The dogs went to Camp David.

Pat Nixon did not need the President around to enjoy herself, she was used to being alone. I'd heard that she'd had a good time touring a crafts exhibit at the Department of Agriculture. She walked through the displays of wood carvings and shriveled-apple dolls and hand-woven cloth from thirty-two states. When she got to one West Virginia exhibit she completely broke up in laughter. It was a banjo made from old auto parts. She said, "Now I know what to do with David's old car."

Incidentally, the First Lady commented when she got back to the White House later that a little grandma doll, with a painted shriveled apple for a head, sold for eight dollars. "It was no apple you'd want to eat," she said.

9/28/69   Doris and I attended church in the East Room of the White House. It was a nice Lutheran sermon by a minister from Minnesota, the Rev. Paul H. A. Noren. The title of the sermon was "This Is My Father's World." I was glad to be reminded who the world belonged to. You tended to forget around the White House. The President and the First Lady shook hands with everyone attending; coffee and cookies were also served. It was very nice, but should a White House become a church? Some people are muttering around the White House that everything must come to the castle, even religion. And if it was democratic to have services at the White House, why couldn't all the White House staff, from the lowest to the highest, attend? You have to be a cabinet officer or a friend. And mixed in are a few employees.

10/26/69   I just returned from a hard seven-day bear hunt. We got two bears. My guide Ronnie Priest had to shoot my bear, as it was about to kill the dogs. While I was away electrician Cliber let the vets take Tim to Walter Reed and they kept Tim a while for treatment of a fungus on his leg. Once President Nixon called for Tim, and Cliber tried to comply. Cliber was told by the Usher's Office to leave the dogs alone and let Manolo and Fina take care of them. The President asked Cliber where I was. He told him I was vacationing in Maine.

The day I got back the big news was that Connie Stuart, a cute thirty-one-year-old former actress, had been hired to "humanize" Pat Nixon, at a salary of $30,000 a year. Her job was supposed to be the same as Liz Carpenter's during the Johnson years.

And the big laugh around the White House was that the Demo-

279

crats were going to have a Halloween Eve party at the Bayou in Georgetown; the main entertainment was going to be a real witch left over from Vice President Spiro Agnew's latest witch-hunt.

10/31/69 The dogs went to Camp David. I gave one of my 35-mm. snapshots of Blanco to Chief Knudsen to give to Fred Blumenthal for his *Parade* story.

11/4/69 Tim returned yesterday. Tricia was being interviewed for the *Today* Show broadcast, linked up with New York, and Connie Stuart, the new Liz Carpenter, replacing Gerry Van der Heuvel, asked me to stroll with the dogs along the walk in front of the President's office to lend atmosphere.

11/5/69 I had the three dogs out when the astronauts who had gone to the moon arrived at the White House. The President and Mrs. Nixon waved to the dogs as they came out of the President's office to meet the astronauts. Later the President took the astronauts out on the Truman Balcony, and they waved at the crowd.

11/6/69 Pasha and Vicky went to Florida. Tim stayed as he has to go to Walter Reed for treatment of his fungus. Electrician Bill Cliber resigned and transferred to the General Services Administration. There was just too much tension with the other electricians; it finally got him down.

11/7/69 Cliber changed his mind; he'd have to take a cut in wages if he leaves the White House, so he will not transfer. He said he would have to eat crow for a while. Tim went to Walter Reed. The dogs were on the *Today* TV program in New York.

By mid-November 1969, the aides around the White House were very gleeful about how clever they and the Boss had been in taking the teeth out of the gigantic November 15 peace demonstration that had been scheduled for months to take place at the Washington Monument grounds.

The aides had given President Nixon ideas on paper and he had accepted the best of them and had done so well that it now seemed unpatriotic to be complaining about his handling of the war in Vietnam. He had announced troop withdrawals, so it looked as if the war might be over fairly soon. And Democrats on Capitol Hill who supported the President—especially Hubert Humphrey—received a lot of telegrams praising them for their dangerous stand, and that hit the papers. The Boss was looking good.

Then on November 15, the day the demonstration was actually

going on, President Nixon had sent word out to the monument grounds that he was peacefully sitting around watching the Ohio State football game on TV.

I didn't know till later that the telegrams sent to Capitol Hill had been fake, in that they had been ordered by the White House. Nor of course did the lawmakers who got them. All I knew was what I picked up around the White House, and in the month of November I was kept busy tending the dogs and thinking about weekend deer-hunting expeditions. Besides, I had my mind on land. I was yearning to get me a piece of land and say farewell to the White House as soon as possible.

11/19/69   Tim came to the White House from Walter Reed, where he was treated for *Tricophyton,* a fungus which is contagious to humans. The vets think he is okay. I got my five-point buck deer yesterday at 12:00 noon. It took me four years. The bullet hit the heart. He then ran about twenty yards before falling.

11/22/69   All the dogs went to Camp David.

11/23/69   The dogs returned to the White House.

11/27/69   The dogs traveled to Florida for the holiday.

11/30/69   The dogs returned.

12/4/69   Doris and I bought a 114-acre farm in Appomattox, Virginia. I'm taking my friend LBJ's advice—"Buy land," he said. Johnson once told me that Lady Bird wanted to buy some land one time at an extremely low price, but his father had ridiculed her, saying it was too high. So they lost the chance and regretted it all their lives. Even at the White House he was mourning the loss of the opportunity to have more land.

What I didn't know about my land when I plunked down my money was that with it came a neighboring farm with seven dogs—one for each day of the week, and no relief on Sunday—all of them noisy and most of them beagles, as if fate wanted me to be reminded every day of LBJ.

However, by the time I found out, it was too late—and besides, I had started to like Jesse Franklin, my dog-loving neighbor to the north.

12/10/69   Helen Smith, Connie's assistant, had me pose the dogs for a Christmas dog picture in front of a fire in the fireplace in the beautiful library. I brought in a Santa Claus standing figure to give it atmosphere.

12/15/69   Mrs. Nixon and Tricia were decorating their Christmas tree in the West Hall. Mrs. Nixon said that she saw a black and white version of the dogs' Christmas picture. She said that the girls wanted to give President Nixon a colored picture of the dogs for a Christmas present. I told Mrs. Nixon I was turning on the wreath lights in the windows. She said Tricia's friend from New York sent the dogs the presents of doggie stockings with doggie toys and candy to hang on the fireplace. I told her I bought the little Santa Claus used in the dog picture from Peoples Drug Store, and it was now in the front window of my camper. She laughed and said that was real Christmas spirit.

12/18/69   I saw Dr. Young in the Executive Office Building. He said he had treated LBJ's hands but didn't say for what, and he had also gone to his hotel and treated him for a cold. He also stated that he would be in charge of LBJ's annual physical examination. Last night I had the two small dogs at the doorway leading out of the ground-floor Diplomatic Room to let the reporters' and photographers' children pet the dogs as they left the Christmas party.

12/19/69   Mamie Eisenhower was a White House guest. She spoke to me this evening as I was working on a chandelier outside the President's bedroom. Pat Nixon was showing her the family Christmas tree on the second floor.

12/21/69   Christmas party for the staff. I was on duty so I didn't attend. I received another nice letter from LBJ chatting about Yuki. I tore a curtain in the Queen's Room when I turned on the Christmas wreath in the window. Very delicate material.

12/22/69   I received a package from LBJ—a bust of LBJ.

I believe I am one of the very few people who got this gift of an almost life-size head by the sculptress Jimilu Mason, and I cherish this gift from my friend.

23

1970 was the year of Prince Charles. And it was the year of Billy Graham's love-in on the Washington Mall. And the year a presidential dog rated an umbrella. But before all that, it was the year a lowly dogkeeper changed the course of White House history —and was proud of it.

It happened when the British prime minister was arriving in January. All the White House policemen were standing self-consciously at attention in garish new uniforms with high-necked white tunics loaded with buttons and gold braid and the most gosh-awful hats I'd ever seen north of the border.

I couldn't resist going over to one of them and whispering into his ear, loud enough for a few others to hear, "Are you the Mexican Army?"

The poor fellow kind of smirked without answering but a young girl reporter overheard me and the next day her newspaper carried the story with my comment. She had cornered Ron Ziegler, the President's press secretary, after the arrival ceremony for Harold Wilson, and had found out that Nixon himself had endorsed the new uniforms.

All the papers picked up the story and made fun of the "Mexican uniform at the White House." Some said it was more a cross between the costumes of the Italian *polizia* and the soldiers of the German *Wehrmacht*. And one paper said the White House police now looked like refugees from a touring company of *The Student Prince* that folded on the road.

Every day more and more fanciful stories and editorials deplored the "Pomp in the White House." Someone suggested that the designer of the royal uniforms immediately hang out a shingle saying, "Tailor to the President's Guard."

I had to take a lot of kidding for a while about what I had started, and the White House Press Information Office was not very pleased with me. But the rest of the White House seemed to be. And so were the ladies and gentlemen of the press—including my old friend, Merriman Smith. Poor Ron Ziegler was nagged until he confessed that the uniforms had cost $23,750 to outfit all the police.

It was too much money to throw away, but the President could stand the heat for only two weeks. Then Ron announced that the White House was keeping the uniform but changing the gaudy cap for something a little more American-looking.

The inside story was that Bob Haldeman and President Nixon had together worked out the design of the new uniform after the President had seen what was worn by palace guards in European capitals. What hurt the President most and caused him to order its change was the question of a congressman of his own party, H. R. Gross of Iowa—"Will they be goose-stepping next?"

After the policemen had the new subdued hats for their dress uniforms, one of them said to me, "Thank God—and you—that's over. I was afraid someone would mistake me for the Good Humor man, a Mexican honcho, or the Statler doorman."

Except for the uniform caper, things were fairly quiet around the White House in the first months of 1970, at least for the dog man.

2/18/70 Tim and the other two dogs returned from Florida. Tricia also returned. She had the measles. King Timahoe has worms. The vets are checking his stool to find out what type of worms to treat for.

A Secret Service man told me that Tim wore himself out chasing sea gulls over a quarter-mile area at the beach. It makes it difficult to put weight on Tim as the Boss wants.

LBJ had wanted his dogs to reduce. President Nixon wanted his to gain weight.

2/24/70 I took the dogs out for a run on the South Lawn today, as it has been a pretty day. We also visited some offices and saw some tourists.

2/26/70 President Nixon motioned to me for Tim as he escorted President Georges Pompidou of France to his limousine. Tim did better than I did—he got to shake hands with Pompidou.

3/16/70 I took Tim to Connie Stuart's office for a birthday party for Pat Nixon. The girls read funny schedules supposedly made up for the First Lady's travels. Mrs. Nixon kissed King Timahoe on the head. She enjoyed the party. We had punch and cookies. I pawprinted a picture of the dogs for Fay Gillis Wells, Storer Broadcasting. Gentle lady.

3/17/70 The President wanted King Tim to meet the Irish ambassador, William Warnock. However, Tim was at Walter Reed. Manolo, the valet, was fit to be tied as Tim didn't get back to the White House until after the St. Patrick's Day celebration. Manolo is getting more nervous than the Boss. Trish took Pasha and Vicky to the second floor yesterday. One of the dogs messed on the rug. Fina can't understand it. She says they were housebroken some time ago. I told her the White House ruins children and dogs.

3/25/70 It's all dogs go. To Florida.

3/30/70 The dogs are back from Florida. As the Nixons got off the helicopter, I tipped my hat to Mrs. Nixon. She spoke and smiled. The President hurried to his office as he has to settle the Post Office strike.

4/8/70 G. Harrold Carswell voted down for Supreme Court. I heard President Nixon comment that he feels it is a personal insult. He returned by chopper from Mount Vernon after a boat ride. He sadly petted all three dogs. Someone told him that on Capitol Hill they were calling Carswell "Child Harrold." At least the dogs were for him—three votes.

4/13/70 Merriman Smith committed suicide this evening. I feel sad as I had many talks with him through the years since 1951. He loved dogs. Starting tomorrow the White House flag will fly at half mast for three days, the night engineer told me. That's a special honor I don't believe any other reporter ever had. He was the dean of the White House press corps. Merv Griffin's assistant called me long distance and asked if I could go on his show taped at night at American University. I told him I couldn't tape an interview at night as I am on night duty at the White House.

The truth of the matter was I had lost all heart for it. My mind was on life and death and Merriman. With Merriman gone, I felt I had lost more than a friend. I had lost my editor for my book, as he was going to pick out the best parts of all my diaries to put together for my manuscript.

He had kept telling me that what I thought about the top political leaders was more important than what columnists like the Alsop brothers thought because, as he put it, "You catch the Presidents with their pants down." He didn't know it, but for a couple of them —Kennedy and Johnson—it was literally true.

4/21/70 2:00 A.M. The President and Mrs. Nixon returned from Hawaii where they greeted the *Apollo 13* astronauts. They petted all three dogs.

Mrs. Nixon said, "It's late for the dogs." I told her they had been asleep. She asked if Tim had been in the fountain. I told her he had.

In the afternoon I had Tim in the fountain swimming with Vicky and Pasha. The President saw and requested that a picture be taken of that scene by the White House photographer. The photographer showed me the ones he had taken for Julie.

4/22/70 .All three dogs had their teeth cleaned at Walter Reed. Fina was crying, because she thought Pasha was sick. I told her Pasha had had a tranquilizer shot so they could clean her teeth; she'd be all right. Later Tricia wanted to see the dogs, but Fina told her that the dogs were having a good time playing on the grounds. Tricia spends most of her time in her room. Even the staff has trouble knowing if she's home.

4/24/70 President Nixon petted the three dogs and then decided to take them with him to Camp David. I told him they were wet. Bebe Rebozo was with him in the White House limousine.

4/28/70 Head Gardener Williams got after me for letting Tim jump in the South Fountain. He said Tim was running through the tulips. I told him that the President and Julie both requested a picture of Tim in the pool, so he couldn't help but run through the tulips that encircle the pool. He didn't like the answer. I finally told him to tell the President that Tim shouldn't jump in the pool. I go through this crap every year.

4/30/70 The President was coming from his office in the Executive Office Building. He stopped close to the new press room and petted the dogs. He had been preparing for his Cambodia speech to justify sending troops to help Cambodia. Photographers made pictures.

Julie and David came in just before the speech. Tim and I met them at the South Portico. I asked Julie if she had received her pool picture. She said she hadn't, but the President had told her about it. Bebe petted Tim also.

5/6/70 I had the three dogs' picture made on the south side of the South Fountain, tulips and the White House in the background.

5/8/70 Pasha and Vicky went to Camp David for the weekend as the college people are having a meeting on the monument grounds. I hope they don't make a try for the White House.

The peace demonstrators did not make a try for the White House. But tension was high there in the days leading up to May 9, the date scheduled for the student antiwar demonstration to be held in front of the White House. The word was Nixon didn't dare try to pretend he didn't care, as he had in the previous November when he sent word out that he was watching a football game on TV and was unconcerned about the mob at the Washington Monument. Peace hadn't happened and the kids were mad.

What he did instead was mighty clever. *He* went to *them.*

In the early predawn of Saturday, May 9, the President made a surprise visit at the Lincoln Memorial where some of the students were asleep waiting for the demonstration. They were so groggy when they woke up at that hour that he was perfectly safe, and he grabbed the headlines by showing he was concerned about the students' thinking and their welfare. He told them special phones had been set up so they could talk with the White House.

Seeing the President of the United States standing there talking to them personally, many of the demonstrators were completely won over. The principle at work was "divide and conquer." The demonstrators that day were split between those who believed in the good faith of Nixon and those who didn't. Many were most impressed that the President was telling them to send delegations right into the White House to talk things over. And if they didn't want to come in, there were those phones.

What President Nixon didn't tell them and what the backstairs hands knew was that he had already assigned a whole group of his youngest, handsomest, and most eloquent aides to talk with the kids who showed up or phoned and explain that the President, their leader, was only trying to *shorten* the war—*that* was why he had ordered the invasion of Cambodia, not to lengthen the war.

Later I again overheard the young aides patting themselves on the back about the damned good job they had done for the Boss in handling those "bastard liberals."

5/10/70   The President and his family were having dinner in the private dining room on the second floor. Manolo was making a fire in the fireplace. He opened the window. A White House policeman had just unloaded a gas device to get rid of it as the trouble with the students was over. The gas fumes drifted through the window as the fireplace damper was open.

The pepper gas came into the room and everyone scattered for the East Hall, where they finished their dinner. The gas set off the fire alarm. The engineers and electrician Cliber got a good whiff of the gas when they investigated the cause for the fire alarm.

5/12/70   David Eisenhower and two male friends were playing whiffle ball. [A whiffle ball is a practice golf ball full of holes which can't be thrown or hit very far.] The ball was batted and David missed. Tim ran over and returned the ball. I yelled at Tim and he dropped it. David picked up the ball and scowled as he examined the ball. It wasn't damaged so the dogs and I went visiting the offices.

Mrs. Nixon also likes to play whiffle ball.

5/19/70   President Nixon played with the dogs on the South Lawn. Usher Pierce called for me to round up the dogs after the President went into the house.

5/20/70   I had the dogs on the south roadway. Julie came by in her car. The driver stopped and Julie let Pasha ride to the South Portico with her.

5/27/70   I met former President Johnson at the South Portico. He came to a luncheon for retiring Speaker of the House McCormack. LBJ got out of a limousine and walked directly to me. He said, "Hello, Mr. Bryant, it's good to see you. Yuki sends his regards." I asked how Yuki was. He said, "Fine, getting a little heavy, as we all are."

3:15 President Nixon escorted LBJ and Mr. McCormack to their cars at South Portico. President Nixon pointed at the three dogs. I walked over and President Johnson petted the two small dogs. He turned to President Nixon and said, looking at me, "He is one of the best." President Nixon answered, "I know." A nice compliment for me.

Mike told me that if LBJ cusses when Yuki jumps in his car, Yuki just jumps out of the car. No cussing, Yuki rides. Yuki is getting to be a puritan in his old age.

Actually, I was shocked at the treatment given the arriving ex-President. It was surprising, if not an outright insult, that the White House and President Nixon failed to have a welcoming committee.

In Johnson's day, when a former Chief Executive arrived, the Chief Usher would rush out with a welcome, and the doorman would be on duty. And sometimes LBJ himself stepped out to greet the former President. But this time no doorman or usher or presidential aide was there to say hello to LBJ when he came to the South Portico. Only me, the dogkeeper, and the regular policeman on duty there. In fact, it was the policeman who, knowing how I felt, tipped me off to stick around and I would see my old friend, LBJ.

To his credit, LBJ acted as if nothing were wrong. He was

beautifully dressed and in wonderful spirits. He came over to me just beaming, with his hand outstretched.

I remembered how the Johnsons had put themselves out to greet the Nixons on January 20, 1969, and earlier at the ranch, right after the election in '68. This was just one year later—just a year or so into the Nixon administration.

5/28/70 I had the two small dogs on the South Grounds for a party for underprivileged children. They enjoyed the dogs.

A young lady came up to me at the lawn party and told me that a miracle had just happened—a young boy clapped his hands after the concert. Before he came to the White House he wasn't moving his body muscles.

Later Mrs. Nixon had a tea. After it was over, I shook hands with J. B. West, who has just returned from a tour of Europe. I talked to Bess Abell and Liz Carpenter, who told me Yuki had gotten upset in the transition from the White House to ranch. She asked me if I had read her book. I told her I would get her to autograph a copy some time when she was in a store. Mrs. Johnson spoke and waved to me from her limousine as she was leaving.

Later the backstairs crowd kidded me because Liz said in her book that I had sulked for two weeks because she hadn't let me get Blanco and Lassie together when Lassie came to White House during the Johnson administration.

I said, "She's right. And I'm still sulking."

Four years later, when I sent a little donation for the thousand trees to be planted in the LBJ Memorial Grove on the Potomac, Liz sent me a nice little note, dated September 16, 1974, thanking me and adding a typically Liz touch in her handwritten P.S. at the bottom of the letter, "What fun to have all those trees for your dogs."

6/1/70 Tim returned from California. He jumped and tried to put his paws on my shoulder. President and Mrs. Nixon stopped and laughed as Tim tried it again. He was so glad to see me. I fed him and put him in his pen for the night.

6/7/70 Tim returned from Camp David. Bebe Rebozo petted Tim at the South Portico. Bebe has the run of the White House.

6/9/70 The President showed the *Apollo 13* astronauts the three dogs after their dinner at the White House. The President and Mrs. Nixon escorted them to the South Portico where the helicopter was waiting to take the guests to Camp David.

289

6/10/70   Candidates for Congress had a cocktail reception and got their picture taken with the President for their campaigns. The candidates and wives petted the three dogs before loading into their buses.

6/11/70   Tim went to Florida.

6/14/70   Tim returned with the President. I had Vicky and Pasha out to meet his chopper. He came over and patted them.

6/23/70   There was almost an international incident. The Russian ambassador's limousine slammed on the brakes and just missed hitting Pasha. This happened about 6:30 P.M., as the car was leaving the White House.

6/25/70   The dogs went to California with the family.

6/26/70   Head Gardener Irvin Williams told me former usher J. B. West wants some pictures of Pushinka. He is writing a White House book. I told him I would have to check, but I am quite sure that I have reserved them for my own book.

July 4, 1970, will go down in history as the day of the great Billy Graham love-in. Graham had come up with the idea himself—people sitting around talking about "what's right with America" on the grounds of the Washington Monument.

Graham made the suggestion to President Nixon, who said, "Great, let's call it, 'Honor America Day.'" The President said he could see it becoming a yearly tradition and everyone at the White House was requested to cooperate with Billy Graham in putting the thing across. Every big gun entertainer on the Republican side was scheduled to appear. They tried, oh how they tried, to make it the kind of love-in that would become an American tradition.

But the event actually proved a bit ridiculous. What happened is that a bunch of hippies were holding a love-in, too, and they were smoking so much pot it became more of a smoke-in. At first they started objecting good-naturedly that they had been there first, but eventually they got stoned and started yelling obscenities and throwing real stones.

That's when it quit being funny. The police threw tear-gas containers, and the hippies, smashed out of their minds, threw the containers back so that the tear gas spilled among the spectators, giving them something to really cry about.

7/14/70   Tricia and her boyfriend's brother, Mr. Cox, were inspecting the dance floor on the South Lawn for a Friday-night entertainment for Prince Charles of England. Pasha and Tim came to me, so I put them in the pen. Vicky wouldn't come to me, so I grabbed her and she let out a little yelp. Tricia said, "Don't you hurt that dog," in an insolent, nasty way. I didn't say anything, as I want to retire in a couple of years, peaceful-like. My wife retires July 31.

7/17/70 Two young men from Kissinger's office tried to crash Tricia's party for the prince. They were dressed in their tuxedos and were with their dates. The Secret Service took their passes away from them in the Map Room. Kissinger and his women are the talk of the White House. The inside story is that he dates all the pretty girls in Hollywood and Washington, including Barbara Howar, but he keeps a change of clothes at the apartment of his girlfriend in New York, Nancy Maginnes.

When Prince Charles came to visit Tricia—bringing his sister Anne as a reluctant chaperone—the rumor around the White House backstairs was that romance was in the air and hopes were high that Tricia would have as spectacular a marriage as her sister, Julie, who had married a presidential grandson in storybook style.

I know that everything humanly possible was done to give the couple a chance to really know each other. And nothing was to distract the prince, not even a dog.

The day he was scheduled to arrive, I went out to the dog pen and found the dogs missing. I went to see Fina to find out what had happened because I planned as usual to have the dogs outside for such an historic event.

Fina said that the First Lady had told her that the dogs were not to be let outside during Prince Charles' arrival or during the time he was at the White House. I was surprised that the First Lady had said that, but knowing the Nixons, I should not have been too surprised. But I was a little worried about the dogs when they were kept shut in all day in Fina and Manolo's small living quarters on the third floor.

To my knowledge, the prince did not get to see the dogs. If he saw them, it was not in the evenings or afternoons or nights when I was around. It would have had to be in the morning, which made it very unlikely.

After the prince and his sister left, the White House help murmured about how bored Princess Anne had been in spite of all the efforts to please and entertain her. Even picnicking on corn on the cob and hot dogs. And somehow, though Tricia and the prince were friendly and polite to each other, the word was that "no sparks flew."

I really didn't know what to expect the heir to the British throne to be like. The Prince had described himself on David Frost's show as "a twit," which in England supposedly means a silly fool.

It was not Tricia who had invited the prince, but her father. The President had also sent Tricia to attend Prince Charles' investiture in 1969. The White House crowd said President Nixon was trying to start something between them if at all possible. He had been going around telling people about the impending visit and saying, "Charles is a nice fellow. You know, that Prince Charles . . ." He'd invited all the governors' children between the ages of twenty-one and thirty to a supper dance at the White House. The age limit of twenty-one had been decided on, he said, because champagne was going to be served. The fact that Tricia was twenty-four would make it unlikely she'd want younger kids around anyway. The Prince was only twenty-one himself. Too young. It was a nice try on Nixon's part, but no go.

The word backstairs was that Charles didn't sound or act royal enough for Tricia. Tricia was much more a little princess than he was a prince. It didn't seem princely, for example, that he said he sometimes almost collapsed with laughter at a ship launching, imagining the ship broke in two but the bottle stayed intact.

The prince enjoyed the American-style picnic at Camp David and everything else, including a talk on Capitol Hill with House Minority Leader Gerald Ford, House Majority Leader Carl Albert, and Speaker of the House John McCormack. But what he seemed to enjoy most, from what I could figure out, was his talk with astronaut Neil Armstrong about what it's like on the moon and how it felt coming down.

Charles said he was an aviator himself, and wanted to know all about the set-down. "Did you come down quite slowly?" he asked. "Did you land where you wanted to?" He waved his arms around excitedly asking his questions and was most intent when Armstrong answered Anne's question about the space suit: "Would it rip?"

"No," said Armstrong, "but the difference between eternity and life is about one-hundredth of an inch of rubber."

Later at the White House, Vice President Spiro Agnew said that Prince Charles had asked him for "three easy lessons in how to become a member of the powerful U.S. Senate."

Agnew told him he didn't know because he was only a lowly Vice President presiding over the Senate, and he'd like the same three easy lessons.

I used to think Hubert Humphrey was not around the White House much during the Johnson years, but Vice President Agnew was around even less. The word was the President didn't like his flamboyant style, though he did need him "to take the heat." Agnew seemed to enjoy making speeches that rubbed the press and TV world the wrong way and stirred up plenty of heat. In the Nixon administration there was enough heat for everyone.

Nor was Pat Nixon close to Judy Agnew. The First Lady seemed to take all her cues from her husband.

I was fascinated to see how the White House was handling the royal visit of Prince Charles and his sister Princess Anne. I know the ladies of the press who had to cover it were furious because Princess Anne would not let herself be interviewed and seemed to be snubbing them. Somewhere along the line, the word was that Anne had called them "the witches of Washington."

Afterwards the story was that "the witches of the White House press" were feeling vindicated because when the prince and princess went to Kenya, some time after their Washington visit, Princess Anne again received a bad press. The princess had stood by and said nothing to the cameraman and reporters except "Get out!" Charles, on the other hand, had joked and laughed and told what it's like to be on foot on a four-day safari in hundred-degree heat, with a bunch of camels: "The camels belch and burp and make an ungodly noise."

The way I see it, maybe there was just too much schedule to encourage any romance—a picnic at Camp David, the tour of Capitol Hill, a boat trip to Mount Vernon on the *Sequoia,* a tremendous ball fit for a king. In all the pictures that I saw of Trish and the prince at Mount Vernon, Prince Charles was walking way ahead of her and seemed completely unaware of her. Altogether the visit was a three-ring circus. There was not a moment for the prince to really get acquainted with Tricia, let alone her dogs. But knowing how the British love dogs, the course of history might have been different if Prince Charles had been permitted to get friendly with King Timahoe and his four-footed sidekicks.

The rumor around the White House was that the President was bitterly disappointed because his daughter had failed to make him a part of the royal set. As I saw it, Trish came out the winner. At least she didn't have to have Anne as a sister-in-law.

24

King Timahoe meant a great deal to the President. Even if Tim didn't reciprocate completely, the President wanted nothing but the best for his noble beast. And Tim certainly knew he had a friend in the Oval Office who was good for a handout. As soon as he got to the President's office Tim made a beeline for the right desk drawer that had his treats and pointed that famous nose. Richard Nixon got the message. Tim got a biscuit.

One time Timahoe grandly chewed up a good-sized strip of the President's office rug, just as Lyndon Johnson's dogs had done. And Nixon had been just as permissive about it. Instead of punishing him, or even saying a harsh word, the President had simply given Timmy some dog biscuits to chew on instead. Henry Kissinger, who was sitting in the President's office, realized Tim might take the treat as a reward and teased the President, saying, "Ah, Mr. President, I see you are *teaching* your dog to chew the rug."

Somehow the President got the impression that Walter Reed Army Hospital wasn't doing right by his dog and he wanted something better; in fact, the best. So he dispatched me to the breeder who had raised Tim at Tirvelda Farms in Middleburg, Virginia, near the place that Jackie and President Kennedy had once used as a hideaway.

My diary tells the story:

7/24/70 Pasha and Vicky went to California with the President. Tim stayed, as he is supposed to go to Walter Reed for two weeks so they can check his fungus. As the President was leaving this morning he told his aide Alex Butterfield that Tim didn't look too good, and then Bill Gulley got in the act and he and the President thought Tim could get better treatment in California. I called Mr. Butterfield on the phone and told him it was difficult for me to continue to treat Tim when he was on a trip for ten days, as it interrupted his treatment. I told him Walter Reed was a first-class place for vet care for Tim. He said he would contact California and ask General Hughes. I told Usher Pierce that all I need now was for four White House ushers to get into the act.

7/25/70 I received a call at home from Bill Gulley. He said that the President wanted E. Irving Eldredge, the famous breeder of Irish setters, to examine Tim, recommend a menu for him, and generally advise.

3:00 P.M. I picked up Tim and brushed him. Usher Pierce called a White House limousine for the trip to Tirvelda. Tim and I rode grandly in the back. It was a one-hour drive each way. Mr. Eldredge met me at his kennel; I had already talked to him on the phone. He has 1,100 acres and showed me his eleven setters. One was Tim's sister. He also showed me his formula and food for his dogs and his new pups. The kennels have air conditioning in summer and heat in the winter. He advised me to leave Tim with his kennel and let his own vet, Dr. John Holland, examine him. He said the vet would charge President Nixon the normal fee. I told him to write a letter to the President after Tim's examination.

Word gets around fast in Washington.

7/27/70 Captain Goodwin from Walter Reed called and he was upset because I took Tim to Middleburg. How did he know, I wonder. He said it was a slap in the face to Walter Reed and to him. I told him that I followed orders from Bill Gulley, the military aide. He said he would take it up with Colonel Asbill, his superior at Walter Reed. I thought it time to let Mr. Butterfield know about Tim going to Middleburg.

7/28/70 I received a call from Bill Gulley. He told me to call Mr. Eldredge. Mr. Eldredge told me that Tim was picking up *too much* weight. He told me to come after Tim on Monday and he advised me to call Abilene, Kansas, and order some meat for Tim. I called Mr. Davis of John Morrel and Company, Abilene, Kansas and ordered Power Plus: two hundred pounds in five-pound packages, 29¢ a pound, to be delivered next week. He is sending it to me and a bill to Mr. Gulley.

Mr. Gulley told Mr. Rotchford of the General Services Administration to get me a deep freeze 4 feet long by 30 in. by 28 in. wide. I told Usher Pierce. He said, "What the hell has Mr. Rotchford got to do with it?" I told him I was only following Mr. Gulley's orders from General Hughes from President Nixon. Pierce told Rex Scouten, and then Pierce came back to me and said Rotchford is not their boss, and the White House would pay for the deep freeze, so Mr. Rotchford won't have any more to do with the deep freeze after it is delivered.

7/31/70 My wife retired today. Captain Goodwin called me and wanted to know how Tim was doing.

10:00 P.M. Mr. Rotchford came over and said that he had a stand-up deep freeze, 6 feet tall. I told him that it would have to be a chest-type deep freeze to hold two hundred pounds of food. He said he would buy one tomorrow. I didn't hurt his feelings by telling him how the White House felt about his help.

8/2/70   7:30 P.M. Julie and David came in. Julie asked me about Tim's condition. I told her that I would go to Middleburg after Tim tomorrow.
   Mr. Rotchford delivered the wrong freezer—upright and too large.

8/3/70   A chauffeur drove me to the Tirvelda farm. Tim had picked up some weight. E. Irving Eldredge showed me how to prepare the Power Plus food. He gave me a frozen block of the food, a bag of Ken-L Ration Kibbles, some medicine spray and ear drops for Tim. I gave him a carton of the President's matches and thanked him for his trouble. He said he had a White House appointment at 12:30 on August 10 with Dwight Chapin. So that's the new dog man—Chapin. Tim was sure glad to see me.
   The President's chopper came in at 11:00 P.M. Mr. and Mrs. Nixon came to me and Timahoe. The President asked about Tim. I told him Mr. Eldredge had sent a letter to California, but he said he didn't receive the letter. I had a copy in my coat pocket, which I gave to the President. He carried it in his hands as he went into the White House. Mrs. Nixon asked about Tim's fungus spots.

The Secret Service men looked at me with awe when the President and I were discussing the letter, especially when they saw the President was hanging onto it himself. One of the first things you learn at the White House is that First Ladies and Presidents do not sully their hands carrying anything, even if it is light as a feather or valuable as solid gold. They hand it immediately to an aide. So the fact that President Nixon carried the letter himself showed me how important Tim was to him.

The significance of this incident became evident the very next day when the military aide, Colonel Coffey, called me and wanted to know what it had been all about and asked for a copy of the letter to put in his own files. He said he wanted to keep abreast of everything to do with the dogs in case there were questions later. And besides all that, he was just plain curious.

8/4/70   Simmons, a White House engineer, got an electric shock while working on the deep freeze. I called Mr. Rotchford and told him about it. He gave me some lip, wanting to know if the White House couldn't fix it. I told him that I had asked him for a three-wire grounded plug so the dogs couldn't get shocked from the freezer. He could tell I was about to blow my stack, so he said, "Come on over here and I will get you a car and let you go out and buy what you want." I told him I would see about it. I asked Rex Scouten about it and he said that he wasn't contacted about a freezer. He called up Bill Gulley and told him that Mr. Rotchford didn't have anything to do with the White House proper. He said that I should see the plumber, Red Arrington. Later he apologized and said he meant Louis Simmons, a White House engineer whom I had already told to contact Mr. Scouten. I then called Mr. Rotchford and told him I would borrow his deep freeze until the White House bought me a new one. Government bureaucracy can "drive you up the wall," to borrow a favorite expression of Jackie Kennedy's.

8/5/70   Captain Goodwin came in with another vet today. He was upset about the dog going to the vet in Middleburg. I told him I wasn't even a private and he was a captain, but if the Commander in Chief wanted to change vets, I would see that the change was made. He said he was going to Colonel Asbill at Walter Reed and resign from the White House charge.

Later I talked to Colonel Coffey and brought him up to date. I walked into Mr. Gulley's office. He was talking to Mr. Eldredge on the phone, asking him about changing vets. Mr. Gulley informed me that the President himself wanted to change vets.

Rex Scouten told me the new freezer would arrive in two weeks. Janet Kemp from the Attorney General's office called and asked me to recommend a kennel in Washington, D.C., for her boss's poodle. I guess he wanted to know what was *good enough* for the President. I didn't tell.

8/11/70   Mrs. Nixon's Secret Service agent called and wanted the dog leashes. They had let the dogs out and Tim had jumped in the South Fountain and Mrs. Nixon said he was too wet to go for a ride. I showed the agent where I kept the leashes under a water pail on top of the doghouse. Pasha and Vicky went. I brought Tim to my shop, so he wouldn't be lonesome. I had an argument with Batey, the storeroom keeper. He bought some scales with weights on them. I had ordered a plain round scale (no weights to adjust). I asked Usher Pierce to send Batey out tomorrow for the correct scales.

8/12/70   The correct scales arrived today.

The Walter Reed vets came in today. I told them that the vet service had definitely been changed. However, I escorted them to Colonel Coffey's office with the dogs' health records, which they brought. Coffey then officially gave the records to me, and I have to turn them over to Dr. John Holland, the new official White House vet, at Middleburg, next week.

8/14/70 I took the three dogs to Dr. Holland in Middleburg for a checkup. He gave the two small dogs rabies shots and treated Tim's ears.

The President and Mrs. Nixon returned from Louisiana about 9:45 P.M. They petted the dogs after landing. I told the President that Tim had gained weight. He said, "Good."

8/16/70 Tonight the American flag flies all night over the White House with three lights shining on the flag. It looks good at night. It's something that should have been done long ago.

8/18/70 I gave the Navy mess thirty pounds of meat and thirty pounds of Kibbles dry food for Tim's trip in California. Usher Pierce was practicing pool in the President's poolroom on the third floor. He is supposed to get me a refrigerator and freezer for Tim's frozen food.

The President, Mrs. Nixon, and Tricia returned from New York at 11:00 P.M. Mrs. Nixon and Tricia petted Tim. The President walked towards C-9 and looked at the lighted flag on the White House. He came to Tim a few minutes later. He said, "Tim, you are going to California tomorrow." He paused and then said, "No, it will be Thursday." I told the President that Tim missed him. Ron Ziegler asked me how Tim's health was. The President is not to know anything about the skin condition. Alexander Butterfield also asked about Tim.

A few years later, when Butterfield headed the Federal Aviation Agency, he startled the Watergate Committee by revealing for the first time that President Nixon's Oval Office had been bugged so that every word spoken was recorded on reels of tape. When I knew Alexander Butterfield, he was in the Communications Division of the White House and was a real nice guy, whom everyone called Alex. Seeing his name scattered through my diary for the Nixon years gives me a strange feeling. There are so many ghostly figures in the diary. Like Chapin and Ehrlichman and Haldeman, and even Jake Jacobsen.

When milk lobbyist Jake Jacobsen was accused of being involved with President Nixon's friend, former Texas Governor John Connally, in an alleged deal to get the President to raise milk prices, and when Jacobsen was indicted on charges of misapplication of $825,000 from the San Angelo, Texas, First Savings and Loan Association, I thought of how I had known Jake when he was at the White House during the Johnson administration.

Jake Jacobsen was one of LBJ's liaison men with Capitol Hill and very likable. I used to bring the dogs by to see him because he enjoyed relaxing for a few minutes to pet the Johnson dogs. I remember once he was too rushed to play with the dogs and he laughed and said, "I have to get up to the Hill fast and do a snow job on a couple of tough senators to get this bill passed."

8/21/70   7:30 P.M. Tim left for California. (Lucky dog.)

8/24/70   Tricia is still at the White House. She complained to her butler about the poor grade of hamburger she was served. (I hope Tim isn't sharing his special mix with her.) Last week Mr. Kissinger's secretary called and asked for a 15-amp fusetron. I told her we didn't have any, and suggested she call the electric shop in the Executive Office Building. Later I got a call from the police stating that it was an emergency. Mr. Kissinger needed the 15-amp fusetron in his home. The EOB electric shop had one, but the man who could release it was missing. The 25¢ fusetron probably cost fifty dollars by the time it was delivered to Kissinger's home by chauffeur-driven limousine.

The White House police, military aides, electricians, telephone operators, secretaries, and drivers all got in the act before the mission was accomplished. "King Kissinger," as we called him, had everyone around the White House jumping almost as much as "King Richard." But I refused to jump for anyone but the President himself or the immediate presidential family.

9/24/70   Doug Lluellyn, WTOP-TV, came in with his cameramen and sound man. The interview was one of our best. The dogs in the South Fountain, Sam Page feeding them, and then the dogs chasing a squirrel. It looked like we had rehearsed it.

9/27/70   President and Mrs. Nixon went to Europe (Rome). The dogs stayed home.

9/29/70   Julie let the dogs out. The police called me and said there was a wire cut in the fence. I got the dogs in line and Julie thanked me. I told her the dogs might be on television. She said she would like to see it.
    Last night it was supposed to be on, but news reports of Nasser's death cancelled it out.

9/30/70   The dogs and I were on WTOP tonight. It looked very good.
    The White House had the play *Oh Calcutta* picked up from a closed circuit television recording today. The maintenance crew got to see it.

10/1/70   Tricia's agent called and said that Tricia wanted the dogs in her room. I took all three dogs to her door and knocked on the door. The little dogs Pasha and Vicky ran into her room as she opened the door. I told her I had Tim too, and she said, "Yes, I want Tim also." She said Julie saw the TV show about my interview and she said she would have liked to have seen it. Forty-five minutes later I got a call from the Usher's Office and I took the dogs outside for their exercise. Julie drove up and said that she had enjoyed the TV interview very much.

10/2/70 Capital Parks Service is moving two large trees east of the tennis court so the court can be extended.

The Nixon administration will surely go down in history as the "tennis administration," just as the Eisenhower administration was the "golf administration." "Tennis anyone?" was the battle cry as Haldeman, Ehrlichman, Chapin, and the rest of the White House "In crowd"—everyone but the President himself—came charging out of the White House from their offices, dressed in their tennis shorts.

10/5/70 President and Mrs. Nixon returned from their European trip. I had all three dogs at the South Portico. When his chopper landed he walked over and patted the dogs. Mrs. Nixon also greeted the dogs. They looked tired.

10/7/70 Usher Stout called and said that Manolo Sanchez requested that the dogs be at South Portico early in the morning. I told Mr. Stout that the workers didn't arrive until 7:30 A.M. I told him that Manolo knew where the dogs stayed. Stout is one of the nicest ushers I've known.

10/8/70 The dogs went to Florida. In an interview Chef Haller stated that President Nixon got his exercise before dinner by mixing a martini. Mr. Haller said I shouldn't laugh, as it could happen to me. He meant the press telling everything you say. Which reminds me, the President's favorite barber, Martini, doesn't cut hair at the White House any more. Mrs. Bailey, the housekeeper, cannot have interviews, by Mrs. Nixon's request. The ladies of the press have been pleading to talk to her about how she takes care of the White House, just like they used to interview Lady Bird's housekeeper, Mary Kaltman. What's Mrs. Nixon trying to hide?

10/11/70 The dogs returned from Florida. The President and Mrs. Nixon waved to Mr. Butterfield after the helicopter landed.

10/20/70 10:45 P.M. The President returned from his campaign trip. As soon as he got off the helicopter at the White House he came over to me and petted all three dogs. Then he went into the Mansion. He appeared to be tired.

A few minutes later Julie and David drove up and they patted the dogs. Julie said that she has been so busy she has neglected the dogs. David said, "They are fine dogs." He and Julie are a loving couple.

10/22/70   Julie and David spoke to me as they came into the White House theater to see *Tora Tora Tora*, the film about the bombing of Pearl Harbor. I didn't care much for the picture, but I sat through it. It reminded me too much of the damaged ships that I worked on as an electrician at the Pearl Harbor shipyard early in "War Two," as it's fashionable to call it around the "WH."

10/24/70   David is in the Navy. Poor Julie.

10/26/70   Julie spoke to me on the second floor. I was checking lights for the dinner for the President of Romania, Nicolae Ceausescu. Vicky was groomed at the dogs' beauty salon—thirteen dollars.

10/27/70   Ron Ziegler was waiting at the South Portico for the President's helicopter. He asked me how Tim was. The President waved to us as he boarded the helicopter for his political trip to Florida and California. From his helicopter window he waved to some children dressed in Halloween costumes on the first-floor balcony. After the chopper left, John Davies—the "Official Greeter," they call him—asked me to bring the dogs up the steps and let the children in the costumes pat them. The children were delighted.

White House police apprehended a young man who climbed over the White House fence below A-1 Post on the east side. What, again?

10/29/70   Ah, memories! Usher Stout, a former Secret Service man, told me that President Johnson used a big convertible to hunt deer in Texas. He said that he would have the driver stop the car, then President Johnson would prop his rifle on the top of the door, aim, and shoot the deer without leaving the car. He said that an agent would go to the deer and cut its throat so it would bleed.

All the dogs are going to California. These days "Texas" is a dirty word.

11/3/70   One of the new Negro White House policemen on F-2 Post near the President's elevator asked, "Where are the dogs?" I replied they went to California to vote. He said, "If Mr. Nixon has anything to do with it, he would see that they voted, all right."

Mr. Scouten asked me if Mr. Williams told me about the south fence repair job. I said no. He informed me that Capital Parks is replacing the mesh fence on the iron fence. He said they are using a heavier gauge for security and painting it black as they install it. I told him not to let Pasha run loose until the fence is completed, as Pasha could go through the iron bars. Tricia was in the White House Saturday, but she later went to California to vote.

11/4/70 I told Usher Hare to notify the Nixons about the loose fencing and to leave the small dogs in the heated room.

The Nixons returned from Andrews Field in their car because the rain and weather was too heavy for a chopper. I was in the small entrance hall at the Diplomatic Entrance. Tricia came in. Her eyes were looking downward. She's sad. The President and Mrs. Nixon spoke to me. Bebe Rebozo followed; he also spoke to me. They looked very tired. I went out under the far end of the canopy and I heard Manolo say to Tim, "There is your Mr. Bryant."

I hollered out, "Hello, Tim, what are you doing out in the rain?" I petted Tim and told Manolo I was going to leave the small dogs in their room. Dr. Walter Tkach, the President's doctor, came running and puffing out of the Diplomatic Room. He said to be very quiet as the President was still in the Oval Office.

Later a Secret Service man came out and asked what the noise was all about. After the Secret Service man left I told the policeman somebody's nerves sure are shot if they are *that* nervous. I took Tim out to his pen, and he ran around like a deer in the woods. He was glad to be home!

11/5/70 Anita Coffelt, publisher and editor of the *Animal Lovers Magazine* from Bridgeville, Pennsylvania, came in today at 2:00 P.M. for an interview with me. Another lady was with her. I showed them the dogs, the Rose Garden, the President's office, the Cabinet Room. I introduced them to Mr. Butterfield, who explained his job at the White House to Anita.

I saw Lord Louis Mountbatten at the White House tonight! I worked on the *Illustrious*, an English aircraft carrier in Norfolk, Virginia, when it was damaged during World War II. He was secretly aboard the carrier while I was working on it. It was very hush-hush.

11/9/70 I talked to Fina. She had been in Spain for over a month.

Fina Sanchez had brought a scarf and a rosebud pin for my wife, which I thought was very nice of her. I was very interested in her description of a house that was just waiting for her and Manolo to retire to in Spain. Fina said it was a lovely stone house which had been left to them by their family, and it was so "peaceful and quiet compared with the White House."

Fina said it was her dream to go back there some day, and she talked of how little it cost to live in Spain.

I escorted the Capital Parks electricians today, wherever they worked at the White House, inside, outside, and on the roof, as the police say they are understaffed and someone has to be with any worker who is not on the White House staff. The electricians have been working on lighting the White House for over two months. It is a surprise for the public driving by and Pat Nixon's first big White House project. LBJ will be gnashing his teeth when he hears how much electricity this is costing. I'd hate to be around to hear him.

Mrs. Nixon and Julie came out on the North Grounds to look at the new gleaming appearance of the White House, with all the spotlights trained on it. They later took Pasha and Vicky upstairs at 10:30 P.M. Usher Pierce told me that Fina said Pasha was starving. I opened a can of Hill's dog food and went to the third floor to feed the two dogs.

The routine was that I had Sam Page, the Capital Parks grounds keeper, feed all three dogs. He would take the food to the dog pen. Fina decreed that the little ones should be fed Alpo, and Tim, of course, had his special mix which I would order shipped in. Fina also saved a few table scraps and had dog candy around for when the dogs visited her. I still gave each dog a tablespoon of bacon and beef drippings mixed in their food, occasionally, to keep their coats nice and shiny.

11/10/70   Nixon returned to White House because De Gaulle died and the President is going to attend the funeral. When he came off the helicopter it was pouring down rain and the President's valet Manolo and doorman Mayfield each held an umbrella over the President. The President wanted Tim protected too. Someone signaled me. Tim rated my umbrella as I met the President.

I had Capital Parks put some hay in Tim's doghouse, to keep it clean.

11/12/70   The President is back from Paris.

12/8/70   Julie Robinson, one of the First Lady's press aides, called and asked me if tomorrow at 11:00 A.M. I could pose the dogs in a sleigh for a Christmas picture. I told her I would do my best. Also, Dog World magazine wants an interview.

12/9/70   Julie Robinson and Helen Smith couldn't locate a sleigh for today. Julie told me Mr. Scouten got a sled but that wouldn't do. I suggested the doghouse could be fixed up very Christmasy and cute. So Capital Parks Service put up a pine tree, the bouquet boys put up a great wreath, and three dummy Christmas packages were strewn about the

303

doghouse. We took several pictures so I'm sure we got a good picture for the press, made by the White House photographers.

John Muffler, a White House electrician, was on the second floor talking to Mrs. Nixon. He told her that he heard that President Johnson was planning on running for President in '72. Sam Houston Johnson, LBJ's brother, had made that wild statement to reporters in Baltimore.

Mrs. Nixon said, "Okay, but isn't he too old to run?" Muffler said the newscaster had said that Dwight Eisenhower was still older when he ran. Muffler couldn't help needling Pat by commenting that LBJ would want the new spotlights on the White House cut off at night.

Muffler said that Mrs. Nixon said, shocked, "He wouldn't do that, would he?"

12/10/70 Stop the show! Julie Robinson made the White House photographers take down the dog Christmas picture they hung in a hall. It has not been released to the press yet. They are afraid of a press leak. Ho, ho.

12/15/70 I pawprinted the Nixon dogs for Manolo. Fina wanted the picture autographed "To Mel, Vicky's hairdresser favorite." Nothing doing.

I thought it over and I decided the poodle beautician would get a thousand dollars' worth of publicity with a picture like that. So I told the social-office engraver to print "To Mel, with Best Wishes."

12/18/70 Evening-at-the-White-House party for three hundred and fifty guests. Mamie Eisenhower stopped and petted Pasha at the South Portico. Mrs. Herb Klein petted Tim as they came to the party. I told my AP friend, Frank Cormier, that the Treasury engravers will have to engrave a new twenty-dollar bill as the east and west parapet pole lights were removed while I was on vacation. You can't fool around with history.

12/27/70 Tricia and her Ed Cox came in earlier in the evening. She spoke to me happily. President and Mrs. Nixon returned from Camp David about 7:15 P.M. The President walked off the helicopter with Tim on leash. The President handed the leash to me. Mrs. Nixon smiled and spoke to me. I will be on leave for one week. Lord give me strength. I wonder if anybody would miss me if I didn't come back from vacation.

25

1971 was the year we really flipped our wigs trying to make the White House into a castle or palace or, at the very least, a princely dwelling. The staff had developed a subservient attitude toward the First Family, and the funniest illustration of it concerned the First Lady and the South Fountain. First Lady Pat said she wanted the South Fountain turned on in the winter because she enjoyed watching it from the White House windows.

The South Fountain had not been turned on in winter in twenty years. But the Usher's Office was apparently afraid to say no to the First Lady. So one night soon after, the White House engineer and a plumber rode around the fountain pool nearly all night long in a rowboat, breaking up the ice, in case the First Lady wanted to see the pretty fountain and looked out the window. I almost collapsed on the ground in laughter. I could not believe my eyes. I'll be merciful and let the midnight boatmen remain nameless. For the historical record, though, the date was February 1, 1971.

Later, an electric cable was installed to heat the fountain in winter. I think we ran out of boatmen.

Even before that historic episode, 1971 had begun to look like a red-letter year. January started out on a note of mystery.

1/14/71 Some airplane personnel called, very concerned but guarded. They said for me to check Pasha when dogs arrived at the White House. They said they couldn't say too much over the radio. Very mysterious. Then, after the President and Mrs. Nixon arrived, Fina arrived separately with the dogs. All of them were excited. She said that just before they left California a German police dog belonging to Coast Guard personnel jumped on Pasha. I checked the dog over for about an hour out on the grounds; Pasha was nervous but all right. I don't think they want the President to find out.

1/15/71 I called Morrel and Company in Kansas for two hundred pounds of meat for Tim.

Tim went to Camp David. Bill Gulley called and asked me if I kept a

305

record of Tim's trips to California. He said it would have to simmer down. He never gave me the details. It was something about Jack Anderson's column telling how elegantly the President is transporting his dogs.

I looked up the column and saw it was more than that, much more. No wonder Anderson had drawn blood. After telling how Nixon had sent Timahoe to San Clemente in a Boeing 707 airliner "with the same pampering accorded high officials," he commented, "This elevation of pets has been a ruler's prerogative since the Emperor Caligula gave his horse, Incitatus, a retinue of slaves and announced the horse would be made a consul."

1/27/71   The White House chauffeur told me on the long ride back that sometimes his job bugged him. Last Saturday night he waited seven hours for Dr. Kissinger. He said several of the wheels in this administration use a White House chauffeur and car for parties, etc. Sometimes they have to wait right there until the party is over. As he was telling me this, we heard the dispatcher call for a car to pick up Herb Klein and his group at a hotel near the White House. The chauffeur said someone must be plastered and unable to navigate on foot as the hotel is only a two-minute walk through Lafayette Park to the White House. The chauffeur said they also have a problem with Nixon wheels who leave home a half-hour late regularly and get angry if the chauffeur refuses to break the speed law. But it's on the chauffeur's record if they get stopped by police, not the big wheel's record.

1/28/71   I took King Timahoe to Mrs. Nixon, who was in the library. She wanted a Cub Scout to see Tim. I could see the First Lady adored that child and was anxious to impress him with something. As he petted Tim, she told the boy that the President of the United States took this dog on most of his trips, but that the first time the dog had boarded a helicopter, he had to be carried on. I helped the First Lady by telling the kid a little more about Tim, including the fact that I had gone on four practice flights in getting him used to the chopper noise, mostly carrying him on.

1/31/71   The President and Pat are in the Virgin Islands watching the *Apollo 14* flight; they will return tomorrow.

The First Family did return the next night—February 1, the night the boatmen pursued the ice in the South Fountain. I met their chopper at 9:30 P.M. with all the dogs and with Pasha tucked into my overcoat because of the cold. Mrs. Nixon, who had just come from a sunnier clime, petted the dogs and commented, "It is cold."

I'm sure she didn't know how cold it was going to be for the two Volga boatmen later in the evening.

2/4/71 I took Pasha and Vicky up to the third floor to see Fina. Julie came into the sitting room. I was sitting on the davenport. I stood up as she petted the dogs and talked. She told me to sit down. She is very considerate and nice to everyone around the White House. Tricia not only would have let me stand, but would have expected a salute. I said, "I am going to have *Julie's* teeth cleaned after she is groomed." I caught my error and corrected myself. If she recognized my "Freudian slip" she never let on.

2/5/71 Jackie Kennedy and her children visited the Nixons. The secret of the year. Even I didn't know it until she was gone. That's better security than for LBJ by far.

2/11/71 All the dogs went to Florida.

2/15/71 The Nixons and the dogs returned at 8:15 P.M. The Nixons waved to me.

2/18/71 The First Lady is the same kind of fussbudget about rugs as First Lady Mamie Eisenhower was. She must have learned it from her.

Mrs. Nixon came out of Tricia's room as I was replacing a light bulb in the chandelier outside the President's bedroom. She put on her "Lady Patricia" voice: "You should use a drop cloth under the ladder, or it will leave dust marks on the hallway rug." I could have argued and told her the ladder is left in a stairwall that goes to the third floor. There is no dust there. Also, there are rubber pads on the legs of the ladder. There is no dust. But I said, "Yes, ma'am."

2/19/71 Dave Powers visited the White House to look at the Kennedy pictures. He asked a press aide about me, a policeman told me. He's doing a book. I'll bet he's leaving out all the best parts. He should be an expert on the amours of JFK, as well as his wit.

2/21/71 President and Mrs. Nixon returned from Camp David. The President waved to me as he entered the Diplomatic Room. The dogs came by car. I have one year to go to get my thirty years in the government. Give me strength. The atmosphere in the Nixon White House is getting me down.

2/23/71 Funny, funny. Engineers Grimes and Webster built a fire in the Queen's Room fireplace for Mrs. Bob Hope. It smoked her out, as the flue is blocked off. Bob Hope had the Lincoln Room. Mrs. Hope had the Queen's Room and she wanted the fire in the fireplace. Usher Hare insisted it be built, but he forgot to check. There are seven blocked-off fireplaces. Fina said that if anyone said Manolo started the fire, they would be fired from their jobs. They had a fire in the Nixon California home, and Manolo Sanchez had jokingly told the press that he wouldn't smoke pot in the basement any more.

The engineers supposedly put the fire out and left the Queen's Room but somehow the logs started to burn and smoke all over again.

A week or so later it was not so funny:

3/1/71 We had a bomb scare last night at 8:00. All clear.

3/11/71 President Nixon returned from a Williamsburg speech. When the helicopter landed I didn't have the dogs out to meet him. He told Manolo to let Tim out of his pen. Tim ran to everyone but the President. It was funny, but the President was really hurt. He winced.

I left Rex Scouten a note last night about the dangerous steam-heating system in Pasha and Vicky's room. President Nixon invited nine women reporters into his office for a small elite press conference, which caused an uproar among the other women reporters. This just wasn't his day. Barbara Walters also interviewed the President tonight.

3/12/71 The dogs went to Florida. The plumbers fixed the dog room as I requested. Mr. Scouten told me to check it out while the dogs are gone. Television commentator Walter Cronkite referred to last night's interview and said, "Hell has no fury like a woman reporter scorned."

3/15/71 Tim returned with the President, Mrs. Nixon, and Julie at 8:00 P.M. Fina brought the small dogs earlier on the baggage plane.

From Tricia's happy look, I should have known a big announcement was coming.

3/16/71 Hurray for Tricia. The day started with a twenty-one-gun salute for the arrival of Prime Minister John Lynch of Ireland. A few hundred people and children petted Tim, and many tourist pictures were made. I held my hands over Tim's ears as the cannon salute was given.

Later, as the President escorted Mr. Lynch to his car, he showed him Timahoe. The prime minister said that Tim had a fine coat. Later in the evening the President announced his daughter Tricia's wedding plans for June 5, 1971.

3/18/71 Fina said sadly that Tricia might take Pasha to New York after she got married. I told her that I doubted it.

3/24/71 The SST (Supersonic Transport) was voted down. Usher Pierce said that the President looked down in the dumps as he came from his office to the White House. I had Pasha under my raincoat, and Tim and Vicky were with me on the iron bench at the South Portico. The President and Mrs. Nixon waved to us from their limousine as they departed for a Republican dinner.

3/25/71 Tim is going to California with President Nixon for some sunshine.

3/30/71 Julie drove up in her car as I was putting out the two roadway lights that shine on the White House. I told her that I saw her on TV today and she did a good job. She thanked me and said it was good to see me. She also asked about her dog Vicky's gums and teeth. I told her they were okay.

4/5/71 Manolo brought Tim from California on the baggage plane. I had Tim at C-11 when the President landed in his chopper. He petted and shook hands with Tim. Manolo told me that Timahoe drank some Pacific Ocean salt water which gave the dog diarrhea and also that Tim got sick on the plane.

4/6/71 Fina called and said that she had Pasha and Vicky back at the White House. It was raining. She wanted me to put the dogs in their house. I told her that I was dressing as we have to wear the dark coat, pants, and a bow tie when the White House has a dinner. I told Fina to put the dogs in their room.

The new rule about dress was a pain, but "King Richard," as he was by now frequently called around the White House, had decreed that everything and everybody his eye fell on had to look just so.

4/12/71 Mrs. Nixon opened the Dutch door and let the dogs loose (LBJ's favorite trick). Pasha went into the house with her, so I rounded up Vicky and Tim. Tricia was the only Nixon out for the Easter Egg Roll.

4/18/71 Julie, David, and another couple petted the dogs. David and the other young man were in uniform. I let the girl have her picture made with Tim. Julie said Pasha was getting in the picture. Then Julie said, "Here comes Vicky, she's a ham."

4/20/71 President Nixon, Pat, and Tricia ate dinner on the Truman Balcony at 7:00 P.M. I had the dogs on the South Grounds near the pool at the request of Fina, who said that the President enjoyed watching the dogs while dining. From where he was observing us, over the balcony, we must have looked like an old pastoral painting—except we moved occasionally.

4/21/71 President Nixon and I showed dogs to 4-H boys and girls on South Lawn. The President said they could tour the Rose Garden, as that is where Tricia will be married. He said that they could "tiptoe through the tulips" but they wouldn't see any roses this time of the year.

I helped Cleave Ryan, the photographic electrician, set up lights in the East Room for the President and Mrs. Nixon's speech to the 4-H people.

One woman almost kicked over one of the lights I was protecting on a tripod. She kept kicking and I told her to please keep her feet away from my light. She gave me more guff. I finally told her, "My boots can kick harder than your slippers." She had been talking to a 4-H photographer on the platform near my light. I always try to be polite to White House visitors, but there is a limit to my politeness.

Once Prince Charles had passed up his chance to put the glass slipper on Richard Nixon's twenty-four-year-old daughter, Tricia, the President resigned himself to taking Ed Cox as his son-in-law. At least that was the story pieced together backstairs at the White House in the days following the President's announcement.

According to the story, Trish met Ed Cox when his mother, Mrs. Anne Cox, chairman of the New York City International Debutante Ball, arranged for her son to escort Tricia in 1964. Mrs. Cox hated people saying she had encouraged the romance between her son and the then eighteen-year-old daughter of the former Vice President, who had moved to New York from California; the date was just one of several arrangements she made as chairman to ensure the success of the ball.

Ed was a law student and his father was a New York lawyer of the old school in an old-fashioned office off Fifth Avenue. The Coxes lived in what was called a "genteel but old" townhouse on East End Avenue. But Ed's family did have one claim to fame that was hard to beat—his mother's ancestor, Robert Livingston, helped write the Declaration of Independence. Trish fell in love with Cox and vice versa, and the story was she had been trying to get permission to marry him for some time.

Backstairs everyone heaved a sigh of relief that Trish was happy at last and was going to have her man. The talk was of how strange it was, history-wise, that twice in a row, for two administrations— Johnson's and Nixon's—the older daughter was marrying last. The help of the White House is as interested in "records" of this kind as the rest of the country is interested in baseball or football firsts.

310

My diary records many funny items about White House weddings, but I have more notes about Tricia's than any other. The kitchen preparations for the June wedding heated up as early as April. First, a mock-up of the cake was constructed. I watched the frame being put together layer by layer with the help of the carpenters. The pipe used in the center came from my electrical shop.

The cake wasn't the only thing the White House staff had to worry about that spring. Larger and larger demonstrations against the war in Vietnam were occurring in Washington, and many of us had to put in extra hours standing by in case of emergency.

4/22/71   The electricians cut an 82-inch length of 1¼-inch pipe to support the tiers for the sample mock-up of Tricia's wedding cake. The tiers, or layers, will be 28, 24, 22, 12, and 6 inches high, with the smallest at the top. The carpenters taped the cardboard layers together, and Tricia, princess-like, inspected it at 3:15 P.M.

4/23/71   Tim went to Camp David by car. I worked twenty-four hours over the weekend on stand-by, as the peace marchers were in Washington. I was on duty twenty-four and a half hours, from Friday 3:30 P.M. until Saturday 4:00 P.M.

Fina gave me a bath towel and two sheets and I took a nap in my electric shop. Luckily we had no trouble. The next night the other electrician, Bill Cliber, had to deal with a partial blackout, as part of the high-tension feeders went out downtown.

4/25/71   The President, Mrs. Nixon, and Julie petted Pasha and Vicky when they arrived on the South Lawn at 8:10 P.M. Tim had gotten loose at Camp David when the President unleashed him before boarding the helicopter. Tim saw a bird and chased it. The President was too nervous to wait. So the dog was rounded up later and brought back to the White House by car. I picked Tim up at C-3 Post under the North Portico; he jumped all over me, he was so glad to see me.

Last week I gave Tim, Pasha, and Vicky a piece of deer meat from the buck I had shot on a hunting trip. Tim almost took off my finger as he snatched it out of my hand. Now maybe the deer in Camp David had better beware.

4/26/71   A White House policeman told me there were two mallards on the South Fountain. I held Tim by his choker and we walked to the South Fountain. We walked halfway round the fountain; then I let Tim loose. Timahoe pointed and ran the ducks to the center of the pool. Then Tim jumped in the pool and swam toward the ducks—one drake and one

311

hen. They took off into the air and went southwest with Tim trying to fly. One of the funniest things I ever saw. The President is a perfectionist. He told the helicopter "teacart" man to have the helicopter land farther away from the White House—several feet south of the normal landing pad—"as the wind from the chopper blows the buds off of the pretty trees in the West Rose Garden."

The "teacart" was the portable radio communications set up by which the White House keeps in touch with the helicopter pilot as well as the air control towers within the Washington, D.C., area.

4/28/71 2:00 A.M. Vicky bit John Gardosik, a night engineer. A policeman had called the engineers about the dogs barking. John went to the George Washington Hospital as the bite from Vicky brought blood.

I talked to Fina, the valet's wife, and she said Vicky wouldn't bite anyone. I told her that John went to the hospital to be treated. She still didn't believe it. Usher Pierce showed me a picture of the Johnsons on the first-floor balcony and the dogs and me below them during the wedding reception of one of LBJ's girls. The Nixon people are looking for ideas for Tricia's wedding. I asked Mr. Pierce to see Rex Scouten (who has the pictures) to get me a copy, as they were taken by Abby Rowe (deceased). He said he would ask, but he doubted if Scouten would give me one. The ushers are so cooperative! I blame it all on the Nixon atmosphere.

Later the word came back that the Nixons couldn't believe that a bite from poor little Vicky could put a man in the hospital. Or that innocent Vicky could bring herself to bite anyone. All I can say is that the White House makes even a dog act arrogant.

4/29/71 Rex Scouten called me to his office. He wanted to know the different foods we were feeding Vicky and Pasha. Later he told me that he was surprised at the low food cost. I took John Gardosik to the White House doctor and had him examine John's leg where Vicky bit him. It was just below his right kneecap. The doctor said it was healing.

On May Day, one of the largest stop-the-war demonstrations ever held began in Washington.

5/3/71 President Nixon, Tricia, and the three dogs returned from California after a four-day trip. The President and Tricia waved and spoke to me as they entered the Diplomatic Room after getting off the helicopter. I have put in thirty-two hours stand-by time. The peace marchers didn't close down the government.

5/7/71   Forty-eight hours overtime this week. I took the dogs for a tour of an agricultural exhibit on the South Lawn. Pasha barked at an 850-pound steer. Everyone laughed—Pasha only weighs five pounds.

5/9/71   Fina, the dogs, and I were checking the animal pens. However, the animals were removed a half-hour earlier as a "women's lib" group threatened to sit down on the White House lawn. So the tour was closed to the public. Tricia and her future husband stopped their car on the south roadway and Tricia petted the dogs. Fina said that Julie may take Vicky with her to her new quarters. I told Fina it would probably be only for a short time.

Rex Scouten sent me the Johnson wedding picture. Well!

5/10/71   Manolo said that Julie wanted to take Tim with her on a walk, but he told her that Tim wouldn't mind her. So Julie and the President took a walk around the Rose Garden outside his office, and then the Kennedy Garden—now called the First Lady's Garden, but always remaining the Jacqueline Kennedy Garden to me—and the South Grounds with the dogs running loose. I was tossing an orange-colored rubber ball for Timahoe and Pasha to retrieve. Mrs. Nixon and Mrs. Agnew came out to their limousine just as I tossed the ball and I almost hit Mrs. Agnew. She looked like she thought I did it on purpose.

5/12/71   The dogs were taking turns getting lost: a Secret Service man told me that two boys found Vicky four miles away.

5/17/71   President Nixon returned from Florida. Tim got lost and a Secret Service man called me and asked me about new tags for Tim, as he had lost his quite a while ago. I called Manolo Sanchez in Florida and I told him to go to a pet shop and get a nameplate and have it stamped: "I belong to Richard Nixon, 1600 Pennsylvania Avenue, N.W."

For some reason I could never refer to Richard Nixon as "the Prez," even in my diary. He was a cool, distant figure, even though he could heat up when angry. He just wasn't the "Prez" type.

5/18/71   I called Dr. Holland in Middleburg. He was in surgery, so I told his wife to please send me new rabies tags and certificates.

5/23/71   I almost sent out an alarm. Wanted to put a new rabies tag on Vicky's collar. I searched the grounds and couldn't find her. I asked Fina to check the second floor. Then we searched all over the South Grounds. Finally Fina called the Secret Service. They told her Tricia and Ed Cox had taken Vicky out for a ride. Only Fina had the nerve to scold Tricia and tell her she should let someone know when she takes a dog out of the White House grounds. Later Tricia said they stopped at Gino's and Vicky ate a hamburger and no one recognized them.

Fina said she was so tired she could die. She has been working on Tricia's winter clothes and trousseau. She was so busy Saturday that she missed her dinner; she just ate a few bites while sewing. I told her that after the wedding maybe her work load would be lighter. She said, "No, Mr. Bryant, it will be like it is with Julie. I will go to their place for a week or two and alter and repair her clothes." She said Manolo, her husband, tried to telephone her from Florida, but she was so busy, she couldn't even take any phone calls.

5/25/71 I saw Julie, David, and Tim's picture in today's papers. They were fishing at Key Biscayne. Pasha and Tim returned from Florida at 3:00 P.M. on a baggage plane as the President went to speak in Alabama. I had all the dogs out to greet the President, Julie, and David. They petted the dogs all at the same time. I told Julie that her picture with Tim in today's paper was good. She thanked me and said, "The one where Tim was barking?" The President scowled. His pet peeve is Timahoe's barking; he can't sleep if he hears a dog bark.

The President's irritation with dog barking eventually got so bad that to escape any sound of it, he tried sleeping in Julie's second-floor bedroom facing Pennsylvania Avenue, on the side opposite the doghouse.

5/26/71 I let a small group of children who were touring the West Rose Garden pet the three dogs, and they made pictures with their personal cameras.

Pat Nixon had a group of fifty-six children in the Kennedy Garden for cookies, punch, and music. She hugged as many as she could and loved every minute of it. As they left the garden and approached the South Portico, Mike Farrell, the aide who arranges White House special tours, told me to keep the dogs away from the children for a few minutes because Mrs. Nixon wanted the kids to come with her for a picture. But Pat called out, "Mr. Bryant, please bring the dogs to the West Steps and let the dogs be in the picture with the children." She directed, "Let this little girl hold Pasha's leash." I let two young boys hold Tim's and Vicky's leashes. The First Lady was also in the picture. I got out of the picture; then Vicky barked and wanted to come to me.

5/31/71 Tim returned from Camp David. Usher Stout called and told me Mrs. Nixon left the dogs out on the South Grounds. As I started out the west end on the ground floor I met Tricia and Ed Cox with Vicky and Pasha. They act very subdued, not like Luci Johnson and Pat, cutting up. They took the dogs. Later they had dinner on the Truman Balcony. The President ate his dinner in the Executive Office Building; he's too busy for family meals these days. He likes stag meals better, so he can talk politics full time.

6/2/71 Two thousand Explorer Scouts visited the White House lawn. The President gave a speech inspiring them to greatness. Then they toured the White House.

6/3/71 Tricia was in the ground-floor kitchen talking to the chefs about wedding preparations. Last night I looked like a clown. I had to wear Bill Cliber's coat and trousers for the lighting of the Grand Stairway picture. I had to roll up the cuffs of the pants and keep my arms raised or in the coat pockets so they wouldn't flop over my hands, as we got our dry cleaning mixed up. I felt like Charlie Chaplin.

My troubles were small compared to Fina's. She had the responsibility for the perfection of Tricia's appearance in her wedding dress, plus the whole trousseau. And she continued to wrestle with certain old problems, especially the pressure on her to go to Camp David. The trouble was Fina hated it. The President would go by helicopter and Manolo and Fina followed by car with the dogs. Fina was deathly afraid of all the wildlife there—plants as well as animals. She particularly feared that some hawk would swoop down from the sky and scoop up Vicky or Pasha, both small dogs. By 1971 she was ready to do almost anything to get out of going, though sometimes she had to give in.

6/5/71 Fina said, "Oh, Mr. Bryant, I have to go to Camp David and I don't like it there." Fina usually tells Mrs. Nixon that she has a sore throat so she won't have to go.

As Tricia's wedding day drew near, the White House released the recipe for the wedding cake to reporters. When other cooks around the country attempted to follow it, they came up with custard, and the matter became a cause célèbre. The pastrymen in the kitchen sweated out the bad publicity as they worked through the nights getting every phase of the cake program ready for the big day.

6/6/71 Heinz Bender has been working nights making Tricia's wedding cake. He told me today that he has to make enough for 1,000 small samples. He showed me the small cardboard boxes that he will put them in. He said, "These people are nuts."

315

The small cake box measures three inches by two inches by one inch deep.

6/9/71   Fina said that she didn't want any more trips to Camp David. She said that she saw a large black snake at Camp David, and that it's a jungle and she's afraid.

A Secret Service man told Usher Hare that he had x-rayed the package containing Tricia's wedding dress, but they didn't want him to open it. Mr. Hare said it's a big secret, but now it's on Tricia's bed. I checked the second-floor lights. I'm glad I didn't check her room. Any leaks to the press will not be mine.

6/11/71   Chef Haller gave me the first sample of the wedding cake. He was busy using a pipe-shaped tool to make a hole through each layer of the cake. It tasted good, but it wasn't worth the publicity. I gave the chief electrician a piece of the cake, as his wife wanted to test it. She was going to make it from the recipe in the newspapers. The Nixons have been active checking the wedding arrangements. The President checked the CBS studio house on the South Grounds. He also turned the dogs loose—LBJ style—and the Secret Service called me to round them up. Heinz Bender licks the cake topping off his fingers as he puts the finishing touches on the wedding cake.

(This explains why I ate the cake but not the frosting the day of the wedding.)

Lynda Bird Robb tried to call me, but I was out of the office watching the chefs put the cake together. The first center hole made in one single layer of cake was too small to go over the next layer, so they had to get a larger pipe-cutter so it would make all the layers go on more smoothly.

6/12/71   Tricia's wedding day. A day fit for a princess, or a duck. We weren't sure which till two minutes beforehand. Today I dressed up at 12:30. Earlier I had gone out and brushed the dogs. I washed their faces and mouths after they ate, just as George Washington used to have his horses groomed. Then I went to the White House Bouquet Room to get the dogs' floral collars. They were put together yesterday. I asked Rusty Young if he had someone who could make them up. He said that William Kistler, who has the American Floral Art School in Chicago, would make them for me. He did a beautiful job.

I took the three dogs to the South Grounds and several women reporters interviewed me and some photographers took pictures. One lady reporter asked me to go to the press tent for an interview. The dogs and I had several interviews outside the tent.

I saw Fran Leighton; she has been busy on another book, on White House cooking through history. One woman reporter annoyed me as she kept pestering Tim, trying to get him to raise his head. He had seen a squirrel at the base of a tree. Even I couldn't have made him raise his head. I finally told the reporter to leave him alone as she was messing up his floral collar. Fran and I acted like she was interviewing me. But we were talking about my diary.

Fina told me that she wanted to show the dogs to the family, so we went to the second floor. I stayed in the kitchen.

She came back ten minutes later and said the family liked the floral collars. But she had an order from the First Lady. She said Mrs. Nixon "doesn't want the dogs to get too much publicity as there are so many poor people in the nation." Does Mrs. Nixon think for a minute the poor people of the nation aren't going to know a lot of money is being spent on this wedding?

I took the dogs to the east end to see the wedding guests. We saw Billy Graham, Red Skelton, Martha Mitchell, Alice Longworth. Luci and Pat Nugent yelled, "How are you, Mr. Bryant?" It was sprinkling and it looked like the wedding would be held inside. I guess each one of us backstairs workers said a silent prayer, asking that the rain would stop so the wedding could go on outside. Guests were standing or sitting outside behind ropes. Everyone felt nervous and was getting wet. The dogs and I went to the east side of the press stand facing the White House, and presidential aide Bruce Whelihan said, "One little whimper and you move the dogs out of here." Julie looked out of the Treaty Room window at the crowd. The rain sort of stopped. A few minutes later the President escorted Tricia down the steps of South Portico. The President saw the dogs and me as he walked by. He smiled and said something to Tricia that I couldn't catch.

During the ceremony I walked the dogs farther east and we sat under a tree. After the ceremony the guests walked by the Jacqueline Kennedy Garden. Luci, Pat, Lynda, and Chuck Robb stopped and Lynda asked me if I had a sister named Zelda. I said yes. She said she had a letter from her, but she didn't have time to explain it then. Baroness Geudo Zerillimarimo from Rome, Italy, stopped and asked if she could pet Tim. I told her it was all right. She said that she liked dogs. The guests went inside for the cake-cutting and dancing. I took the dogs back to their home and took off the floral collars. The wedding was over for dogs and dogkeeper.

About 7:30 P.M. as I was leaving the White House, I saw Fran Leighton coming from the North Portico in front of the White House where the press watched Mr. and Mrs. Cox leave for their honeymoon. She saw that I was carrying a little paper bag. She said, "Oh-oh, did you save me a piece of cake?" I said "Yes." I had been waiting a couple of minutes to see if she was returning. I walked down West Executive Avenue with her, borrowed a knife from a TV technician, walked inside the trailer, and cut off a piece of the cake that Heinz Bender had given me early this morning. Fran took a bite and said it was good. Fran was lucky, as it is almost impossible to get a piece of the wedding cake after the ceremony is over; in fact, they did run short. Many people were griping they didn't get to the cake in time.

Earlier, just before they cut the cake, I had to go to the East Room and fix some lights in a hurry. On my way I had to pass the line of people coming from the ground floor to the first floor. Clement Conger, the White House Curator, called out, "Mr. Bryant, it was a delight to see the dogs in their decorations on the grounds during the wedding ceremonies." But there was no reward. Backstairs we griped. When Lynda had her wedding in the White House, after the ceremony was over, the White House help was invited to the first floor, where we had champagne, shrimp, a piece of the wedding cake, and lots to eat—a nice gesture from LBJ. This time I was just lucky to grab a piece of cake and get started home.

I have put in over eighty-two hours overtime during the last two weeks, so at least I will have a heavy paycheck to soothe my hurt feelings.

6/15/71 Rose Mary Woods, the President's secretary, was looking at wedding pictures on the ground floor west end. She said, "Where are the wedding pictures with the dogs?" I told her the press made pictures, but I didn't think that the White House photographers made any wedding shots with the dogs. She looked disappointed. Now she knows how it feels.

26

After Tricia's wedding was over, I felt a great sense of relief, and so did the rest of the backstairs crowd, especially Fina, who put down her needle and thread and said she could go to sleep for a month. The lethargy of summer set in, broken only by a few small incidents. One event seemed big to me—my own sitdown strike. It was a warm-up for the day I would retire from dogkeeping chores forever.

6/27/71   The dogs returned from Camp David by *car.* The President and Mrs. Nixon returned by *helicopter* 7:30 P.M. Dogs and people don't mix—or mingle—in the Nixon administration.

7/1/71   Sammy Davis visited the President. A White House policeman asked one of the men with Sammy if he carried a gun. He said he had one. The White House policeman made him check it at the desk and told him he could recover it as he left the White House. I asked the policeman who spotted the gun whether Sammy had a bodyguard. He said that he wouldn't be surprised.

7/3/71   President and Mrs. Nixon and Mr. and Mrs. Cox were on the Truman Balcony. They called and called to the dogs and Tim and Vicky were going in circles. Pasha was the only dog smart enough to spot them. I put Pasha in the South Fountain and Tim jumped in. I picked up Pasha and was almost bitten by her. I discovered a tick under her right leg joint. I took Pasha to the third floor. Fina held Pasha while I took the bloated tick off. Pasha looked so contented after it was over. Ticks in the White House trees?

7/4/71   I received a package from my old favorite, Mrs. Pat Nugent of Austin, Texas. It was x-rayed by the Secret Service, just as if someone else had sent it. After all, anyone could have written her name. It was a wooden plaque painting of Yuki singing and dancing and a girl who looked like Luci, with the White House in the background. It said, "To Traphes Bryant, my guardian and friend, Yuki." I was very pleased.

7/5/71   The President and Mrs. Nixon returned from Camp David for the signing of the bill allowing eighteen-year-olds to vote. The President

319

unleashed Tim after they got off the helicopter. I had to ask the President for the leash as he had it balled up in his hand. He is very nervous. Historic bill-signing in East Room.

Tricia and Ed Cox went to New York. Fina is going for a week to help them.

My last Fourth of July celebration observed from the White House—I feel nostalgic. As usual I took the dogs among the White House spectators and let them pet the dogs. Parents made many pictures of the dogs posing with their children. I saw several old friends on the grounds who had gathered to watch the fireworks display at the monument grounds, which was held a day late because of the weather.

Every year White House staffers bring their families to watch the fireworks from the South Grounds. The dogs and I sat on the iron bench on C-11 Post at South Portico, and at every burst of noise Pasha hid behind me. I let Vicky hide her head under my coat. Tim was braver. I should have taken them to the basement electric shop, as the noise is too much for a dog's sensitive ears. But they didn't mind too much as they knew I was protecting them.

7/6/71 All the dogs went to California.

7/9/71 Tricia and Ed Cox returned to the White House. Fina also returned.

7/11/71 Ed Cox left at 8:20 P.M. The bride is still in residence.

7/14/71 The bride has taken to her room. Word is Tricia is a little ill. Someone said, "From the way she looks, I don't think marriage is agreeing with her." She did look a little peaked. The "Little Princess" is learning about life.

7/18/71 I went to the third floor to replace a light. Fina asked me to zip up the back of her dress. She was going to Andrews Field to meet Manolo and the dogs. The President, Mrs. Nixon, and Dr. Kissinger got off the chopper and waved to Julie, Tricia, and Ed on Truman Balcony. Mrs. Nixon came over and petted only the small dogs. The President petted only Tim. Just before the chopper arrived, Julie hollered at Pasha from the Truman Balcony. I held Pasha in my arms so Pasha could look at Julie, who was leaning on the iron railing. Julie would holler. Tricia never would do such a "lowbrow" thing.

7/19/71 President Nixon and Mrs. Nixon were dining on the Truman Balcony. I took the dogs to the south fence and let the tourists pet and take pictures of the dogs. Tim and Pasha took a swim. We walked to C-11 Post under the canopy at the South Portico.

The President whistled to Tim. Tim heard but he didn't care. He can be snobbish too. The President said something in Spanish to Tim. I finally made Tim sit and I tilted his head up so he could see the President who was now standing near the iron railing and really desperate to get Timahoe's attention. The smaller dogs ran up the stairway under the balcony, but of course they couldn't go beyond the first floor.

7/20/71   I had the three dogs out on the South Lawn. A policeman told me that Vicky had killed a squirrel on the east side. She knew she had done a bad thing. I was looking for her but she hid and stayed quiet. Yelling for the dogs, Mrs. Nixon and Julie came out on the grounds. I talked to them. Mrs. Nixon told me that a Spanish photographer had taken a picture of me and the dogs under a tree at the wedding and it was used in Spain. She said that she would see that I received a copy. I told her I would appreciate it. Pat is nice. I wish she could be happy!

Julie asked me if her dog minded me now. All three dogs were wet as I'd had them in the fountain. I said to Mrs. Nixon and Julie, "You all can take the dogs for a walk if you want to." They did. A few minutes later the President came out and played with the dogs. He picked up Tricia's dog, Pasha, held it close to his chest, and got his suit coat wet. Mrs. Nixon informed him and he said, "It's all right." I told the President that Tim was a wonderful dog. He told me that Tim ran so gracefully, that he enjoyed the dog's company, just watching him. I told him to use Tim's name first, then give the command: "Tim, come!" "Tim, sit!" "Tim, stay!" Then I showed him how to rub Tim's tail underneath to make Tim point with his tail straight. President Nixon said to Julie, "See, Tim points beautifully, with his tail straight out." The President told Mrs. Nixon and Julie, "We will have a nice time." Then they left by car for the baseball game at the stadium. Anyway, *he* will have a nice time. He loves baseball.

7/23/71   Julie went to Florida. Tricia went to New York.

7/24/71   President and Mrs. Nixon and the dogs went to Camp David.

7/26/71   The Nixons returned after wishing a new group of astronauts Godspeed.

7/28/71   The President and Mrs. Nixon had about twenty guests; Mr. Scouten and Dr. Tkach were among the dinner guests. Later they went out on the Truman Balcony. I got a call that the President wanted the dogs to run the grounds. The dogs and I got wet playing around the South Fountain, but the President likes to see the dogs romp and I aim to please. Damn the flowers, full speed ahead.

321

8/8/71 President and Mrs. Nixon returned from Maine at 7:45 P.M. The President took the leash off Tim as he got off the helicopter. Tim ran to me to lick my face. Mrs. Nixon had stopped walking as she watched Tim.

On August 9, some cross-country cyclists arrived at the White House and were received by the President. As usual, I had the dogs in the background, but the photographers for some reason were turning their cameras on me and the dogs and away from the President and the cyclists. A presidential aide, Dwight Chapin, told me quickly to move on, and I did. I saw him huddling with other aides about it. Two days later, a phone call came from the Usher's Office that so upset me that right or wrong, I went on a sit-down strike, abandoning all dogkeeping duties and confining myself to my electrical work. My diary tells the story.

8/11/71 Now I'm really disgusted! Usher Scouten wanted to see me in his office. He said that the Nixon people think that I am overexposing the dogs to the cameras and reporters. He said, "You know how it was in the last administration. They want to cool it now and later on they will call on you again." I told him that I would be careful and wouldn't get the dogs any more recognition.

Later I thought it over and got good and sore. I called Usher Pierce. I told him to go back to the "Nixon people" and tell them that I preferred to stop caring for the dogs. I said they can let someone else take care of the dogs as I was too close to retirement to have any trouble with some kookie advisor. I also said that Nixon will need lots of publicity between now and November 1972. Scouten said to hold on, he would see if he could make some kind of an arrangement. I doubt it though. I am through. I will stick to my electricity and let someone else chase dogs and take stool samples. I'll just enjoy the dogs now and then, like the rest of the people around here.

Mayor John Lindsay of New York switched to the Democratic party. The President's expensive sauna bath made the newspapers. Bank rates are up. There must be some connection.

The news said that the sauna in the Executive Office Building was a Roman-style romper room—cost, $100,000. Nixon has a low popularity rating in the polls.

My little feud with the Nixon staffers began on August 11, 1971. I didn't know it at the time, but these men were uptight with problems of their own, mainly the undercover investigation into the leaking of the Pentagon Papers. John Ehrlichman later said in court that on August 11 he initialed a memo approving "covert action"—which turned out to be the break-in of the office of Daniel Ellsberg's psychiatrist, Dr. Lewis Fielding.

I suppose I might have been more tolerant about the way I was being treated if I'd understood the tensions behind the scenes. On the other hand, if the Nixon staffers had been the sort of people to discuss their affairs with a dogkeeper, Watergate never would have happened in the first place.

A few days later I recorded an incident in my diary that says a lot about presidential children.

8/15/71   Usher Ray Hare got an order for pillows and cushions for the East Garden chairs from Tricia Cox. He told me that he carried the cushions to the garden. Mr. Cox didn't offer to help him. Mr. Hare told me that he lifted up Ed Cox's feet as he put a cushion under them for a hassock. I told him I would be damned before I did that.

As I said, the White House had become a castle.

8/20/71   The doctor's office is being remodeled. The South Grounds are torn up for the new manholes for power and communications. The last two weeks I've worked ninety-six hours overtime.

8/29/71   Julie and Mrs. Nixon returned to the White House. Julie has a damaged toe. The South Grounds are torn up, so they came in the North Grounds. Pasha and Vicky also came back. I fed them.

Later Julie used her toe as a reason for not continuing her job as a teacher. She taught only one day, as I recall.

9/1/71   Fina told me that the reason her hair is cut short is that she got oil in her hair on the California beach from a Navy ship.

She said that Tim got so much oil on his hair that they had to cut some of it off. She says she warned everyone that Mr. Bryant wouldn't like it. I said the dogs are not my responsibility any more.

9/3/71   Tim has returned from California.

This was the night Ellsberg's psychiatrist's office was broken into, yet all my diary has is that simple statement—"Tim has returned from California."

9/6/71   Usher Stout asked me to call Fina about the dogs' fleas. I told her to tell Sam to spray the doghouses and the dogs.

Last night Usher Stout called me and informed me that Manolo was coming in the South Gate with the dogs. I told Mr. Stout that Manolo knew where the dog pen was.

9/8/71 Irvin Williams called and told me that Fina slept with Pasha, and the dogs have fleas. I told him that I had already heard. I asked Mr. Batey, the storeroom supplier, to buy four cans of spray for fleas.

I felt the most I could do was give a little advice. After all, this was a complete sit-down strike. There could be no more brushing of the dogs' coats. No more running with them for exercise. No more doggie treats on the lawn. No more spraying for fleas. No more dogs standing by to greet the President and his family as they climbed into or descended from the helicopter. No more walks to the gates with the dogs to thrill the tourists waiting in line, often with cameras, to tour the White House. No more delivery of dogs on demand and responding to calls to pick them up.

I guess I was a little haughty, maybe even childish at times, in the way I turned down requests for help. For example, when Fina notified me that the dogs had arrived back at the White House and were ready to be put away, I replied, "Yes, well, I'm sure you'll have no trouble finding the doghouse."

But while I stood my ground and secretly felt sorry for myself, I also felt sorry for the dogs, who were not getting their exercise. And I honestly missed them so much, I sometimes sneaked into their pens at night for a short visit. They were really happy to see me.

Meanwhile, my one-man sit-down strike was causing a bit of consternation. The President had liked to see the dogs when he came off the helicopter, and now he missed them. He also liked to watch the dogs running about when he dined at 8:00 P.M. on the Truman Balcony, and sometimes called to them in Spanish, which he was learning from Manolo and Fina. Now he didn't see them.

By the middle of September, when my strike had gone on for about a month, several people were trying to get me to show an interest in the dogs again. Dwight Chapin's secretary, for example, called me at home, of all places, to come get Tim out of the President's office. It was a Saturday, however, and my day off, as I explained to her, and I was miles from the White House. But I was touched. I was also starting to miss the dogs very much.

9/13/71 I went out to the dogs' pen after dark and played with them. They were glad to see me. The dogs miss their evening runs in the South Grounds chasing the squirrels and birds.

The next day Colonel Coffey, the President's military aide, called me while I was on duty in my shop. "The President is a little concerned about Tim having a skin infection," he told me. So I said, "I have been told the Nixon people said I was overexposing the dogs, and I haven't been fooling with them these days. If I had been taking care of them, I would have been able to spot the infection."

Colonel Coffey ended the conversation in a way that meant things were happening. "Well, the President is concerned," Colonel Coffey said. "I think you can expect a call from his personal physician, Dr. Tkach."

A few minutes later, the telephone rang, and Dr. Walter Tkach asked me to come to his office. He gave me a nice welcome and he told me about the President being really worried about the dogs and the fungus infection.

I repeated to Dr. Tkach what I had said to Colonel Coffey—that I had been told the President didn't want me to overexpose the dogs, and that I was just staying away from the dogs. I knew he'd have to report to "the Boss," and I wanted the President finally to hear *my* side of it. So I explained again that I knew only one way to handle *dogs* and *people*, and that was just to be friendly with everyone. I could not change at this stage of life, and so it was just better for me to stay away from the dogs altogether.

But I added that since the President himself was concerned about Tim's health I would be happy to take the dogs to the vet's the next day.

Suddenly, I also got a concerned and friendly call from Fina, who told me that the poor dogs all had fleas, and that Vicky especially was suffering extreme discomfort because of them.

I told Fina not to worry, I would take care of it. I said, "You know, they told me the President felt I was overexposing the dogs. So I haven't been taking care of them for fleas."

She said, "Oh, the President is not the one. I will have Manolo ask the President."

Complete vindication came later when I took the dogs to Fina's room. Manolo told me the President said he had never issued an order for me to stop overexposing the dogs, and had never said that I was overexposing them. "You go ahead and take care of the dogs as you always did and don't pay attention to anybody," Manolo said. Later, I found out H. R. Haldeman had issued the order.

325

9/15/71   I got a station wagon with two chauffeurs and I took the dogs in style to Dr. Holland's emporium in Middleburg. He gave the dogs the works—distemper shots, blood samples for heartworms, their ears cleaned. He treated Tim for the skin ailment. I brought Dr. Tkach a statement of the work Dr. Holland and his wife had completed.

But I did not bring the dogs home. Dr. Holland found the skin of all the dogs in such bad shape he had to keep them overnight for treatment. And poor Tim was under medication for his fungus for some time after that. I had to treat him twice a day until it cleared up.

But the happiest moment came when President Nixon called for me to bring the dogs to the South Lawn. He was having dinner on the Truman Balcony and wanted to watch them romp and play as he ate. He gave me a nice grin and wave. Everything was back to normal.

So the big feud was over. But meanwhile life hadn't been standing still at the White House, and I summarized it in one day's entry:

9/10/71   This week AP man Frank Cormier broke a chair as he sat in it at a news conference. So there was a ceremony and the White House presented Frank with the remains. I received a card from Fran Leighton, who is on assignment-vacation in India, doing a story on Indira Gandhi, who is coming on a state visit.

A White House electrician showed porno stag movies three days this week. The film belongs to another White House employee, who bought the film from a White House policeman. No names, please.

9/20/71   The President has a new tradition—he eats dinner on the balcony regularly. And I have to turn the dogs loose so he can see them. His private floor show at dinner is a dog act. The poor President is a lonely man. Now even his daughters are both married and gone on their own.

9/21/71   New trouble. Mr. Pierce called and said that Manolo said that the two small dogs bark at night and keep the President awake, so I put Vicky and Pasha in their winter quarters. Five more months and I will have my thirty years of service. Then any President's dog can howl all night.

9/24/71   Manolo told me that the President wants Tim to be turned loose in the South Grounds every night. Manolo said that Tim barked while he was in his pen, which kept the President awake at night. He said that the President tried to sleep on the third floor one night. Manolo said that the President felt like killing Pasha and Vicky as they barked so much.

Now we had a new problem. In keeping Timahoe quiet, we had the Secret Service and police in an uproar.

9/27/71 Rex Scouten told Mr. Williams to tell me to keep Tim in his pen, as Tim was setting off the White House night alarms and was driving the police nuts. Mr. Scouten said that he would take full responsibility for the order. I told him that the President said to let Tim roam. Later Mr. Scouten called and said that he had talked to Manolo and for me to let Tim roam in the South Grounds. The President and Mrs. Nixon returned about 9:00 P.M. from Alaska. After they got off the helicopter, Mrs. Nixon petted Pasha and Vicky while the President petted Tim. The President and Mrs. Nixon again petted the dogs about 12:00 P.M. after they returned from Mamie Eisenhower's seventy-fifth birthday. The President was talking about how he played the piano at the party.

9/28/71 The President spoke before the National League of Families of American Prisoners. He petted Tim at C-11 on his return. I told the President to beware, as Tim was wet because he had been in the pool.

Three White House policemen and a girl were bitten yesterday by a stray dog loose in the North Grounds of the White House. Who can they sue?

9/29/71 All the dogs have gone to Florida.

10/10/71 I returned from a week's leave moving furniture to my farm at Appomattox. Electrician Bill Cliber tried to get out of taking care of the dogs, but Ray Hare and Chief Electrician Martin said the electricians were going to be stuck with taking care of the dogs.

10/18/71 John Eisenhower and his wife are houseguests of President and Mrs. Nixon during the dedication of the Eisenhower Theater of the Kennedy Center. When they were going to the dedication, John's wife petted the dogs and said she knew Pasha, but Pasha probably didn't remember her. President Nixon also petted the dogs as they entered their limousine. I told President Nixon's chauffeur, a Secret Service man, to be careful because Tim would be running in the grounds when they returned. He said, "I hope he doesn't get in my way." Another Secret Service man told the chauffeur sharply that President Nixon wouldn't appreciate it if Tim was hit by his car.

11/10/71 I sent the dogs to Dr. Holland for an overnight checkup. The small dogs get their teeth cleaned. I am breaking in a new electrician, Arthur Baum, to replace me while I am on a three-week visit to my farm in Appomattox.

12/5/71 Trouble as soon as I returned from Appomattox. I checked the small dogs' room. It was 110 degrees. A steam or hot-water heater had been defective for days. I told Arthur Baum that he wouldn't last here very long if the dogs suffocated from the hot room.

I had an interview Friday at 3:00 with Nancy Ball from the *Newsweek* magazine. Cute girl.

I worked sixteen hours a day from Monday through Friday, twelve on Saturday and sixteen on Sunday decorating the house for Christmas. We were decorating the Green Room chandelier. Mr. Scouten told me to have the dogs on the second floor at 10:30 A.M. for a picture of the family at their tree with the dogs.

Julie asked me to let the dogs be in the tree scene with Tricia and herself and their husbands. I posed the dogs. One of Nixon's press nuts came up and said the dog scene was only for the President. Julie told him that she asked me to have the dogs in the picture. He told me to get the dogs out of the room. I said I will after I get them leashed. After working such long hours I wasn't in any mood for a fight. Everyone here is getting a little nuts—nuts and mean. I had already posed the dogs at the tree for a press picture by the White House photographers to be released to the press later on.

During the morning Mrs. Nixon, Julie, and Tricia helped John Muffler and Mr. Fischer, the movie projector operator, hang some old Christmas balls on the tree. Mrs. Nixon and the girls had me put wire hooks on the balls and let them hang some of the balls. I asked if the balls were very old. Mrs. Nixon said yes, the girls had them years ago as babies. She'd saved them. Fischer found a bird's nest in the top rear of the tree. There was a little excitement over that. Mrs. Nixon and Julie climbed our ladder to peek in.

Just before the President came on the scene preparing for his appearance on TV, Tim jumped up and almost knocked Mrs. Nixon down as she reached for his leash. I told her to take the two small dogs' leashes, and as I gave the President Tim's leash, Tim jumped up on the President. I scolded Tim and pulled him back. The President said, "No, let him jump. That's what I want." They walked into the TV set up. Tim didn't behave too well with all the lights and people.

Pasha saw me in the kitchen doorway of the second floor and barked, trying to run to me. Mrs. Nixon motioned for me to get out of the doorway so Pasha couldn't see me. The President tried to get Tim to sit on a two-person seat. The President said, "No, Mr. Bryant, don't push him." He said, "If Manolo were here, he would talk Spanish to them and they would mind." Manolo stepped into the picture and with all his Spanish lingo, Tim still didn't listen. The President apologized to the camera people and said if there weren't any extra people in here the dogs would be perfect and not all over the tree.

Tricia's husband told me later that the President was not pleased, there were too many people and it distracted the dogs. I tuned him out.

I told Julie that I had one of President Eisenhower's old golf balls. David said it was a collector's item. David was reading a newspaper while we were in the hall next to the President's bedroom. Julie asked him if he was reading the sports page. He was, and he kidded her, saying, "That's where the important news is." Later Mrs. Nixon went to the first floor and inspected the Christmas decorations.

The President left for the Azores. Manolo told me he and Fina were going for a drive. He said, "This is my third day off in one year." I laughed—the day was already half gone.

The dogs are in Florida.

12/11/71 Mrs. Bender, the White House housekeeper, was sipping eggnog. She said, "I have seen more urinals than any woman in the nation." She checks to see that everything is clean. She said, "I just barge in the men's rooms, shouting, 'Housekeeper!' "

Her assistant, Mrs. Bowen, who was also sipping eggnog, was playing the piano, which is temporarily in the small private dining room on the first floor. She played so loudly that I didn't dare open the door, as it might disturb the First Lady on the second floor. Mrs. Nixon earlier had the ushers and the two housekeepers on the second floor for a Merry Christmas thank-you and some drinks. Usher Hare said, "Now they appreciate us."

1/9/72 The dogs returned from California.

We had small write-ups in *Newsweek,* the *Evening Star* and the *Post.*

1/28/72 Usher Hare called and said that a table lamp was out in the Green Room. I went to the Green Room and Mrs. Bender, the housekeeper, was there. Mr. Phillips had disconnected the lamp plug from the wall so he could plug in his floor waxer. I told Mrs. Bender that she should look before calling an electrician. She got all upset. I told her, "I will see Mr. Bender and see if he can straighten you out." She blew her top and said, "I will get someone to straighten *you* out." I finally told her I was only kidding.

Looking back, it seems ironic that while the Nixon administration was getting ready to collapse, I was recording such things as:

1/29/72 The dogs went to Camp David.

1/30/72 The dogs came back from Camp David.

But I had no premonition of the Watergate dramatics to come when I prepared to leave government service early in 1972. All I knew was that I couldn't take it any longer. The atmosphere at the White House had lost its friendliness. I felt a stranger at the place that had been my home for twenty years.

The cast of characters was certainly changing. And there was a scary note injected. G. Gordon Liddy had come on the scene as some kind of legal counsel, and I heard he had been showing some people how you could kill a man with a sharp pencil jammed into the neck —an eerie kind of thing for a legal advisor to be talking about.

I had gotten out just in time to avoid having to witness the words of the Bible, "How are the mighty fallen," and I'm grateful for that. But I had stayed long enough to know the truth of the joke we started with—"The dogs will enjoy the White House more than you."

2/6/72 The dogs returned from Florida.

Mr. Haldeman's speech on President Nixon's policy made him very much talked about on TV. They're saying he's "overexposed" as he once said about me and the dogs.

I had a little fun with the kitchen crowd last week. I told Carl Beam, the florist, to ask Frank Blair, the kitchen clean-up man, in front of Chef Haller, if it was true what he had read in the newspapers, that President Nixon was taking Frank to China to serve his food. Chef Haller jumped up and immediately went upstairs to check the newspapers.

A little later I walked through the kitchen and said, "Hello, Chef Blair." Haller gave me a dirty look.

2/17/72 President and Mrs. Nixon were leaving for China. I asked Stephen Bull if I could have the dogs out to see the President off. He said no. I guess he didn't want the dogs and me to overexpose the President. Ha, ha.

3/13/72 Fina gave me a flower ornament for my wife. She said she wished I would not retire from my job. I told her that she would be in the White House for four more years. The Florida primary is tomorrow.

3/14/72 I met Tricia, Luci Nugent, and Lyn, her son, in the theater hallway. Luci told Lyn to shake hands with me, then for Lyn to give me a hug. I told Luci to tell her father and mother hello for me. She said she would and she gave me a hug and a kiss. Luci looks even prettier. Motherhood agrees with her.

Later tonight the President took the dogs and drove up to Camp David at about 9:30 P.M.

3/15/72   I signed for my retirement today at 11:00 A.M.

3/16/72   It was pouring rain when the President and Tim came off the chopper; Mayfield the doorman held an umbrella over the President. I stayed under the canopy with my raincoat on at the door to the Diplomatic Room. The President grinned as he walked up and gave me Tim's leash. I later told the engineers that if they ever do that—staying under a canopy around here—they damn well better have their thirty years in and the papers signed.

Epilogue

The story goes that God spoke to President Nixon as he was packing to leave the White House. And the Lord said, "You see, Richard, my son, I was right. The dogs did have more fun than you."

Index

Abell, Bess, 106, 109, 169, 227, 289
Adams (engineer), 28
Adams, Abigail, 74
Adams, John Quincy, 74
Adams, Sherman, 21
Agnew, Judy, 293, 313
Agnew, Spiro, 280, 292–293
Air Force I, 229, 256
Albert, Carl, 292
Alexandra, Princess, 198
Algonquin (pony), 29
Alsop brothers (columnists), 285
American Kennel Club, 97
American Society for the Prevention
  of Cruelty to Animals, 97
Americans for Democratic Action, 103
Amy (dog), 278
Anders, William, 226
Anderson, Christine, 177
Anderson, Jack, 306
Angelo, Bonnie, 272
Animal Lovers' Magazine, 302
Anne, Princess, 291–293
Anne Marie, Princess, 114
Apollo 8, 226
Apollo 13, 285, 289
Apollo 14, 306
Armstrong, Neil, 292
Army Signal Corps, 40, 148, 192
Arrington, Red, 297
Asbill, Colonel (Walter Reed), 221,
  230, 264, 295, 297
Astro (dog), 180, 212
Atkins, Ollie, 69, 253
Atoka, Va., 23
Atticus (dog), 55
Ayub Khan, Mohammed, 57

Baker, Bobby, 99
Bailey, House, 300
Ball, Nancy, 328
Batey (storeroom keeper), 297, 324
Baum, Arthur, 327, 328
Beagle (dog), 137, 158, 165, 170,
  180
Beagle Breeders' Association, 122
Beam, Carl, 166, 176, 330
Bean, Orson, 165
Beauregard, "Bo" (dog), 172, 178
Bender, Heinz, 315–316, 318, 329
Bender, Mrs. Heinz (housekeeper),
  329
Benedikte, Princess, 121
Benson Animal Hospital, 194
Bernstein, Aruthur M., 31
Bernstein, Leonard, 249
Bersbach, F. John, 108
Bethesda Naval Hospital, 227
Betz, Paul, 113, 115, 122
Blackie (dog), 30, 44
Blair, Frank, 91, 271, 330
Blair House, 9, 13, 79, 249
Blanco (dog), 86–87, 89–92, 98, 101,
  104, 117–130, 135–159, 161–163,
  165, 167, 170–172, 176, 179,
  184, 187–188, 195, 198–199, 201–
  202, 208, 211–213, 216, 223–
  230, 280, 289
Blauvelt Family Genealogy, The,
  108
Blauvelt, Louis, 108
Blumenthal, Fred, 275, 280
Boozer, Yolanda, 147
Boris, Jr. (hamster), 145
Borman, Frank, 226

Bowen, Mrs. (assistant housekeeper), 329
Bradley, Omar, 162
Brambletide (Cape Cod), 32
Brandt, Willy, 119
Bremer, Arthur, 78
Bricker, Zelda, 317
Bridget (dog), 144, 147, 153
Brooks, Jack, 132
Brooks, Dame Mabel, 139
Brooks, R. Max, 94, 103
Bruce (doorman), 200
Bryant, Bill, 55, 56
Bryant, Doris ("Dot"), 3, 24, 39, 54, 61, 73–74, 128, 145, 156, 171, 186, 202, 206, 222, 279, 281, 291, 297
Bryant, Douglas, 55
Buchanan, Pat, 250
Buell, Bradford E., 188, 193, 201
Bull, Stephen, 254, 330
Bundy, McGeorge, 152
Bunshaft, Gordon, 94
Burger, Warren E., 273
Burkette, Chester, 180
Butterfield, Alexander, 294–295, 298, 300, 302
Butterfly (dog), 30, 44
Byrd, Harry F., 122, 125
Byrd, Harry F., Jr., 270

Calder, Alexander, 130
Caldwell (Secret Service agent), 128
Califano, Joseph, 71, 173, 179, 180–182, 184, 187, 193, 195–198, 208, 214, 217, 219–220, 222
Camp David, 118, 120–122, 124, 130, 138, 159, 164, 167, 222, 224–225, 260, 267, 270–274, 276–281, 289, 292, 304–305, 307, 311, 314–316, 319, 321, 329, 330
Canine Defense League, 97
Capital Parks Service, 11, 158, 177, 179, 199, 218, 226, 229, 301, 303
Capitol Hill, see Congress

Carlisle, Kitty, 165
Carpenter, Elizabeth ("Liz"), 73, 80, 88, 106, 109, 136, 144, 153, 162–164, 169, 172, 177–179, 192, 202, 210, 222, 229–230, 279–280, 289
Carson, Johnny, 157
Carswell, G. Harrold, 285
Carter (usher), 117–118, 138, 145, 193, 197, 203, 205–206
Caruso, Enrico, 131
Cash, Johnny, 243
Cass, Peggy, 165
Castro, Nash, 177, 179
Catella, Tony, 122
Ceausescu, Nicolae, 301
"Cell 326," 133
Centaur, The, 128
Chadwick, Ralph, 88, 92, 118–119, 121, 123, 125, 128, 136
Channing, Carol, 86
Chapin, Dwight, 254, 261, 262, 296, 298, 300, 322, 324
Charles, Prince, 51, 240, 283, 290–293, 310
Charlie (dog), 15, 19, 26–31, 40–41, 44, 55, 58, 61–63, 85, 91
Checkers (dog), 55, 228
Chicago Tribune, 163
Child Development and Diagnostic Center of Georgetown, 244
Chinkapen (dog), 172
Christian, George, 96, 198, 217, 226, 228
Cindy (dog), 162
Cleveland, Grover, 35, 36
Cliber, Bill, 257, 279–280, 287, 311, 315, 327
Clipper (dog), 26, 28–29, 31–33, 40–41, 44, 79, 91
Coffelt, Anita, 302
Coffey, Lieutenant Colonel (Military aide), 229–230, 261, 273–274, 296–297, 325
Collins, Bud, 165
Colson, Chuck, 244
Conger, Clement ("Clem"), 268, 318

Congress, 65, 99, 103, 107–108, 124,
142, 153, 176–177, 185, 229–231
Conniff, Ray, 257
Connally, John, 77, 298
Cook, Mrs. (secretary), 146
Cooke, Terence Cardinal, 252
Coolidge, Calvin, 75
Cormier, Frank, 304, 326
Cornell University, 189
Cox, Mrs. Anne, 310
Cox, Edward ("Ed") Finch, 51, 277,
290, 304, 310, 313–314, 317,
319–320, 323, 328
Cox, Tricia, see Nixon, Tricia
Crim, Howell G., 9, 10
Cronkite, Walter, 308
Cub scouts, 306

Daniel, Clifton, 214
Daniel, Mrs. Clifton, see Truman,
Margaret
Daniel, W. T., 229
Davies, John, 301
Davis, Sammy, Jr., 319
Dean, John, 254
Deason, Willard, 71, 144, 155–156
170–171, 175, 177, 179, 187, 197–
198, 207, 210, 212, 214, 217, 228
DeGaulle, General Charles, 303
de Valera, Eamon, 28
Dickerson, Nancy, 143
Disneyland, 254
Dog World, 303
Dottie (dog), 278
Doud, Mrs. (Mamie Eisenhower's
mother), 17
Douglas, Cathy, 169
Douglas, Justice William O., 169
Doyle, Sarah, 269
Dumpling (dog), 179, 185, 191, 195,
199, 211–212, 217
Dunn (chauffeur), 166
Dunn, Commander (Camp David),
274
Dupont family, 172, 175–176

Duprey, Marty, 192

Eagleton, Tom, 55
Edgar (dog), 170–171, 176 177,
179–180, 197–199, 201, 211, 226,
228–230, 262
Ehrlichman, John, 246, 266, 273, 298,
300, 322
Eisenhower, David, 20, 44, 240, 265–
266, 270, 275–276, 278–279, 286,
288, 296, 301, 309, 314, 328–329
Eisenhower, Dwight D. ("Ike"), 9–
11, 14–15, 17–18, 20, 33, 36, 44–
45, 53–54, 64, 67, 72, 78, 125,
137, 145, 163, 187, 266, 304, 329
Eisenhower, John, 36, 327
Eisenhower, Mrs. John, 327
Eisenhower, Julie, see Nixon, Julie
Eisenhower, Mamie, 9, 17, 36, 44–
45, 52–53, 56, 185, 240, 266, 282,
304, 307, 327
Eldredge, E. Irving, 238, 295–297
Eldorado, 185
Ellsberg, Daniel, 323
Elms, The, 90, 94
Enterprise, The (aircraft carrier),
200
Erhard, Chancellor Ludwig, 152
Explorer Scouts, 315

Fala (dog), 143
Fanfani, Amintore, 124
Farrell, Mike, 314
Farrow, Julia, 271
Fehmer, Marie, 130, 142–143, 183,
195, 197, 199, 207, 212, 228
Ferdinand (pastry chef), 186
Feraci, Carole, 257
Few, Robert, 109
Fielding, Lewis, 323
Fighting Catbird, The, 175, 188
Fischer, Paul, 18, 137, 185, 276, 328
Flanigan, Peter, 254
Fleming, Robert, 173, 216
Folsom, Frances, 35–36
Ford, Betty, 241, 255

Ford, Cristina, 255
Ford, Gerald, 15–16, 37, 64–65, 75, 164, 292
Ford, Susan, 16
Fort Myer, 88, 92, 119–121, 125–126, 128, 145, 159, 171–172, 176, 180, 186, 188, 193–195, 202–204, 206
Foster, Robert, 278
4-H Club, 310
Fox, Dr. (physician, White House Medical Unit), 157
Fox, Sandy, 202
Franklin, Jesse, 281
Freckles (dog), 153–155, 157, 159–160, 162, 167, 171–172, 175, 177–179, 185, 191, 195–201, 203, 205, 207, 212, 217, 220, 259
Freeman, Lieutenant (White House policeman), 216
Friends of Japan, 167–168
Friendship Animal Hospital, 92, 188, 194
Frost, David, 292
Fsurdies Clementine (dog), 91

G-Boy (dog), 162
Gabor, Zsa Zsa, 157
Gaddis (valet), 202
Galbraith, John Kenneth, 39, 71
Gallagher, Mary Barelli, 5, 29
Galt, Edith Bolling, 35
Gandhi, Indira, 159, 326
Ganns, Helen, 142
Gardosik, John, 312
General (doorman), 191
George (deer), 87
George (dog), 179–180, 194–195, 197, 214, 219–220, 222
Gettysburg Farm, 45, 53, 222
Gibson, Officer (White House policeman), 191
Ginger Boy (dog), 162
Glenn, John, 129
Glynn, Paul, 152, 206, 210, 214
Gold Bug, The, 128–130

Goldwater, Barry, 101
Goldwater, Barry, Jr., 270, 277
Gonella, Ashton, 180–184, 186, 195–196, 198–199, 201, 211–215, 217, 219–221, 229, 265
Good Housekeeping, 129
Goodwin, Captain (veterinarian), 213, 295, 297
Gorton, Prime Minister, 270
Graham, Billy, 252, 283, 290, 317
Grayson, Cary, 35
Grey, Zane, 18
Griffin, Merv, 285
Grimes (engineer), 307
Gross, H. R., 284
GSA (General Services Administration), 5, 278
Gulley, Bill, 294–295, 297, 305
Guys, Morgan, 136

Hagerty, James, see photo insert
Haldeman, H. R., 239, 245, 250–251, 253, 261, 266, 273, 278, 284, 298, 300, 325, 330
Haldeman, Mrs. H. R., 278
Haller, Chef, 50–51, 218–219, 224, 264, 271, 300, 316, 330
Hamilton, Alexander, 95
Hamilton, George, 51, 86, 111–113, 115, 153, 170, 173–174, 185, 189, 190, 203
Hanson, Officer (White House policeman), 77
Harder, Howard, see photo insert
Harding, Warren G., 26–27, 87
Hare (usher), 129, 170, 177, 192–193, 196–197, 200, 207–208, 210, 265, 276, 278, 302, 307, 316, 323, 327, 329
Harkness, Rebekah, 200
Harriman, Averell, 165
Harriman, Mrs. Averell, 165
Harrison (doorman), 93
Harwell, Ray, 165
Heidi (dog), 10, 44–45, 52, 187

Her (dog), 88, 91–92, 156
Herblock (cartoonist), 103
Hill, Lieutenant (White House
    policeman), 61, 165–166
Hill, Clint, 46, 215
Him (dog), 86, 88–92, 96–98, 100–
    101, 118–130, 134–135, 137, 139–
    147, 149–159, 161–163, 166–167,
    170, 173, 176, 313
Holland, Dr. (veterinarian), 295,
    297–298, 313, 326–327
Hollstein, E. D., 88
Holt, Prime Minister, 184
Honey (dog), 180–181, 183–184,
    186, 195–196, 199, 211, 213, 215,
    220, 229–230
Honey Fitz (yacht), 42
Hoover, J. Edgar, 162, 170
Hope, Bob, 70, 307
Hope, Mrs. Bob, 307
Hornet (aircraft carrier), 277
Hough, Nancy, 72–73
Howar, Barbara, 109, 117, 169, 221,
    255, 291
Howard University, 108, 127
Hoxie, Peggy, 179, 195
Hughes, General (military aide),
    294–295
Hughes, Howard, 242
Hume, Paul, 114
Humphrey, Hubert H., 67, 102, 124–
    125, 157, 159, 177, 186, 196, 215,
    221–222, 224–225, 280, 293
Humphrey, Mrs. Hubert, 185
Hyannis Port, 30, 46, 59

Illustrious (English aircraft carrier),
    302

Jackson 11th (dog), 91
Jacobsen, Jake, 298
Jacqueline Bouvier Kennedy (book),
    149
Jeff (butler), 124
Jefferson, Thomas, 74, 87
Jenkins (engineer), 148

Jenkins, Beth, 99, 115–116
Jenkins, Walter, 99, 115
Jet Star (airplane), 147
Jezebel (dog), 198
John Birch Society, 103
John F. Kennedy (aircraft carrier),
    39, 186, 218, 221
Johnny (butler), 193
Johns (Secret Service agent), 136,
    138, 145, 158, 198
Johns, Mrs. (agent's wife), 145
Johnson, Clarence, 149–150
Johnson, Johnny, 148
Johnson, Lady Bird, 36–37, 41, 52–
    54, 56, 65, 71, 85, 92–93, 95,
    106–107, 109–110, 117–118, 120–
    122, 124, 126, 128–131, 135–136,
    138, 149–152, 155–156, 164–165,
    167, 170–173, 176–178, 181–182,
    184–185, 189, 192–194, 196–199,
    201–203, 207–212, 214, 217–219,
    222–224, 226–228, 230–231, 240–
    242, 248, 269, 275, 281, 289
Johnson, Luci (Mrs. Patrick J.
    Nugent), 42–43, 47, 50, 54, 56, 88–
    90, 92, 99, 104, 106, 109, 111–
    117, 120, 122, 125–126, 129, 134–
    138, 142–146, 148–153, 155–161,
    164, 166–176, 178, 180, 182, 185,
    187–190, 193, 195, 197, 199–202,
    205, 207, 212–213, 218–219, 221,
    223–227, 229–231, 314, 317, 319,
    330
Johnson, Lynda Bird (Mrs. Charles
    S. Robb), 47, 51, 56, 81, 86, 92,
    98, 103, 106, 111–114, 120–121,
    127–128, 135–136, 138, 152–153,
    155, 161, 165–166, 170–175, 185,
    187–190, 193, 195–196, 198, 201–
    203, 205–206, 208, 211, 214, 216,
    222–227, 230–231, 316–318
Johnson, Lyndon Baines, 10, 12–18,
    20, 28–29, 36–37, 40, 49, 51, 54,
    56, 64–69, 71–74, 78, 80–81, 85–
    233, 237, 239–240, 245–246, 248–
    253, 255, 260–262, 268–272, 274,

276, 281–282, 284–285, 288, 294, 298, 301, 303–304, 307, 309, 312, 318

Johnson, Sam Houston, 13, 105, 131–133, 304

Johnson, Tom, 203–204, 225, 228

Jones, Jim, 156, 158, 183, 203, 214–216, 221–222

Kaltman, Mary, 146, 154, 274, 300

Kearns, Doris, 223

Keene, Barbara, 170

Kemp, Janet, 297

Kennedy, Caroline, 15, 25, 27–31, 41–46, 56, 58, 61–62, 73–74, 85–86, 186, 221, 224, 278

Kennedy, Edward ("Ted"), 44

Kennedy, Jacqueline, 4, 13, 17, 19, 22–28, 30–33, 38–39, 41, 45–47, 52–53, 56–63, 65–66, 72–73, 78–80, 85, 106, 111, 161, 186, 206, 221–222, 224, 269, 275, 278, 294, 297, 307

Kennedy, John Fitzgerald, 3, 10, 12–13, 15, 17, 19–33, 35–45, 55, 58–59, 62–67, 70–71, 77–79, 85, 91, 96, 102, 108, 118, 221, 243–244, 250, 255, 269, 285, 294, 307

Kennedy, John F., Jr. ("John-John"), 27–28, 30–31, 41–43, 56, 221, 224

Kennedy, Joseph P. (ambassador), 15, 28, 32, 38, 108

Kennedy, Patrick Bouvier, 32, 72

Kennedy, Robert ("Bobby"), 23, 44, 102, 118, 186, 218

Kennedy, Robert Jr., 44

Kennerly, David, 16

Ketchum (curator), 157

Key Biscayne, 243

Kilduff, Mac, 142

Kim (dog), 155–156, 159–160, 162, 167, 171–173, 176, 180, 212

King (masseur), 200, 208

King, Coretta Scott, 142

King, Dr. Martin Luther, 142, 213–214

King Timahoe (dog), 15–16, 41, 51, 70, 163, 238, 242, 245–246, 252–253, 259–260, 262–267, 270–281, 283–286, 288–290, 293–303, 306, 308–309, 311–314, 317, 319–328, 331

Kissinger, Henry, 250–251, 255–256, 272–273, 291, 294, 299, 306, 320

Kissinger, Nancy Maginnes, 255, 291

Kistler, William, 316

Kivett, Jerry, 178

Klein, Herb, 253–254, 306

Klein, Mrs. Herb, 304

Knudsen, Chief (photographer), 101, 199, 280

Kraskin, Robert A., 134–135, 176

Khrushchev, Nikita, 27–28

Laddie Boy (dog), 26–27

Lafayette, General, 73–74

Laitin, Joe, 68, 95, 137, 144, 152, 155

Lanier, Major (White House policeman), 216, 263

Lasker, Mary, 130, 228

Lassie (dog), 43, 184, 289

Lawford, Patricia, 46, 60

Lawford, Peter, 46

LBJ Ranch, 166, 224, 232

Leader Blair Jamie of Edlin (dog), 91 (See also Blanco)

Lee, Gypsy Rose, 209

LeFeve, David, 127, 128

Leighton, Frances Spatz, 5, 317–318, 326

Leprechaun (pony), 28

Liberty (dog), 16, 164

Liddy, J. Gordon, 330

Lincoln, Abe, 48–49, 53, 74

Lincoln, Anne, 125, 138, 140

Lincoln, Evelyn, 41

Lincoln, Tad, 48, 74

Lincoln, Willie, 74

Lindsay, John, 322

Linn (veterinarian), 261

Little Beagle (dog), 91

338

Little Chap (dog), 177, 185, 193, 195–196, 198, 212
Livingston, Robert, 310
Lluellyn, Doug, 299
Lodge, Henry Cabot, 40, 137, 162
Longworth, Alice, 74, 223, 317
Look, 208, 210
Love Story, 253
Lovell, James, Jr., 226
Lucke, Jane, 243
Lulu (dog), 276
Luns, Joseph, 274
Lynch, John (Prime Minister), 308
Lyndon B. Johnson Library, 94, 96

McCall's, 115
McCormack, John W., 99, 125, 288, 292
McCormack, Mrs. John, 125, 166
McGovern, George, 55
McGrory, Mary, 96
McKinley, William, 36, 74
McNamara, Robert, 39, 43, 80, 124, 221
McNamara, Mrs. Robert, 80
MacArthur, General Douglas, 12
MacDougal, Kristie, 221
Macaroni (pony), 28, 29
Mackenna's Gold, 272
Maddox, Marcia, 202, 212, 217, 220
Maggie (maid), 27
Maginnes, Nancy, *see* Kissinger, Nancy
Magnuson, Warren G., 273
Magruder, Jeb, 254
Major (dog), 143
Malcolm, Durie (Kerr), 108
March, Frederic, 139
Markel, Hazel, *see photo insert*
Marshall, General George, 36
Martin (electrician), 210, 275
Martini (barber), 300
Mason, Jimilu, 282
Masters, George, 115
Mayfield (doorman), 303, 331
Means, Marianne, 144, 200

Meir, Golda, 248–249
Mel (dog's beautician), 304
Mellon, Mrs. Paul, 63
Menzies, Prime Minister, 139
Mesta, Perle, 85, 90
Michael, Peggy, 262
Mike (Secret Service agent), 205, 225, 288
Miller (photographer), 120
Miller, Merle, 65
Miller, Scooter, 85
Miller, Tom, 208
Milton (Secret Service agent), 128
Miss Emily Spinach (snake), 74
Mitchell, James, 228–229
Mitchell, John, 256–257
Mitchell, Martha, 256–257, 317
Mitchum, Robert, 18
Moaney (valet), 11–12, 33
Monroe, Marilyn, 22, 38
Montgomery, Robert, *see photo insert*
Moore (General Services Administration), 156
Moreman, Dr., 213, 218, 226, 261
Moro, Aldo, 119
Mosbacher, Emil, *see photo insert*
Motion Picture Association, 102, 161
Mountbatten, Louis, 302
Muffler, John (electrician), 304, 328
Murphy, Robin, 117
My Thirty Years Backstairs at the White House, 4

Nader, Ralph, 254
Nasser (President of Egypt), 299
Natasha (hamster), 142
Natasha Jr. (hamster), 145
National Beagle Club, 97
National Cathedral School, 104, 125
National Council of Jewish Women, 244
National Federation of Republican Women, 244
National League of Families of American Prisoners, 327

National Symphony Orchestra, 104

NBC-TV, 126

Nehru, Prime Minister, *see photo insert*

Nelson (of License Bureau), 162

Nelson, Jimmy (florist), 152, 158, 176

New Republic, 223

New York Herald Tribune, 19

Newsweek, 99, 328–329

Nip (canary), 75

Nixon, Frank, 247

Nixon, Julie (Mrs. David Eisenhower), 43–44, 51, 163, 240, 242, 263–266, 270, 272, 274–278, 286, 288, 291, 296, 299–301, 303, 307–309, 311, 313–314, 317, 320–321, 323, 328–329

Nixon, Patricia, 5, 16, 19, 37, 41, 51, 53, 56, 163, 231, 238, 240–244, 247–250, 253, 256, 262–264, 266–270, 272–280, 282, 284–286, 288–289, 291, 293, 296–300, 302–311, 313–317, 319–323, 327–330

Nixon, Richard M., 5, 10, 12, 14, 16, 18–19, 37, 51, 55, 64–65, 67, 69–70, 72, 76–78, 97, 102, 106, 163–164, 220–221, 225, 228, 231, 237–332

Nixon, Tricia (Mrs. Edward F. Cox), 43, 50–51, 56, 163, 231, 240, 242, 249, 256, 263–264, 267–268, 272, 274, 276–278, 280, 282, 285–286, 290–293, 298–299, 302, 304, 307–317, 319–321, 323, 328–330

Nolan (engineer), 138, 147

Noren, Paul H. A., 279

Norman (dog), 212

Nugent, Lyn, 187, 212–213, 218, 224–228, 230, 330

Nugent, Patrick J. (Pat), 113, 115, 122, 126, 143–150, 156–161, 168, 170–172, 174, 176, 185, 188, 194, 199–200, 202, 212–213, 232, 314, 317

Nunn, Amy (*See also* Luci Johnson), 115

Oh Calcutta, 299

Oberon, Merle, 203

O'Brian, Hugh, 86

O'Brien, Larry, 58

Odle, Bob, 254

Okamoto, Yoichi, 69, 215

Old Beagle (dog), 87, 90

Old Whitey (horse), 57

Olsen, Jack, 113

Onassis, Aristotle, 39, 224

Onassis, Mrs. Aristotle, *see* Kennedy, Jacqueline

Oswald, Lee Harvey, 77

Page, Sam, 202, 230, 261, 299, 303

Pahlavi, Rezashah (Shah of Iran), 192

Pakenham, Mary, 163

Parade, 275, 280

Park, Chung Hee, 122

Parks, Lillian Rogers, 4–5, 27

Pasha (dog), 16, 163–164, 230–231, 261–267, 273–274, 276–278, 280, 286, 288, 290, 294, 297, 300–301, 303, 305–309, 311–315, 319–321, 323–324, 326–328

Patsy (dog), 278

Pearl Harbor, 5, 301

Pearson, Drew, 114–115

Pecora, Charles, 63

Peters, Officer (White House policeman), 29

Pelkey, John, 209–210

Peterson, Chris, *see photo insert*

Phenner, Michael, 190

Phillips (carpenter), 329

Pickle, Jake, 132

Pierce (usher), 131, 135, 172, 177, 179–180, 188, 194, 205, 210, 216, 288, 294–295, 297–298, 303, 308, 312, 322, 326

Plutto, Officer (White House policeman), 216

Pompidou, Georges, 284

Pokie (dog), 278

Poorhouse Fair, The, 128

Porter, Herbert ("Bart"), 254
Poulain, Simone, 177, 225
Powers, Dave, 15, 37, 70–71, 255, 307
President Johnson's Hill Country, 160
President's Analyst, The, 55
Prettyman, Mr. (valet), 11
Priest, Ronnie, 279
Princess (dog), 136, 145, 158
Prudence Prim (dog), 75
Pushinka (dog), 19, 23, 27–31, 40–41, 44–45, 58–61, 91, 161, 180, 206, 259, 290
Pustka, John, 89, 126, 138, 140, 162, 164

Rabbit, Run, 128
Radziwill, Anthony T., 27
Radziwill, Prince, 27
Radziwill, Princess, 27, 31, 39
Rather, Mary, 132, 229
Raye, Martha, 185
Rayburn, Sam, 52
RCA, 17, 18
Readers' Digest, 257
Reardon, Ted, 108, 155–156
Rebozo, Bebe, 72, 241–243, 245, 249, 252, 257, 273, 286, 289, 302
Red River, 223
Reedy, George, 129, 142, 222
Rob Roy (dog), 75
Robb, Charles S. ("Chuck"), 188–190, 196, 202, 205, 208, 211, 224, 230, 317
Robb, Lucinda Desha ("Cindy"), 224, 226
Roberts, Juanita, 120, 126, 128–130, 136, 146, 149–150, 161–163, 193–194, 208, 218, 265
Robin (canary), 29, 74
Robinson, Julie, 303–304
Robinson, Major (military aide), 204, 206, 208, 220, 229
Rockefeller, Nelson, 273
Roosevelt, Alice, *see* Longworth, Alice
Roosevelt, Archie, 29

Roosevelt, Eleanor, 143, 156
Roosevelt, Franklin D., 66, 138, 143, 233
Roosevelt, Frankin D., Jr., 42
Roosevelt, Theodore ("Teddy"), 29, 53, 74, 131, 223
Rosenbach, Bernard, 113
Rotchford, Charles, 156, 278, 295–297
Rowe, Abby, 312
Ruback, William, 180
Rusk, Dean, 147
Ryan, Cleave, 146, 226, 310
Rysavy, Francois, 265

St. John, Jill, 255
Salinger, Pierre, 33, 55, 60, 71, 102, 142
Sam (janitor), 118
San Clemente, 278, 306
Sanchez, Fina, 230, 251–252, 258, 260, 262, 264, 271, 273–276, 278–279, 285–286, 291, 302–305, 307–309, 312–316, 319–320, 323–325, 329–330
Sanchez, Manolo, 230, 239, 251–252, 258, 260–263, 267, 272–279, 285, 287, 291, 300, 302–304, 308–309, 313, 315, 320, 323–326, 327–329
Sardar (horse), 57
Saturday Evening Post, 69
Schweiker, Richard, 178
Schweiker, Mrs. Richard, 178
Scouten, Rex, 10, 27, 88, 117–119, 125, 137, 179, 229–230, 264, 266, 269, 275, 295, 297, 303, 308, 312, 321–322, 327–328
Sears, Roebuck, 167, 187
Secret Service, 30, 46, 51, 54, 78, 80, 93, 96, 115, 122, 128, 130, 137, 144, 162, 164–165, 168, 177–178, 180, 192, 211–212, 214–216, 231–232, 291, 302, 327
Seley, Jason, 129
Selassie, Haile, 276
Sellers, Peter, 256

Senz, Eddie, 107
Sequoia (yacht), 110, 293
Sevilla-Secasa, Ambassador, 143
Shah of Iran, *See* Pahlavi, Rezashah
Shan (cat), 75
Shannon (dog), 29, 31, 44, 91
Shaw, Maud, 27
Shriver, Eunice, 44
Shriver, Sargent, 146
Siegal, Wally, 162
Signal Corps (Army), 40, 148, 192, 205
Simmons (engineer), 120, 224, 296–297
Sinatra, Frank, 85
Sinatra, Frank, Jr., 85
Skelton, Red, 317
Smathers, George, 243
Smith, Colonel Haywood (military aide), 229
Smith, Helen, 281, 303
Smith, Jean, 44
Smith, Margaret, 264
Smith, Merriman, 227, 284–285
Smith, Mrs. Merriman, 227
Smith, Warrie Lynn, 189
Sobel, George, 144
Solomonson, Vicky, 177
Spandorf, Lily, 127–128, 136
Spring Valley, 249
Spunky (dog), 44–45, 265
Squaw Island, 32
Starkoff, Captain (White House policeman), 177, 216
Stern, Isaac, 249
Stevenson, Adlai, 136–137
Stout (usher), 300–301, 314, 323, 324
Stoughton, Cecil, *see photo insert*
Strachan, Gordon, 254
Streaker (dog), 30, 44
Strelka (dog), 28
Stuart, Connie, 279–280, 284
Student Prince, 283
Summersby, Kay, 36
Sylvester, Tony, 153–154

Tames, George, 123, 126
Taylor (Secret Service agent), 214
Taylor, Elizabeth (Liz), 256
Taylor, Willie Day, 122, 125, 136, 147–148, 160–161, 172, 185, 210, 214, 223
Taylor, Zachary, 57
Tex (pony), 28
Thayer, Mary Van Rensselaer, 149
Thomas, Helen, 57–59, 144, 151
Thrift, Virginia, 143
This Week, 174
Tiger (cat), 75
Time, 272
Tirvelda Farms, 238, 294–296
Tkach, Walter, 261, 302, 321, 325
To Tell the Truth, 162, 164–165, 173
Today Show, 173, 280
Tom Kitten (cat), 29
Tora, Tora, Tora, 301
Tower, John, 77
Truman, Bess, 9–10, 13, 20, 56, 81, 214, 240
Truman Center for the Advancement of Peace in Israel, 154
Truman, Harry, 9–13, 15, 20, 64–67, 69, 76, 79, 114, 214, 240, 250, 253
Truman Library, 154
Truman, Margaret, 15, 20, 42, 51, 62, 111, 114, 214
Tuck (canary), 75
Tuckerman, Nancy, 72–73
Turner, Alley, 211

United Nations, 136–137, 165
Updike, John, 128

Valenti, Courtney, 123–124, 132, 137, 142–143, 147, 154–159, 161, 169–170, 179, 187
Valenti, Jack, 102–103, 123–125, 142–143, 151, 155, 157–158, 160–161, 165, 170–171, 180–182, 187, 246
Valenti, Mary Margaret, 103, 123–124, 132, 143, 157–158, 161, 170

Van der Heuvel, Gerry, 280
Vantage Point, The, 54
Vicky (dog), 16, 51, 163, 230–231,
    261–264, 266–267, 272, 276–278,
    280, 285–286, 290, 294, 297, 300–
    301, 303–304, 307–309, 311–315,
    319–321, 323, 325–327
Vicky (secretary), 158, 203

Wall Street Journal, 210
Wallace, George, 78, 139
Wallace, Henry, 66
Wallace, Mrs. (Bess Truman's mother),
    13
Walter Reed Hospital, 125, 206–208,
    218, 221, 226, 261, 263–264, 266–
    267, 277, 279–281, 285, 294–295,
    297
Walters, Barbara, 308
Warnock, William, 285
Washington Evening Star, The, 125,
    164, 329
Washington, George, 57, 87, 316
Washington Post, The, 103, 144, 162,
    164
Washington, Walter, 222
Watergate, 58, 250, 256, 272, 298,
    330
Watson, W. Marvin, 87, 95, 117, 119,
    143, 155, 160, 172, 183, 192–193,
    200, 208
Wayne, John, 223
Webb, James, 226
Webster (engineer), 307
Wells, Fay Gillis, 285
Wells, Officer (White House police-
    man), 165
West (chauffeur), 43
West, J. B., 10, 72, 151, 177, 180,
    208, 210, 220, 229, 264, 289, 290
West, Zella, 264
Westmoreland, William C., 185, 213
What's New, Pussycat, 137
Whelihan, Bruce, 317

White House Police, 144, 147–148,
    152, 165, 168, 207, 217, 301
White Tip (dog), 30, 44
Whittington, Geraldine, 108–109, 127
Wiggins, Pearl, 148
Wiggles (dog), 274
Wilkinson, Bud, 261
Wilkinson, Jay, 261
Williams, Irvin (Whitey), 61, 151,
    158–159, 177, 180, 229, 286, 290,
    301, 327
Williamson, Officer (White House
    policeman), 274
Wilson, Cynthia, 207
Wilson, Harold, 151–152, 283
Wilson, Lois, 226–227
Wilson, Woodrow, 35, 53, 202
Winchester, Lucy, 264–265
Wolf (dog), 28, 31, 44, 79, 85, 91
Wolfe, Frank (photographer), 158,
    172
Woods, Captain (White House police-
    man), 265
Woods, Joe, 251
Woods, Rose Mary, 237–238, 242,
    251, 265, 267, 270, 272, 318
Woodward, President of American
    Airlines, 171
Workman, Bernard, 97
Wright, Zephyr, 87, 139, 219, 221

Yarmouth Animal Hospital, 31
Young, Dr. (to Lyndon B. Johnson),
    142, 282
Young, Rusty (florist), 176, 316
Youngblood (Secret Service agent),
    126, 137, 147
Yuki (dog), 74 90–91, 104, 166–167,
    175, 183, 188, 191–203, 206–231,
    233, 261–262, 282, 288–289, 319

Zerillimarimo, Baroness Geudo, 317
Ziegler, Ron, 70, 244, 254, 283–284,
    298, 301